The New Guide to
Dakini Land

Also by Geshe Kelsang Gyatso

Meaningful to Behold

Clear Light of Bliss

Universal Compassion

Joyful Path of Good Fortune

The Bodhisattva Vow

Heart Jewel

Great Treasury of Merit

Introduction to Buddhism

Understanding the Mind

Tantric Grounds and Paths

Ocean of Nectar

Essence of Vajrayana

Living Meaningfully, Dying Joyfully

Eight Steps to Happiness

Transform Your Life

The New Meditation Handbook

How to Solve Our Human Problems

Mahamudra Tantra

Modern Buddhism

The New Heart of Wisdom

Profits from the sale of this book are designated to the
NKT-IKBU International Temples Project Fund
according to the guidelines in *A Money Handbook*
[Reg. Charity number 1015054 (England)]
A Buddhist Charity, Building for World Peace
www.kadampa.org/temples

GESHE KELSANG GYATSO

The New Guide to Dakini Land

THE HIGHEST YOGA TANTRA
PRACTICE OF BUDDHA
VAJRAYOGINI

THARPA PUBLICATIONS
UK • USA • CANADA
AUSTRALIA • ASIA

First published as *Guide to Dakini Land* in 1991
Second edition revised and reset 1996
Reprinted 1999, 2005, 2008
Third edition revised and published as
The New Guide to Dakini Land 2012

Tharpa Publications UK Office   Tharpa Publications US Office
Conishead Priory   47 Sweeney Road
Ulverston, Cumbria   Glen Spey
LA12 9QQ, England   NY 12737, USA

Tharpa Publications has offices around the world,
and Tharpa books are published in most major languages.
See page 565 for contact details.

© The New Kadampa Tradition – International Kadampa Buddhist
Union 1991, 1996, 2012

The cover image is Buddha Vajradharma.

Library of Congress Control Number: 2012953550

ISBN 978-1-906665-50-0 – hardback
ISBN 978-1-906665-49-4 – paperback
ISBN 978-1-906665-51-7 – e-book
ISBN 978-1-906665-53-1 – Adobe Portable Document format (.pdf)

Set in Palatino by Tharpa Publications.
Printed on Munken Pure by CPI Antony Rowe Ltd.,
Chippenham, Wiltshire, SN14 6LH, England.

Paper supplied from well-managed forests and other controlled
sources, and certified in accordance with the rules of the
Forest Stewardship Council.

Contents

Illustrations

Introduction

I have prepared this book, *The New Guide to Dakini Land*, to clarify many profound meanings, and to make it easy to understand and practise this precious holy Dharma. Please enjoy!

We should know that living beings have many different capacities for spiritual understanding and practice. For this reason, out of his compassion, Buddha the Blessed One gave teachings on many levels, just as a skilful doctor administers a variety of remedies to treat different types of sick people.

For those who wish merely to attain human happiness Buddha gave teachings revealing actions and their effects, or karma; and he taught moral discipline as their main practice. For those who wish to experience the permanent inner peace of liberation, or nirvana, for themselves, Buddha gave teachings on the disadvantages of samsara, the cycle of contaminated rebirth; and he taught the three higher trainings – training in higher moral discipline, training in higher concentration and training in higher wisdom – as their main practice. For those who wish to attain the ultimate goal of full enlightenment Buddha gave teachings on learning to cherish others, great compassion and the supreme good heart, bodhichitta; and he taught the six perfections – the perfections of giving, moral discipline, patience, effort, concentration and wisdom – as their main practice. All these teachings are open to anyone who wishes to study and practise them. The experiences that are gained from practising them are called the 'common spiritual paths'.

Besides these teachings, Buddha also gave teachings on Tantra. These may be practised only by those who have received Tantric empowerments. The experiences gained by practising these teachings are called the 'uncommon spiritual paths'.

Venerable Vajrayogini

In the Tantric teachings Buddha revealed four classes of Tantra. The practices explained in this book, *The New Guide to Dakini Land*, are included within the highest of these, Highest Yoga Tantra. These are the very essence of Buddha's teachings. They include special methods for preventing ordinary appearance and ordinary conception, special methods for preventing ordinary death, intermediate state and rebirth, and uncommon methods for transforming all daily experiences into higher spiritual paths. By transforming ordinary experience in this way we can prevent all the problems we experience in our daily life and swiftly attain the ultimate happiness of full enlightenment. In this context, 'Dakini' refers to Vajrayogini, and her Pure Land of Keajra is called 'Dakini Land' or 'Keajra Heaven'.

The source of all the essential meanings contained in *The New Guide to Dakini Land* is *Illuminating All Hidden Meanings* (Tib. Be don kun sel), which is a precious commentary to the practice of Heruka and Vajrayogini Tantra by Je Tsongkhapa. Through the kindness of my root Guru, Dorjechang Trijang Rinpoche, I have had the opportunity to study and practise the instructions of Heruka and Vajrayogini. Now I have written this book as a special offering, mainly for practitioners of the modern world.

To practise the instructions explained in this book we require special inner conditions. First we should train in the common spiritual paths, the practice of Kadam Lamrim, and then receive the empowerments of Heruka and Vajrayogini. Having received these empowerments we should strive to maintain our vows and commitments purely.

If we have a pure motivation and read the entire book carefully, concentrating deeply on its meaning without rushing to finish it, we will gain profound realizations of Buddhadharma.

Geshe Kelsang Gyatso

Mandala of Vajrayogini

Preliminary Explanation

The commentary to the Highest Yoga Tantra practice of Venerable Vajrayogini consists of the preliminary explanation, the main commentary to the generation and completion stages, and the dedication. The first of these, the preliminary explanation, has seven parts:

1 Generating a correct motivation
2 The origin and lineage of these instructions
3 The benefits of these instructions
4 Biographies of past Buddhist practitioners who gained realizations through practising these instructions
5 The qualifications necessary for practising these instructions
6 The four special causes of swift attainments
7 What are outer and inner Dakini Lands?

GENERATING A CORRECT MOTIVATION

These instructions concern the extraordinary spiritual path of Tantra, or Secret Mantra, which is the quickest and most profound method for attaining great enlightenment. We should rejoice in this precious opportunity to study these instructions which, if put into practice, can lead to full enlightenment within one short human life. However, studying these instructions will be truly meaningful only if our motivation is pure. If we read this book merely out of intellectual curiosity we will not experience its real meaning. To receive the maximum benefit from these instructions, each time we study or practise them we should begin by generating a pure, altruistic motivation. We can do this by reciting the following prayer three times while concentrating on its meaning:

1

I and all sentient beings, the migrators as extensive
as space, from this time forth until we reach the
essence of enlightenment,
Go for refuge to the glorious, sacred Gurus,
Go for refuge to the complete Buddhas, the Blessed
Ones,
Go for refuge to the sacred Dharmas,
Go for refuge to the superior Sanghas.

We should then recite three times:

Once I have attained the state of a complete Buddha, I
shall free all sentient beings from the ocean of samsara's
suffering and lead them to the bliss of full enlightenment.
For this purpose I shall practise the stages of Vajrayogini's
path.

THE ORIGIN AND LINEAGE OF THESE INSTRUCTIONS

The two stages of the practice of Vajrayogini were originally
taught by Buddha Vajradhara. He manifested in the form of
Heruka to expound the *Root Tantra of Heruka*, and it was in this
Tantra that he explained the practice of Vajrayogini. All the
many lineages of instructions on Vajrayogini can be traced back
to this original revelation. Of these lineages, there are three that
are most commonly practised: the Narokhachö lineage, which
was transmitted from Vajrayogini to Naropa; the Maitrikhachö
lineage, which was transmitted from Vajrayogini to Maitripa;
and the Indrakhachö lineage, which was transmitted from
Vajrayogini to Indrabodhi. This commentary to the generation
and completion stages of the Highest Yoga Tantra practice of
Vajrayogini is based on the instructions of the Narokhachö
lineage.

THE ORIGIN OF HERUKA TANTRA

At one time this universe was controlled by the worldly deity
Ishvara. His mandalas and lingams existed in many places
in this world, the most important ones being in the twenty-
four holy places. Ishvara's followers sacrificed innumerable

animals as offerings to him. This greatly pleased Ishvara and in return he helped them to obtain wealth and worldly success, but he obstructed anyone who tried to attain liberation or enlightenment. Under the influence of Ishvara the people of this world slaughtered thousands of animals every day, thinking that they were performing virtuous actions. In reality however they were accumulating heavy negative karma and depriving themselves of the opportunity to attain liberation.

The Heroes and Heroines of the five Buddha families found this situation intolerable and asked Buddha Vajradhara to intervene. Buddha Vajradhara manifested in the form of Heruka and through the power of his blessings subdued Ishvara and transformed Ishvara's mandalas, or worlds, into Heruka's mandalas. The other Deities of Heruka's mandala subdued Ishvara's retinue by converting them to followers of Heruka.

Heruka did not reabsorb the mandalas, his pure worlds, that he had emanated in the twenty-four places in this human world but left them intact, and to this day beings with especially pure karma are able to see these mandalas and the Heroes and Heroines who abide within them. For practitioners of Heruka and Vajrayogini these blessed places are particularly powerful sites for meditation.

After subduing Ishvara and his retinue, Heruka expounded the condensed, middling and extensive root Tantras of Heruka. Of these, only the *Condensed Root Tantra of Heruka* has been translated from Sanskrit into Tibetan. Buddha Vajradhara also expounded many explanatory Tantras, which are commentaries to the root Tantras, and a number of these have been translated into Tibetan. It is in these root and explanatory Tantras, especially in the forty-seventh and forty-eighth chapters of the fifty-one chapters of the *Condensed Root Tantra of Heruka*, that Buddha Vajradhara gave clear instructions on the practice of Vajrayogini.

THE LINEAGE OF THESE INSTRUCTIONS

The first Guru in the lineage of these instructions is Buddha Vajradharma and the second is Buddha Vajrayogini. Vajrayogini transmitted these instructions directly to Naropa, who diligently put them into practice and as a result gained great realizations. Although Naropa had many disciples he kept his practice of Vajrayogini secret, transmitting it only to two brothers from the Nepalese town of Pamting, now called Pharping. He recognized that the Pamtingpa brothers, Jigme Dragpa and his younger brother Ngawang Dragpa, had a particularly strong karmic connection with these instructions. Sakya Pandita Kunga Gyaltsen and other famous Teachers have remarked on the fact that even Naropa's most famous disciple, the great Tibetan Master Marpa, did not receive these instructions.

The Pamtingpa brothers passed these instructions to the Tibetan translators Lokya Sherab Tseg and then Malgyur Lotsawa. It was Malgyur Lotsawa who translated the *Condensed Root Tantra of Heruka* from Sanskrit into Tibetan. Through his kindness many Tibetans in the past became great Yogis and Yoginis, and today many people have the opportunity to study and practise the Heruka and Vajrayogini Tantras. Malgyur Lotsawa himself reached the supreme Union of Vajradhara and attained Dakini Land in that life.

From Malgyur Lotsawa these instructions were passed down in unbroken succession to Je Phabongkhapa, and then to the most Venerable Dorjechang Trijang Rinpoche, holder of the lineage. It was from this great Master that I, the author, received these instructions.

From Buddha Vajradharma to Dorjechang Trijang Rinpoche there have been thirty-seven lineage Gurus. The lineage of these instructions is unbroken and the blessings passed down from Buddha Vajradharma are intact. Each lineage Guru attained complete experience of these instructions, thereby ensuring that their power has not decreased. These instructions are completely authentic and are clearly presented. If we put them into practice with deep conviction and joyous effort we will definitely gain realizations. We should know that Buddha Vajradharma, Buddha Vajradhara and Buddha Shakyamuni are the same person with different aspects. Vajradhara is the manifestation of all Buddhas' minds, Vajradharma is the manifestation of all Buddhas' speech, and Shakyamuni is the manifestation of all Buddhas' bodies.

4

THE BENEFITS OF THESE INSTRUCTIONS

It is said in the *Condensed Root Tantra of Heruka* that the benefits to be gained from engaging in the practice of Vajrayogini are limitless and that a thousand voices could never fully enumerate them. Here we will consider ten principal benefits.

BY PRACTISING THESE INSTRUCTIONS WE QUICKLY RECEIVE GREAT AND POWERFUL BLESSINGS

When we practise these instructions we quickly receive great and profound blessings from all the Buddhas. These blessings help us temporarily, and eventually enable us to attain the ultimate goal of full enlightenment.

THESE INSTRUCTIONS ARE A SYNTHESIS OF ALL ESSENTIAL INSTRUCTIONS

The instructions on the practice of Vajrayogini are a synthesis of all the essential instructions contained within the Tantras of Heruka, Yamantaka and Guhyasamaja. All the essential points of the stages of Secret Mantra are included within the practice of Vajrayogini.

THESE INSTRUCTIONS ARE EASY TO PRACTISE

The instructions on the practice of Vajrayogini contain concise and clearly presented meditations that are relatively easy to practise. The mantra is short and easy to recite, and the visualizations of the mandala, the Deity and the body mandala are simple compared with those of other Highest Yoga Tantra Deities. Even practitioners with limited abilities and little wisdom can engage in these practices.

BY PRACTISING THESE INSTRUCTIONS WE CAN SWIFTLY ACCOMPLISH ATTAINMENTS

Many great Teachers such as Dorjechang Trijang Rinpoche have said that through the practice of Vajrayogini those with only middling fortune can attain Dakini Land in this life. Those with greater fortune will attain this with ease, and even those with lesser fortune can attain Dakini Land in the intermediate state between death and rebirth. If we continually recite Vajrayogini's mantra we will remember the mantra when we are dying, and then, as if in a dream, we will hear Vajrayogini and her retinue of Dakinis calling us and inviting us to her Pure Land. In this way Vajrayogini will guide us through death and the intermediate state and lead us to the Pure Land of the Dakinis.

It is said that even those with the least fortune who do not attain Dakini Land in the intermediate state will be led by Vajrayogini to her Pure Land within seven lives. Even if such practitioners find themselves in the deepest hell, Vajrayogini will bless their minds and cause their previously accumulated virtuous actions to ripen. In this way they will be released from hell and guided directly to the Pure Land of the Dakinis.

Thus through keeping our commitments purely and practising these instructions sincerely we can attain Dakini Land in this life, in the intermediate state, or certainly within seven lives. 'Dakini Land' refers to the pure world of Heruka and Vajrayogini, commonly known as 'Keajra Pure Land' or 'Keajra Heaven'. A detailed explanation of Keajra Pure Land can be found in Part Two of *Modern Buddhism*. As our main commitment we should emphasize practising the nineteen commitments of the five Buddha families, an explanation of which can be found in *Condensed Six-session Yoga*, in Appendix II.

THESE INSTRUCTIONS INCLUDE A SPECIAL BODY MANDALA PRACTICE

Body mandalas are not included within all Deity practices. A practice that contains a body mandala is more profound than one that does not, and the most profound of all body mandalas is that of Vajrayogini.

THESE INSTRUCTIONS INCLUDE AN UNCOMMON
YOGA OF INCONCEIVABILITY

The uncommon yoga of inconceivability is a special method, unique to the practice of Vajrayogini, whereby we can attain Dakini Land within this life without abandoning our present body. The sadhana or ritual prayer for the attainment of the Pure Land of Keajra, *The Uncommon Yoga of Inconceivability*, can be found in Appendix II.

WE CAN PRACTISE BOTH GENERATION STAGE
AND COMPLETION STAGE TOGETHER

In practices such as Yamantaka and Guhyasamaja, practitioners can meditate on completion stage only after they have gained experience of generation stage; but in the practice of Vajrayogini we can train in completion stage meditations, and even gain certain completion stage realizations, while we are still training in generation stage.

THESE INSTRUCTIONS ARE ESPECIALLY SUITABLE FOR
THOSE WITH STRONG DESIROUS ATTACHMENT

In general it is difficult for those with strong desirous attachment to practise Dharma, but this is not so with the practice of Vajrayogini. Throughout this world there exist countless emanations of Heruka and Vajrayogini manifesting as ordinary men and women. These emanations help pure practitioners of Vajrayogini to transform their desirous attachment into the spiritual path. If such practitioners conscientiously keep their commitments and faithfully practise the eleven yogas, eventually they will meet an emanation of Vajrayogini manifesting as an attractive man or woman. By causing desirous attachment to arise in the practitioner, that emanation will bless their channels, drops and winds. Then, by entering into union with the emanation, the practitioner will be able to transform his or her desire into spontaneous great bliss. With this blissful mind the practitioner will meditate on emptiness and eventually eradicate all delusions, including desirous attachment.

In this way he or she will swiftly attain full enlightenment. Just as fire that is produced from wood eventually consumes the wood that produced it, so too Tantric bliss, which is developed from desirous attachment, eventually consumes the desirous attachment that gave rise to it. This skilful method of transforming attachment into the spiritual path was adopted by Masters such as Ghantapa and Tilopa.

The essence of Highest Yoga Tantra practice is to generate a mind of spontaneous great bliss and use that blissful mind to meditate on emptiness. We attain the mind of spontaneous great bliss by gathering the inner winds into the central channel through completion stage meditation. For completion stage meditation to be successful, the channels, drops and winds of our body must be blessed by Deities. We accomplish this through generation stage practice.

THESE INSTRUCTIONS ARE PARTICULARLY APPROPRIATE FOR THIS DEGENERATE AGE

The practice of Vajrayogini quickly brings blessings, especially during this spiritually degenerate age. It is said that as the general level of spirituality decreases, it becomes increasingly difficult for practitioners to receive the blessings of other Deities; but the opposite is the case with Heruka and Vajrayogini – the more times degenerate, the more easily practitioners can receive their blessings.

Whenever Vajradhara expounded a Tantra he emanated the mandala associated with it, but after completing the discourse he would usually reabsorb the mandala. For example, when he expounded the *Root Tantra of Kalachakra* he emanated the Kalachakra mandala, and when he had finished he reabsorbed it. However, he did not reabsorb the mandalas of Heruka or Vajrayogini. These mandalas still exist at various places throughout this world, such as in the twenty-four holy places. Because of this, human beings in this world have a special relationship with Heruka and Vajrayogini and can quickly receive their blessings. Furthermore, in the *Root Tantra of Heruka* Vajradhara promised that in the future, when times

8

became spiritually degenerate, Heruka and Vajrayogini would bestow their blessings on those with strong attachment.

In general, as the number of lineage Gurus of a Deity's practice increases, the blessings of that Deity take longer to reach practitioners; but the greater the number of lineage Gurus of Heruka and Vajrayogini, the more quickly practitioners receive their blessings.

VAJRAYOGINI'S MANTRA HAS MANY SPECIAL QUALITIES

In the *Root Tantra of Heruka* Vajradhara says that we can gain attainments merely by reciting Vajrayogini's mantra, even with poor concentration. Nowadays this is not possible when reciting the mantras of other Deities. However, we need to have very strong faith in Vajrayogini and her mantra if we are to gain realizations by mantra recitation alone.

If we think deeply about the benefits and special qualities of these instructions we will realize that we now have a very precious opportunity to study and practise them. We will generate a feeling of great joy which will give us great confidence in the instructions and encourage us to put them into practice.

BIOGRAPHIES OF PAST BUDDHIST PRACTITIONERS WHO GAINED REALIZATIONS THROUGH PRACTISING THESE INSTRUCTIONS

Many people have accomplished the highest attainments through Vajrayogini practice. Of the Eighty-four Mahasiddhas of ancient India, many gained their attainments through the practices of Heruka and Vajrayogini, and since the time when these Tantras were introduced into Tibet many Tibetans have also gained similar realizations. It is still possible to emulate these practitioners and accomplish the same attainments.

There now follow brief biographies of five great practitioners who received special care and guidance from Vajrayogini and as a result reached Dakini Land.

LUYIPA

Luyipa was a great Indian Mahasiddha who relied upon Heruka and Vajrayogini. One day, on the tenth day of the month, he went to a charnel ground to meditate. When he arrived he saw a group of men and women having a picnic. One of the women gave him a piece of meat, which he ate, and as a result his mind was blessed and instantly purified of ordinary appearance. He attained a vision of Heruka and Vajrayogini, and realized that the men and women were in reality Heroes and Heroines. His previous pure practice of Vajrayogini had caused her to manifest as the woman who offered him the meat. In this way Vajrayogini helped him to attain both outer and inner Dakini Land.

GHANTAPA

The Mahasiddha Ghantapa lived deep in a forest in Odivisha (present-day Orissa) in India, where he engaged in intensive meditation on Heruka and Vajrayogini. Since he was living in such an isolated place his diet was poor and his body became emaciated. One day the king of Odivisha was out hunting in the forest when he came across Ghantapa. Seeing how thin and weak he was, the king asked Ghantapa why he lived in the forest on such a poor diet, and encouraged him to return with him to the city where he would give him food and shelter. Ghantapa replied that just as a great elephant could not be led from the forest by a fine thread, so he could not be tempted to leave the forest by the riches of a king. Angered by Ghantapa's refusal, the king returned to his palace threatening revenge.

Such was the king's anger that he summoned a number of women from the city and told them about the arrogant monk in the forest. He offered great wealth to any one of them who could seduce him and force him to break his vows of celibacy. One woman, a wine-seller, boasted that she could do this and she set out for the forest to look for Ghantapa. When eventually she found him she asked if she could become his servant. Ghantapa had no need of a servant, but he realized that they had a strong relationship from previous lives

10

and so he allowed her to stay. Ghantapa gave her spiritual instructions and empowerments and they engaged sincerely in meditation. After twelve years they both attained the Union of No More Learning, full enlightenment.

One day Ghantapa and the former wine-seller decided to encourage the people of the city to develop a greater interest in Dharma. Accordingly, the woman returned to the king and reported that she had seduced the monk. At first the king doubted the truth of her story, but when she explained that she and Ghantapa now had two children, a son and a daughter, the king was delighted with the news and told her to bring Ghantapa to the city on a particular day. He then issued a proclamation disparaging Ghantapa, and ordered his subjects to assemble on the appointed day to insult and humiliate the monk.

When the day came, Ghantapa and the woman left the forest with their children, the son on Ghantapa's right and the daughter on his left. As they entered the city Ghantapa was walking as if he were drunk, holding a bowl into which the woman was pouring wine. All the people who had gathered laughed and jeered, hurling abuse and insults at him. 'Long ago', they taunted him, 'our king invited you to the city but you arrogantly refused his invitation. Now you come drunk and with a wine-seller. What a bad example of a Buddhist and a monk!' When they had finished, Ghantapa appeared to become angry and threw his bowl to the ground. The bowl sank into the earth, splitting the ground and causing a spring of water to appear. Ghantapa immediately transformed into Heruka and the woman into Vajrayogini. The boy transformed into a vajra which Ghantapa held in his right hand, and the girl into a bell which he held in his left hand. Ghantapa and his consort then embraced and flew into the sky.

The people were astonished and immediately developed deep regret for their disrespect. They prostrated to Ghantapa, begging him and the emanation of Vajrayogini to return. Ghantapa and his consort refused, but told the people that if their regret was sincere they should make confession to Mahakaruna, the embodiment of Buddha's great compassion.

Through the deep remorse of the people of Odivisha and the force of their prayers a statue of Mahakaruna arose from the spring water. The people of Odivisha became very devoted Dharma practitioners and many of them gained realizations. The statue of Mahakaruna can still be seen today.

Because of Ghantapa's pure practice of Heruka and Vajrayogini in the forest, Vajrayogini saw that it was the right time for him to receive her blessings and so she manifested as the wine-seller. Through living with her Ghantapa attained the state of full enlightenment.

DARIKAPA

King Darikapa was another of the Eighty-four Mahasiddhas. He received empowerments and instructions on Heruka and Vajrayogini from Luyipa. Luyipa predicted that if Darikapa were to abandon his kingdom and apply great effort in the practice of Vajrayogini and Heruka he would swiftly attain enlightenment. Darikapa immediately left his palace and wandered from place to place as a beggar, practising meditation at every opportunity. In a city in South India he met a wealthy courtesan who was an emanation of Vajrayogini. The woman owned a large mansion and she took Darikapa in as her servant, where he worked for twelve years. During the day he performed menial tasks in and around the house, and at night he practised Luyipa's instructions. After twelve years he attained the fifth stage of completion stage, the union that needs learning. It is said that Darikapa and the courtesan's entire entourage of fourteen thousand all attained the Pure Land of Keajra with their human bodies. In this way Darikapa received the guidance of Vajrayogini.

KUSALI

A novice monk called Kusali also came under Vajrayogini's care. One day, while travelling along the banks of the River Ganges, he met an old leper woman in great pain, who wanted to cross the river. Kusali was overcome with compassion for

12

her. He bound her onto his back with his upper garment and started to ford the river but, when they were half way across, the leper woman transformed into Vajrayogini and led him to Dakini Land.

PURANG LOTSAWA

Purang Lotsawa was a great Teacher who lived near Shiri Monastery in western Tibet and who had many spiritually advanced students. When he became aware through various signs that he was ready to attain the Pure Land of Keajra, he dug out a small cave in a hillside where he planned to live in solitary retreat. As he entered the cave at the start of his retreat he announced that if he left before attaining the Pure Land his throat should be cut by the Dharma Protectors. He told his assistant to seal the entrance of his cave, leaving only a small hole through which food and drink could be passed.

Some time later a Tantric Yogi accompanied by eight women arrived and asked to see Purang. The assistant turned them away, but that evening, when he told Purang about the visitors, Purang told him not to dismiss anyone who asked to see him. The visitors returned the next day and so the assistant showed them to the cave. Suspecting that they were not ordinary people, he looked for a place to hide so that he could see what would happen, but by the time he had found a suitable place the visitors had unaccountably entered the cave. The assistant crept up to the small hole in the side of the cave and looked in. The cave was full of radiant light. The eight women were sitting in a row with the Yogi at one end and Purang at the other. The Yogi was rolling letters of gold, which he passed to the women. They in turn passed them to Purang, who appeared to be eating them. Purang became aware of his assistant looking through the hole and shouted at him to go away. The assistant left immediately. Later, when he returned with Purang's supper, Purang was sitting alone with no sign of the Yogi or the eight women. That night Purang went to Dakini Land, the Pure Land of Vajrayogini.

The next morning the assistant took Purang his breakfast but found the cave empty. Although he was convinced that Purang had attained Dakini Land he was afraid that others might think that he had been the cause of Purang's disappearance. To allay such suspicions he called together a number of people and showed them that the seal to Purang's cave had not been broken. Although some people were convinced and believed that Purang had attained Dakini Land, others still suspected the assistant of murder.

To resolve the matter a Tibetan translator was sent to Nepal to consult a famous Vajrayogini practitioner who had great powers of clairvoyance. After the translator had explained what had happened to Purang, the Nepalese practitioner replied that on the day of the disappearance, while in meditation, he had seen through his clairvoyance that Purang had been invited to Dakini Land by a Hero and eight Heroines. The Hero was Heruka and the eight Heroines were the eight Goddesses of the doorways of Heruka's mandala. As a result of Purang's pure practice, Heruka and Vajrayogini had come to his cave and taken him to Dakini Land.

Many great practitioners of the Gelug tradition such as Takbu Tenpai Gyaltsen, Drubchen Cho Dorje, Changkya Rolpai Dorje, and many of their disciples have attained Dakini Land. Such things happen even today. For example, in recent years there was a Tibetan layman called Gonche who lived in eastern Tibet in a place called Chatring. To all appearances he was an evil man, always fighting and stealing, and generally engaging in many negative actions. The Chinese invasion of Tibet eventually forced him to flee from his motherland. One day, on his journey into exile, he saw a boat crossing a stretch of water carrying about thirty Chinese soldiers. He shot holes in the boat, causing it to sink, and all the soldiers drowned. When he finally reached the Nepalese border he joined the Tibetan resistance.

Some years later, as an elderly man, he travelled to Dharamsala in India where he visited Dorjechang Trijang Rinpoche, who advised him to abandon all negative actions and to devote himself to spiritual practice. From that day

Gonche's mind changed. He developed strong regret for all his past harmful actions and promised to practise Dharma sincerely. Some time later, Trijang Rinpoche gave a Vajrayogini empowerment to a large group of his disciples, and Gonche was among them.

Trijang Rinpoche advised Gonche to go to Nepal to do a long retreat on Vajrayogini. Receiving material assistance from his family and spiritual advice from some local Geshes, Gonche entered into retreat; but during his retreat he died. At the time of his death many people saw a rainbow above his retreat hut. Three days later he was cremated and this time a rainbow appeared over the funeral pyre. These rainbows were seen by the local people as well as by the monks who had assembled to pray for him. High Lamas said later that the rainbows were signs that Vajrayogini had led Gonche to her Pure Land while he was in the intermediate state.

Many female Vajrayogini practitioners have also attained enlightenment through this practice. These accounts of the attainments of past practitioners demonstrate the great value of the practice of Vajrayogini and are a source of inspiration for our own practice.

THE QUALIFICATIONS NECESSARY FOR PRACTISING THESE INSTRUCTIONS

Before we can practise the two stages of Vajrayogini Tantra we must have certain qualifications. Through the study and practice of the stages of the path, Lamrim, we should have gained at least some experience of the three principal aspects of the path: renunciation, bodhichitta and the correct view of emptiness. These are sometimes known as 'paths common to both Sutra and Tantra'. Once we have built the foundation of experience in the common paths we are qualified to enter the special path of Tantra. The gateway to Tantric practice is empowerment. Before we can engage in Vajrayogini practice we must receive from a qualified Tantric Spiritual Guide the empowerment of Heruka, and the empowerment of Vajrayogini in her sindhura mandala. These empowerments place special, virtuous potentials on our consciousness which, when nurtured by subsequent spiritual practice, eventually ripen into the realizations of generation stage and completion stage. During the empowerments we take certain vows and commitments, which we must observe scrupulously. Upon this basis, if we practise Vajrayogini's instructions continuously and sincerely we will receive all the benefits mentioned above.

THE FOUR SPECIAL CAUSES OF SWIFT ATTAINMENTS

To gain swiftly the realizations associated with Vajrayogini practice we need four special causes. These are:

1 Having unwavering faith
2 Having wisdom that overcomes doubts and
   misgivings concerning the practice
3 Integrating all our spiritual training into the
   practice of one Yidam, or Enlightened Deity
4 Practising in secret

HAVING UNWAVERING FAITH

We should not become discouraged if after only a few days or months of intense effort we do not attain any special results. We should train consistently, with unshakeable conviction in the benefits of our practice. Our practice should be like a broad river that flows steadily and continuously.

HAVING WISDOM THAT OVERCOMES DOUBTS AND MISGIVINGS CONCERNING THE PRACTICE

We should have a clear understanding of the eleven yogas of generation stage and of the meditations of completion stage. In general, whenever we practise Dharma we should first overcome all doubts about the instructions we have received and reach clear conclusions about them. By listening to and studying complete and correct instructions we develop the wisdom arisen from listening, and through thinking about the meaning of the instructions we develop the wisdom arisen from contemplation. Only then can we proceed to meditate single-pointedly on the conclusions we have reached.

It is most important that while we are engaged in Dharma practice our concentration should be single-pointed. If we practise with a distracted mind and do not gain realizations it is not the fault of Dharma, Buddha or our Gurus. Even when we are not engaged in formal meditation we should be able to focus our mind clearly on any virtuous object we choose. If our mind continually wanders to a multitude of extraneous objects our progress will be hampered. As we begin to control our mind and gain the ability to direct it at will, we will experience results from our meditation and make swift progress along the spiritual path. Our mind should be like a fine, well-trained horse that is powerful but easy to control and direct. Such a horse will take a rider wherever he or she wishes to go, whereas an unruly horse will follow only its own wishes and disregard the wishes of its rider.

Once we can direct our mind to a specific object and keep it focused on that object we will have a well-controlled mind and our life will not be wasted through distracted thoughts. Even in worldly activities, success comes only as a result of single-minded concentration, so how much more important is strong concentration for successful Dharma practice? In Dharma we gain realizations only by practising with single-pointed concentration, and this is possible only if we have understood the instructions thoroughly.

INTEGRATING ALL OUR SPIRITUAL TRAINING INTO THE PRACTICE OF ONE YIDAM, OR ENLIGHTENED DEITY

Je Tsongkhapa showed how all the essential practices of Tantra can be included within the practice of a single Yidam. Following Je Tsongkhapa's instructions, later Teachers composed the Vajrayogini sadhana, the ritual prayer that we now practise. When we practise this sadhana we practise the essential meaning of all the Tantras.

Our progress towards gaining Tantric realizations will be seriously obstructed if doubts and dissatisfaction cause us to switch continually from one Deity to another. We should be like a wise blind person who relies totally upon one trusted guide instead of attempting to follow a number of people at once. There is a traditional Tibetan analogy that illustrates this point. Tibetan farmers used to allow their cows to roam freely during the day, mixing with the cows belonging to other farmers, but every evening all the cows would return to the right farm. If a blind person wished to go to a particular farm, all he or she had to do was to hold on to the tail of a cow that belonged to that farm. If he did this he would definitely reach the right farm, but if he kept switching from one cow to another he would soon be completely lost. Similarly, by following the practice of one particular Deity wholeheartedly we will definitely attain enlightenment, but if we keep switching from one to another we will never reach our goal, no matter how much effort we make.

During his stay in Tibet the Indian Buddhist Master Atisha met the renowned translator Lama Rinchen Sangpo and was greatly impressed by his knowledge of Dharma. One day Rinchen Sangpo invited Atisha to visit him to discuss Dharma. Atisha realized that Rinchen Sangpo was a very erudite scholar and said to him, 'You are such a wonderful Teacher that it seems unnecessary for me to stay in Tibet.' Rinchen Sangpo then showed Atisha his four meditation cushions and four different Tantric mandalas. Atisha asked why he had four cushions and four mandalas, and Rinchen Sangpo replied that every day he practised in four sessions. The first session, on the first cushion, was to accomplish the mandala of an Action Tantra Deity; the second session, on the second cushion, was to accomplish the mandala of a Performance Tantra Deity; the third session, on the third cushion, was to accomplish the mandala of a Yoga Tantra Deity; and the last session, on the fourth cushion, was to accomplish the mandala of a Highest Yoga Tantra Deity. Atisha asked why he did not incorporate all these Deity practices into one sadhana, accomplishing the mandalas of all these Deities within the mandala of one Deity.

When Rinchen Sangpo asked how he could do this, Atisha exclaimed, 'Yes, I do need to stay in Tibet!'

Atisha advised Rinchen Sangpo that when he was visualizing the mandala of his personal Deity he should invite all the other Deities together with their mandalas to dissolve into his personal Deity and mandala. By maintaining the recognition that his personal Deity was the synthesis of all the Deities of the four classes of Tantra he could complete the practices of all other Deities by completing the practice of his personal Deity. Atisha used to say, 'Some of you Tibetans have tried to accomplish a hundred Deities but have failed to gain a single attainment, while some Indian Buddhists have gained the attainments of a hundred Deities by accomplishing the practice of just one.'

Although we should concentrate on the practice of one particular Deity we should not neglect to practise others if we have a commitment to do so. For practitioners who are dedicated to the practice of Vajrayogini, who see it as their main practice, and who are striving to gain generation stage and completion stage realizations by depending upon this practice, there is a special method to keep their commitments to other Deities. This involves realizing that all Tantric Deities have the same nature, differing only in appearance. For example, suppose that such a practitioner, in addition to his or her daily Vajrayogini practice, has commitments to recite the long sadhanas of Heruka, Yamantaka and Guhyasamaja every day. If he recites the words of all these sadhanas every day he will have little opportunity to do any serious meditation. His Tantric practice will be largely verbal, and although he might place many virtuous imprints on his mindstream he will not attain genuine experience of meditation, and so the real purpose of Deity practice will be lost. For this reason, great Masters such as Atisha, Je Phabongkhapa and Dorjechang Trijang Rinpoche advise serious Vajrayogini practitioners to integrate all their Tantric practices into the Vajrayogini sadhana by realizing that all Tantric Deities have the same nature, differing only in appearance.

The essential meaning of the practices of all Highest Yoga Tantra Deities is the same – to transform ordinary death, intermediate state and rebirth into the three bodies of a Buddha. This transformation is accomplished first in the imagination using the meditations and visualizations of generation stage, and then in reality by controlling the subtle winds, drops and mind through completion stage meditation. All the methods necessary to do this are contained within the practice of Vajrayogini. With this understanding, committed Vajrayogini practitioners should apply themselves wholeheartedly to the generation and completion stages of Vajrayogini, knowing that by doing so they are fulfilling the real purpose of all their commitments to other Deities, even if they neglect to say the words of the sadhanas of other Deities.

This advice should not be used as an excuse for laziness. Its purpose is to give dedicated practitioners more time to concentrate on their personal Deity practice and thereby gain the essential realizations of all Deity practices. For those who are not yet able to devote themselves wholeheartedly to the practice of a particular Tantric Deity it is better that they continue to recite the words of all the sadhanas to which they have committed themselves.

PRACTISING IN SECRET

If we do not conceal our practice from others the blessings we have received during the empowerments will be dissipated. Talking openly about our meditation experiences is a fault. It may cause us to develop attachment to being respected and praised by others. Such attachment to reputation is a mara – a demonic interference that is a serious obstacle to pure Dharma practice and spiritual attainment. A good reputation may help us to obtain external wealth and possessions, but these things deplete our merit and are obstacles to gaining the internal wealth of pure Dharma realizations. The attainment of bodhichitta, the attainment of the six perfections, and the realizations of generation stage and completion stage are our real wealth; we should not waste our merit on external possessions. As Shantideva says in *Guide to the Bodhisattva's Way of Life*:

I, who seek liberation, have no need for wealth or
  a good reputation
For they only keep me bound in samsara.

It is helpful to recall these words frequently. We should remain indifferent to our reputation while acting in accordance with Dharma. The equilibrium of our mind should not be disturbed by praise or blame, gain or loss. If we are attached to these things we will constantly be distracted from our spiritual practice. We will waste energy trying to acquire possessions and a good reputation, and when we fail in these endeavours we will become overly disheartened. For these reasons it was the custom of the ancient Kadampa Teachers and of Je Tsongkhapa to praise others but to declare their own faults and limitations.

Talking carelessly about our meditation experiences or practice attracts hindrances and obstacles, just as talking openly about our wealth attracts thieves. Although we should strive assiduously in our practice of Tantra we should not reveal our practice to others. There are only two exceptions to this rule: we should confide in our Gurus, and we can discuss aspects of our practice with friends engaged in similar practices provided that they have faith and keep their commitments purely.

If we create these four special causes and fulfil all the conditions for successful practice that have been explained, we will definitely gain realizations quickly through practising the instructions of Vajrayogini.

WHAT ARE OUTER AND INNER DAKINI LANDS?

In general, 'Dakini' refers to a female Tantric Deity, and in this context is synonymous with Yogini and Heroine. Outer Dakini Land is beyond the world of ordinary experience. It is the Pure Land of Buddha Vajrayogini and Buddha Heruka, known as 'Keajra Pure Land'. A Pure Land is a world that is free from true sufferings. Nowhere in samsara is without true sufferings, because the samsaric environment itself acts as a condition to experience suffering. Ordinary beings are born in samsara without choice and continually have to experience dissatisfaction and misery. However, if we purify our mind we purify our experience of the world and thereby attain a Pure Land free from all suffering.

There are different Pure Lands associated with different Buddhas. Dakini Land is similar to the Pure Lands of Tushita and Sukhavati, except that Heruka and Vajrayogini's Pure Land is the only one in which beings can receive teachings on Highest Yoga Tantra and put them into practice.

When through Vajrayogini's guidance those who are very old and infirm reach her Pure Land they will no longer experience the sufferings of old age and sickness. All signs of their old age will disappear and they will be transformed into sixteen-year-olds of great beauty and vitality, enjoying an endless lifespan. All the enjoyments they desire will appear spontaneously. They will never be reborn in samsara again, unless they choose to for compassionate reasons. Everyone who reaches this Pure Land will receive teachings on Highest Yoga Tantra directly from Heruka and Vajrayogini and thereby attain enlightenment quickly.

Outer Dakini Land can also be explained in terms of an individual practitioner's personal experience. From this point of view we attain outer Dakini Land by completing the practices of the generation stage of Vajrayogini. During our training in generation stage meditation we visualize our body as the pure body of Buddha Vajrayogini, our immediate surroundings as the mandala of Vajrayogini, and our world as Dakini Land. If we engage in generation stage practice continuously, the ordinary, impure appearances to our mind will gradually diminish and finally cease altogether. Once we have gained a firm realization of generation stage we will experience only pure appearances and our world will be transformed into Dakini Land. The great Teacher Tenpa Rabgye said that Dakini Land is not some faraway place, nor is it necessary to disappear from this world to reach it.

Pure appearances are experienced only by realized practitioners. It is generally accepted in both Sutra and Tantra that the world appears to our mind as faulty, imperfect and unsatisfactory because our mind is impure – polluted by the delusions and their imprints. In *Ornament for Clear Realization* Venerable Maitreya says that when the minds of sentient beings become completely pure, their environment becomes a Buddha's Pure Land.

A Pure Land can be attained only by purifying the mind. Even when we have attained outer Dakini Land through a firm realization of generation stage we will still appear to others as an ordinary, impure being. Ordinary people cannot recognize that another person is in a Pure Land because they cannot perceive that person's Pure Land and cannot share their experience of it. Someone once asked Milarepa in which Pure Land he had attained enlightenment and Milarepa pointed to his cave. The questioner could see only a cold, empty cave, but for Milarepa that cave was a Pure Land.

Because the minds of ordinary beings are impure, whatever appears to them is seen as ordinary. As ordinary beings with ordinary appearance we cannot experience anything as totally pure and perfect. Even an emanation of Buddha appears to us to have faults. It is because we have ordinary appearance that we view ourself and others as imperfect – subject to faults such as sickness and ageing.

According to Sutra teachings the root of samsara is self-grasping and the delusions that arise from it. However, according to Secret Mantra teachings the root of samsara is ordinary appearances and ordinary conceptions. The self-grasping recognized by Sutra practitioners is only a gross ordinary conception.

In this context, any being who is not a Buddha, and any environment, enjoyment, body or mind that is not a Buddha's, is ordinary. Perceptions of these objects as ordinary due to impure minds are ordinary appearances, and the minds that conceive of objects in this way are ordinary conceptions. According to Secret Mantra teachings, ordinary appearances are obstructions to omniscience and ordinary conceptions are obstructions to liberation. Both ordinary appearances and ordinary conceptions have many levels of subtlety.

One of the main purposes of practising generation stage meditation is to overcome ordinary appearances and ordinary conceptions. We can overcome ordinary appearances by developing clear appearance of being Vajrayogini, and we can overcome ordinary conceptions by developing divine pride of being Vajrayogini.

Because of our ordinary appearances and ordinary conceptions we experience an endless cycle of ordinary death, ordinary intermediate state and ordinary rebirth. This endless cycle, known as 'samsara', must be broken. Through generation and completion stage practice we can purify the three ordinary states of death, intermediate state and rebirth, and thereby attain the three bodies of a Buddha.

When we gain a full realization of the generation stage of Vajrayogini we experience our environment as Dakini Land; and when we attain the illusory body in the aspect of Vajrayogini our body becomes the actual body of the Deity. When we attain full enlightenment in the form of Vajrayogini we become a newly born Buddha Vajrayogini, our place of residence becomes a newly developed mandala of Vajrayogini, and our world becomes a newly developed Dakini Land.

With a superficial realization of generation stage meditation we will attain only a similitude of Dakini Land. By gradually increasing the power of our generation stage meditation this similitude will be strengthened and stabilized and we will move closer to attaining actual Dakini Land. By practising the generation stage and completion stage meditations continuously and enthusiastically we will complete the spiritual path by relying upon Vajrayogini.

At first we may doubt the existence of Dakini Land or doubt that it is possible to reach it. To overcome such doubts we can consider dreams. Sincere practitioners familiar with Vajrayogini practice may dream of reaching a Pure Land. In their dream they will see all places as pure and themselves as Vajrayogini. At that time they do not think they are dreaming; they believe they are in a Pure Land and therefore experience great joy and happiness. If they were to remain in that happy state without ever waking up it would be valid to say that, according to their experience, they were in Dakini Land.

Through studying the correct view of emptiness we can understand that everything is merely an appearance to the mind and, like a dream, merely imputed by conceptual thought. This understanding is extremely helpful for developing conviction in the existence of Pure Lands. Clear and deep understanding of the nature of outer Dakini Land will help us to gain a firm faith in Buddhadharma. Through this we will practise with greater power and enthusiasm.

Inner Dakini Land is meaning clear light. We attain this only through completion stage meditation. Through completion stage meditation we develop spontaneous great bliss, and when this mind meditates on emptiness and gains a direct realization it is called 'meaning clear light'. This is the fourth of the five stages of completion stage. When we attain inner Dakini Land through Vajrayogini practice we also attain outer Dakini Land. This is explained more fully later in this book.

The way to train in the two stages of Vajrayogini Tantra is explained in the instructions that follow. First there is an explanation of how to train in generation stage, and then there is an explanation of how to train in completion stage.

The instructions on generation stage are in two parts: an explanation of how to practise the eleven yogas of generation stage, and an explanation of how to attain outer Dakini Land through the practice of generation stage. The eleven yogas of generation stage are:

1 The yoga of sleeping
2 The yoga of rising
3 The yoga of experiencing nectar
4 The yoga of immeasurables
5 The yoga of the Guru
6 The yoga of self-generation
7 The yoga of purifying migrators
8 The yoga of being blessed by Heroes and Heroines
9 The yoga of verbal and mental recitation
10 The yoga of inconceivability
11 The yoga of daily actions

The instructions that follow explain how to practise each of these eleven yogas. We first need to study these instructions carefully to ensure that we understand clearly each of the yogas. Then, when we feel ready to put them into practice, we should begin with the yoga of sleeping and continue through to the eleventh yoga, the yoga of daily actions. If we repeat this cycle of practices every day, all our actions will be included within the eleven yogas.

The Yogas of Sleeping, Rising, and Experiencing Nectar

The first three of the eleven yogas, the yogas of sleeping, rising, and experiencing nectar, are methods for purifying our body, speech and mind. Collectively they are known as the 'yogas of three joys' or the 'yogas of the three purifications'. The latter title is more correct as it is the one given in the sadhanas of Heruka. The yogas of sleeping and rising purify our mind and body, transforming them into the mind and body of Vajrayogini, and the yoga of experiencing nectar purifies our speech, transforming it into the speech of Vajrayogini.

THE YOGA OF SLEEPING

In general, the yoga of sleeping is included within the eleventh yoga, the yoga of daily actions, along with the yoga of eating and other daily activities. However, there are good reasons why the practice of Vajrayogini begins at night, with the yoga of sleeping considered as a separate practice. One reason is that during the night the Dakinis of the twenty-four places visit sincere Vajrayogini practitioners and bestow their blessings. In *Vajradaka Tantra* it says:

> The Ladies of these places
> Bestow attainments upon practitioners.
> They always come at night,
> They always go at night.

Here 'The Ladies of these places' are the Dakinis of the twenty-four holy places of Heruka and Vajrayogini, which are listed in the extensive sadhana of Heruka body mandala. We can visit these places today.

Buddha Vajradharma

If we are not accomplished meditators we cannot maintain mindfulness and alertness during sleep. This leaves our mind unguarded and exposed to unseen influences. For example, we may fall asleep with a positive mind but wake up feeling bad because during the night we were disturbed by evil spirits who took advantage of our defenceless state. Sincere practitioners of Vajrayogini, however, may find the opposite happening. They may go to bed with a mind preoccupied with the problems of the day, but wake up refreshed, with a clear and positive mind. Although the external situation may be much the same, they are now able to face it with a peaceful mind. They may also find that obstacles to their Dharma practice inexplicably disappear overnight. These are signs that during the night they have been visited by Dakinis from the twenty-four holy places, who blessed their mind and subtle body. Dakinis are able to help a practitioner in this way when he or she establishes a connection with them through pure Vajrayogini practice.

Another reason for beginning the practice of Vajrayogini at night is that during sleep the clear light mind of sleep manifests naturally and, with training, this mind can be used to progress along the spiritual path towards the realizations of example clear light and meaning clear light. One of the main reasons for practising Vajrayogini Tantra is to gain these realizations.

During the day we perceive many different things, but in the darkness of night all these appearances vanish. The day therefore symbolizes conventional truth and the night symbolizes emptiness, or ultimate truth. Beginning our practice at night reminds us that the main purpose of training in these instructions is to develop a mind of clear light that directly realizes emptiness. Remembering this, we begin our practice of the eleven yogas of Vajrayogini with the yoga of sleeping. Other texts present different reasons but the ones given here are the most accurate.

Since we all spend a large portion of our time asleep it is important that we have a method for transforming sleep into the spiritual path. Sleeping, dreaming and waking are similar to death, the intermediate state and rebirth. Through continual training in the yogas of sleeping and rising we will gain the ability to purify and transform our death, intermediate state and rebirth into the spiritual path. This is the main purpose of generation stage meditation.

Briefly, there are seven principal benefits to be gained from practising the yoga of sleeping:

1 We accumulate great merit
2 All our hindrances and obstacles are dispelled
3 We will receive direct care and guidance from Vajrayogini in all our future lives
4 We will be blessed by the Heroines of the twenty-four holy places of Heruka
5 Our practice of generation stage meditation will be strengthened and stabilized
6 We will attain both outer and inner Dakini Lands
7 We will attain enlightenment quickly

There are two ways to practise the yoga of sleeping: according to generation stage and according to completion stage. We may choose either method.

THE YOGA OF SLEEPING ACCORDING TO GENERATION STAGE

Sleeping according to generation stage creates great merit and is a cause to attain the Form Body of Vajrayogini. Successful practice of the yoga of sleeping depends upon having gained proficiency in the sixth yoga, the yoga of self-generation.

When the time for sleep approaches we should regard our surroundings as the Pure Land of the Dakinis and our room as Vajrayogini's phenomena source mandala. The phenomena source is the nature of Vajrayogini's wisdom. It is made of red light in the shape of a double tetrahedron, and we should visualize it as large as possible. Inside the phenomena source we visualize a precious jewelled throne supported by eight snow lions. Covering the surface of the throne there is an eight-petalled lotus, and on top of this there is either a sun cushion, a circular cushion of yellow light, or a moon cushion, a circular cushion of white light. When we lie down to sleep we visualize ourself clearly as Vajrayogini, only without the usual ornaments and hand implements.

If we wish to sleep lightly and wake quickly, or if we wish to sleep with strong concentration, we visualize ourself lying on a cool moon cushion. If we feel cold, or if we wish to sleep deeply or for a long time, we visualize ourself lying on a warm sun cushion. Usually, however, we need a balanced sleep. If we sleep too lightly we may wake too readily, but if we sleep too deeply we will be unable to maintain mindfulness during our dreams. To achieve a balanced sleep we visualize ourself lying on a sun cushion but without imagining it to be warm.

We should lie facing west with our head towards the north. Facing west is auspicious because we invite the Dakinis to visit us from the land of Odiyana, which is in the west. The soles of our feet should point towards the south. This is auspicious for a long life because it symbolizes our wish to subdue Yama, the Lord of Death, who is said to live in the south. Our practice is enhanced by sleeping in this position, but if it is not practical because of the shape of our room or the position of our bed we can simply imagine that we are doing this. Directions are merely imputed.

On the northern petal of the lotus flower we visualize our root Guru in the aspect of Buddha Vajradharma. Visualizing our Guru in the aspect of a Buddha is a practice unique to Secret Mantra. According to the Vinaya the Guru should be regarded as like a Buddha, but according to Secret Mantra the Guru should be regarded as a Buddha.

Although some texts state that we should visualize our Guru in the aspect of Hero Vajradharma, there are in fact three ways in which we can visualize him: in his outer aspect as Hero Vajradharma, in his inner aspect as Buddha Vajradharma, or in his secret aspect as Buddha Vajradharma with consort. In essence there is no difference between these three aspects of the Guru because Hero Vajradharma, Buddha Vajradharma without consort, and Buddha Vajradharma with consort are exactly the same nature. Whichever aspect we choose to visualize, we should regard him as our root Guru, the synthesis of all the Buddhas.

Hero Vajradharma is red. His left hand holds at the level of his heart a skullcup filled with nectar, his right hand is raised holding a damaru, and his left shoulder supports a khatanga. Buddha Vajradharma looks exactly like Buddha Vajradhara, except that Buddha Vajradharma is red and adorned with six bone ornaments whereas Buddha Vajradhara is blue and wears ornaments made of jewels.

Buddha Vajradharma is similar to Buddha Amitabha in that he is a manifestation of the speech of all the Buddhas. It is primarily through receiving teachings from our Guru that we receive the blessings of Buddha's speech, so for us our Guru functions as the manifestation of Buddha's speech. To help us develop this recognition we visualize our Guru as Buddha Vajradharma.

When we practise the yoga of sleeping according to generation stage the most important thing is to maintain strong divine pride that we are Vajrayogini, that our room is the phenomena source, and that our bed is a sun cushion or moon cushion. As we lie on our bed we imagine that we rest our head in Guru Vajradharma's lap, and then with strong faith in our Guru we go to sleep. As we fall asleep we should prevent all ordinary appearances and maintain only pure appearances.

When we wake up we should immediately recollect that we are Vajrayogini, that our room is the phenomena source mandala, and that our root Guru is on the northern petal of the lotus in the aspect of Buddha Vajradharma.

THE YOGA OF SLEEPING ACCORDING
TO COMPLETION STAGE

In the completion stage yoga of sleeping, before we go to sleep we imagine that the entire world system and all its inhabitants melt into light and that this light dissolves into our body. Our body then gradually melts into light and diminishes in size until it dissolves into the letter BAM at our heart. At this stage only the letter BAM appears to our mind; we perceive nothing else. Then the letter BAM gradually dissolves into its head, or upper horizontal line, the head dissolves into the crescent moon, the crescent moon into the drop, and the drop into the nada – the three-curved line at the top of the letter. The nada then gradually decreases in size until finally it dissolves into clear light emptiness.

Now only emptiness appears. It is important to feel that our mind of clear light has become one with emptiness, like water mixed with water. This inseparable union of our very subtle mind and emptiness is called 'clear light emptiness'. We identify this as the Dharmakaya, or Truth Body, of Vajrayogini, and then fall asleep maintaining this recognition throughout our sleep. When we wake up the next morning we immediately remember emptiness. This practice increases our wisdom, causing us to gain experience of the clear light and eventually to attain the Truth Body of a Buddha.

The clear light mind manifests automatically during sleep and death, but only those proficient in completion stage meditation are able to retain mindfulness at these times. Most people are unable to recognize either the clear light of sleep or the clear light of death. Besides sleep and death, the only other time the clear light manifests is when all the winds are deliberately gathered and dissolved within the central channel through the force of completion stage meditation. Yogis or Yoginis who can cause the clear light mind to manifest in this way are able to use this mind to meditate on emptiness. When they fall asleep they remain mindful throughout their sleep and use the clear light of sleep to deepen their experience of emptiness. In deep sleep the winds naturally and forcefully gather and dissolve within the central channel, and the clear light that manifests at that time is purer than that which a novice completion stage meditator can induce through meditation alone. Therefore, sleep becomes extremely valuable for these Yogis. Their most profound experience of emptiness occurs during deep sleep.

Meditators who are familiar with transforming the clear light of sleep into the spiritual path will also be able to transform the clear light of death. They will remain mindful throughout their death process, and when the clear light of death dawns they will be able to transform it into the mind of ultimate example clear light. This realization directly prevents ordinary death. For this reason, transforming sleep into the path is one of the principal practices of Secret Mantra and one of the most important methods for attaining enlightenment.

THE YOGA OF RISING

There are two ways to practise the yoga of rising, depending upon the way in which we practise the yoga of sleeping. If we sleep according to generation stage we should practise the yoga of rising according to generation stage, and if we sleep according to completion stage we should practise the yoga of rising according to completion stage.

THE YOGA OF RISING ACCORDING TO GENERATION STAGE

Immediately upon waking we should recall our visualization from the previous night and try to prevent ordinary appearances. We should develop three recognitions: (1) the world is the Pure Land of the Dakinis, with our room as the phenomena source mandala; (2) we are Vajrayogini; and (3) all other beings are Heroes and Heroines. We imagine that in the space around us Dakas and Dakinis are reciting Vajrayogini's mantra. This causes us to rise with the joyful motivation to benefit others. Throughout the day we regard any sound we hear as the sound of this mantra.

While dressing, instead of putting on ordinary clothes we imagine that we are offering the five ornaments, such as the crown and the earrings, to ourself generated as Vajrayogini. We then prostrate three times to our root Guru on the northern petal of the lotus, which causes him to generate a joyful wish to enter our body and mind. We imagine that he melts into light and diminishes to the size of a small egg. He then enters through our crown and dissolves into the letter BAM at our heart.

Throughout the day we should remember that our Guru is at our heart in the aspect of a letter BAM. We should also maintain the divine pride of our body and mind as Vajrayogini's body and mind, our room as the phenomena source mandala, the world as the Pure Land of Vajrayogini, and all beings as Heroes or Heroines. If we find that we are about to develop negative states of mind we should immediately recall these recognitions. If we can maintain this pure appearance there will be no basis for delusions to arise. We should try to maintain these three recognitions until we go to sleep, when we once again practise the yoga of sleeping.

The yoga of rising is practised continuously throughout the day, and the yoga of sleeping is practised continuously throughout the night. If we practise these two yogas diligently, all our daily actions become a quick path to enlightenment and we will definitely attain Buddhahood before very long.

THE YOGA OF RISING ACCORDING TO COMPLETION STAGE

If we have slept according to completion stage yoga, absorbed in the clear light of emptiness, then upon waking we imagine that from that state of emptiness we arise instantly in the form of Vajrayogini, just as clouds might suddenly appear in a clear sky. As in the practice of generation stage we should develop the three recognitions: ourself as Vajrayogini, the world as the Pure Land of Keajra with our room as the phenomena source mandala, and all other beings as Heroes, Tantric male Deities, and Heroines, Tantric female Deities. The previous night we dissolved all phenomena into emptiness, and our mind of clear light was mixed inseparably with this emptiness and identified as the Dharmakaya. From this union of bliss and emptiness a new world now appears, arising from the substance of our blissful mind and having the same nature as our mind. If we think like this it will be easy to generate pure appearance and develop the three recognitions.

We should maintain the three recognitions strongly throughout the day, recalling them again and again until we go to sleep. To sustain this practice we need both mindfulness and alertness. By relying upon mindfulness we should maintain the motivation and the three recognitions that we generated upon rising. From time to time we should apply alertness to check that we are still holding these recognitions. If we fail to apply alertness our practice of maintaining the three recognitions will quickly degenerate. We will lose pure appearance and revert to viewing ourself as ordinary. This happens because we are so accustomed to ordinary appearance. Whenever we find that we have forgotten our initial motivation or the three recognitions we should recall them immediately. To maintain pure appearance we do not need to recite words or sit on a cushion. If we perform our daily actions with mindfulness of the three recognitions they all become a method for attaining enlightenment quickly.

When we are able to maintain these three recognitions all the time, everything we see will help us to develop great bliss. Nothing will appear as ugly, irritating, or disgusting; rather everything experienced by our senses will seem attractive and will stimulate pure pleasure. Because at this stage we will be very familiar with meditating on the union of bliss and emptiness, even our sense pleasures will remind us of emptiness. Thus, by maintaining the three recognitions all our daily experiences can be transformed into the wisdom of great bliss and emptiness. The practice of the three recognitions is the supreme moral discipline of the Vajrayana. If we understand and really believe that our self, our world and all other phenomena that we normally perceive do not exist, as explained in detail in *Modern Buddhism,* we will not find it difficult to maintain these three recognitions day and night.

THE YOGA OF EXPERIENCING NECTAR

The main purpose of practising the yoga of experiencing nectar is to transform pleasures into the spiritual path. Because we are beings of the desire realm we always take delight in seeing attractive forms, listening to beautiful sounds, smelling fragrant scents, tasting delicious food, and touching smooth and sensuous objects. These five objects of enjoyment are known as the 'five objects of desire'. We usually enjoy them with a mind of attachment, and so most of our actions related to these objects are non-virtuous and lead to experiences of suffering in the future.

It is only through Dharma practice, particularly the practice of Secret Mantra, that our experience of these five objects of desire can be transformed into a spiritual path. According to Sutra teachings we prevent attachment to the five objects of desire by recognizing their faults and avoiding contact with them. In the practice of Secret Mantra, however, we transform our enjoyment of desirable objects into the spiritual path. This transformation is one of the special attributes of Secret Mantra.

The practice of transforming enjoyments is very extensive because it applies to every object of desire. One method is to regard all visual forms as being in essence Rupavajra Goddesses, all sounds as Shaptavajra Goddesses, all smells as Gändhavajra Goddesses, all tastes as Rasavajra Goddesses, and all tactile objects as Parshavajra Goddesses. When enjoying a delicious meal, for example, we should overcome our ordinary appearance of the food by dissolving it into emptiness, and then in its place visualize Rasavajra Goddesses who offer us pure nectar that induces spontaneous great bliss. We can transform the enjoyments of the other senses in a similar way.

Another way to transform our experience of pleasant objects into the spiritual path is to consider them to be by nature indivisible spontaneous great bliss and emptiness. We should regard every visual form, sound, smell, taste and tactile object as having this nature.

Among the many Tantric methods for transforming pleasant experiences into the spiritual path, the yoga of experiencing nectar is a method for transforming our enjoyment of food and drink, thereby enhancing our practice of Secret Mantra. There are three ways to practise the yoga of experiencing nectar. The first is to taste and swallow a nectar pill that has been made in the traditional way, the second is to taste nectar that has been made by dissolving a nectar pill into inner offering, and the third is to regard our daily food and drink as nectar.

We should try to obtain a genuine nectar pill that has been blessed by our Spiritual Guide. There are various types of nectar pill that are produced according to the different traditions of Mahayana Buddhism. In all traditions the ingredients are first blessed through meditative concentration and mantra recitation and then they are made into pills. A meditation similar to that for blessing the inner offering is then used to consecrate the pills, and the mantra OM AH HUM is recited many times with strong concentration until certain signs of accomplishment occur.

At the beginning of the consecration the ingredients of the pills are visualizeds five 'meats' and five 'nectars'. The five meats that are visualized are the corpses of a cow, a dog, an elephant, a horse and a human; and the five nectars that are visualized are excrement, brains, sperm, blood and urine. These base ingredients are then transformed into precious nectar.

A highly realized meditator can transform the actual five meats and five nectars into the substance of precious nectar pills. When the first Panchen Lama, Losang Chogyan, made nectar pills, there were clear signs of this transformation. Through the power of his concentration, fire blazed beneath the container and the ingredients boiled. However, only someone of exceptional accomplishment can transform impure substances such as urine and excrement into precious nectar pills; it is impossible for an untrained person with few realizations to do this. It has been known for some practitioners to make pills from actual meats and nectars and to distribute them even though they have received no signs that the ingredients have been transformed. We are warned in various Tantric texts not to accept such pills, otherwise we may find ourself eating excrement! Instead we should try to obtain pills made from medicinal herbs by a qualified Tantric Master who is known for his or her accomplishment and integrity. We can then be confident that the pills we are given are both wholesome and genuine.

If possible we should try to obtain blessed pills that originate from those of the first Panchen Lama. These pills are known as 'fire-blessed nectar pills'. Nowadays it is difficult to find pills that are entirely made by the first Panchen Lama. However it is possible to obtain pills that have been made by later accomplished meditators who mixed a portion of a pill made by the Panchen Lama with fresh substances, and continued doing this with all subsequent pills so that each pill contains part of a pill blessed by the Panchen Lama. If we obtain one of these pills we can use it as the basis of our practice of the yoga of experiencing nectar, and also for making more pills.

If we are unable to make new nectar pills ourself, we should pour some alcohol or tea into a skullcup, or some other small, clean container, and into this dissolve a pill blessed by a qualified Master. Every morning we should bless this nectar as an inner offering, as explained on pages 57-63, and then taste it. To do this we dip our left ring finger into the inner offering nectar and draw a triangle counter-clockwise on the palm of our right hand, with one point towards our wrist. We then dip the same finger into the inner offering three times, each time placing a drop in the centre of the triangle so that they coalesce to form a single drop. We bless this nectar by reciting the mantra OM AH HUM three times. We imagine that the blessed nectar now has three qualities: it is medicine nectar that prevents sickness, it is life nectar that overcomes death, and it is wisdom nectar that purifies all delusions. We then taste the nectar, regarding it as an offering to ourself, the Deity Vajrayogini. As we taste the nectar we imagine that we experience spontaneous great bliss and with this mind we meditate on emptiness, or at least remember emptiness briefly.

If neither a nectar pill nor inner offering is available, as may be the case for instance when we are travelling, we can use our first drink of the day as the nectar offering. We lift the cup with our left hand and bless the contents by reciting OM AH HUM three times. We imagine that the drink transforms into nectar with the three qualities and we offer this to ourself generated as Vajrayogini. As we drink we imagine that we experience great bliss and then we meditate on emptiness, or recall emptiness according to our own understanding.

We should practise the yoga of experiencing nectar first in the morning and then throughout the day whenever we eat or drink. In this way all our daily actions of eating and drinking become the yoga of experiencing nectar. When practising this yoga, practitioners of the body mandala of Vajrayogini should recall the thirty-seven Heroines at their heart and offer the nectar to them.

There are many benefits from practising this yoga. For example, even if we are old we will retain a youthful vitality because every time we eat or drink we accumulate great merit and create the cause to enjoy a long and happy life. Furthermore, the practice of the yoga of experiencing nectar is a cause to gain Tantric realizations such as spontaneous great bliss. Tasting nectar pills and inner offering reminds us that all eating and drinking is to be transformed into the yoga of experiencing nectar. If we meditate on bliss and emptiness every time we eat or drink, our experience of the essential point of Secret Mantra, the union of spontaneous great bliss and emptiness, will rapidly increase.

An explanation of how to practise the yogas of sleeping, rising and experiencing nectar in a simple manner can be found in Part Two of *Modern Buddhism*.

The Yoga of Immeasurables

This fourth yoga and the remaining seven yogas should be practised in conjunction with the precious sadhana called *Quick Path to Great Bliss*, which can be found in Appendix II. This sadhana was composed by Je Phabongkhapa who is a manifestation of Buddha Heruka. It contains the essential practices of all the Highest Yoga Tantra Deities in general and the practice of Je Tsongkhapa's oral instructions of Sutra and Tantra in particular. We should rejoice in our great good fortune at having met this precious Buddhadharma.

The main practices of the yoga of immeasurables are going for refuge, generating bodhichitta, and meditation and recitation of Vajrasattva. Going for refuge is called 'immeasurable' because during this practice we concentrate on an immeasurable number of objects of refuge; cultivating the altruistic mind of bodhichitta is called 'immeasurable' because we focus our mind of compassion on immeasurable living beings; and meditation and recitation of Vajrasattva is called 'immeasurable' because it purifies the non-virtuous actions we have accumulated over an immeasurably long period of time.

The commentary to the yoga of immeasurables is presented under the following seven headings:

1 Going for refuge
2 Generating the supreme good heart, bodhichitta
3 Receiving blessings
4 Instantaneous self-generation as Vajrayogini
5 Blessing the inner offering
6 Blessing the outer offerings
7 Meditation and recitation of Vajrasattva

Venerable Vajrayogini

Within the eleven yogas, the fourth yoga – the yoga of immeasurables – and the fifth yoga – the yoga of the Guru – contain the practices of the four great preliminary guides: the great guide of going for refuge and generating bodhichitta, the great guide of meditation and recitation of Vajrasattva, the great guide of Guru yoga, and the great guide of making mandala offerings. The first two are included in the yoga of immeasurables and the second two are included in the yoga of the Guru.

These practices are called 'guides' because by engaging in them we are guided to the actual spiritual paths of Secret Mantra. We should know that training in generation stage and completion stage is the supreme inner vehicle by which we will quickly reach the enlightened world. The four wheels of this vehicle are the four great preliminary guides. Through this we can understand that practising the four great preliminary guides is extremely important for the effectiveness of our training in generation stage and completion stage.

Going for refuge is the gateway to Buddhism in general and generating bodhichitta is the gateway to Mahayana Buddhism in particular; meditation and recitation of Vajrasattva is the gateway to purifying negativities and downfalls; Guru yoga is the gateway to receiving blessings; and making mandala offerings is the gateway to accumulating a collection of merit.

GOING FOR REFUGE

This has two parts:

1 General explanation
2 The practice of refuge

GENERAL EXPLANATION

In this context, 'going for refuge' means seeking refuge in Buddha, Dharma and Sangha. The purpose of this practice is to protect ourself permanently from taking lower rebirth. At present, because we are human, we are free from rebirth as an animal, hungry ghost or hell being, but this is only temporary. We are like a prisoner who gets permission to stay at home for a week, but then has to return to prison. We need permanent liberation from the sufferings of this life and countless future lives. This depends upon entering, making progress on and completing the Buddhist path to liberation, which in turn depends upon entering Buddhism.

We enter Buddhism through the practice of going for refuge. For our practice of refuge to be qualified, while visualizing Buddha in front of us we should verbally or mentally make the promise to seek refuge in Buddha, Dharma and Sangha throughout our life. This promise is our refuge vow, and is the gateway through which we enter Buddhism. For as long as we keep this promise we are inside Buddhism, but if we break this promise we are outside. By entering and remaining inside Buddhism we have the opportunity to begin, make progress on and complete the Buddhist path to liberation and enlightenment.

We should never give up our promise to seek refuge in Buddha, Dharma and Sangha throughout our life. Going for refuge to Buddha, Dharma and Sangha means that we apply effort to receiving Buddha's blessings, putting Dharma into practice and receiving help from Sangha, pure spiritual friends, mainly our Spiritual Teachers. These are the three principal commitments of the refuge vow. Through maintaining and sincerely practising these three principal commitments of refuge we can fulfil our final goal.

The main reason why we need to make the determination and promise to seek refuge in Buddha, Dharma and Sangha throughout our life is that we need to attain permanent liberation from suffering. At present we may be free from physical suffering and mental pain, but this freedom is only temporary. Later in this life and in our countless future lives we will have to experience unbearable physical suffering and mental pain continually, in life after life without end.

When our life is in danger or we are threatened by someone, we usually seek refuge in the police. Of course, sometimes the police can protect us from a particular danger, but they cannot give us permanent liberation from death. When we are seriously ill we seek refuge in doctors. Sometimes doctors can cure a particular illness, but no doctor can give us permanent liberation from sickness. What we really need is permanent liberation from all sufferings, and as human beings we can achieve this by seeking refuge in Buddha, Dharma and Sangha.

Buddhas are 'awakened', which means that they have awakened from the sleep of ignorance and are free from the dreams of samsara, the cycle of impure life. They are completely pure beings who are permanently free from all delusions and mistaken appearance. The function of Buddhas is to bestow mental peace on each and every living being every day by giving blessings. We know that we are happy when our mind is peaceful, and unhappy when it is not. It is therefore clear that our happiness depends upon our having a peaceful mind and not on good external conditions. Even if our external conditions are poor, if we maintain a peaceful mind all the time we will always be happy. Through continually receiving the Buddhas' blessings we can maintain a peaceful mind all the time. Buddhas are therefore the source of our happiness. Dharma is the actual protection through which we are permanently released from the sufferings of sickness, ageing, death and rebirth; and Sangha are the supreme spiritual friends who guide us to correct spiritual paths. Through these three precious wishfulfilling jewels, Buddha, Dharma and Sangha – known as the 'Three Jewels' – we can fulfil our own wishes as well as the wishes of all living beings.

Every day from the depths of our heart we should recite requesting prayers to the enlightened Buddhas, while maintaining deep faith in them. This is a simple method for us to receive the Buddhas' blessings continually. We should also join group prayers, known as 'pujas', organized at Buddhist Temples or prayer halls; which are powerful methods to receive the Buddhas' blessings and protection.

In summary, first we engage in the following contemplation:

I want to protect and liberate myself permanently from the sufferings of this life and countless future lives. I can accomplish this only by receiving Buddha's blessings, putting Dharma into practice and receiving help from Sangha – the supreme spiritual friends.

Thinking deeply in this way, we make the strong determination and then the promise to seek refuge sincerely in Buddha, Dharma and Sangha throughout our life. We should meditate on this determination every day and maintain our promise continually for the rest of our life. As the commitments of our refuge vow we should always apply effort to receiving Buddha's blessings, putting Dharma into practice and receiving help from Sangha, our pure spiritual friends including our Spiritual Teachers. This is how we go for refuge to Buddha, Dharma and Sangha. Through this we will accomplish our aim – permanent liberation from all the sufferings of this life and countless future lives, the real meaning of our human life.

To maintain our promise to go for refuge to Buddha, Dharma and Sangha throughout our life, and so that we and all living beings may receive Buddha's blessings and protection, we should recite refuge prayers every day with strong faith.

THE PRACTICE OF REFUGE

This has five parts:

1 Visualizing the objects of refuge
2 Developing renunciation
3 Developing compassion
4 Developing conviction in the power of the Three Jewels
5 Reciting the refuge prayer

VISUALIZING THE OBJECTS OF REFUGE

In the space in front of us, level with our eyebrows, we visualize a vast jewelled throne supported by eight snow lions. Completely covering the surface of the throne is a four-petalled lotus. The eastern petal, which is closest to us, is white;

the northern petal, to our right, is green; the western petal is red; and the southern petal is yellow. The centre of the lotus is green. Upon this is a smaller throne and upon this is a moon cushion and a sun cushion, with the sun cushion uppermost.

Sitting on the sun cushion is our root Guru in the aspect of Buddha Vajradharma. He has a red-coloured body, one face, and two hands, which are crossed at his heart and hold a vajra and bell. At Guru Vajradharma's heart, on a sun cushion, stand Father Heruka and Mother Vajrayogini. Heruka is blue with four faces and twelve arms. He embraces his consort Vajrayogini, who is red with one face and two arms. In the sadhana it says, 'In the space before me appear Guru Chakrasambara Father and Mother.' According to Je Phabongkhapa's intention, 'Guru' here refers to Guru Vajradharma, and 'Chakrasambara' refers to the Deity Heruka embracing Vajrayogini at Guru Vajradharma's heart.

Around Guru Vajradharma, on the yellow anthers of the lotus, are the Gurus of the Narokhachö lineage and all the other lineage Gurus of Sutra and Tantra. From the heart of Guru Vajradharma all the other objects of refuge emanate and fill the entire surface of the four-petalled lotus.

At the centre of the eastern petal stands Vajrayogini, surrounded by all the Deities of the four classes of Tantra. They are in four concentric circles with the Deities of Highest Yoga Tantra nearest the centre, surrounded by the Deities of Yoga Tantra, the Deities of Performance Tantra, and the Deities of Action Tantra respectively.

At the centre of the southern petal is Buddha Shakyamuni, surrounded by all the Emanation Bodies and Enjoyment Bodies of the Buddhas.

At the centre of the western petal are Dharma Jewels in the symbolic form of books composed by the Gurus, Buddhas and Bodhisattvas. These include the Kangyur and Tengyur texts, such as the Tantric texts of Heruka, as well as countless other texts together with their commentaries composed by other Buddhas. We should imagine that these books appear in the aspect of light but are by nature the inner realizations of the Gurus, Buddhas and Bodhisattvas. Holy beings benefit all living beings by displaying their realizations in the form of books that can be studied and put into practice.

At the centre of the northern petal is Manjushri, surrounded by all the superior Bodhisattvas, Emanated Foe Destroyers, Heroes and Heroines. Around the outer edge of the four petals are the Dharma Protectors.

Each refuge being is either sitting or standing on a moon or sun cushion. We imagine that each one is a real living being, not lifeless like a statue or painting.

All the countless refuge objects on the throne in front of us are included within the Three Jewels – the Buddha Jewel, the Dharma Jewel and the Sangha Jewel. The Gurus, Yidams and Buddhas are all Buddha Jewels; the Bodhisattvas, Emanated Foe Destroyers, Heroes, Heroines and Dharma Protectors are all Sangha Jewels; and the Dharma books represent the Dharma Jewel. We should also regard all the refuge objects as manifestations of our root Guru, Guru Vajradharma. The Buddha Jewels are all manifestations of his mind, the Dharma Jewels manifestations of his speech, and the Sangha Jewels manifestations of his body.

We should not expect to be able to visualize the refuge assembly clearly from the beginning. To start with it is sufficient simply to imagine that they are in the space in front of us. The most important thing is to have strong conviction that they are actually present. Even though we may not be able to see them we can be certain that they are appearing before us in subtle forms and that we are actually in their presence. Gradually we will be able to bring to mind a rough mental image of the whole assembly, and as we become more familiar with the visualization we will naturally attain a more detailed image. However, we should not be concerned with detail at the beginning. For example, when we think of a friend we simply bring to mind a general image of him; we do not try to achieve a detailed image of all his features such as his face, his legs, and his arms. In the same way, when we begin to visualize the refuge assembly we should be satisfied with a general image of the holy beings and not try to see all their specific details.

DEVELOPING RENUNCIATION

When we practise the yoga of rising we wake with the divine pride of being Vajrayogini, but when we go for refuge or engage in practices such as Vajrasattva purification we should temporarily give up this divine pride.

To develop renunciation we should first remember the preciousness of our human life. Because of their previous deluded views denying the value of spiritual practice, those who have taken rebirth as animals, for example, have no opportunity to engage in spiritual practice, which alone gives rise to a meaningful life. Since it is impossible for them to listen to, understand, contemplate and meditate on spiritual instructions, their present animal rebirth itself is an obstacle. Only human beings are free from such obstacles and have all the necessary conditions for engaging in spiritual paths, which alone lead to everlasting peace and happiness. This combination of freedom and the possession of necessary conditions is the special characteristic that makes our human life so precious.

In conclusion, we should think:

I should not be satisfied with merely temporary freedom from particular sufferings, which even animals can experience. I must attain permanent freedom from self-grasping ignorance – the root of suffering – through sincerely practising the three higher trainings.

We should meditate on this determination every day, and put our determination into practice. In this way we guide ourself to the liberating path.

DEVELOPING COMPASSION

Next we contemplate the sufferings of all other living beings. We think:

I am not alone in having to experience suffering. There are countless living beings, all of whom have experiences and problems similar to my own, so how can I think of working

*solely for my own liberation? Every living being has at some
time in the past been my dear mother. Again and again each one
of them has had to experience the sufferings of birth, sickness,
ageing, death, having to part with what they like, having to
encounter what they do not like, and failing to satisfy their
desires. At some time or other they all have to endure hunger,
thirst, conflict, uncertainty, and the repeated loss of status and
companions. Until now they have been unable to find security
or satisfaction and have been forced to give up body after body,
taking rebirth again and again. I cannot bear the misery of all
these beings drowning in the ocean of samsara, each one having
no choice but to experience immense suffering. I must work to
liberate them all.*

DEVELOPING CONVICTION IN THE POWER
OF THE THREE JEWELS

Without the protection and guidance of enlightened beings it
is impossible for confused living beings to escape from samsara, the cycle of miserable lives. If we think deeply we will
come to realize that only the Three Jewels, Buddha, Dharma
and Sangha have the complete power to guide and protect us.
Buddhas can protect us because they have four special attributes: they are free from all fear and suffering, they have skill
in liberating all living beings, they have great compassion for
all living beings, and they are without partiality. The Dharma
that is revealed by Buddha is the actual method for gaining
release from samsara, and the Sangha help us to gain realizations of Dharma. In summary, through receiving Buddha's
blessings and help from Sangha, and gaining Dharma realizations, we will be permanently free from suffering and fear. If
we repeatedly contemplate these facts we will develop strong
faith and conviction in the Three Jewels.

RECITING THE REFUGE PRAYER

First we visualize the refuge assembly and generate the causes
of refuge: renunciation, compassion, and faith in the Three

Jewels, and imagine that we are surrounded by the countless living beings of the six realms of samsara. We visualize them all in human form, but remember that in reality each one is experiencing the sufferings of his or her particular realm. Closest to us are our parents, family, and friends. We then imagine that we all recite the refuge prayer together. If we practise in this way, the benefit we receive from going for refuge will be equal to the number of all living beings.

With our prayer to the Gurus we request them to bestow their blessings upon us and to transform all our actions of body, speech and mind into spiritual paths; with our prayer to the Buddhas we request their guidance on the path to liberation and enlightenment; with our prayer to Dharma we remember the special qualities of the Dharma Jewel and generate a strong wish to gain Dharma realizations quickly; and with our prayer to the superior Sanghas we request their assistance on the spiritual path and the removal of all obstacles preventing our attainment of liberation and enlightenment.

If we are collecting a hundred thousand refuge prayers as the first of the four great preliminary guides we can count refuge prayers at this point. We can collect either the prayer from the sadhana or the following short prayer:

I go for refuge to the Gurus, Buddhas, Dharma and
    Sangha.

After reciting the prayer a hundred times, or as many times as we wish, we imagine that five-coloured lights and nectars descend from each of the refuge objects. These dissolve into us and purify all our negative actions, especially those committed against our Gurus, the Buddhas, Dharma and Sangha. We have committed many such negative actions. We may have been angry with our Gurus or the Buddhas, or behaved disrespectfully towards them. We may have lost our faith in them or broken the commitments and promises we made to them. We may have temporarily abandoned Dharma, or developed an aversion to listening to Dharma teachings or to practising Dharma. We may have been critical of Sangha, pure spiritual friends, or behaved disrespectfully towards them. As we recite the prayers and visualize the lights and nectars descending we imagine that all these non-virtuous actions, created in this and all our previous lives, are purified, and that our life span, merit and Dharma realizations increase.

GENERATING THE SUPREME GOOD HEART, BODHICHITTA

The practice of Mahayana refuge includes developing renunciation and compassion, both of which are essential causes of generating bodhichitta. The more we train in Mahayana refuge, the stronger our bodhichitta becomes.

The root of bodhichitta is compassion. The principal method for developing compassion is contemplating the suffering of others and developing a wish to free all living beings from their suffering. We need to develop this compassionate wish again and again until it arises spontaneously, and continuously influences all our thoughts and actions.

Compassion induces a superior intention. Realizing that simply wishing to free others from suffering is not sufficient, we make a definite decision to act to free them ourself. We then think, 'To liberate all living beings from their suffering I must first attain enlightenment myself. Only then will I have the power to bring lasting happiness to all other living beings.' This strong desire, rooted in compassion, to attain enlightenment to benefit all living beings is bodhichitta. When it arises spontaneously in our mind we enter the actual Mahayana paths. Je Tsongkhapa said that to enter the Mahayana it is not enough merely to study Mahayana teachings; the only gateway to the Mahayana paths is actually to generate the spontaneous mind of bodhichitta.

We should generate and enhance our mind of bodhichitta by reciting the bodhichitta prayer from the sadhana. This prayer contains the practices of aspiring bodhichitta, engaging bodhichitta and the four immeasurables. The phrase 'Once I have attained the state of a complete Buddha' refers to the practice of aspiring bodhichitta; the phrase 'I shall free all sentient beings' refers to immeasurable equanimity, indicating that our compassion embraces all living beings without partiality; the phrase 'from the ocean of samsara's suffering' refers to immeasurable compassion; the phrase 'and lead them to the bliss of full enlightenment' refers to immeasurable love and immeasurable joy; and finally the phrase 'For this purpose I shall practise the stages of Vajrayogini's path' refers to engaging bodhichitta. By practising the two stages of Vajrayogini's path we are actively engaging in the methods to attain enlightenment for the benefit of others.

The purpose of reciting prayers is to remind ourself of their meaning. Because our mind is weak in Dharma understanding we must rely upon the support of verbal prayers. Just as a feeble, old person needs a walking stick, so we need to recite prayers to remind us to improve our bodhichitta.

Before practising Secret Mantra we should train well in Lamrim, the stages of the path common to both Sutra and Tantra; and in particular we should become familiar with the methods for generating bodhichitta. The main foundation of successful practice of the two stages of Vajrayogini is to have developed the three principal realizations – the three principal aspects of the path: renunciation, bodhichitta and the correct view of emptiness. In addition to these we need to engage in the preliminary practices. Just as we need a firm foundation to build a good house, so we need the firm foundation of training in the preliminaries and in the three principal aspects of the path if we are to be successful in our Secret Mantra practice. If our practice of the generation and completion stages of Secret Mantra has such a firm foundation it will become a quick method for attaining enlightenment.

Our present state of mind is not permanent. It can change into either a negative mind such as anger or a positive mind such as the altruistic wish to attain enlightenment. At present our bodhichitta may be artificial because it is generated with effort, but with practice we can transform our primary mind into a real bodhichitta that arises spontaneously. However, we cannot develop compassion and bodhichitta merely by listening to teachings. We should be prepared to spend a long time training in the methods to develop them, both in and out of meditation. More detailed explanations of going for refuge, generating bodhichitta, and so forth can be found in *Modern Buddhism* and *Joyful Path of Good Fortune*.

Throughout our practice of the two stages of Vajrayogini we should continue to improve our bodhichitta. We should not discourage ourself by thinking that we cannot practise Secret Mantra because we have not yet developed bodhichitta; we can train in both simultaneously. If we practise Secret Mantra and Lamrim together we will eventually gain realizations of both simultaneously. For example, if we sow an apple seed and a pear seed at the same time and we water and nourish them equally, they will grow together and ripen together. Similarly, from now on we should begin to practise both Secret Mantra and Lamrim, and in the future we will accomplish their results together. These two practices are like friends who help and support each other. Both are indispensable if we are to progress to full enlightenment.

Tantric teachings explain special methods to improve our bodhichitta and our understanding of emptiness. For example, there is one practice called 'generating the mind of all yogas' which is explained during Highest Yoga Tantra empowerments. To generate this mind we first generate great compassion focusing on all suffering sentient beings and then develop a strong wish to attain Buddhahood for their sake. This is conventional bodhichitta. Without losing this wish we then remember that all phenomena lack inherent existence. This is ultimate bodhichitta. At our heart we visualize our conventional bodhichitta in the form of a very small moon cushion lying flat. At the centre of the moon cushion we visualize our ultimate bodhichitta in the form of a white five-pronged vajra standing vertically. Imagining the moon and vajra to be firm, stable and radiating light, we hold this visualization without distraction for as long as possible. We should recall this experience constantly throughout the day.

For skilful meditators the practices of generation stage and completion stage are the supreme methods for improving their conventional and ultimate bodhichitta.

RECEIVING BLESSINGS

As mentioned before, the Gurus, Yidams and Buddhas are emanations of Guru Vajradharma's mind, the assembled Dharma Jewels are emanations of his speech, and the assembled Sangha Jewels are emanations of his body. With this in mind we recite from the sadhana the special request prayer to receive the blessings of the Three Jewels.

We imagine that as a result of making these requests with strong faith, the assembly of Sangha Jewels melts into white light. This light dissolves into our crown and our body receives the blessings of Guru Vajradharma's body. The assembly of Dharma Jewels then melts into red light. This light dissolves into our throat and our speech receives the blessings of Guru Vajradharma's speech. The Gurus, Yidams and Buddhas then melt into blue light. This light dissolves into our heart and our mind receives the blessings of Guru Vajradharma's mind. By receiving these blessings all our faults and negative actions of body, speech and mind are purified, and our actions of body, speech and mind transform into spiritual paths.

INSTANTANEOUS SELF-GENERATION AS VAJRAYOGINI

After receiving the blessings of Guru Vajradharma's body, speech and mind we imagine that the entire world and its inhabitants melt into light and dissolve into our body. Our body also melts into light and slowly diminishes in size until finally it dissolves into emptiness. This resembles the way in which all the appearances of this life dissolve at death. We meditate single-pointedly on emptiness without permitting any conventional appearance to arise. We imagine that our mind mixes completely with emptiness and we develop the recognition 'I am Truth Body Vajrayogini.' This practice is called 'bringing death into the path to the Truth Body.'

From the Truth Body we instantly transform into an oval of red light about twelve inches high and six inches wide, standing vertically on an eight-petalled lotus and a sun cushion. This resembles the way in which the body of the intermediate state being arises out of the clear light of death. We develop the recognition 'I am Enjoyment Body Vajrayogini.' This practice is called 'bringing the intermediate state into the path to the Enjoyment Body.'

The red oval of light, in nature our own mind, now increases in size and transforms into the Emanation Body of Vajrayogini. We develop the divine pride 'I am Emanation Body Vajrayogini.' This resembles leaving the intermediate state and taking rebirth. This practice is called 'bringing rebirth into the path to the Emanation Body.'

If we wish to practise Vajrayogini Tantra daily but have insufficient time or ability to practise either the extensive or the middling sadhana, we can fulfil the commitment taken during the Vajrayogini empowerment to generate ourself as the Deity by practising the following sequence. First we go for refuge, generate bodhichitta, and dissolve the objects of refuge, as explained earlier. We then meditate on bringing death, the intermediate state and rebirth into the path and generate as the Deity Vajrayogini, as just described. We then visualize that at our heart, inside a red phenomena source and on top of a moon cushion, there is a red letter BAM. Standing in a circle counter-clockwise around this is the mantra of Vajrayogini: OM OM OM SARWA BUDDHA DAKINIYE VAJRA WARNANIYE VAJRA BEROTZANIYE HUM HUM HUM PHAT PHAT PHAT SÖHA. With strong faith we concentrate on the BAM and mantra letters and recite the mantra as many times as possible, or at least as many times as we promised to when we received the Vajrayogini empowerment. Finally, we recite a short prayer of dedication. A condensed self-generation sadhana, *The Blissful Path,* can be found in Appendix II.

It is also possible to do a middling self-generation practice in conjunction with the sadhana called *Dakini Yoga,* which can be found in Appendix II. However we should not be satisfied with only short practices. If we wish to attain Buddhahood by relying upon Vajrayogini we definitely need to practise the eleven yogas extensively.

BLESSING THE INNER OFFERING

This has five parts:

1 The benefits
2 The basis of the inner offering
3 The visual object of the inner offering
4 How to bless the inner offering
5 The significance of the inner offering

THE BENEFITS

The practice of inner offering is found only in Highest Yoga Tantra. Inner offering can be used as an offering to the holy beings, for ourself as in the yoga of experiencing nectar, or to avert external or internal obstacles. Blessing and tasting the inner offering is a cause of many levels of completion stage realization. Through this practice we can purify our five contaminated aggregates and elements and transform them into the five Buddha families, and we can purify the five delusions and transform them into the five omniscient wisdoms. Making the inner offering is a cause of increasing our life span, accumulating merit and experiencing great bliss.

THE BASIS OF THE INNER OFFERING

The inner offering is so called because its basis is a collection of five meats and five nectars, all of which are inner substances, or substances derived from the bodies of sentient beings. Torma and tsog offerings are based upon external substances which are not obtained from the body and so they are called 'outer offerings'. For the inner offering, the basis and the visual object are different, whereas for the outer offerings they are the same.

THE VISUAL OBJECT OF THE INNER OFFERING

We set up in front of us a skullcup, or a vessel of similar shape, or any small container that has a lid. Into this container we pour black tea or alcohol, and into this we put a nectar pill that has been blessed by our Spiritual Guide or received from a Dharma practitioner of the same lineage as ourself. This is the visual object. Focusing on this we proceed to bless the inner offering.

HOW TO BLESS THE INNER OFFERING

This has four parts:

1 Clearance
2 Purification
3 Generation
4 Transformation

CLEARANCE

Here, clearance means clearing or driving away obstacles such as harmful spirits who might interfere with the blessing of the inner offering. This is done by reciting the mantra OM KHANDAROHI HUM HUM PHAT. Among the many Deities of the Heruka mandala, the wrathful female Deity Khandarohi is the one responsible for dispelling obstacles and hindrances. She is also known as the 'Goddess of Action' and her mantra is called the 'action mantra'. While reciting this mantra we imagine countless red Khandarohi Goddesses emanating from our heart. They disperse in all directions and drive away any negative forces that might obstruct the blessing of the inner offering. We then reabsorb the Goddesses into our heart.

PURIFICATION

In this context, purification means purifying our ordinary appearances and ordinary conceptions, including self-grasping, by means of meditation. We need to purify the ten substances before we can transform them into nectar. To do this we focus on the visual object of the inner offering and contemplate that it and all other phenomena, including our self that we normally perceive, do not exist. At the same time we recite the mantra: OM SÖBHAWA SHUDDHA SARWA DHARMA SÖBHAWA SHUDDHO HAM, followed by the phrase 'Everything becomes emptiness.' The mantra summarizes the meditation on emptiness – OM refers to the visual object of the inner offering, SARWA DHARMA means 'all phenomena', and SÖBHAWA SHUDDHO means 'lack inherent existence'. The whole mantra, therefore, means: 'All phenomena, including the visual object of the inner offering, lack inherent existence.'

After reciting 'Everything becomes emptiness' we meditate briefly on emptiness, the mere absence of all phenomena that we normally perceive. We imagine that all conventional appearances have dissolved into emptiness, identify this emptiness as lack of inherent existence, and then try to mix our mind with this emptiness.

GENERATION

This has two parts:

1 Generating the container
2 Generating the contained substances

GENERATING THE CONTAINER

We visualize:

From the state of emptiness appears a blue letter YAM. This is the seed of the wind element and its nature is the wisdom of great bliss and emptiness. The YAM transforms into a huge wind mandala, which is blue, bow-shaped, and lies flat with its curved edge furthest from us. At both corners there is a white banner. The movement of the banners activates the wind mandala, causing the wind to blow.

Above the wind mandala appears a red letter RAM. This is the seed of the fire element and its nature is the wisdom of great bliss and emptiness. The RAM transforms into a triangular fire mandala, which is flat and red. One of its corners points towards us, directly above the straight edge of the wind mandala, and the other two corners are above the curved edge of the wind mandala. This red triangle, which is slightly smaller than the wind mandala, is the core of the fire mandala. When this core is fanned by the wind, red-hot flames blaze and cover the whole wind mandala.

Above the fire mandala appear three AH letters of different colours. The letter AH above the eastern point, the point closest to us, is white; the letter above the northern point, to our right, is red; and the letter above the southern point, to our left, is blue. These letters transform into three large human heads, which are the same colours as the letters from which they developed.

Above the centre of the three heads appears a large white letter AH, which symbolizes emptiness. The AH transforms into a vast skullcup, white outside and red inside, which rests on top of the heads.

GENERATING THE CONTAINED SUBSTANCES

To generate the contained substances we should visualize the following:

Inside the skullcup there instantly appear the ten letters OM, KHAM, AM, TRAM, HUM, LAM, MAM, PAM, TAM, BAM. Gradually these letters transform into the five meats and the five nectars. In the east, the part of the skullcup nearest to us, the white letter OM transforms into yellow excrement, which is marked by a radiant white OM, the seed-letter of Vairochana. In the north, to our right, the green letter KHAM transforms into white brains marked by a radiant green KHAM, the seed-letter of Amoghasiddhi. In the west the red letter AM transforms into white sperm marked by a radiant red AM, the seed-letter of Amitabha. In the south the yellow letter TRAM transforms into red blood marked by a radiant yellow TRAM, the seed-letter of Ratnasambhava. In the centre the blue letter HUM transforms into blue urine marked by a radiant blue HUM, the seed-letter of Akshobya.

In the south-east the white letter LAM transforms into the black corpse of a cow marked by a radiant white LAM, the seed-letter of Lochana. In the south-west the blue letter MAM transforms into the red corpse of a dog marked by a radiant blue MAM, the seed-letter of Mamaki. In the north-west the red letter PAM transforms into the white corpse of an elephant marked by a radiant red PAM, the seed-letter of Benzarahi. In the north-east the green letter TAM transforms into the green corpse of a horse marked by a radiant green TAM, the seed-letter of Tara. In the centre the red letter BAM transforms into a red human corpse marked by a radiant red BAM, the seed-letter of Vajravarahi.

All the corpses lie on their backs and are marked at the heart by their respective letters. The human corpse lies in the urine with its head pointing away from us. All the other corpses lie with their heads pointing towards the centre of the skullcup.

In summary, from inside the vast skullcup arise the ten letters – the seed-letters of the five Buddha Fathers and the five Buddha Mothers. These ten letters transform into the ten inner substances that constitute the basis of the inner offering.

Those with no understanding of emptiness should not try to visualize the ten substances too clearly or they might feel that they are visualizing real excrement and urine, and instead of being able to transform it into nectar they will feel disgusted!

TRANSFORMATION

This has three parts:

1 Purifying faults
2 Transforming into nectar
3 Increasing

PURIFYING FAULTS

We contemplate:

Light rays radiate from the letter BAM at our heart and strike the two banners of the wind mandala, causing them to flutter. This causes the wind mandala to blow, which in turn causes the fire mandala to blaze. The heat from the fire mandala causes the ten seed-letters that mark the substances and the ten substances themselves to boil. They all melt together into a hot, orange liquid. As the letters mix with the ten substances, the unpleasant colours, tastes, and smells of the substances are purified.

TRANSFORMING INTO NECTAR

We contemplate:

Above the orange liquid appears a white letter HUM, which is the nature of Heruka's mind, the wisdom of indivisible great bliss and emptiness. The HUM transforms into a white upside-down khatanga. The substance of the khatanga is white bodhichitta and its nature is Heruka's mind.

Due to the heat of the boiling liquid below, the white khatanga begins to melt and drip into the skullcup, as butter melts when it is held close to steam. The melted white khatanga swirls three times counter-clockwise inside the skullcup and then mixes completely with the liquid. The liquid becomes cool and sweet, and takes on the colour of mercury. Due to the mixing of the khatanga, the liquid transforms into nectar possessing three qualities: medicine nectar that prevents all diseases, life nectar that destroys death, and wisdom nectar that eradicates all delusions.

While we are imagining that the liquid is transforming into nectar with the three qualities we need very firm and strong concentration.

INCREASING

Directly above the nectar we visualize a row of Sanskrit vowels and consonants, which are white in colour. In the centre is the letter OM. Starting from the right of the OM and extending from right to left are the vowels in the following sequence: A AA I II U UU RI RII LI LII E AI O AU AM AH. Starting to the left of the OM and extending from left to right are all the consonants in the following sequence: KA KHA GA GHA NGA CHA CHHA JA JHA NYA DA THA TA DHA NA DRA THRA TRA DHRA NA BA PHA PA BHA MA YA RA LA WA SHA KA SA HA KYA.

Above this row of white letters is a similar row of red letters, and above this is a row of blue letters. The letters of each row are the same, differing only in colour. All three rows of letters are made of radiant light.

We imagine that the row of white vowels and consonants gradually dissolves from both ends towards the centre and transforms into a white OM. In the same way, the row of red letters transforms into a red AH, and the row of blue letters transforms into a blue HUM. Now there is a white letter OM, a red letter AH, and a blue letter HUM, one above the other, above the nectar.

These three letters radiate brilliant light rays to the Buddha Lands of the ten directions, invoking the enjoyments of all the Buddhas, Heroes and Yoginis, and drawing back all their wisdom nectars into the three letters. The blue HUM turns upside-down, descends, and dissolves into the nectar, followed in the same way by the red AH and the white OM. The three letters mix with the nectar, causing it to become inexhaustible. To stabilize the transformation of the nectar we recite OM AH HUM three times.

We do all these inner offering practices while reciting the appropriate words from the sadhana. At the conclusion of the blessing we should develop a strong conviction that in front of us there is a special wisdom nectar possessing the three qualities. This nectar can now be used either for our own purposes or to benefit others.

THE SIGNIFICANCE OF THE INNER OFFERING

When advanced meditators bless their inner offering they visualize the various stages as external transformations, but at the same time internally they engage in completion stage practices that correspond to the stages of the blessing. Knowing the symbolism of the inner offering, they use the process of blessing it to greatly enhance their completion stage practice.

The wind mandala symbolizes the downward-voiding winds that are located below the navel. The triangular-shaped fire mandala symbolizes the inner fire, or tummo, at the navel. The three human heads symbolize the minds of white appearance, red increase and black near-attainment – the fifth, sixth and seventh of the eight signs that occur when the winds have dissolved within the central channel. The skullcup symbolizes the mind of clear light, the eighth sign. The skullcup is white outside and red inside, symbolizing emptiness and great bliss respectively. The skullcup itself symbolizes the indivisible union of bliss and emptiness. The five nectars inside the skullcup symbolize the five contaminated aggregates, and the five meats symbolize the five elements – earth, water, fire, wind and space, as well as the five principal delusions – confusion, miserliness, attachment, jealousy and self-grasping. The contaminated aggregates and elements are the principal basis to be purified during completion stage practice. Their generation inside the skullcup of bliss and emptiness symbolizes their purification and transformation.

In general, meat symbolizes the flesh of the four maras that are slain by Tantric practitioners with the weapon of their wisdom. Each of the five meats also has a special significance. Cows are very dull and stupid, so the meat of the cow symbolizes confusion. Dog meat symbolizes miserliness because dogs are very possessive and miserly. Although a dog usually cannot enjoy its owner's possessions it will nevertheless guard them diligently and attack anyone who threatens them. Elephant meat symbolizes attachment. Horse meat symbolizes jealousy because horses are very competitive. When they run together and one horse moves ahead, the others jealously chase after it.

Human flesh symbolizes self-grasping because most humans have an inflated sense of their own importance. These delusions must be purified because they are the main cause of developing both contaminated aggregates and contaminated elements.

The fluttering of the banners on the wind mandala symbolizes the downward-voiding winds ascending. The blazing fire symbolizes the blazing of the inner fire. Through the blazing of the inner fire the winds gather and dissolve within the central channel, inducing the three signs symbolized by the three human heads on top of the fire mandala. When the energy winds have completely dissolved within the central channel the mind of clear light arises. This is symbolized by the skullcup on top of the three heads. Through meditating on the clear light the five contaminated aggregates are purified and transform into the five Buddha Fathers, and the five contaminated elements are purified and transform into the five Buddha Mothers. This is symbolized by the ten substances transforming into wisdom nectar.

In summary, blessing the inner offering indicates the basis that needs to be purified, the path that purifies and the results of purification – the basis, path and result of completion stage practice. When we have understood this and can combine our understanding with the practice of blessing the inner offering, we will begin to appreciate the real significance of this profound practice. Marpa Lotsawa said that tasting the nectar of his inner offering was more powerful than receiving a hundred initiations from other Lamas. This may seem to be a boastful statement, but when we thoroughly understand the special qualities of the inner offering we will realize the profound truth of Marpa's words.

When we bless our inner offering, the basis of the offering is the ten inner substances, but the visual object of the offering is a nectar pill dissolved in alcohol or tea. When we bless torma and tsog offerings, the visual object of the offerings and the basis of the offerings are the same, both having the aspect of nectar for eating. Apart from these differences, the four stages of clearance, purification, generation and transformation are the same when blessing the inner offering, the tsog offerings and the torma offerings.

The procedure for making nectar pills that was mentioned in the yoga of experiencing nectar is also similar to the procedure for blessing the inner offering. However, there are some differences with respect to the visualized basis upon which the pills are established, the substances that are used, and the number of OM AH HUM mantras that are recited during the blessing.

BLESSING THE OUTER OFFERINGS

This has two parts:

1 General explanation
2 How to bless the outer offerings

GENERAL EXPLANATION

Traditionally there are eight outer offerings, which are sometimes followed by a further six. Listed in the order in which they are offered, the eight offerings are: nectar for drinking, water for bathing the feet, flowers, incense, light, perfume, food and music. The purpose of making these offerings to the Gurus, Yidams, Buddhas and Bodhisattvas is to increase our merit, or good fortune, and thereby create the cause for our wishes to be fulfilled. In particular, by offering food and nectar we will gain freedom from the suffering of poverty and obtain the enjoyments of the Buddhas. By offering bathing water and perfume we will become free from samsaric rebirths and attain the Form Body of a Buddha. By offering beautiful flowers we will become free from sickness, ageing, and other bodily ailments, and we will attain the special attributes of the body of a Buddha. By offering incense we create the cause to keep pure moral discipline and attain pure concentration. By offering lights we will become free from the inner darkness of ignorance and attain omniscient wisdom.

By offering beautiful music we create the cause never to have to hear unpleasant sounds but only to hear pleasant sounds, especially the sound of Dharma; and to receive only good news. It is also a cause of attaining the speech of a Buddha. Knowing these benefits we should try to make outer offerings every day, at least mentally.

All Buddhist practitioners should keep a statue or a picture of Buddha Shakyamuni and regard this as the living Buddha. Practitioners of these special Vajrayogini instructions should also keep statues or pictures of Je Tsongkhapa and Vajrayogini and regard these as they would the living Je Tsongkhapa and Vajrayogini. In front of these representations of the Buddhas, Gurus and Yidams we arrange three rows of offering bowls. The first row, closest to the shrine, is for the Field for Accumulating Merit visualized in the practice of Guru yoga; the second row is for the in-front-generated Deity visualized during the torma offering; and the third row is for ourself generated as the Deity. We can arrange more than three rows if we wish. We can set out a hundred rows of offerings, or even more, if we have the time.

According to Mother Tantra, offerings are made starting from the left hand of the Deity. Thus, offerings to the self-generated Deity should be set out starting from our left and offerings to the in-front-generated Deities should be arranged starting from our right, and placed in the order already explained. Traditionally we use water for the first two offerings and the sixth, but we regard it as nectar.

In front of us, on a small table, we place in a row from our right to our left a damaru, a bell, a vajra and the inner offering. The bell faces us with the vajra to its right, just touching it. The other ritual objects should be placed a little apart. The bell symbolizes emptiness and the vajra symbolizes great bliss; together they remind us that when we received the empowerment we made a commitment to train in great bliss and emptiness, and in the union of these two. 'Great bliss' refers to the bliss that arises through the melting of the drops inside the central channel through the power of meditation.

HOW TO BLESS THE OUTER OFFERINGS

This has four parts:

1 Clearance
2 Purification
3 Generation
4 Actual blessing

CLEARANCE

For the clearance stage of the blessing we recite OM KHANDAROHI HUM HUM PHAT and visualize either ten or countless wrathful Khandarohi Goddesses emanating from the letter BAM at our heart. These Goddesses drive away all spirits who try to interrupt us. We then reabsorb the Goddesses into our heart.

PURIFICATION

While reciting the mantra OM SÖBHAWA SHUDDHA SARWA DHARMA SÖBHAWA SHUDDHO HAM we meditate on the lack of inherent existence of the eight offering substances and of all phenomena. This practice purifies our ordinary appearances and ordinary conceptions.

GENERATION

We visualize the following:

From the state of emptiness eight KAM letters instantaneously appear in the space in front of us. These eight letters, which have the nature of great bliss and emptiness, transform into eight skullcups. Inside each skullcup a letter HUM appears. These letters, which are in nature indivisible bliss and emptiness, transform into the individual offerings: water for drinking, water for bathing the feet, and so on. Each offering has three attributes: its nature is the wisdom union of great bliss and emptiness, its aspect is that of the individual outer offering, and its function is to cause those who enjoy it to experience special, uncontaminated bliss.

ACTUAL BLESSING

Above each skullcup we visualize the three letters OM AH HUM, one above the other, and we then recite the appropriate blessing mantra. For each blessing mantra we insert the Sanskrit name of the offering between OM and AH HUM. The Sanskrit names of the eight outer offerings are: AHRGHAM, water for drinking; PADÄM, water for bathing the feet; VAJRA PUPE, flowers; VAJRA DHUPE, incense; VAJRA DIWE, light; VAJRA GÄNDHE, perfume; VAJRA NEWIDE, food; and VAJRA SHAPTA, music. Thus to bless the water for drinking, for example, we recite the blessing mantra OM AHRGHAM AH HUM.

After verbally blessing each offering in this way we imagine that the letter HUM above each skullcup dissolves into the offering, followed by the letters AH and then OM. In this way the offerings are blessed and transform into the nature of the wisdom union of great bliss and emptiness possessing the three attributes.

OM is the seed-letter of all Buddhas' bodies, AH the seed-letter of all Buddhas' speech, and HUM the seed-letter of all Buddhas' minds. The letters OM AH HUM therefore symbolize the body, speech and mind of all the Buddhas. These three letters are the source of all the mantras of the Gurus, Buddhas, Yidams and Dharma Protectors, and when we recite this mantra we invoke the great power of all these holy beings. Despite its brevity, this is one of the most blessed and powerful of all mantras. If we recite it with conviction and strong faith we will receive the blessings of all the Buddhas.

While we recite the blessing mantra we can perform the accompanying hand gestures, or mudras, which symbolize and bless each offering. Illustrations of the various hand gestures can be found in Appendix III. As we recite the blessing mantra for the music offering we play the damaru and bell. We hold the bell in our left hand and play it at the level of our heart to symbolize the experience of clear light, which arises through the dissolution of the inner winds within the central channel at the heart. To attain the wisdom of clear light through meditation we need to ignite the inner fire and cause it to increase, and this is symbolized by playing the damaru. We hold the vajra and damaru in our right hand. We play the damaru at the level of the navel because we ignite the inner fire by concentrating on our navel channel wheel. We begin by playing the damaru and imagining that it ignites our inner fire, and then we accompany it by playing the bell briefly, signifying the subsequent experience of clear light. Playing the instruments in this way sows in our mind a special potential to accomplish these attainments in the future.

The six additional outer offerings are also known by their Sanskrit names. They are: VAJRA ADARSHE, indestructible form – we imagine that all visual forms arise as Rupavajra Goddesses; VAJRA WINI, indestructible sound – all sounds arise as Shaptavajra Goddesses; VAJRA GÄNDHE, indestructible scents – all smells arise as Gändhavajra Goddesses; VAJRA RASE, indestructible tastes – all tastes arise as Rasavajra Goddesses; VAJRA PARSHE, indestructible objects of touch – all tactile objects arise as Parshavajra Goddesses; and VAJRA DHARME, indestructible phenomena – all other phenomena arise as Dharmadhatuvajra Goddesses.

MEDITATION AND RECITATION OF VAJRASATTVA

This has three parts:

1 Developing the intention to purify
2 Visualizing Vajrasattva
3 Reciting the mantra

DEVELOPING THE INTENTION TO PURIFY

Sometimes we feel that our relatives and friends cause our happiness and that our enemies cause our suffering and problems, but in fact all our happiness is the result of our own virtuous actions and all our suffering is the result of our own negative actions. Although, even in our dreams, it is our constant wish to be free from misery, suffering, fear and danger, we will never enjoy these freedoms until we have purified all the negative actions we have accumulated in this and previous lives.

Purification is very important for everyone, but it is especially important for Dharma practitioners who wish to gain realizations of Sutra and Tantra. The negative actions we have created in the past are the main obstacles to our gaining Dharma realizations and fulfilling our spiritual wishes.

Out of his compassion for living beings Buddha taught many methods for purifying negative actions. Among these, one supremely powerful method is meditation and recitation of Vajrasattva. In *The Main Path of the Conquerors, the Root Text of the Mahamudra*, the first Panchen Lama says:

> And since the realization of the ultimate nature of the
>   mind
> Depends upon accumulating merit and purifying
>   obstructions,
> You should first recite the hundred-letter mantra
>   a hundred thousand times
> And make as many hundreds of prostrations as
>   possible while reciting *Confession of Moral Downfalls*,
> And then from the depths of your heart you should
>   make requests again and again to your root Guru
> Who is inseparable from all the Buddhas of the three
>   times.

Powerful purification practices such as training in taking and giving motivated by compassion for all living beings will cause suffering in general, and the sufferings of sickness such as cancer in particular, to cease completely. This is because it will cause self-cherishing and self-grasping, the root of all these sufferings, to cease.

VISUALIZING VAJRASATTVA

We imagine that above our crown appears a white, thousand-petalled lotus and a moon cushion. Upon the moon cushion sit Vajrasattva Father and Mother. They have white-coloured bodies and are in nature one with Guru Heruka. The Father holds a vajra in his right hand and a bell in his left. His arms are crossed embracing his consort Vajramanani, and he sits in the vajra posture. He is adorned with six types of bone mudra-ornament: crown ornament, earrings, necklace, heart ornament, bracelets and anklets, and ashes of bone spread on his body. Vajramanani holds a curved knife in her right hand and a skullcup in her left. She is adorned with the first five mudra-ornaments, but not with the ashes. She sits in the lotus posture, so called because her legs make a shape similar to a lotus as she embraces Vajrasattva.

We should regard them as the real, living Vajrasattva and consort. Their bodies are the synthesis of all Sangha Jewels, their speech the synthesis of all Dharma Jewels, and their minds the synthesis of all Buddha Jewels. We should visualize them about three inches above our crown and ideally about six inches in height, but if we find this difficult we can visualize them whatever size is most comfortable.

RECITING THE MANTRA

This has three parts:

1 The mantra to be recited
2 How to combine recitation with purification
3 Conclusion

THE MANTRA TO BE RECITED

There are four kinds of hundred-letter mantra: the hundred-letter mantras of Heruka, Yamantaka, Vajrasattva, and the Pema lineage. All four mantras are the same for the most part, the main difference being the name of the Yidam at the beginning of the mantra. Thus, in the hundred-letter mantra

of Heruka we recite OM VAJRA HERUKA SAMAYA . . . and
so on; in the hundred-letter mantra of Yamantaka we recite
OM YAMANTAKA SAMAYA . . . ; in the hundred-letter mantra
of Vajrasattva we recite OM VAJRASATTÖ SAMAYA . . . ; and
in the hundred-letter mantra of the Pema lineage we recite
OM PÄMASATTÖ SAMAYA . . . . The remaining letters of the
mantras are mostly the same. In the practices of Heruka and
Vajrayogini we recite the hundred-letter mantra of Heruka.

In general, Vajrasattva and Vajradhara have the same
nature, differing only in shape, colour and ornaments. This is
like someone expressing different aspects of their nature by
wearing different clothes. In *Guhyasamaja Tantra* Vajradhara
says that there are one hundred Buddha families. These
hundred families can be condensed into five, these can be
condensed into three, and these in turn can be condensed into
one – Vajradhara, or Vajrasattva. The hundred-letter mantra
symbolizes the hundred Buddha families and has the same
nature as these families.

HOW TO COMBINE RECITATION WITH PURIFICATION

This has two parts:

1 General explanation
2 Purification in seven rounds

GENERAL EXPLANATION

To combine the recitation of the mantra with purification we
must first develop a strong sense of regret for all the negative
actions we have created in this life and in countless previous
lives.

As mentioned before, all unhappiness, problems, fears,
dangers and unfulfilled wishes are the result of our harmful
actions. In what way do negative actions produce suffering?
We can take a single action of killing as an example. This action
will result in four effects of great suffering. As its ripened
effect we will take rebirth in an unfortunate realm. As its

environmental effect, when we are born human, for example, our birthplace and living environment will be very poor and barren, and we will meet many hazards and problems. As the experience similar to the cause, when we take a human form, for example, our body will be ugly and deformed, we will have to undergo much physical pain, and our life span will be short. Finally, as the tendency similar to the cause, in future lives we will have a natural tendency to kill, taking delight in hunting, warfare, and so forth. These impulses will lead us to create the causes to be reborn in the lower realms again and again. All non-virtuous actions, even the tiniest, produce these four great sufferings.

However much we may wish to advance spiritually, we will find it difficult to make any progress until we have purified these negative actions. Through contemplating the faults and dangers of negative actions we develop intense regret and make a firm determination not to commit negative actions in the future. We keep this regret and determination in our mind and then go for refuge to Guru Vajrasattva at our crown, regarding him as the synthesis of the Three Jewels. Remembering Shantideva's words in *Guide to the Bodhisattva's Way of Life*:

> But I might die before I purify
> All my negativities;
> O Please protect me so that I
> May swiftly and surely be freed from them.

we mentally supplicate Vajrasattva:

> *Please protect me and all living beings from the dangers of negative actions and their effects.*

We then recite the mantra. We first visualize on a moon cushion at Father Vajrasattva's heart a white letter HUM encircled by the white hundred-letter mantra standing counter-clockwise. All the letters radiate light and have the wisdom nature of Guru Vajrasattva. We remember that the hundred letters of the mantra are inseparable from the hundred Buddha families. While reciting the mantra we mentally request Vajrasattva to protect us and all living beings from the misery of our negative actions and their effects.

For this purification practice to be effective we must correctly apply the four opponent powers. Developing regret for the negative actions we have created in the past is the power of destruction, making the determination not to repeat these actions is the power of promise, going for refuge to Guru Vajrasattva is the power of reliance, and reciting the mantra is the power of the opponent force.

PURIFICATION IN SEVEN ROUNDS

We can combine mantra recitation with purification in seven rounds. These are:

1 Dispelling negativity from above
2 Dispelling negativity from below
3 Destroying negativity at the heart
4 Purification through receiving the vase empowerment
5 Purification through receiving the secret empowerment
6 Purification through receiving the wisdom-mudra empowerment
7 Purification through receiving the word empowerment

The first three rounds are general practices and the remaining four are practices unique to Highest Yoga Tantra.

DISPELLING NEGATIVITY FROM ABOVE

To practise the first round we begin by recollecting the feeling of regret and the determination not to commit negative actions in the future. We then focus our attention on the hundred-letter mantra at Guru Vajrasattva's heart and generate strong conviction and faith in Guru Vajrasattva and the power of his mantra. We recite the mantra verbally or mentally seven times or more and then imagine that white wisdom lights and nectars descend from the mantra letters. These leave through the point of union of Guru Vajrasattva Father and Mother and enter our body through our crown. We visualize all our negative actions and delusions in the aspect of sooty liquid, all our ailments and sufferings in the aspect of pus, blood and mucus, and all hindrances from spirits in the aspect of poisonous snakes, spiders and scorpions. As our body fills with lights and nectars we imagine that all these impurities are pushed down from the upper part of our body and leave through our lower doors. They descend to the depths of the earth where they enter the mouth of the Lord of Death. We imagine that he is fully satiated. Our body fills with wisdom lights and nectars and transforms into a body of light, free from all faults of sickness, ageing and death. We meditate on this pure body of light single-pointedly.

DISPELLING NEGATIVITY FROM BELOW

We recollect our previously generated regret, determination and faith in the power of this practice to purify negativities, and we then recite the mantra seven times or more. As before, we visualize wisdom lights and nectars descending and filling our body. We imagine that this causes all our negative actions, sickness, sufferings and delusions in the form of smoke, pus, blood, mucus, snakes, spiders and scorpions to rise up from the lower part of our body and leave through our mouth and nostrils. These then disperse and disappear completely into space. This method is like cleaning the inside of a dirty bottle – as water is poured in from the top and the water level inside rises, the dirt floating on the surface is forced out through the mouth of the bottle, leaving it completely clean inside.

DESTROYING NEGATIVITY AT THE HEART

We visualize all our bad karma, sickness, sufferings and delusions in the form of a mass of black light at our heart and then recollect the three necessary conditions of regret, determination and faith. We recite the mantra seven times or more. We then visualize wisdom lights and nectars descending and entering our body through our crown. When these reach our heart all our negative actions, sicknesses and so forth are dispelled, disappearing all at once, just as darkness is instantly dispelled the moment a light is switched on.

PURIFICATION THROUGH RECEIVING
THE VASE EMPOWERMENT

To receive the vase empowerment and the blessings of Guru Vajrasattva's body we first recollect the three conditions and recite the mantra for a short time. We then imagine that wisdom lights and nectars descend and fill our entire body, purifying all our negative actions of body such as killing, stealing, beating and other ways of physically harming others. We generate a feeling of great bliss and recognize that this feeling is the essence of the vase empowerment. This empowerment ripens the seeds of our generation stage realizations, as well as our potential to attain the Emanation Body of a Buddha.

PURIFICATION THROUGH RECEIVING
THE SECRET EMPOWERMENT

To receive the secret empowerment and the blessings of Guru Vajrasattva's speech we first recollect the three conditions and recite the mantra as before. We then imagine that wisdom lights and nectars fill our body, purifying all our negative actions of speech such as harsh words, lying, criticism and verbal retaliation. This induces an experience of great bliss, which is the essence of the secret empowerment. This empowerment ripens the seeds of our attainment of the illusory body and our potential to attain the Enjoyment Body of a Buddha.

PURIFICATION THROUGH RECEIVING THE
WISDOM-MUDRA EMPOWERMENT

To receive the wisdom-mudra empowerment we recollect the three conditions, recite the mantra, and then imagine that wisdom lights and nectars fill our body, purifying all our negative actions of mind such as harmful thoughts, wrong views, negative intentions, lack of faith, and disrespect to holy beings. The wisdom lights and nectars confer upon us the blessings of Guru Vajrasattva's mind, inducing an experience of great bliss, which is the essence of the wisdom-mudra empowerment. This empowerment ripens the seeds of our realization of clear light and our potential to attain the Truth Body of a Buddha.

PURIFICATION THROUGH RECEIVING
THE WORD EMPOWERMENT

To receive the word empowerment we recollect the three conditions, recite the mantra, and then imagine that wisdom lights and nectars fill our body, purifying all our downfalls, broken commitments and transgressions of the Bodhisattva and Tantric vows. The wisdom lights and nectars confer upon us the blessings of Guru Vajrasattva's body, speech and mind, inducing an experience of great bliss, which is the essence of the word empowerment. This empowerment ripens the seeds of our completion stage realizations of the union that needs learning and the Union of No More Learning.

Sometimes we can practise the first three rounds and at other times the remaining four rounds. For practitioners emphasizing meditation on gathering and dissolving the inner winds within the central channel it is not necessary to practise the first two rounds.

CONCLUSION

When we have finished the meditation and recitation we feel that Guru Vajrasattva is delighted with us. We imagine that he slowly diminishes in size, dissolves into light, and enters our body through our crown. When he reaches our heart he dissolves into our subtle mind, and our subtle body, speech and mind become one with Vajrasattva's body, speech and mind.

We can do the meditation and recitation of Vajrasattva in conjunction with the short prayers from the Vajrayogini sadhana, or separately with the Vajrasattva sadhana. When we do this practice as one of the four great preliminary guides we collect a hundred thousand recitations of the hundred-letter mantra. If we have the opportunity we should try to do a long retreat on Vajrasattva. The most important thing is to do this practice every day until we perceive signs that our negative actions have actually been purified.

If our practice of purification is successful we may experience recurring dreams in which we are washing ourself or wearing new, clean clothes, or we may dream that we are flying, or that unclean substances are being expelled from our body. Other effects of having purified negative karma are that our mind becomes more and more peaceful, and it becomes increasingly easy for us to attain deep experience of Dharma.

Naropa

The Yoga of the Guru

This has two parts:

1 General explanation
2 The practice of Guru yoga

GENERAL EXPLANATION

Practising Guru yoga sincerely is relying upon the Spiritual Guide, the root of the spiritual path. As practitioners of Highest Yoga Tantra we have a commitment to practise Guru yoga six times every day. Guru yoga is an especially powerful method for receiving the blessings of the Buddhas and increasing our merit. By following the Sutra path alone it would take a thousand aeons to accumulate the vast amount of merit needed to attain Buddhahood, but, as Sakya Pandita observed, by wholeheartedly practising Guru yoga we can accumulate the same amount of merit in the brief span of one human life.

Our mind is like a field, purifying negative karma and accumulating merit are like clearing the field of obstructions and fertilizing it, and meditating on generation stage and completion stage is like sowing good seeds. However, these seeds will grow into a harvest of realizations only if they are watered by a rain of blessings from the Yidams and Buddhas. Practising Guru yoga is the means by which we receive these blessings.

The practice of relying upon our Spiritual Guide, as explained in *Joyful Path of Good Fortune*, is the best way to enhance our practice of Guru yoga. Yeshe Tsondru, a highly accomplished Teacher, says in *Essence of Nectar*:

When disciples rely sincerely upon their Spiritual Guide
All the Buddhas naturally enter and abide within the
    Spiritual Guide's body,
And he, delighted with his disciples, accepts their
    offerings
And blesses their mental continuums.

At that time the minds of the faithful disciples
Receive the blessings of all the Buddhas.
Thus maras, evil spirits and delusions will not harm
    them,
And they will naturally gain the realizations of the
    spiritual grounds and paths.

Many Dharma practitioners, such as Naropa, Dromtonpa and
Geshe Jayulwa, have gained instant, pure realizations of Sutra
and Tantra through receiving the blessings of their Spiritual
Guides.

Animals are generally unable to generate virtuous
minds, but occasionally, through receiving the blessings of
the Buddhas, they spontaneously develop minds such as
compassion, love, and the wish to help others. If this happens
when an animal is about to die, its mind will become peaceful
and positive, and this will help it to obtain rebirth as a human
or a god. Nagarjuna said that there is no living being who has
not experienced the happiness of humans or gods through
receiving the blessings of the Buddhas.

Whether or not we receive the Buddhas' blessings through
our Spiritual Guide depends upon how we view him or her.
If we view our Spiritual Guide as a Buddha we will receive
the blessings of a Buddha, if we view him as a Bodhisattva
we will receive the blessings of a Bodhisattva, and if we see
him as an ordinary being we will receive no blessings. Geshe
Potowa said that whether or not our Spiritual Guide is precious depends upon our own view and not upon the Spiritual
Guide's qualities. It does not matter whether or not our
Spiritual Guide is an actual Buddha. If we lack faith in our
Spiritual Guide we will gain nothing from him, even if he is a

living Buddha. Conversely, if our Spiritual Guide is an ordinary being but we regard him as a Buddha we will definitely receive Buddha's blessings. The benefits of relying upon our Spiritual Guide and the methods for doing so in thought and in deed are explained in detail in Lamrim. It is important that we train in relying upon our Spiritual Guide in accordance with the Lamrim instructions.

Who is our root Guru? As Tantric practitioners our root Guru is the Spiritual Teacher from whom we receive the empowerment, transmission and complete commentary of our main Yidam practice. Thus if our main practice is Vajrayogini our root Guru is the Teacher who gave us the empowerment, transmission and complete commentary of Vajrayogini. Some Vajrayogini practitioners may have more than one root Guru, but when they practise Guru yoga they should visualize Buddha Vajradharma and regard him as being the essence of all their Gurus; and with this recognition make prostrations, offerings, requests and so forth.

THE PRACTICE OF GURU YOGA

This has six parts:

1 Visualization
2 Prostration
3 Offerings
4 Requesting the lineage Gurus
5 Receiving the blessings of the four empowerments
6 Absorbing the Gurus

VISUALIZATION

In the space in front of us, arisen from the omniscient wisdom of Guru Vajradharma and inseparable from emptiness, is a celestial mansion which is square with four doorways, ornaments and archways. It possesses all the essential architectural and ornamental features. In the centre of this mansion is a precious jewelled throne supported by eight snow lions. Upon this, on a lotus of various colours, a moon, and a sun cushion, sits our root Guru in the aspect of Buddha

Vajradharma. He has a red-coloured body, one face, and two hands, which are crossed at his heart and hold a vajra and bell. He is in the prime of his youth, adorned with silk garments and the appropriate jewel and bone ornaments.

Around Guru Vajradharma are the lineage Gurus. They are arranged in a counter-clockwise sequence, forming a square around Guru Vajradharma. In front of Guru Vajradharma is the first lineage Guru, Buddha Vajradharma. In the sadhana it says 'Buddha Vajradhara'. Buddha Vajradhara and Buddha Vajradharma are the same nature. Here, Buddha Vajradhara is appearing in the aspect of Buddha Vajradharma.

To Buddha Vajradharma's left is Vajrayogini, followed by Naropa, Pamtingpa, and Sherab Tseg. The next nine lineage Gurus from Malgyur Lotsawa to Sonam Gyaltsen are to Guru Vajradharma's left, the next nine Gurus from Yarlungpa to Wangchug Rabten are behind him, the next nine Gurus from Jetsun Kangyurpa to Ganden Dargyay are to his right, and the last five Gurus from Dharmabhadra to Losang Yeshe are in front of him and to the right of Buddha Vajradharma. The complete list of the lineage Gurus can be found in the extensive sadhana, *Quick Path to Great Bliss*, in Appendix II.

From Buddha Vajradharma to Lama Losang Yeshe Dorjechang Trijang Rinpoche there are thirty-seven lineage Gurus, but the total number of lineage Gurus can vary for different disciples. For example, if a practitioner's root Guru is Dorjechang Trijang Rinpoche, Trijang Rinpoche should be at the centre of his or her visualization in the aspect of Guru Vajradharma. For that practitioner the last lineage Guru would then be Je Phabongkhapa Dechen Nyingpo and the lineage Gurus would number thirty-six. Therefore, the number of lineage Gurus is not fixed.

We should visualize Buddha Vajradharma and Vajrayogini in their usual aspects. The remaining lineage Gurus are in the aspect of Hero Vajradharma. In the prime of their youth, they have red-coloured bodies with one face and two hands. They sit in the vajra posture wearing the six bone ornaments. With their right hands they play damarus and with their left hands they hold at the level of their hearts skullcups filled with nectar. Khatangas rest against the inside of their left elbows.

At the crown of each Guru is a white letter OM, the symbol of the body of all Buddhas; at their throat a red AH, the symbol of the speech of all Buddhas; and at their heart a blue HUM, the symbol of the mind of all Buddhas. These three letters show that these Gurus are the synthesis of the Three Jewels. Visualizing our root and lineage Gurus in this way is called 'generating the commitment beings'.

From the HUM at the heart of our root Guru, light rays radiate and invite all the Gurus, Yidams, Buddhas and Dharma Protectors to come from their natural abodes. The natural abode of all Buddhas is the Nature Body, the ultimate nature of their omniscient mind. We then recite:

OM VAJRA SAMADZA DZA HUM BAM HO
Each becomes a nature which is the synthesis of all objects of refuge.

and we imagine that the invited wisdom beings dissolve into the commitment beings.

PROSTRATION

Focusing on our Spiritual Guide on the central throne we generate three recognitions: (1) he or she is the embodiment of all Buddhas, (2) he or she is inseparable from Vajrayogini, and (3) his or her kindness exceeds that of all other Buddhas. In this way we generate deep faith and respect for our Spiritual Guide. With this mind of faith and respect we imagine that we emanate countless replicas of our body pervading the entire world, and that with these emanated bodies we make physical prostrations to our Guru. At the same time, with our palms pressed together, we recite the following praise while contemplating its meaning:

Vajra Holder, my jewel-like Guru,
Through whose kindness I can accomplish
The state of great bliss in an instant,
At your lotus feet humbly I bow.

In this verse of praise our Guru is compared to a wish-granting jewel because if we develop unshakeable faith in him he will help us to attain the wisdom of spontaneous great bliss. This bliss is the supreme, quick path to Buddhahood that enables us to fulfil all our own wishes and those of all other living beings. The phrase 'accomplish the state of great bliss in an instant' means that by practising Guru yoga purely we can attain spontaneous great bliss and Buddhahood within the brief span of one human life. If we constantly make prostrations to our Guru with our body, speech and mind, every moment of our human life will have great meaning.

OFFERINGS

We make the following seven offerings:

1 Outer offerings
2 Inner offering
3 Secret offering
4 Thatness offering
5 Offering our spiritual practice
6 Kusali tsog offering
7 Offering the mandala

OUTER OFFERINGS

To make the eight outer offerings we recite the offering prayers from the sadhana. As we offer each substance we imagine that countless offering goddesses emanate from the letter BAM at our heart and make the offering to the Gurus. First innumerable white Ahrghamvajra Goddesses emanate, each one holding a vessel of nectar. These are followed by white Padämvajra Goddesses holding vessels of bathing water, white Pupevajra Goddesses holding flowers, smoke-coloured Dhupevajra Goddesses holding incense, orange Diwevajra Goddesses holding lights, green Gändhavajra Goddesses holding vessels of perfume, multicoloured Newidevajra Goddesses holding precious bowls of food, and multicoloured Shaptavajra Goddesses playing musical instruments.

As we make each offering we perform the accompanying mudra and recite the appropriate offering mantra. Thus, when we make the first offering, nectar for drinking, we emanate the Ahrghamvajra Goddesses, perform the mudra of offering nectar for drinking, and recite OM AHRGHAM PARTITZA SŌHA. We then reabsorb the Ahrghamvajra Goddesses into our heart and emanate the next set of goddesses, the Padāmvajra Goddesses. We perform the accompanying mudra and recite the appropriate offering mantra. Each of the eight offerings follows the same pattern.

Next we offer the objects of enjoyment of the six senses, such as beautiful forms and melodious sounds. We imagine that countless vajra goddesses such as Rupavajra Goddesses emanate from the BAM at our heart to make the offerings. Each offering that the Gurus receive causes them to experience uncontaminated great bliss. The different vajra goddesses are named after the Sanskrit word for their offering and they all have different aspects. Rupavajra Goddesses are white and hold jewelled mirrors reflecting all the visible forms of the universe; Shaptavajra Goddesses are blue and play various instruments such as flutes; Gāndhavajra Goddesses are yellow and hold jewelled vessels filled with perfume; Rasavajra Goddesses are red and hold jewelled containers filled with various foods; Parshavajra Goddesses are green and hold an assortment of precious cloths, delightful to the touch, and Dharmadhatuvajra Goddesses are white and hold phenomena sources symbolizing the ultimate nature of phenomena. While visualizing these goddesses making the offerings we recite the offering mantras from OM AH VAJRA ADARSHE HUM up to OM AH VAJRA DHARME HUM and perform the accompanying mudras. All the various mudras are illustrated in Appendix III.

Whenever we make these offerings we imagine that all the visual forms that exist in the universe transform into Rupavajra Goddesses, all sounds transform into Shaptavajra Goddesses, all smells transform into Gāndhavajra Goddesses, all tastes transform into Rasavajra Goddesses, all objects of touch transform into Parshavajra Goddesses, and all other phenomena transform into Dharmadhatuvajra Goddesses. These goddesses make offerings to the assembled Gurus and Deities, to the self-generated Deity, or to the assembly of the Deities of the body mandala.

INNER OFFERING

To offer the inner offering we imagine that red offering goddesses emanate from our heart, scoop up some nectar from the inner offering in front of us, and offer it to the Gurus. At the same time we dip our left ring finger into the nectar and flick some nectar into space while reciting the inner offering mantra: OM GURU VAJRA DHARMA SAPARIWARA OM AH HUM. We imagine that the Gurus accept this offering and as a result experience spontaneous great bliss. We then reabsorb the goddesses into our heart.

SECRET OFFERING

While reciting the prayers from the sadhana we imagine that countless attractive knowledge goddesses in the aspect of Vajrayogini emanate from our heart. These knowledge goddesses serve as Tantric consorts, or mudras. They are of three types: (1) Dakinis of the twenty-four places, (2) mudras with realizations of generation stage or the first stages of completion stage, and (3) mudras with realizations of the union that needs learning or the Union of No More Learning. The goddesses absorb into one another to become one single Deity. She then embraces Guru Vajradharma, causing both of them to experience uncontaminated bliss.

THATNESS OFFERING

Through embracing, Guru Vajradharma Father and Mother experience an uncontaminated bliss that realizes thatness, the emptiness of all phenomena. This realization of indivisible bliss and emptiness is the thatness offering.

OFFERING OUR SPIRITUAL PRACTICE

At this point we offer our practice of the Tantric seven limbs. This is the supreme offering that delights our Spiritual Guide more than any other. The Tantric seven limbs are our practices of purifying, rejoicing, ultimate bodhichitta, refuge, aspiring bodhichitta, engaging bodhichitta and dedication.

The practice of the seven limbs is indispensable for practitioners of Highest Yoga Tantra. According to the teaching of Highest Yoga Tantra, ultimate bodhichitta is the wisdom of spontaneous bliss that realizes emptiness directly. This is the actual quick path leading to the Union of No More Learning. Before we can realize ultimate bodhichitta we must generate the two types of conventional bodhichitta – aspiring bodhichitta and engaging bodhichitta; and all these attainments depend upon going for refuge, accumulating merit, purifying negative actions and dedicating virtue.

We can offer these seven limbs with the Tantric prayer of seven limbs from the sadhana:

I go for refuge to the Three Jewels
And confess individually all negative actions.
I rejoice in the virtues of all beings
And promise to accomplish a Buddha's
 enlightenment.

I go for refuge until I am enlightened
To Buddha, Dharma and the Supreme Assembly,
And to accomplish the aims of myself and others
I shall generate the mind of enlightenment.

Having generated the mind of supreme enlightenment,
I shall invite all sentient beings to be my guests
And engage in the pleasing, supreme practices of
 enlightenment.
May I attain Buddhahood to benefit migrators.

The first four lines of this prayer come from *Vajrapanjara Tantra*. According to the Highest Yoga Tantra interpretation the first two lines indicate purification, the third rejoicing, and the fourth training in ultimate bodhichitta. The phrase 'promise to accomplish a Buddha's enlightenment' means to train in developing the wisdom of spontaneous bliss inseparable from emptiness, which is the main cause of the enlightened mind of a Buddha. The first two lines of the second verse indicate Mahayana refuge, and the last two indicate the practice of aspiring bodhichitta. In the last verse, the first three lines indicate engaging bodhichitta and the Bodhisattva vows, and the last line is a dedication prayer.

Sometimes we can offer our experience of these seven limbs by imagining that our inner experiences transform into a variety of offerings such as flowers, beautiful gardens, parks, mountains and lakes. We can offer to the Gurus any of our virtuous actions, such as moral discipline, giving, patience, mental stabilization, or wisdom. All these offerings of our spiritual practice are called 'sublime offerings'.

<h2 style="text-align:center">KUSALI TSOG OFFERING</h2>

'Kusali' literally means 'possessor of virtue'. It is the name given to very special Dharma practitioners, like Shantideva, who appear to engage in little spiritual practice but who in fact practise extensively and powerfully in secret. In the kusali tsog offering we use our imagination to offer our own body rather than offering external things. Because it is our most precious possession, it is far more powerful to offer our body to our Spiritual Guide by performing the kusali tsog offering than it is to offer other material things. The kusali tsog offering is said to resemble the secret practices of kusali Yogis because it is made only mentally and other people cannot see it. The literal meaning of the word 'tsog' is 'collection'. In this context it refers to the vast collection of merit that we accumulate by making this offering.

There are two ways to offer our body to our Spiritual Guides and the Buddhas. One way is to offer our body as a servant, as did Naropa, Milarepa, and Geshe Jayulwa. The other way is to generate a strong and clear determination to offer our body, mentally to transform it into nectar, and then to offer it to the holy beings and give it to all sentient beings. This method is similar to the 'white distribution' of the 'chod', or 'cutting', practice – the principal difference being that in the kusali tsog offering we do not use ritual objects such as a large drum or a thigh-bone trumpet.

The kusali tsog offering is an especially powerful practice of giving that can sever our self-cherishing and self-grasping. A similar effect can also be attained through the practice of taking and giving. Both practices greatly increase our collection of merit.

To practise the kusali tsog offering we temporarily abandon our clear appearance of being the Deity and resume our ordinary form. We then generate a special motivation by contemplating the following:

From beginningless time until now I have taken countless rebirths, and each time I had a body. Of all these bodies, my present body is the only one that remains. All my previous bodies have disappeared. Some were reduced to ashes by fire, some were buried in the ground, some were thrown into water, and some were eaten. To have taken all those forms would have been worthwhile if I had extracted some meaning from my past lives, but most of my lives were wasted. In the same way, to have taken this present form will prove just as futile if I do not use it in a meaningful way.

My main aim is to attain enlightenment as soon as possible so that I can benefit all living beings. To accomplish this I must use my body to create a great wealth of merit. Whether I use it in a meaningful way or not, this body will be destroyed sooner or later, as were all my previous bodies. Therefore I must use my body now while I still have the opportunity. The best way to do this is by practising the kusali tsog offering. I shall transform my body into nectar, offer it to the Gurus and Three Jewels, and give it to all living beings. Through this practice I will cut my self-cherishing and self-grasping and attain Buddhahood to protect all living beings.

Having generated this motivation we visualize that our mind is in the aspect of a letter BAM at our heart. We then develop a strong wish to separate our mind from our body. Our mind, the letter BAM at our heart, transforms into a thumb-sized Vajrayogini, referred to in the sadhana as the 'powerful Lady of Dakini Land'. In this form our mind shoots up from our heart like an arrow, leaves our body through the crown of our head, and flies towards our root Guru. Coming face to face with our root Guru, our mind-Vajrayogini then increases to the size of a woman of average height. We retain this form for the remainder of the kusali tsog offering.

Now we transform our old body into a form that is suitable to offer. We imagine that we turn to look back at it and see that it has fallen to the ground, where it has become fat and oily, and as huge as a mountain. Those who are ordained should visualize their old body in the aspect of a lay person and not as a monk or nun. As we move closer to this gigantic corpse three enormous human heads spontaneously appear. They are arranged in a triangle, like three stones arranged to support a cooking pot. We touch the forehead of the corpse with our curved knife and instantly the skin peels away and the skull cracks open. The skullcap falls away to form a giant cup, or kapala, which is placed on the grate of three human heads. We chop the rest of the corpse into pieces and heap these into the skullcup. The pile of dismembered flesh and bones in the skullcup is as large as a mountain, and it is surrounded by an ocean of blood, pus and other bodily liquids. Our mind-Vajrayogini stares with wide open eyes at the skullcup and the substances inside. As it is inappropriate to offer such impure substances to the holy beings we must now bless these substances and transform them into nectar.

The blessing of the kusali tsog offering includes all the profound meaning of the blessing of the inner offering and the visualization is very similar. The main difference is that on this occasion we need recite only OM AH HUM HA HO HRIH three times while performing the accompanying mudras. These six letters accompanied by the mudras contain the four stages of blessing that are found in the blessing of the inner offering.

Clearance, usually the first stage, is the last stage in the blessing of the kusali tsog offering, and it is accomplished through a mudra. Purification and generation are accomplished in association with the letters OM AH HUM, and transformation is accomplished in association with the letters HA HO HRIH.

When we say OM, we should make our right hand into a fist at heart level. On top of this we place our left hand, which is open with the palm facing outwards, the fingers pointing upwards, and the thumb tucked in. This mudra symbolizes the wisdom of clear light realizing emptiness. Generally in Secret Mantra the left side or left hand signifies wisdom realizing emptiness and the right signifies method. Mother Tantras such as Vajrayogini Tantra emphasize the development of the clear light of emptiness, and to remind us of this we should try to begin each physical action with our left. For example, when we start to eat we should pick up the cutlery with our left hand and recall clear light emptiness. This helps us to maintain mindfulness throughout the day.

The letter OM symbolizes the ultimate nature of our body and all other phenomena. By reciting OM, performing the accompanying mudra, and briefly meditating on the lack of inherent existence of the skullcup and its contents we overcome our ordinary appearances and ordinary conceptions and thereby purify the skullcup and its contents.

When we say AH, we make a similar mudra but with our left hand in a fist and our right hand upright. This mudra symbolizes method, indicating the generation of the conventionally existent offering container. When we focus our mind on the huge skullcup on top of the three human heads, this is similar to generating the skullcup from the syllable AH in the blessing of the inner offering.

When we say HUM, we imagine that from a HUM inside the large skullcup the substances of our former body appear in the form of the five meats and five nectars. At the same time we perform the mudra symbolizing the ten substances. To do this we hold our hands at the level of our heart with the palms facing outwards, the tips of the thumbs touching, and the fingers outstretched.

Inside the kapala are the five meats and the five nectars. By reciting HA HO HRIH we transform them into nectar. The letters HA HO HRIH have the same nature and the same meaning as the letters OM AH HUM which are used to bless the inner offering. Both signify the three Vajra Buddhas: Akshobya, Amitabha and Vairochana. Akshobya is the Vajra Mind Buddha, the Buddha whose nature is the mind of all Buddhas; Amitabha is the Vajra Speech Buddha, whose nature is the speech of all Buddhas; and Vairochana is the Vajra Body Buddha, whose nature is the bodies of all Buddhas. HRIH and HUM are the seed-letters of Buddha Akshobya, HA and AH are the seed-letters of Buddha Amitabha, and HO and OM are the seed-letters of Buddha Vairochana.

In the space directly above the kapala we visualize a blue letter HRIH. This symbolizes the vajra mind, the nature of all Buddhas' minds. To the right of the HRIH we visualize a red letter HA, the symbol of the vajra speech, the nature of all Buddhas' speech; and to the left of the HRIH we visualize a white letter HO, the symbol of the vajra body, the nature of all Buddhas' bodies.

As we recite HA HO HRIH these letters melt and fall into the skullcup, mixing with the ten substances. As the letters and substances mix together they transform into nectar possessing the three qualities, as explained in the inner offering. While reciting HA HO HRIH we perform the mudra of clearance, known as the 'Garuda Mudra'. This mudra symbolizes the Deity, Garuda, who appears as a terrifying bird. At one time the people of this world were afflicted with many terrible diseases, caused by harmful naga-spirits, which were extremely difficult to cure. After being requested by Vajrapani, Buddha Shakyamuni manifested as the Garuda and completely pacified the harmful actions of these malevolent beings.

To perform the Garuda mudra we touch the middle finger and thumb of each hand together and then touch the joined middle fingers and thumbs of both hands together. The tip of the right ring finger then crosses on top of the nail of the left ring finger and both little fingers touch at the tips and point away from us. The two index fingers point upwards. The spaces inside the touching middle finger and thumb symbolize the Garuda's eyes, the index fingers the Garuda's horns, the two ring fingers the Garuda's tucked-in wings, and the two little fingers the Garuda's tail. Seeing this mudra, naga-spirits remember the Garuda and immediately flee in panic. This mudra also drives away the many other spirits who harbour harmful thoughts against practitioners, as well as the spirits who try to interfere with the blessing of the kusali tsog offering. An illustration of this mudra can be found in Appendix III.

Now our old body has been blessed and transformed into nectar, and is ready to be offered to the holy beings and given to ordinary beings. First we offer the nectar to the principal guest, our root Guru, Guru Vajradharma. To make offerings to our root Guru we hold the inner offering container at the level of our forehead and recite the offering verse from the sadhana:

I offer this nectar of commitment substance
To my root Guru, the nature of the four [Buddha]
  bodies;
May you be pleased.

At the same time we visualize that seven leading offering goddesses, together with many other goddesses, emanate from our heart. With their skullcups they scoop up nectar from the huge skullcup and offer it to our root Guru. At the end of the verse we say OM AH HUM seven times. Each time we say OM AH HUM we dip our left ring finger into the nectar and flick a drop of nectar into space. We imagine that our root Guru is delighted with our offering and accepts it by drawing the nectar through his tongue of vajra-light. This causes him to experience spontaneous great bliss. We then reabsorb all the offering goddesses into our heart.

After making offerings to our root Guru we offer the nectar to the lineage Gurus of these instructions. Holding the inner offering as before, we recite the next verse while imagining that many offering goddesses emanate from our heart. With their skullcups they scoop up nectar from the huge skullcup and offer it to the lineage Gurus who surround our root Guru. At the end of the verse we say OM AH HUM once and flick a drop of nectar away from us. We imagine that the lineage Gurus are delighted to accept our offering and we then reabsorb the offering goddesses.

Next we focus on the Three Jewels. Visualizing them as in the Lamrim Merit Field, we make offerings to all the other lineage Gurus of Sutra and Tantra, to the Buddhas, to the Yidams of the four classes of Tantra, and to the Bodhisattvas. Holding the inner offering at the level of our throat we recite the next verse while imagining that many offering goddesses emanate from our heart. With their skullcups they scoop up nectar and offer it to the Three Jewels. At the end of the verse we say OM AH HUM and flick the nectar once. We imagine that the Three Jewels are delighted to accept our offering and we then reabsorb the offering goddesses.

Next we offer the nectar to the different types of guardian. We visualize all the local guardians, regional guardians and directional guardians throughout the universe, concentrating especially on those who protect our own country and the area in which we live or are doing retreat. We also visualize all the peaceful and wrathful spirits and nagas – those who help, those who harm, and those who are neutral. Holding the inner offering at the level of our heart we recite the next verse, emanating offering goddesses who scoop up the nectar and offer it to the guardians. At the end of the verse we say OM AH HUM and flick the nectar once. We imagine that the guardians accept our offering and we then reabsorb the offering goddesses.

Lastly we offer the nectar to all sentient beings in the six realms and the intermediate state. Holding the inner offering at the level of our navel we recite the next verse, emanating offering goddesses who scoop up the nectar and give it to all these beings. At the end of the verse we say OM AH HUM and flick the nectar once.

We imagine that all the guests are completely satisfied and enjoy uncontaminated bliss. All sentient beings receive whatever they wish for – food, drink, beautiful things – and their mental and physical faults are purified. Their environment is purified and transforms into outer Dakini Land, their bodies transform into the form of Vajrayogini, and their minds transform into the supreme inner Dakini Land, the clear light Truth Body.

After making the offering we reabsorb the offering goddesses and contemplate that the three circles of the offering – the guests, the offering, and ourself – are empty of inherent existence and have the nature of the union of bliss and emptiness.

There are other ways of mentally giving our body. For example, in *Guide to the Bodhisattva's Way of Life* Shantideva teaches a method of giving our body in which we imagine that it transforms into a wish-granting jewel that radiates light throughout the universe, fulfilling the wishes of all living beings and causing them to experience great happiness and satisfaction.

OFFERING THE MANDALA

In general 'mandala' means 'universe', but a literal translation of the Tibetan equivalent, 'kyil khor', is 'taking the essence'. By making mandala offerings we create the cause to experience outer and inner Dakini Land, and so we are taking the essence of this precious human life.

In *Guhyasamaja Tantra* Vajradhara says:

Those who wish for attainments
Should mentally and skilfully fill this universe
With the seven precious objects.
By offering them every day,
Their wishes will be fulfilled.

This verse reveals the mandala offering. Although it explicitly mentions only seven points, implicitly it refers to the full thirty-seven-point mandala.

It is important for practitioners to obtain a traditional mandala set, which consists of a base, three rings and a top jewel. The base and rings are used to support heaps of rice, or some other grain, which represent the various features of the mandala. Such simple things may seem useless to those who do not know their significance, but they can be very valuable in the hands of a practitioner who knows how to use them to accumulate a vast collection of merit.

To construct the thirty-seven-point mandala we first take a little rice in our left hand and hold the mandala base with that hand. With our right hand we scoop up more rice and sprinkle a little onto the base. With the inside of our right wrist we rub the base three times clockwise, which symbolizes purification of the universal ground. As a result all rocky and uneven ground becomes smooth and level, and all our delusions are purified. We then rub the base three times counter-clockwise and imagine that all the blessings of the body, speech and mind of all the Buddhas gather into us. We think that the whole ground has been blessed and we recite the mantra for blessing the ground: OM VAJRA BHUMI AH HUM. We then sprinkle the rice that remains in our right hand onto the base and visualize that the ground throughout the entire universe transforms into a pure golden ground.

While reciting OM VAJRA REKHE AH HUM we now put the largest ring on the base and, in a clockwise direction, pour a ring of rice inside it to symbolize the precious iron fence. We then place a heap of rice in the centre of the ring to symbolize Mount Meru, visualizing it as a huge mountain made of precious jewels. We then place another heap of rice in the east, the part of the mandala base nearest to us, to symbolize the eastern continent. Proceeding clockwise around the ring we place heaps of rice in the three remaining cardinal directions to symbolize the southern, western and northern continents.

We then place eight small heaps of rice to symbolize the eight sub-continents. Beginning with the eastern continent and proceeding in a clockwise direction we place one heap a little to the left and one a little to the right of each continent.

We then place four small heaps of rice inside the eastern, southern, western and northern continents to symbolize respectively the mountain of jewels, the wish-granting tree, the wish-granting cow and the unsown harvest. We imagine that there are countless continents and sub-continents, each possessing their own special wealth of resources and riches.

We now put the second ring on top of the rice and place a heap of rice clockwise in each of the cardinal directions – east, south, west and north – to symbolize respectively the precious wheel, the precious jewel, the precious queen and the precious minister. We then place a heap of rice clockwise in each of the intermediate directions – south-east, south-west, north-west and north-east – to symbolize respectively the precious elephant, the precious supreme horse, the precious general and the great treasure vase. We imagine countless numbers of each of these filling all of space. Again we place heaps of rice clockwise in each of the four cardinal directions – east, south, west and north – to symbolize the goddess of beauty, the goddess of garlands, the goddess of song and the goddess of dance; and then clockwise in each of the four intermediate directions – south-east, south-west, north-west and north-east – to symbolize the goddess of flowers, the goddess of incense, the goddess of light and the goddess of scent. We imagine that there are countless offering gods and goddesses filling space.

We now put the third ring on top of the rice and place a heap of rice in the east for the sun, one in the west for the moon, one in the south for the precious umbrella, and one in the north for the banner of victory. We imagine that all of space is filled with innumerable precious objects.

As we place the top jewel, which is the last thing we place on the mandala, we imagine an abundance of other precious jewels and resources enjoyed by both humans and gods. In the space above Mount Meru are the environments of the desire realm gods and above these are the form realms. These god realms transform into Pure Lands and the enjoyments of the gods become pure enjoyments.

Having constructed the mandala we take a little rice in our right hand and hold the base with both hands. We imagine that all the innumerable world systems and everything contained within them have completely transformed into Pure Lands and pure enjoyments. We imagine that all these are present on the base in our hands, and yet the base does not increase in size and the universe does not become smaller. Just as a mirror can reflect huge mountains, or a small television screen can show images of entire cities, so we imagine that the mandala in our hands contains the entire universe. We concentrate single-pointedly on these countless pure worlds, enjoyments and beings, and with firm faith offer them all to our Gurus and the Buddhas.

While we construct this mandala we recite the offering prayer from the sadhana. When we have recited the long mandala offering prayer we can continue, while still holding the base, to offer the twenty-three-point mandala. We do not need to construct a new mandala because the twenty-three precious objects are included among the precious objects of the thirty-seven-point mandala. The twenty-three precious objects are: Mount Meru, the four continents, the eight sub-continents, the seven precious objects (from the precious wheel up to the precious general), the treasure vase, the sun and the moon.

To offer the twenty-three-point mandala we recite the verse from the sadhana:

O Treasure of Compassion, my Refuge and Protector,
I offer you the mountain, continents, precious objects,
treasure vase, sun and moon,
Which have arisen from my aggregates, sources and
elements
As aspects of the exalted wisdom of spontaneous
bliss and emptiness.

With this verse we make outer, inner, secret and thatness mandala offerings. We offer the outer mandala by visualizing the mountain, continents, precious objects, treasure vase, sun and moon. We offer the inner mandala by mentally transforming our aggregates and elements into the form of the outer mandala. We offer the secret and thatness mandalas by imagining that our mind of indivisible bliss and emptiness transforms into the mandala. From the point of view of its having the nature of great bliss the mandala is the secret mandala, and from the point of view of its being a manifestation of emptiness it is the thatness mandala. If we wish to collect twenty-three-point mandalas as one of the great preliminary guides we can construct them using the base, with or without the rings, and recite this verse.

Offering the mandala is the best method for freeing ourself from future poverty and for creating the cause of rebirth in a Buddha's Pure Land. By making mandala offerings we lessen our attachment to worldly enjoyments and possessions and accumulate a vast collection of merit. As a result we experience a gradual increase of our enjoyments, wealth and good conditions. Our temporary wishes are fulfilled and finally we will attain our ultimate goal, full enlightenment. If we wish to experience these benefits we should familiarize ourself with the practice of offering the mandala.

Je Tsongkhapa was an enlightened being who did not need to accumulate merit, but to show a good example to other practitioners he offered a million mandalas during one of his long retreats in the south of central Tibet, in the cave called Ölga Cholung. For a base he used a flat stone, and through offering so many mandalas he rubbed the inside of his wrist until it was raw and bleeding.

Many practitioners have received visions of holy beings as a result of making mandala offerings. Khedrubje, a disciple of Je Tsongkhapa, would take his mandala base with him wherever he went because mandala offerings were so important to him. After Je Tsongkhapa had passed away Khedrubje received many visions of him while he was making mandala offerings. The nun Bhikshuni Palmo also emphasized the practice of mandala offerings and she received a vision of Avalokiteshvara as a result. Whenever Atisha offered a mandala to Tara he would immediately receive a vision of her, and when Chandragomin made mandala offerings he received visions of Avalokiteshvara. These examples indicate the power and importance of this practice.

If we are strongly attached to someone or something we can imagine the object of our attachment on the mandala base, transform it into a pure object, and then offer it while praying,

'May I be free from all attachment.' In a similar way we can offer all the objects of our ignorance, anger, jealousy, pride, and so forth. While reciting the verse from the sadhana we can offer all the objects of our delusions and pray to be free from those delusions.

To make mandala offerings as one of the great preliminary guides we collect a hundred thousand mandala offerings. At the beginning of each session we offer a thirty-seven-point mandala, and we then collect seven-point mandalas. To construct and count seven-point mandala offerings we place a loosely threaded mala over the fingers of our left hand, take some rice in that hand, and then hold the mandala base with it. We then take some rice in our right hand and recite refuge and bodhichitta prayers while constructing the mandala. To do this we sprinkle a little rice on the base, and with the inside of the right wrist rub three times clockwise and three times counter-clockwise. We then place one heap of rice in the centre of the base, one in the east, one in the south, one in the west and one in the north, to symbolize Mount Meru and the four continents. We then place a heap of rice in the east for the sun and one in the west for the moon. We then take a little rice in our right hand and hold the base with both hands while reciting the following mandala offering prayer:

The ground sprinkled with perfume and spread with
    flowers,
The Great Mountain, four lands, sun and moon,
Seen as a Buddha Land and offered thus,
May all beings enjoy such Pure Lands.

IDAM GURU RATNA MANDALAKAM NIRYATAYAMI

After reciting the prayer we tip the rice towards us into a cloth on our lap. This is counted as one mandala offering and so we move one bead along the mala. We make as many mandala offerings as we wish during each session. At the end of the session we make a long mandala offering of thirty-seven points and then dedicate our merit.

REQUESTING THE LINEAGE GURUS

We make this request by using the prayer from the extensive sadhana. As we recite the prayer we should focus our mind on the Gurus mentioned in each verse, generate strong faith in them, and request their blessings. Our principal request is for the realization of spontaneously born exalted wisdom, which is the essence of Highest Yoga Tantra. This wisdom is attained when the very subtle mind of spontaneous great bliss realizes emptiness. It is only by attaining spontaneously born exalted wisdom that we can attain Buddhahood in a single human life, and it is because of this wisdom that Highest Yoga Tantra is the quick path to enlightenment. This wisdom is the real ultimate bodhichitta. When we train in methods to develop spontaneously born exalted wisdom we are practising the fourth offering of the Tantric seven limbs explained earlier.

In *Song of the Spring Queen* Je Tsongkhapa says:

You who have the characteristic of the liberation of great
  bliss
Do not say that deliverance can be gained in one
  lifetime
Through various ascetic practices having abandoned
  great bliss,
But that great bliss resides in the centre of the supreme
  lotus.

This clearly indicates that spontaneously born exalted wisdom is the heart of Tantric practice. Other accomplished Yogis such as the Mahasiddhas Saraha, Nagarjuna, Naropa and Tilopa have also praised highly the realization of spontaneously born exalted wisdom and emphasized the importance of the practices that lead to its attainment. At this point in the sadhana we request each lineage Guru to bless our mind to help us to attain this essential realization.

Merely gaining an intellectual understanding of the real nature, function, quality and characteristics of spontaneously born exalted wisdom will give us great encouragement to study and practise the methods to develop it. If we listen to teachings on this wisdom our mind will become happier and more peaceful, our ignorance will diminish, and our desire to practise Highest Yoga Tantra will increase.

It is important to distinguish between ordinary bliss, the pure bliss mentioned in the Sutras and the lower Tantras, and the spontaneous bliss described in Highest Yoga Tantra. We should also understand the difference between the bliss attained through generation stage practice and the spontaneous bliss attained through completion stage practice. By studying authentic commentaries on completion stage practice we will come to understand what spontaneous bliss is, and thereby understand the real nature and function of ultimate bodhichitta. More detailed explanations of these essential points can be found in *Clear Light of Bliss* and *Tantric Grounds and Paths*.

In *Clear Light of Bliss* four distinct experiences of great bliss are explained. The foremost of these is spontaneous great bliss. It is only through attaining a mind of spontaneous great bliss realizing emptiness that we can attain Buddhahood. Through completion stage meditation we can cause the subtle winds to dissolve into the indestructible drop inside the central channel at the heart. Then when the bodhichittas melt within the central channel we experience great bliss. We generate several levels of bliss in this way, but the most sublime is spontaneous great bliss. When spontaneous great bliss realizes emptiness, either directly or conceptually, this wisdom is called 'spontaneously born exalted wisdom'. We should try to understand the importance of this wisdom and how to attain it. The main purpose of Tantric practice is to develop this wisdom. When we have generated an intense wish to gain this special realization we should request our Gurus to grant their blessings to help us to do so.

We should firmly believe that the living Gurus are sitting in front of us, and cultivate strong faith in them. As we recite the words of request we concentrate on their meaning and imagine that the Gurus listen attentively. After reciting the last verse, the verse to Losang Yeshe Dorjechang Trijang Rinpoche, we focus our mind on our root Guru on the central throne and recite the following two verses:

My kind root Guru, Vajradharma,
You are the embodiment of all the Conquerors,
Who grant the blessings of all Buddhas' speech,
I request you, please bestow the spontaneously born
    exalted wisdom.

Please bless me so that through the force of
    meditation
On the Dakini yoga of the profound generation stage,
And the central channel yoga of completion stage,
I may generate the exalted wisdom of spontaneous
    great bliss and attain the enlightened Dakini state.

We should not be satisfied with merely reciting these requests but should make a strong determination actually to engage in the practices of generation stage and completion stage. The attainment of the enlightened Dakini state, Buddhahood, depends upon spontaneously born exalted wisdom, which depends upon the central channel yoga of completion stage, which in turn depends upon the self-generation practices of generation stage. Having understood the purpose of the two Tantric stages we should conclude our request by making a strong determination to practise them.

RECEIVING THE BLESSINGS OF THE FOUR EMPOWERMENTS

The first of the four empowerments is the vase empowerment, through which we receive the blessings of all Buddhas' bodies. This empowerment purifies the negative karma we have created with our body and sows the seed for us to attain generation stage realizations and the Emanation Body of a Buddha. Through the second empowerment, the secret empowerment, we receive the blessings of all Buddhas' speech. This empowerment purifies our negative karma of speech and sows the seed for us to attain the illusory body of completion stage and the Enjoyment Body of a Buddha. Through the third empowerment, the wisdom-mudra empowerment, we receive the blessings of all Buddhas' minds. This empowerment purifies our negative karma of mind and sows the seed for us to attain the clear light of completion stage and the Truth Body of a Buddha. Through the fourth empowerment, the precious word empowerment, we receive the blessings of all Buddhas' body, speech and mind. This empowerment purifies all our negative karma of body, speech and mind and sows the seed for us to attain the union that needs learning and the Union of No More Learning. We take the four empowerments in order to obtain these blessings and realizations.

We receive the four empowerments directly from our Guru during the actual Highest Yoga Tantra empowerment. The purpose of receiving the blessings of the four empowerments when we practise the sadhana is to prevent the blessings that we received directly from our Guru from degenerating. We first request our root Guru to grant the four empowerments, by reciting the following verse three times:

> **I request you O Guru incorporating all objects of refuge,**
> **Please grant me your blessings,**
> **Please grant me the four empowerments completely,**
> **And bestow on me, please, the state of the four bodies.**

We then visualize that from the letter OM at our Guru's forehead white light rays and nectars radiate. Each tiny particle of the lights and nectars appears in the form of a radiant white letter OM, which is the nature of all Buddhas' bodies. The lights and nectars dissolve into our forehead, purifying all the negativities and obstructions of our body. We receive the vase empowerment and the blessings of our Guru's body enter our body. These cause the seeds of the generation stage realizations and the Emanation Body to ripen.

From the letter AH at our Guru's throat, red light rays and nectars radiate. Each particle of the lights and nectars appears in the form of a radiant red letter AH, the nature of all Buddhas' speech. These dissolve into our throat, purifying all the negativities and obstructions of our speech. We receive the secret empowerment and the blessings of our Guru's speech enter our speech. These cause the seeds of the illusory body and the Enjoyment Body to ripen.

From the letter HUM at our Guru's heart, blue light rays and nectars radiate. Each particle of the lights and nectars appears in the form of a radiant blue letter HUM, the nature of all Buddhas' minds. These dissolve into our heart, purifying all the negativities and obstructions of our mind. We receive the wisdom-mudra empowerment and the blessings of our Guru's mind enter our mind. These cause the seeds of the clear light of completion stage and the Truth Body to ripen.

From the letters OM, AH and HUM at the three places of our Guru, white, red and blue light rays and nectars radiate and dissolve into our three places, purifying all the negativities and obstructions of our body, speech and mind. We receive the fourth empowerment, the precious word empowerment, and the blessings of our Guru's body, speech and mind enter our body, speech and mind. These cause the seeds of the union that needs learning and of the Union of No More Learning to ripen.

Finally we recite the following brief request to our Guru three times:

I request you my precious Guru, the essence of all Buddhas of the three times, please bless my mental continuum.

If we wish to do the great preliminary guide of Guru yoga we can recite this request a hundred thousand times. Alternatively we can recite the same number of either the name mantra of our Guru or the mantra of Guru Sumati Buddha Heruka: OM GURU SUMATI BUDDHA HERUKA SARWA SIDDHI HUM.

ABSORBING THE GURUS

As a result of our making this request the celestial mansion dissolves into the lineage Gurus, and the lineage Gurus, together with their thrones, dissolve into each other. Beginning with Buddha Vajradharma, each Guru dissolves into the Guru to his left. Finally the last lineage Guru, Losang Yeshe Dorjechang Trijang Rinpoche, dissolves into our root Guru. Out of his affection for us, our root Guru develops a wish to unite with us, and we from our side also wish strongly for this to happen. We imagine that our Guru melts into red light from below and above, diminishing to the size of a thumb. He then enters through the crown of our head and descends through our central channel to our heart, where he mixes inseparably with our mind. Since the real nature of our Guru is the spontaneous great bliss of all Buddhas, we imagine that by merging with him our mind transforms into spontaneous great bliss. We meditate single-pointedly on the feeling that we experience spontaneous great bliss, which is our Guru's mind. This meditation is definitive Guru yoga. It is the heart of Tantric practice.

The Yoga of Self-Generation and the Yoga of Purifying Migrators

THE YOGA OF SELF-GENERATION

This yoga is explained in three parts:

1 Bringing the three bodies into the path
2 Checking meditation on the mandala and the beings within it
3 The actual generation stage meditation

BRINGING THE THREE BODIES INTO THE PATH

This has two parts:

1 General explanation
2 The practice of bringing the three bodies into the path

GENERAL EXPLANATION

In the yoga of self-generation the three bodies that are brought into the path are the basic truth body, the basic enjoyment body and the basic emanation body. These are so called because they are the bases from which the resultant bodies of a Buddha develop. Buddhas have three bodies: the Truth Body, or Dharmakaya; the Enjoyment Body, or Sambhogakaya; and the Emanation Body, or Nirmanakaya. The Truth Body is the omniscient mind of a Buddha, which is mixed inseparably with emptiness. This mind is experienced only by Buddhas. The Enjoyment Body is a Buddha's subtle Form Body, and can be seen only by Superior Bodhisattvas and Buddhas. The Emanation Body is a Buddha's gross Form Body, and can be seen even by ordinary beings. The actual Truth Body, the actual Enjoyment Body, and the actual Emanation Body are possessed only by Buddhas. These three bodies are called the 'three resultant bodies' or the 'three results of purification'.

The basic truth body is our clear light of sleep and clear light of death. At the moment neither of these minds is an actual Truth Body but they are the bases of the Truth Body because they are similar in aspect to the Truth Body and they are the bases that are brought into the path and transformed into the actual Truth Body of a Buddha. The basic enjoyment body is our dream body and intermediate state body. They are the bases of the Enjoyment Body because they are similar in aspect to the Enjoyment Body, and because by bringing the dream body and the intermediate state body into the path we will eventually transform them into the actual Enjoyment Body of a Buddha. The basic emanation body is our waking from sleep and our rebirth. They are the bases of the actual Emanation Body because they are similar in aspect to the way in which an Emanation Body develops, and because by bringing waking and rebirth into the path we will eventually attain the actual Emanation Body of a Buddha.

We attain the three resultant bodies of a Buddha – the actual Truth Body, the actual Enjoyment Body and the actual Emanation Body – through the generation and completion stage practices of Highest Yoga Tantra. First we must attain the three bodies of the path: ultimate example clear light, which directly prevents ordinary death; the illusory body, which directly prevents ordinary intermediate state; and the gross Deity body that arises from the illusory body, which directly prevents ordinary rebirth. We attain these three path bodies through completion stage practice.

To attain the three path bodies we need to train in bringing the basic truth body into the path that prevents ordinary death, bringing the basic enjoyment body into the path that prevents ordinary intermediate state, and bringing the basic emanation body into the path that prevents ordinary rebirth.

We can meditate on bringing the three basic bodies into the path according to generation stage or according to completion stage. Before we gain actual completion stage realizations we need constantly to improve our meditation on bringing the three basic bodies into the path according to generation stage. Once we have gained experience in this, and have also gained some experience of completion stage, we should emphasize the meditations on bringing the three basic bodies into the path according to completion stage. Finally we will attain the actual three path bodies.

To summarize, the bases to be purified are death, intermediate state and samsaric rebirth; the methods to purify them are the practices of bringing the three basic bodies into the path and the three path bodies; and the results of purification are the three bodies of a Buddha.

Since beginningless time we have experienced an uninterrupted cycle of death, intermediate state and rebirth. For as long as we remain in this cycle we will be imprisoned within samsara and we will continue to experience misery without choice. Until we purify death, intermediate state and rebirth we will not attain Buddhahood. The principal function of generation stage and completion stage is to purify these three states and thereby to attain the three resultant bodies. We accomplish this by engaging in the meditations on bringing the three basic bodies into the path.

THE PRACTICE OF BRINGING THE THREE BODIES INTO THE PATH

This has three parts:

1 Bringing death into the path to the Truth Body
2 Bringing the intermediate state into the path to the Enjoyment Body
3 Bringing rebirth into the path to the Emanation Body

Pamtingpa

BRINGING DEATH INTO THE PATH TO THE TRUTH BODY

This practice has three main functions: it purifies ordinary death, it causes the realization of clear light to ripen, and it increases our collection of wisdom. In this meditation we cultivate experiences similar to those we have when we die by imagining that we perceive the signs that occur during the death process, from the mirage-like appearance to the appearance of clear light.

Having requested our Guru to bless our mind and imagined that he has entered our heart we develop three recognitions: (1) the nature of our Guru's mind is the union of great bliss and emptiness; (2) our Guru's mind has mixed inseparably with our own mind, transforming it into the union of great bliss and emptiness; and (3) our mind of great bliss is in the aspect of a red letter BAM at our heart. We meditate on these three recognitions for a while.

The letter BAM then begins to increase in size, gradually melting our body into blissful red light, just as warm water melts ice when it is poured onto it. The letter BAM expands until it has absorbed our whole body. Continuing to expand, it gradually absorbs our room, our house, our town, our country, our continent, our world, and finally the whole universe, including all the living beings who inhabit it. Everything is absorbed and transformed into an infinitely large letter BAM, which pervades the whole of space, and which in nature is our mind of great bliss that has mixed with emptiness. We perceive nothing but this letter BAM and we meditate on it single-pointedly for a while. We think, 'I have purified all living beings together with their environments.'

After a while the letter BAM begins to contract, gradually gathering inwards from the edges of infinite space and leaving behind only emptiness. It becomes smaller and smaller until there remains only a minute letter BAM. Then this minute letter BAM gradually dissolves, from the bottom up to the horizontal line at the head of the BAM. Throughout this meditation we imagine that we undergo experiences similar to those experienced by a dying person. At this point we imagine that we perceive the mirage-like appearance that arises due to the dissolution of the earth element. The head of the BAM then dissolves into the crescent moon, and we imagine that we perceive the smoke-like appearance that arises due to the dissolution of the water element. The crescent moon then dissolves into the drop, and we imagine that we perceive the sparkling-fireflies-like appearance that arises due to the dissolution of the fire element. The drop then dissolves into the nada, and we imagine that we perceive the candle-flame-like appearance that arises due to the dissolution of the wind element.

These four appearances are the inner signs of the dissolution of the winds that support our four bodily elements. When we die, these four winds gradually absorb, and because of this we experience these four signs. Normally when the fourth sign of the death process, the candle-flame-like appearance, is perceived, all gross memory, gross inner winds and gross appearances cease, and the external breathing stops. At this point in the meditation all that remains is the nada. After a while we imagine that we experience the fifth sign, the mind of white appearance. With each successive dissolution the mind becomes increasingly subtle. When the lower curve of the nada dissolves upwards into the middle curve we imagine that we experience the mind of red increase, and when the middle curve dissolves into the upper curve we imagine that we experience the mind of black near-attainment. Finally the upper curve dissolves into emptiness and we imagine that we experience the most subtle mind, the mind of clear light.

At this point we should have four recognitions: (1) we imagine that our mind of clear light has actually manifested and that it is experiencing great bliss; (2) only emptiness appears to our mind; (3) we identify this emptiness as the lack of inherently existent phenomena; and (4) we imagine that we have attained the Truth Body of a Buddha and think, 'I am Truth Body Vajrayogini, definitive Vajrayogini.' We then meditate on the mind of clear light while trying to maintain these four recognitions constantly.

Without being distracted from the main meditation, from time to time we should use one part of our mind to check that none of these recognitions is missing. If we find that we have lost one or more of them we should apply skilful effort to re-establish them. If we meditate in this way every day, even with weak concentration, we will increase our collection of wisdom. A collection of wisdom is defined as any virtuous mental action that principally causes the attainment of a Buddha's Truth Body. A collection of merit is defined as any virtuous action that principally causes the attainment of a Buddha's Form Body. By completing these two collections we will attain Buddhahood. 'Definitive Vajrayogini' refers to Vajrayogini that is imputed upon Buddha's Truth Body, or Dharmakaya.

For the beginner there is a simplified meditation on bringing death into the path. When we have dissolved the nada into emptiness we imagine that we perceive the eighth sign, the clear light, and we imagine that this mind is experiencing great bliss. With this mind of bliss we then meditate on emptiness. Without losing this experience of the blissful mind of clear light meditating on emptiness, with one part of our mind we imagine that our mind of bliss has completely mixed with emptiness like water mixing with water, and we identify this union of bliss and emptiness as the Truth Body of Vajrayogini. We then meditate on this recognition single-pointedly.

When through completion stage meditation we are able to cause our inner winds to enter, abide and dissolve within our central channel at the heart channel wheel, we experience the isolated mind of example clear light. Once we have attained this realization our death will no longer be an uncontrolled, samsaric process, but we will be able to control the process of dying by transforming the clear light of death into the mind of ultimate example clear light. This is the quick path to enlightenment. When we rise from this clear light, instead of entering the ordinary intermediate state with an intermediate state body we will attain the illusory body. From this subtle body, instead of having to take an ordinary rebirth we will emanate a gross Deity body similar to the Emanation Body of a Buddha.

In summary, from the moment we attain ultimate example clear light we will be able to control death, intermediate state and rebirth. The attainment of ultimate example clear light depends upon training in meditation on bringing death into the path of the Truth Body. To meditate on bringing death into the path of the Truth Body we must first prevent all ordinary appearances by perceiving everything as empty. We should identify this emptiness as lack of inherent existence, and imagine that our mind merges with this emptiness. Then, with a feeling that our mind is completely one with emptiness, we should try to develop the divine pride of being the Truth Body. If we are successful in this meditation, our meditations on generating ourself as a Deity will also be successful.

Once a practitioner told Longdol Lama that even though he tried hard to generate himself as a Deity, he was still conscious of his ordinary body, his friends, his house and all the things he usually did. He asked what he should do to correct this. Longdol Lama replied that he could solve the problem by training in the meditation on bringing death into the path to the Truth Body. If we imagine that everything dissolves into emptiness we can overcome ordinary appearances, and this will make it easy for us to generate new, pure appearances. 'Truth Body' refers to a Buddha's mind – the Wisdom Truth Body – and the emptiness of a Buddha's mind – the Nature Truth Body. They are also known as the 'Dharmakaya'. In this context body means the basis of imputation of a person.

BRINGING THE INTERMEDIATE STATE INTO THE PATH TO THE ENJOYMENT BODY

Immediately after an experience of clear light has ceased and the mind has become slightly grosser, a subtle body manifests. For ordinary beings a dream body arises when the clear light of sleep ceases, and a bardo body arises when the clear light of death ceases. For Tantric practitioners the impure illusory body arises from the mind of ultimate example clear light, and the pure illusory body arises from the mind of meaning clear light. For Buddhas the Enjoyment Body arises from the clear light of the Truth Body.

When we meditate on bringing death into the path of the Truth Body we develop divine pride thinking, 'I am the Truth

Body.' While maintaining this divine pride, one part of our mind should think:

If I remain only as the Truth Body I cannot benefit living beings because they are unable to see me. Therefore I must arise in a Form Body, a Buddha's Enjoyment Body.

With this thought we imagine that from the clear light of emptiness our mind instantly transforms into an Enjoyment Body in the aspect of the red letter BAM. We generate divine pride thinking, 'I am Enjoyment Body Vajrayogini', and meditate briefly on this feeling. At this stage it is more important to meditate on the feeling of being the Enjoyment Body of a Buddha than it is to dwell on the aspect of the letter BAM. 'Enjoyment Body Vajrayogini' refers to Vajrayogini imputed upon Buddha's subtle Form Body, Buddha's illusory body. The nature of our mind is great bliss and its aspect is a red letter BAM. The letter BAM has three parts: the BA, the drop and the nada. These symbolize the body, speech and mind of the bardo being, and the body, speech and mind of the Enjoyment Body. This indicates that meditation on bringing the intermediate state into the path purifies the intermediate state and causes the ripening of the illusory body, which eventually transforms into the Enjoyment Body of a Buddha.

BRINGING REBIRTH INTO THE PATH TO THE EMANATION BODY

For ordinary beings the waking state arises from the dream body, and after death their next rebirth arises from the bardo body. Similarly, for Tantric practitioners the gross Deity body arises from the illusory body, and for Buddhas the Emanation Body arises from the Enjoyment Body. When we meditate on bringing rebirth into the path to the Emanation Body we imagine a similar process. While we are in the form of the red letter BAM standing in space, which we identify as being the Enjoyment Body, one part of our mind thinks:

If I remain only in this form I cannot benefit ordinary beings because they are unable to see a Buddha's Enjoyment Body. Therefore I must be born in an Emanation Body so that even ordinary beings can see me.

With this motivation we look for a place in which to take rebirth. Looking down through the space beneath us we see two red EH letters, one above the other, appearing from the state of emptiness. These transform into a phenomena source, which is shaped like a double tetrahedron standing with its fine tip pointing downwards and its broad neck facing upwards. There is an outer tetrahedron, which is white, and an inner one, which is red. They are both made of light and so they interpenetrate without obstruction. Looked at from above, the top of the double tetrahedron resembles a six-pointed star with one point of the inner tetrahedron pointing towards the front and one point of the outer tetrahedron pointing towards the back. The triangular segments at the front and the back are empty, but in each of the four remaining segments there is a pink joy swirl spinning counter-clockwise.

Inside the phenomena source there appears a white letter AH which transforms into a white moon disc. Standing around the edge of the moon disc are the letters of the three-OM mantra: OM OM OM SARWA BUDDHA DAKINIYE VAJRA WARNANIYE VAJRA BEROTZANIYE HUM HUM HUM PHAT PHAT PHAT SÖHA. The letters are red and are arrayed counter-clockwise, starting from the front. The centre of the moon disc is empty. Our mind, the red letter BAM, observes these developments from above.

The outer phenomena source symbolizes the rebirth environment, the inner phenomena source the mother's womb, the white moon disc the white bodhichitta of Father Heruka, and the red mantra rosary the red bodhichitta of Mother Vajrayogini. Because the mantra rosary is reflected in the moon, the moon is tinged with red. The moon and mantra rosary together symbolize the union of the germ cells of the father and mother at the moment of conception.

Just before a bardo being takes rebirth it sees its future parents engaged in intercourse. Similarly we, in the aspect of the red letter BAM, observe below us the union of Father Heruka and Mother Vajrayogini in the symbolic forms of the moon and mantra rosary, and we generate a strong motivation to take rebirth there. With this motivation we, the letter BAM, descend and alight upon the centre of the moon disc inside the phenomena source. This is similar to a bardo being taking rebirth in the womb of its future mother.

Then from the letter BAM and the mantra rosary, rays of light radiate throughout space. On the tip of each ray is a Deity of Heruka's mandala. These Heroes and Heroines bestow blessings and empowerments upon all beings throughout the universe. They purify all samsaric beings and those who have entered solitary nirvana, as well as their environments, and transform them into pure beings in Vajrayogini's Pure Land. Then the transformed beings, their worlds, the phenomena source, and the moon disc all melt into light and dissolve into our mind, the letter BAM. This and the mantra rosary then instantly transform into the supporting mandala and the supported Deities of Vajrayogini. We become Vajrayogini with a pure body, speech and mind, abiding in the Pure Land of Vajrayogini, and experiencing pure enjoyments. We strongly think, 'I am Emanation Body Vajrayogini' and we meditate on this divine pride. 'Emanation Body Vajrayogini' refers to Vajrayogini imputed upon the Emanation Body, the gross Form Body of a Buddha.

CHECKING MEDITATION ON THE MANDALA AND THE BEINGS WITHIN IT

With the divine pride of being the Emanation Body of Buddha Vajrayogini, and viewing our environment as the Pure Land of Vajrayogini, we now improve our clear appearance of the mandala, the celestial mansion and the beings within it by contemplating the following:

The mandala is supported by a vast and extensive vajra ground, which is composed entirely of indestructible vajras. Each vajra consists of vajra-shaped atoms. Enclosing the entire vajra ground is the circular vajra fence. The vajra fence has three layers of huge five-pronged vajras. The first layer lies horizontally. Upon this the second layer stands vertically, and upon this the third layer lies horizontally. The vajra fence is impenetrable and indestructible, with not even the smallest gap. On top of the vajra fence is the vajra canopy, which serves as a ceiling. Above this is the cone-shaped vajra tent. The impenetrable canopy and tent, which have the shape of a Mongolian tent, are also composed of vajras. Each vajra is composed of tiny atom-like vajras, which allow no intervening space. Although all the tiny vajra-atoms are clear and distinct, not one single atom can be removed. The vajra ground, fence, canopy and tent are blue in colour and are entirely surrounded by five-coloured flames of wisdom-fire which swirl counter-clockwise. The flames are real and have the power to protect us from all harm from evil spirits.

If we repeatedly contemplate the details of the protection circle, the clarity of our visualization will gradually improve and we will develop firm conviction that the protection circle actually exists and is effective in protecting us from harm and hindrances. We continue our checking meditation:

Just inside the protection circle, situated in the cardinal and intermediate directions, are the eight great charnel grounds. The charnel ground in the east is called Ferocious One, in the north, Very Dense Forest, in the west, Blazing Vajra, and in the south, Possessing Bone and Marrow. The charnel ground in the south-east is called Auspicious Guardian, in the south-west, Fearful Darkness, in the north-west, Making the Sound Kili Kili, and in the north-east, Wrathful Laughter. Each charnel ground has eight features: a tree, a directional guardian, a regional guardian, a lake, a naga, a cloud, a fire and a stupa.

In the eastern charnel ground the tree is called Naga Tree. At its foot is the guardian of the east called Indra, who is yellow, holds a vajra and skullcup, and rides a white elephant. At the top of the tree is a white regional guardian called Elephant

Face. In each of the eight charnel grounds the regional guardian holds a red triangular-shaped torma and skullcup, and sits in the top of the tree with the upper half of his body emerging above the branches. Below there is a lake called Water of Compassion in which there is a white naga called Increasing Wealth. In the sky above there is a cloud called Making Sounds. A fire called Wisdom Fire blazes at the base of a precious mountain called Mount Meru. At the crest of the mountain is a white stupa called Stupa of Enlightenment.

In the northern charnel ground the tree is called Ashuta. At its foot is the guardian of the north called Vaishravana, who is yellow, holds a mongoose and skullcup, and rides on the back of a man. At the top of the tree is a yellow regional guardian called Human Face. In the lake below is a naga called Jogpo, and in the sky above is a cloud called Making Loud Sounds. A fire of wisdom blazes at the base of a green mountain called Mandara. At the crest of the mountain is a white stupa. The lake, fire, and stupa in each charnel ground have the same names as those in the eastern charnel ground.

In the western charnel ground the tree is called Kangkela. At its foot is the guardian of the west called Water Deity, or Varuna in Sanskrit. He is white, with a hood of seven snakes, holds a snake-rope and skullcup, and rides on a crocodile. At the top of the tree is a red regional guardian called Crocodile Face. In the lake below is a blue naga called Karakota, and in the sky above is a cloud called Wrathful. A fire of wisdom blazes at the base of a white mountain called Kailash. At the crest of the mountain is a white stupa.

In the southern charnel ground the tree is called Tsuta. At its foot is the guardian of the south called Yama, who is blue, holds a staff and skullcup, and rides on a buffalo. At the top of the tree is a black regional guardian called Buffalo Face. In the lake below is a white naga called Lotus, and in the sky above is a cloud called Moving. A fire of wisdom blazes at the base of a yellow mountain called Malaya. At the crest of the mountain is a white stupa.

In the south-eastern charnel ground the tree is called Karanza. At its foot is the guardian of the south-east called

Fire Deity, or Agni in Sanskrit. He is red, holds a mala, long-necked vase and skullcup, and rides on a goat. At the top of the tree is a red regional guardian called Goat Face. In the lake below is a yellow naga called Carrying a Conch-shell, and in the sky above is a cloud called Completely Full. A fire of wisdom blazes at the base of a yellow mountain called Fragrant Incense. At the crest of the mountain is a white stupa.

In the south-western charnel ground the tree is called Padreyaga. At its foot is the guardian of the south-west called Possessing a Rosary of Human Heads, or Kardava in Sanskrit. He is naked, blue in colour, holds a sword and skullcup, and rides on a zombie. At the top of the tree is a black regional guardian called Zombie Face. In the lake below is a white naga called Possessing Lineage, and in the sky above is a cloud called Descending. A fire of wisdom blazes at the base of a white mountain called Possessing Snow. At the crest of the mountain is a white stupa.

In the north-western charnel ground the tree is called Parthipa. At its foot is the guardian of the north-west called Wind Deity, or Vayuni in Sanskrit. He is smoke-coloured, holds a yellow banner and skullcup, and rides on a deer. At the top of the tree is a green regional guardian called Deer Face. In the lake below is a red naga called Boundless, and in the sky above is a cloud called Wrathful. A fire of wisdom blazes at the base of a blue mountain called Mountain of Glory. At the crest of the mountain is a white stupa.

In the north-eastern charnel ground the tree is called Nadota. At its foot is the guardian of the north-east called Ishvara. He is white, holds a trident and skullcup, and rides on a bull. At the top of the tree is a white regional guardian called Bull Face. In the lake below is a white naga called Great Lotus, and in the sky above is a cloud called Unmoving. A fire of wisdom blazes at the base of a black mountain called Great Power. At the crest of the mountain is a white stupa.

In addition to these eight features, in each charnel ground there are various creatures such as crows, owls, eagles, foxes, snakes and bull-headed snakes, as well as other emanations *such as spirits, zombies and flesh-eating spirits. There are also many different Tantric meditators in the aspect of humans and gods, and many Yogis and Yoginis manifesting in various forms. Everything inside the charnel grounds, including the lakes, clouds and animals, is an emanation of Vajrayogini.*

In general, the eight directional guardians and the eight regional guardians are worldly deities who control the eight directions of this world and all the major regions within it. In the Mahakala sadhana it says that each directional guardian has a retinue of a hundred thousand, and this is also true of the regional guardians. The directional guardians are like officers of the whole country and the regional guardians are like district officers who control regions within the country. In addition, every city, town and village has a local guardian spirit who controls that area. Usually they try to help the humans living there, but sometimes due to discontent or anger they cause problems such as hail storms and hurricanes.

The directional guardians and regional guardians in the charnel grounds of Vajrayogini's mandala, however, are not worldly deities but emanations of Vajrayogini. In the preliminary torma offering prayer in the self-initiation sadhana eleven different assemblies of guardians are mentioned, such as gods, nagas and givers of harm. The directional guardians and regional guardians in the charnel grounds appear in these eleven different aspects. Some appear as gods, some as nagas, and so forth. When we offer tormas to the mundane Dakas and Dakinis we invite these eleven groups from the eight charnel grounds to receive the torma.

Continuing our checking meditation on the mandala we now contemplate:

In the centre of the circle of eight charnel grounds is the celestial mansion, a red phenomena source standing on its tip on the vajra ground. Within each of its four side corners is a pink joy swirl spinning counter-clockwise. Inside the phenomena source is an eight-petalled lotus of various colours. The lotus petals in the cardinal directions are red. The colours of the petals in the intermediate directions are: in the south-east, yellow, in the south-west, green, in the north-west, yellow, and in the north-east, black. The centre of the lotus is green and is encircled by yellow anthers. In the centre of the lotus is a sun mandala. Upon this I arise in the form of Venerable Vajrayogini.

My outstretched right leg treads on the breast of red Kalarati. She has one face and lies on her back with her two hands pressed together. My bent left leg treads on the forehead of black Bhairawa. He has one face and lies on his front with his head bent backwards, touching his back, and his two hands pressed together. I have a red-coloured body which shines with a brilliance like that of the fire at the end of an aeon. I have one face, two hands, and three eyes looking up towards the Pure Land of the Dakinis. My right hand, outstretched and pointing downwards, holds a curved knife marked with a vajra. My left holds up a skullcup filled with blood which I partake of with my upturned mouth. My left shoulder supports a khatanga marked with a vajra from which hang a damaru, bell and triple banner. My black hair hanging straight covers my back down to my waist. I am in the prime of my youth. My aroused breasts are full and I show the manner of generating bliss. My head is adorned with five human skulls and I wear a long necklace of fifty human skulls. Naked, I am adorned with five mudras and stand in the centre of a blazing fire of exalted wisdom.

The protection circle, charnel grounds and phenomena source are extremely vast and in the nature of uncontaminated wisdom. This is the Pure Land of the Dakinis. I have now been born here in the aspect of Vajrayogini.

To overcome ordinary appearances we should repeatedly contemplate the symbolism of the protection circle, the charnel grounds, the mandala, and all the beings within them. The five-coloured fire of the protection circle is a manifestation of the five omniscient wisdoms of Vajrayogini and symbolizes ultimate bodhichitta. The vajra fence and so forth symbolize conventional bodhichitta, and the charnel grounds symbolize renunciation. Together these three teach us that first we should gain experience of the three principal aspects of the path.

The red, inner phenomena source symbolizes great bliss and the white, outer phenomena source symbolizes emptiness. Together they teach us that we should develop the union of great bliss and emptiness.

The phenomena source gradually increases in width from the bottom upwards, showing that high Tantric realizations cannot be gained instantly but develop gradually. By constantly improving our small Dharma experience we will eventually accomplish the supreme attainment of Buddhahood.

The three points of the top of each tetrahedron symbolize the three doors of perfect liberation: the emptiness of the entity of all phenomena, the emptiness of causes, and the emptiness of effects. These teach us that the nature of all phenomena, as well as all causes and all effects, are simply manifestations of emptiness. The empty front and back corners symbolize selflessness of persons and selflessness of phenomena. The pink joy swirls in the other four corners symbolize the four joys. Together all six corners teach us that we should combine the practice of emptiness with the practice of the four joys.

The sun mandala upon which we stand symbolizes the method for ripening the virtuous crop of generation and completion stage realizations, and for attaining the harvest of Vajrayogini's faultless Form Body, her Pure Land, and her pure enjoyments. The lotus symbolizes that Vajrayogini's body, speech and mind are free from faults and completely pure. Our right leg treads on the breast of red Kalarati, the principal worldly goddess, and our left leg treads on the forehead of black Bhairawa, or wrathful Ishvara, the principal worldly god. These are not the actual sentient beings, Kalarati and Bhairawa, but manifestations of Vajrayogini's wisdom of bliss and emptiness appearing in the aspect of Kalarati and Bhairawa. They symbolize the maras of the delusions. Vajrayogini treads on Kalarati and Bhairawa to demonstrate that she has destroyed her attachment, hatred and ignorance, and to show that she is free from the fears of samsara and solitary peace and can lead all living beings to the same freedom.

The brilliance of Vajrayogini's red-coloured body, which shines like the fire at the end of an aeon, symbolizes the blazing of her inner fire. Her inner fire causes her body to be pervaded by spontaneous great bliss through which she completely destroys the two obstructions. Her single face symbolizes that she has realized that ultimately all phenomena are of one taste, or of one nature. Her two arms symbolize her complete realization of the two truths. Her three eyes symbolize her ability to see everything in the past, present and future. She looks up to space, demonstrating her attainment of outer and inner Dakini Land, and indicating that she leads her followers to these attainments. Her right hand holds a curved knife to show her power to cut the continuum of the delusions and obstacles of her followers and of all living beings. Her left hand holds a skullcup filled with blood, which symbolizes her experience of the clear light of bliss.

Vajrayogini's left shoulder supports a khatanga, symbolizing that she is never separated from Father Heruka. Heruka is the manifestation of the blissful mind of all Buddhas, and Vajrayogini is the manifestation of the wisdom mind of all Buddhas. Since these two minds are one entity, Heruka and Vajrayogini are one person showing different aspects; they are not like an ordinary couple. The khatanga is Heruka himself, and the various features of the khatanga are the sixty-two Deities of Heruka's mandala. The khatanga is octagonal in cross-section, symbolizing the eight great charnel grounds of Heruka's mandala. At its lower tip is a single-pronged vajra symbolizing the protection circle of Heruka's mandala. Towards the upper end of the khatanga is a vase symbolizing Heruka's celestial mansion. Above this is a crossed vajra symbolizing the eight Deities of the commitment wheel, a blue human head symbolizing the sixteen Deities of the heart wheel, a red human head symbolizing the sixteen Deities of the speech wheel, and a white human head symbolizing the sixteen Deities of the body wheel. At the very top of the khatanga is a five-pronged vajra symbolizing the five Deities of the great bliss wheel.

Vajrayogini's body is in nature the perfection of wisdom of all the Buddhas. Her five mudra-ornaments of bone are the other five perfections of all the Buddhas. Adorning her crown is a horizontal eight-spoked wheel made from bone, and at its centre is a precious red jewel with nine facets. On top of this is a blue five-pronged vajra. At the front edge of the wheel is a tiara of five human skulls and on top of each skull is a jewel. The five jewels symbolize the five Buddha families. All these together constitute Vajrayogini's head ornament, which is the perfection of effort of all the Buddhas. The other ornaments are: the ear ornaments, the perfection of patience; the neck ornaments, the perfection of giving; the heart ornaments, the perfection of mental stabilization; and the ornaments of the arms and legs, the perfection of moral discipline.

Vajrayogini's five purified aggregates appear in the form of the five human skulls. Her fifty purified inner winds, the seeds of speech, appear in the form of a garland of fifty human skulls which she wears hanging from her neck. Her hair is black, symbolizing the unchangeable nature of her Truth Body. It falls freely down her back, symbolizing that she is free from the fetters of self-grasping. In the long dedication prayer in the sadhana it says that her hair is vermilion, but this refers mainly to her human emanations who have appeared with vermilion hair, as witnessed by Tsarchen Losel Gyatso and others.

Vajrayogini is naked and her breasts are full and aroused, showing that she herself experiences great bliss and also that she bestows the attainment of great bliss upon practitioners.

By contemplating this symbolism we should try to prevent ordinary appearance of ourself, our environment and our enjoyments, and think strongly, 'I am newly born in my own Pure Land as Emanation Body Vajrayogini.'

THE ACTUAL GENERATION STAGE MEDITATION

The third part of the yoga of self-generation, actual generation stage meditation, is explained after the next two yogas.

THE YOGA OF PURIFYING MIGRATORS

If we continually practise the sixth yoga, the yoga of self-generation, we will improve our familiarity with the recognition that we have attained Buddhahood in the aspect of Vajrayogini. After having generated ourself as Vajrayogini abiding in her Pure Land we should think:

> *I have compassion and love for all beings of the six realms. Now I can lead them all to enlightenment by purifying their environments, enjoyments, bodies and minds, and transforming them into the environment, enjoyments, body and mind of Vajrayogini.*

We then recite the appropriate words from the sadhana while meditating on their meaning as follows:

> *At my heart inside a red phenomena source, a double tetrahedron, is a moon mandala. In the centre of this is a letter BAM encircled by a mantra rosary. Light rays radiate from the moon, letter BAM and mantra rosary, and leave my body through the pores of my skin. The light rays touch all living beings of the six realms, purifying their negativities and obstructions together with their imprints, and transforming them all into the form of Vajrayogini.*

When we generate bodhichitta we have two wishes: to attain Buddhahood ourself and to lead all living beings to the same state. We imagine that we have already fulfilled our first wish by practising the sixth yoga, the yoga of self-generation. Now we fulfil our second wish by practising the seventh yoga, the yoga of purifying migrators. Both practices are the main cause to fulfil these two wishes.

The Yoga of being Blessed by
Heroes and Heroines

This has six parts:

1 Meditation on the body mandala
2 Absorbing the wisdom beings and mixing the three
  messengers
3 Putting on the armour
4 Granting empowerment and adorning the crown
5 Making offerings to the self-generation
6 Eight lines of praise to the Mother

MEDITATION ON THE BODY MANDALA

This has two parts:

1 General explanation
2 The actual meditation

GENERAL EXPLANATION

In this context, 'mandala' refers to an assembly of Deities and
not to a celestial mansion. A body mandala is so called because
the original substance that transforms into a body mandala
is part of the body of a self-generated Deity. This is similar to
calling a vase a golden vase because the substance of the vase
is gold.

A body mandala is defined as the transformation of any
part of the body of a self-generated Deity into a Deity. Merely
visualizing Deities marked on the body, as in the practice of
Yamantaka, is not a body mandala practice. Moreover, the

self-generated Deity itself is not a body mandala because its substantial cause is not a part of our body. During the practice of bringing death into the path we mentally dissolve our ordinary body into emptiness, and from emptiness we arise in the form of the letter BAM, which is the nature of our own mind. This BAM then transforms into Vajrayogini. It is only when a *part* of the body of the self-generation transforms into a Deity that it becomes a body mandala. This is not easy to understand at first and there are different interpretations in various texts as to what is and what is not a body mandala.

Recognizing its superiority over the body mandala practices of other Deities, many highly realized practitioners have praised the profound body mandala practice of Vajrayogini. It is an especially powerful method for blessing our channels, drops and winds. Through such blessings our inner winds will gather and dissolve within the central channel at our heart, and this will cause us to experience the clear light of bliss, the actual quick path leading to Buddhahood. Je Tsongkhapa said that the attainment of spontaneous great bliss depends upon the channels and drops being blessed by Heroes and Heroines. Meditating on the body mandala enables us to receive these blessings. When we visualize our channels and drops in the aspect of Heroines, the Heroines of the twenty-four holy places actually enter into our channels and drops and bless them. This helps us to develop great bliss.

The body mandala of Vajrayogini has thirty-seven Deities generated from thirty-seven parts of her body. These thirty-seven parts are the twenty-four channels of the twenty-four inner places, the eight channels of the eight doors of the sense powers, the four channels of the heart channel wheel, and the very subtle indestructible drop at the heart.

Shortly after conception, when the body begins to take form, the first channel to develop is the central channel at the level of the heart. From the central channel the eight channels of the heart branch out, and from these the twenty-four channels develop. The central channel can be likened to the central rod of an umbrella and the twenty-four channels to its spokes. The inner tips of the twenty-four channels join the central channel at the heart channel wheel and the outer tips terminate at the twenty-four inner places.

The twenty-four inner places of the body are: (1) the hairline, (2) the crown, (3) the right ear, (4) the back of the neck, (5) the left ear, (6) the brow (the point between the eyebrows), (7) the two eyes, (8) the two shoulders, (9) the two armpits, (10) the two breasts, (11) the navel, (12) the tip of the nose, (13) the mouth, (14) the throat, (15) the heart (the point midway between the two breasts), (16) the two testicles for men, or the two sides of the vagina for women, (17) the tip of the sex organ, (18) the anus, (19) the two thighs, (20) the two calves, (21) the eight fingers and eight toes, (22) the tops of the feet, (23) the two thumbs and two big toes, and (24) the two knees. These correspond to the twenty-four outer Pure Lands of Heruka and Vajrayogini that exist in this world.

In the practice of Heruka's body mandala, Deities are generated at the outer tips of the twenty-four channels, at the twenty-four inner places. In Vajrayogini's body mandala, however, the Deities are generated at the inner tips of the twenty-four channels, inside the central channel at the heart channel wheel. This is the main reason why Vajrayogini's body mandala is more profound than those of other Yidams.

The eight channels are those of the eight doors of the sense powers. These eight doors are tiny openings or vacuoles at the outer tip of each of the eight channels. They are located at: (1) the root of the tongue, (2) the navel, (3) the sex organ, (4) the anus, (5) the point between the eyebrows, (6) the two ears, (7) the two eyes, and (8) the nostrils. The inner tips of these eight channels join the central channel at the heart channel wheel, together with the inner tips of the twenty-four channels, the inner tips of the four channels of the heart channel wheel, and the indestructible drop.

These thirty-seven parts of the body transform into the thirty-seven female Deities of the sixty-two Deities of Heruka's mandala. The sixty-two Deities are included within five 'wheels': the six Deities of the great bliss wheel, the sixteen Deities of the heart wheel, the sixteen Deities of the speech wheel, the sixteen Deities of the body wheel, and the eight Deities of the commitment wheel. However, we visualize directly only the eight Heroines of the commitment wheel, the eight Heroines of the body wheel, the eight Heroines of the speech wheel, the eight Heroines of the heart wheel, and the five female Deities of the great bliss wheel (the Goddesses of the four directions and the main Deity of the body mandala, Vajrayogini). The remaining twenty-five Deities, the male Deities, are not visualized directly but appear as the khatangas that are held by Vajrayogini and each of the Heroines of the body, speech and mind wheels.

All the Heroines of the body mandala are generated inside the central channel of the heart channel wheel. The central channel is flanked on both sides by the right and left channels. At the heart channel wheel these two channels loop around the central channel three times, forming six knots in the central channel. At the centre of these knots, inside the central channel, there is a tiny vacuole. This is where we visualize the body mandala of Vajrayogini. The centre of the heart channel wheel is one of the ten doors through which winds can enter the central channel. It is very important to locate accurately the place of the body mandala meditation.

If we practise the body mandala every day, visualizing the Heroines and their khatangas at the inner tips of the twenty-four channels and regarding these channels as the twenty-four inner places, all the Heroes and Heroines of the twenty-four outer places will enter our body. There is no need to go to the twenty-four outer places to receive blessings from these Deities.

THE ACTUAL MEDITATION

At the centre of the heart channel wheel we visualize a phenomena source, in the centre of which is a tiny moon cushion, smaller than a fingernail or as small as we can visualize it. On top of the moon cushion are the thirty-six channels and the indestructible drop. Beginning from the front of the moon cushion and arranged counter-clockwise are the twenty-four channels of the twenty-four inner places and the eight channels of the eight doors of the sense powers, making a circle of thirty-two channels. This arrangement is similar to the way in which the thirty-two letters of the three-OM mantra are arranged on the moon cushion during mantra recitation. The channels stand upright. They are slightly thicker than a needle, very short, transparent, and filled with red and white drops. Inside the circle of the thirty-two channels, the four channels of the heart channel wheel stand in the cardinal directions. In the centre of these is the very subtle indestructible drop, which is about the size of a mustard seed. The top half is white and the bottom half is red, and it is clear and translucent. It is important to believe that these visualized channels and drops are the actual channels and drops of our own body.

The thirty-two channels form a circle around the edge of the moon disc. Inside these are the four channels of the four directions, and in the very centre of these is the indestructible drop. The thirty-two channels instantaneously transform into the thirty-two letters of the three-OM mantra, which are standing upright. The four channels, starting from the left, or the north, and standing counter-clockwise, transform respectively into the green letter YA, the red letter RA, the yellow letter LA, and the white letter WA. The central drop transforms into the letter short-AH, the top half of which is white and the bottom half of which is red. We try to focus our mind clearly on these thirty-seven letters. They are in essence our thirty-six channels and our indestructible drop but they have the aspect of the letters of the three-OM mantra.

After focusing on these letters for a while, we imagine that they transform simultaneously into the Heroines of Heruka's mandala. In the centre is Vajrayogini. She is surrounded by the four Heroines of the four cardinal directions, and these in turn are surrounded by the thirty-two Heroines who stand around the edge of the moon cushion. They are all in the aspect of Vajrayogini and face the principal Deity in the centre.

Around the edge of the moon cushion, starting from the front and standing counter-clockwise, are the eight Heroines of the heart wheel of Heruka: Partzandi, Tzändriakiya, Parbhawatiya, Mahanasa, Biramatiya, Karwariya, Lamkeshöriya and Drumatzaya. They are followed by the eight Heroines of the speech wheel of Heruka: Airawatiya, Mahabhairawi, Bayubega, Surabhakiya, Shamadewi, Suwatre, Hayakarne and Khaganane. They are followed by the eight Heroines of the body wheel of Heruka: Tzatrabega, Khandarohi, Shaundini, Tzatrawarmini, Subira, Mahabala, Tzatrawartini and Mahabire. These are the twenty-four Heroines of the twenty-four places. Completing the circle of the thirty-two Heroines are the eight Heroines of the commitment wheel of Heruka: Kakase, Ulukase, Shonase, Shukarase, Yamadhathi, Yamaduti, Yamadangtrini and Yamamatani.

We imagine that the thirty-two letters of the three-OM mantra transform into these Heroines. For example, the first OM of the mantra transforms into the Heroine Partzandi, the second OM transforms into Tzändriakiya, the third OM transforms into Parbhawatiya, the SAR transforms into Mahanasa, the WA transforms into Biramatiya, and so on, finishing with the third PHAT which transforms into Yamaduti, the SÖ which transforms into Yamadangtrini, and the HA which transforms into Yamamatani.

Inside the circle of thirty-two Heroines the four letters YA, RA, LA and WA transform into the four Goddesses. In the north the letter YA transforms into green Lama, in the west the letter RA transforms into red Khandarohi, in the south the letter LA transforms into yellow Rupini, and in the east the letter WA transforms into white Dakini. These four Goddesses look exactly like Vajrayogini except for their different colours. In the very centre the red and white short-AH transforms into Vajrayogini herself. The four Goddesses of the four cardinal directions together with Vajrayogini are the Heroines of the great bliss wheel of Heruka.

All the Heroes, the male Buddhas of Secret Mantra, and all the Heroines, the female Buddhas of Secret Mantra, are included within the Heroes and Heroines of the twenty-four places. Therefore, when we visualize the Heroes and Heroines of the twenty-four places in the form of the thirty-seven Heroines of the body mandala and their khatangas, in effect we visualize all the Buddhas. If we have strong faith that the thirty-seven Heroines are really at the centre of our heart, all the Buddhas will enter our heart and remain there, and our body will become very precious.

Buddhas' bodies are not obstructed by matter. Wherever we visualize them, whether it be in front of us or at our heart, they will be there immediately. If we harbour doubts about this we deny ourself the chance of receiving their blessings. When doing these practices we need firm conviction in the existence of enlightened beings and in their ability to appear wherever and whenever we visualize them. In the Sutras Buddha said that he would be present whenever someone with faith visualized him. We ordinary beings cannot see Buddhas directly because we do not have sufficient merit. Our minds are obscured by delusions and the propensities of non-virtuous actions, just like a sun obscured by clouds. Although Buddhas exist we will not be able to see them until we have dispelled our own mental obscurations. Until that time we should try to develop conviction that Buddhas are actually present whenever we visualize them. Without this conviction our practice of Secret Mantra, and especially that of the body mandala, will be unsuccessful. If we believe firmly that the Heroes and Heroines are at the centre of our heart channel wheel they will definitely enter and bless our channels, drops and winds. We will draw closer to them and receive their care and guidance, and they will help us to develop spontaneous great bliss.

There are two important points to remember when we meditate on the body mandala. The first is that the thirty-seven Heroines at the centre of our heart channel wheel are the real Heroines of Vajrayogini's Pure Land. The second is that their nature, or essence, is that of the purified channels, drops and elements of our own body. If we do not recollect the first point we will not receive direct blessings from the Heroines, and if we do not recollect the second point our meditation will not be a body mandala practice.

During the actual meditation on the body mandala we first focus on the principal Deity Vajrayogini at the centre of the moon cushion at our heart inside the central channel and remember that she is in essence our own purified indestructible drop. We then focus on each of the four Heroines in turn, remembering that their nature is that of the purified four channels of the four directions at the heart. We then focus on the thirty-two Heroines, remembering that their nature is that of the purified twenty-four channels of the twenty-four places and the purified eight channels of the eight doors of the sense powers.

Having briefly focused on the thirty-two Heroines we again focus on the four Heroines, and then on the main Deity. We repeat this cycle of analytical meditation several times, gradually building up a visualization of the entire assembly. When we have a rough image of the assembly of thirty-seven Heroines we hold it with single-pointed concentration in placement meditation. At first we will not perceive each Heroine clearly and individually. We should be satisfied with a rough image of the whole assembly and focus single-pointedly on this. With placement meditation we try to merge our mind with the assembly of Heroines so that we lose the feeling of our mind and the assembly being separate. First we observe the assembly as if we were separate from it, and then we dissolve our mind into the assembly so that our mind and the assembly become one. We then meditate on it single-pointedly.

To begin with, until we become familiar with the practice, we should do this meditation for only a short time. It is not advisable to concentrate for too long on subtle objects at the beginning. After meditating for a short time we rest for a while and then we begin analytical meditation again. We check from the central Vajrayogini to the four Heroines, to the thirty-two Heroines, and back again; and when we gain an image of the entire assembly we place our mind on this single-pointedly. This is how to train gradually in the body mandala meditation.

During the meditation our attention should not wander outside the central channel. Keeping our attention focused within the central channel will cause our winds to enter, abide and dissolve there. When this happens we will experience each of the signs of dissolution, from the mirage-like appearance up to the clear light.

There are other ways of generating the body mandala but the method explained here is the most succinct. It was taught by Je Phabongkhapa and Dorjechang Trijang Rinpoche.

ABSORBING THE WISDOM BEINGS AND MIXING THE THREE MESSENGERS

This has two parts:

1 Absorbing the wisdom beings into the commitment beings
2 Mixing the three messengers

ABSORBING THE WISDOM BEINGS INTO THE COMMITMENT BEINGS

In this practice there are two types of commitment being: ourself generated as Vajrayogini together with the thirty-seven Deities of the body mandala, and the visualized protection circle, charnel grounds and phenomena source. They are called 'commitment beings' because we have made a commitment to generate all these when we received the Vajrayogini empowerment. The wisdom beings are the male and female Buddhas of the ten directions. When we invite them we imagine that they arrive in the space before us in the same aspect as the commitment beings and then dissolve into the commitment beings, becoming one with them. While visualizing this we recite the following lines from the sadhana:

PHAIM
Light rays radiate from the letter BAM at my heart and, leaving from between my eyebrows, go to the ten directions. They invite all the Tathagatas, Heroes and Yoginis of the ten directions in the aspect of Vajrayogini.

We recite 'PHAIM' quite loudly to exhort the wisdom beings to come to us. While doing so we mentally recall bliss and emptiness and physically perform the hand gesture called the 'blazing mudra'. To perform this mudra we first place the two tips of the thumbs together and, with our palms facing outwards, loosely hook the two index fingers together, with the right index finger crossing over the left. The two middle fingers slightly touch and the ring fingers and little fingers of both hands stretch upwards. The shape formed by the index fingers and thumbs is said to resemble the shape of a vagina, which symbolizes great bliss. The empty space between these fingers symbolizes emptiness. The combination of these two symbolizes the union of great bliss and emptiness; together they remind us to experience the union of great bliss and emptiness. The ring fingers and little fingers stretching upwards symbolizes the blazing of the inner fire. This mudra reminds us to generate the experience of great bliss and emptiness. Initially we hold our hands in this way at our left knee and then, while reciting 'PHAIM', we bring both hands up in an arc to the level of our forehead and make nine small circular movements of the hands – three counter-clockwise, three clockwise, and again three counter-clockwise. We then bring our hands down to our right knee.

With the verbal exhortation PHAIM we invoke the wisdom beings. We imagine that all male and female Buddhas, the Heroes and Heroines of the ten directions appearing in the aspect of Vajrayogini, together with the entire mandala and Deities, come to the space above our visualized mandala. The wisdom beings are identical in aspect to the commitment beings.

We then recite 'DZA HUM BAM HO'. As we say 'DZA' the wisdom beings appear above the commitment beings. At the same time we perform the hooking mudra. To do this we extend the index fingers and little fingers of each hand and tuck the middle fingers and ring fingers of each hand into their respective palms and hold them there with the thumbs. Then, holding the right hand palm downwards and the left hand palm upwards, we place the tip of the right index finger on the tip of the little finger of the left hand.

As we say 'HUM' the wisdom beings dissolve into the commitment beings. At the same time we perform the rope mudra, or binding mudra, which is a mirror image of the hooking mudra. Thus we hold the left hand palm downwards and the right hand palm upwards and place the left index finger on the little finger of the right hand.

As we say 'BAM' the wisdom beings and commitment beings become inseparably mixed. At the same time we perform the iron chain mudra. For this mudra we hold the fingers as before but both palms face upwards and the index fingers and little fingers are loosely hooked together.

As we say 'HO' the inseparable mixing of the wisdom beings and the commitment beings is stabilized. At the same time we perform the bell mudra. We continue to hold down the middle finger and ring finger of each hand with the thumbs, and extend the index and little fingers as before. We then cross our arms with the left forearm closest to our body, hold our left hand with the fingers pointing upwards, and turn our right wrist so that the fingers point downwards with the palm facing outwards. Both wrists are touching with the inside of our right wrist against the outside of our left wrist. All these mudras are illustrated in Appendix III.

This invocation is similar to the way in which an oracle invites a Deity to enter his body by means of his concentration. On such occasions there are many valid signs that the Deity actually enters the oracle's body. In a similar way, when we invoke the wisdom beings of Vajrayogini and invite them to enter the body of the self-generation we should have no doubt that we have become unified with the wisdom being Vajrayogini and that our environment is Vajrayogini's Pure Land.

The scriptures say that if we verbally recite PHAIM, perform the mudra, and recollect great bliss and emptiness, all the Buddhas will definitely come to us. Vajradhara himself promised that he would come with all the Buddhas whenever faithful practitioners called him. We need have no doubt about this. If we regularly make this powerful invocation our mental continuum will receive the blessings of the Heroes and Heroines and we will gain confidence that the wisdom beings actually dissolve into us and remain with us always.

We accomplish Highest Yoga Tantra attainments largely through the power of faith and imagination. By vividly imagining that the wisdom beings dissolve into our body and mind and believing that this actually happens, both our divine pride of being Vajrayogini and the clarity of our visualization will improve. Through this practice we will overcome ordinary conceptions and ordinary appearances and gain Tantric realizations. Even though the absorption of the wisdom beings is imagined to start with, it still has these effects. Through continued practice, eventually the wisdom beings will actually enter our body and mind whenever we invoke them, exactly as happens with an oracle. I would like to encourage practitioners of Vajrayogini or Heruka to become qualified oracles of Vajrayogini or Heruka by maintaining the wisdom being in their heart all the time. In this way they will become emanations of Vajrayogini or Heruka.

Having dissolved the wisdom beings of Vajrayogini into ourself we then recite the mantra 'OM YOGA SHUDDHA SARWA DHARMA YOGA SHUDDHO HAM', which means, 'I am the nature of the yoga of completely purified all phenomena.' In this context 'yoga' refers to the union of bliss and emptiness. From the ultimate point of view all phenomena are in essence the union of great bliss and emptiness. Observing this all-embracing union of bliss and emptiness we generate divine pride, thinking 'This is me.' 'Completely purified all phenomena' means that all phenomena are completely purified of mistaken appearance.

While reciting this mantra we perform the giving the essence mudra. To do this we perform the lotus-turning mudra three times – first from the left side of the chest, then from the right side of the chest, then at the heart – and we then perform the embracing mudra. The first mudra symbolizes the inner winds of the left channel gathering into the central channel, the second symbolizes the inner winds of the right channel gathering into the central channel, the third symbolizes all the winds dissolving within the central channel at the heart, and the fourth symbolizes the union of Father and Mother in embrace. We hold this mudra briefly while we recall great bliss inseparable from emptiness, which is the secret Vajrayogini generated during the Vajrayogini empowerment. While reciting the mantra and performing the mudra we imagine that our mind of great bliss mixes with the ultimate nature of all phenomena. We then take this union of great bliss and emptiness as the basis upon which to impute I, and generate divine pride of being Truth Body Vajrayogini. At the same time we recite, 'I am the nature of the yoga of completely purified all phenomena.' This experience is very profound and its real meaning is not easy to understand.

Correct practice of this meditation entails the mixing of the outer, inner and secret messengers. In the sixth yoga, the yoga of self-generation, we visualize the inner Vajrayogini, the letter BAM. Now, in the yoga of being blessed by Heroes and Heroines, we first absorb the outer Vajrayoginis, the Dakinis of the twenty-four holy places, and we then identify the secret Vajrayogini, or the definitive Vajrayogini, which is the union of bliss and emptiness.

MIXING THE THREE MESSENGERS

Mixing the three messengers means that we invite the outer messengers, the Heroines of the twenty-four places of Heruka and the Pure Land of Keajra, dissolve them into the inner messengers, the thirty-seven Deities of the body mandala of Vajrayogini, who are the nature of our channels and indestructible drop, and through this, experience the secret messenger, the union of great bliss and emptiness.

Generally, a messenger is someone who fulfils the wishes of two people by relaying a message between them. In this practice there are said to be three kinds of messenger: outer messengers, inner messengers and secret messengers. The outer messengers are the Heroines who reside in the twenty-four places of Heruka and in the Pure Land of the Dakinis. They are invited when we invoke the wisdom beings to dissolve into the commitment beings. They are called 'messengers' because they fulfil the wishes of those practitioners who want to attain spontaneous great bliss. The inner messengers are the thirty-six channels and the indestructible drop of our body that appear in the aspect of the Heroines of the body mandala. Through concentration we can penetrate these channels, cause the winds to enter, abide and dissolve within the central channel, and thereby generate spontaneous great bliss. The secret messengers are the many levels of realization of spontaneously born exalted wisdom, which are the main cause of Buddhahood, our ultimate aim. Inner messengers are the observed objects of completion stage meditation, and secret messengers are the realizations that result from such meditation.

In the practice of mixing the three messengers we invite the outer messengers, the Heroines of the twenty-four places and the Pure Land of the Dakinis, to dissolve into the inner messengers, the channels of our body, and we then imagine that we generate the secret messenger, a mind of great bliss indivisibly mixed with emptiness. In one Vajrayogini prayer it says:

O Venerable and beautiful Lady of Dakini Land,
Through receiving assistance from the three outer
    messengers
And meditating on the three inner messengers,
May I attain the three secret messengers.

An outer messenger is anyone who helps us to generate great bliss. There are three types of outer messenger: supreme, middling and minor. A supreme outer messenger is one who has attained the union that needs learning or the Union of No More Learning, a middling outer messenger is one who has attained completion stage realizations but not union, and a minor outer messenger is one who has some experience of generation stage but not of completion stage.

There are also three types of inner messenger. The supreme inner messengers are the central channel and the four heart channels; the middling inner messengers are the twenty-four channels of the twenty-four places of the body; and the minor inner messengers are the eight channels of the eight doors of the sense powers. Meditation on the central channel and four heart channels is the quickest and most powerful method to centralize the winds and to experience spontaneous great bliss. Meditative penetration of the twenty-four channels of the twenty-four inner places is a less powerful method for centralizing the winds than meditating on the central channel itself, but it is more powerful than meditating on other channels such as the eight channels of the eight doors of the sense powers. Meditative penetration of the eight channels will also cause the winds to enter the central channel, but because this is the least powerful method for experiencing spontaneous great bliss, the eight channels are called the 'minor inner messengers'.

The meditations on the three inner messengers include meditations on the winds and the drops as well as on the channels. An example of the first is vajra recitation, also called the 'yoga of wind', which is explained in detail in *Tantric Grounds and Paths*. This is an excellent method for bringing the winds into the central channel and causing spontaneous great bliss to arise. An example of meditation on the drops is the inner fire meditation, also called 'tummo meditation' or the 'yoga of drops', which is another excellent method to experience spontaneous great bliss. In this meditation we focus on the red blood cell, or drop, which is located at the navel and has the nature of inner fire. Any method that causes the experience of spontaneous great bliss is called a messenger.

There are also three types of secret messenger. A supreme secret messenger is a mind of spontaneous great bliss directly realizing emptiness; a middling secret messenger is a mind of spontaneous great bliss meditating on a generic image of emptiness; and a minor secret messenger is a mind of meditation that simply imagines that we have a mind of great bliss indivisible from emptiness. Even though this last meditation is not a complete realization it is called a secret messenger because it helps us to develop the actual realization of the union of great bliss and emptiness.

In summary, we attain the three secret messengers by penetrating the three inner messengers with the assistance of the three outer messengers. To penetrate the inner messengers it is necessary to meditate on our channels, drops and winds.

There are many outer messengers who will assist us in our practice, but it is very important that our meditation on the channels, drops and winds is done correctly.

We can loosen the knots of the heart channel wheel by means of completion stage meditation in which the inner winds enter and dissolve within the central channel at the heart and cause us to experience great bliss. However, although we can partially loosen the knots through solitary meditation, we cannot loosen them completely without relying upon an outer messenger. At the time of death the knots of the heart channel wheel loosen completely through the force of karma and allow our consciousness to leave the body; but to loosen the knots completely before death we need the assistance of an outer messenger, or action mudra, with whom we can strengthen and improve our experience of great bliss. When we have completely loosened all the knots of the heart channel wheel through meditation and relying upon an action mudra, we will attain the isolated mind of ultimate example clear light. This clear light of great bliss is a secret messenger. Once we have gained this realization we will definitely attain enlightenment before death.

By relying upon the outer messengers and meditating on the inner messengers we generate the secret messengers. Unifying the three kinds of messenger in this way is called 'mixing the three messengers'.

PUTTING ON THE ARMOUR

There are three main reasons for putting on the armour: (1) to stabilize the absorption of the wisdom beings into the commitment beings; (2) to safeguard against external obstacles such as harmful spirits; and (3) to protect ourself from inner obstacles such as delusions and sickness, which disturb our concentration on generation stage practice. Just as warriors used armour to protect themselves in battle, so meditators need armour to defend themselves against obstacles and hindrances.

There are two systems for wearing the armour. One is to visualize Deities marked on the body, and the other is to visualize the seed-letters of Deities marked on the body. When we do the practice elaborately, as in the extensive Heruka sadhana, we visualize Deities marked on the body, but in both the extensive and condensed sadhanas of Vajrayogini we visualize only the seed-letters of the Deities.

In Secret Mantra it is important to recognize that Deities and their seed-letters have the same nature. For instance, the thirty-two letters of the three-OM mantra are the same nature as the thirty-two Deities of Vajrayogini's body mandala. We will not accomplish supramundane attainments if we regard mantras and Deities as being different in nature.

In the practice of Vajrayogini we visualize the seed-letters of six Goddesses at various points of the body, between the skin and flesh. The six Goddesses are: Vajravarahi, the consort of Buddha Akshobya; Yamani, the wrathful aspect of Lochana, the consort of Buddha Vairochana; Mohani, the wrathful aspect of Benzarahi, the consort of Buddha Amitabha; Sachalani, the wrathful aspect of Vajradhatuishvari, the consort of Buddha Vajradhara; Samtrasani, the wrathful aspect of Mamaki, the consort of Buddha Ratnasambhava; and Chandika, the wrathful aspect of Tara, the consort of Buddha Amoghasiddhi.

At the level of our navel we visualize a moon mandala which is standing upright, and at its centre we visualize the red letters OM BAM, on the right and left respectively. Although they have the aspect of letters they are in essence Vajravarahi. At the level of our heart is an upright moon mandala which has at its centre the blue letters HAM YOM, on the right and left respectively. They are in essence Yamani. At the top of our neck, just under our chin, is an upright moon mandala which has at its centre the white letters HRIM MOM, on the right and left respectively. They are in essence Mohani. At our forehead is an upright moon mandala which has at its centre the yellow letters HRIM HRIM. They are in essence Sachalani. At our crown is a moon mandala lying flat which has at its centre the green letters HUM HUM. They are in essence Samtrasani. At both shoulders, both wrists, both hips, and both ankles, at the centre of upright moon mandalas, are the smoke-coloured letters PHAT PHAT. They are in essence Chandika. In the sadhana it says that these letters are 'at all my limbs' but the meaning is that they are at the eight places mentioned here. These places are known as the 'eight great joints'.

In each case the two letters at each point symbolize the Father and Mother of each Buddha family. The letters on the right symbolize the Father, and the ones on the left symbolize the Mother. For instance, at our navel the OM symbolizes Akshobya, the Father of the Vajra family, and the BAM symbolizes Vajravarahi, the Mother of that family.

From the green letters HUM HUM at our crown, green light radiates between the skin and flesh, causing the surface of our skull above the forehead to be protected by a layer of green light. However, this does not alter the colour of the outer layer of our skin, which remains red because we have generated ourself as Vajrayogini. From the yellow letters HRIM HRIM at our forehead, yellow light radiates between the skin and flesh down to our neck. From the white letters HRIM MOM at our neck, white light radiates down and around our body to the level of our heart. From the blue letters HAM YOM at the level of our heart, blue light radiates down to our navel. From the red letters OM BAM at our navel, red light radiates down to our hips. From the letters PHAT PHAT at our hips, smoke-coloured light radiates down to our ankles; and from the letters PHAT PHAT at our ankles, smoke-coloured light radiates down to the tips of our toes. From the letters PHAT PHAT at our shoulders, smoke-coloured light radiates down to our wrists; and from the letters PHAT PHAT at our wrists, smoke-coloured light radiates down to our fingertips. There are no gaps between the different coloured lights so that every part of our body between the skin and flesh is suffused with these radiant lights.

In summary, we imagine that our body is enclosed within a protective layer of light, which is in essence the five Buddha families. Our body and mind are filled with their wisdom. In this way the wisdom beings remain one with us and prevent any obstacles from penetrating our body and mind. It is important to have strong faith that these lights are the same nature as the great bliss and emptiness of the five Buddha families. This conviction will protect us from harm. In effect, we are creating an inner protection circle.

GRANTING EMPOWERMENT AND ADORNING THE CROWN

There now follows an explanation of three practices: (1) granting empowerment and adorning the crown, (2) making offerings to the self-generation, and (3) the eight lines of praise to the Mother. Although these are not directly listed within the eleven yogas they are an important part of the self-generation practice.

From the point of view of uncommon appearances, when Buddha Shakyamuni was born the five Buddha families of the ten directions anointed his body with the five nectars. Here we imagine that we, the newly-born Vajrayogini, receive a similar empowerment.

We first recite 'PHAIM' while performing the blazing mudra. We visualize light rays radiating from the letter BAM at our heart and inviting the empowering Deities of Heruka's mandala to appear in the space above us. We then request these Deities, together with all the Buddhas, to grant us the empowerment. The eight Goddesses of the doorways respond to our request by driving away all hindrances, the twenty-four Heroes such as Khandakapala chant auspicious verses, the twenty-four Heroines such as Partzandi sing vajra songs on emptiness, and the offering goddesses such as Rupavajra and Shaptavajra make offerings to the principal Deity Heruka. The principal Deity consents to grant the empowerment, and Vajravarahi and the four Mothers – Lama, Khandarohi, Rupini and Dakini – hold aloft precious jewelled vases filled with the five wisdom nectars and pour the nectar onto our crown. The nectar enters through our crown channel wheel and fills our entire body, purifying all obstructions and negative actions of body, speech and mind.

A little nectar overflows through our crown channel wheel and transforms into Buddha Vairochana-Heruka together with his consort who sit within the multi-faceted jewel of our crown ornament. Buddha Vairochana-Heruka and his consort are both white. The Father sits in the vajra posture holding a wheel in his right hand and a bell in his left hand at the level of his heart. Vairochana-Heruka is the method aspect of all Buddhas appearing in the form of a Deity, and Vajrayogini is the wisdom aspect of all Buddhas appearing as a Deity. Vajrayogini actually belongs to the family of Akshobya, but here she is adorned by Vairochana-Heruka to demonstrate the union of method and wisdom. This is one of many symbols of the union of method and wisdom to be found throughout the practice of Vajrayogini.

MAKING OFFERINGS TO THE SELF-GENERATION

According to some traditions it is not necessary to make offerings to ourself generated as the Deity; offerings to the in-front-generated Deity are said to suffice. Je Tsongkhapa, however, gave many explanations showing the importance of making offerings to the self-generation and cited Tantras to support his reasoning. In the *Root Tantra of Heruka* Vajradhara says:

Making offerings to ourself
Becomes an offering to all Buddhas.

This is because when we absorbed the wisdom beings all the Buddhas dissolved into and merged inseparably with ourself generated as Vajrayogini. Moreover, during the practice of bringing death into the path of the Truth Body we dissolved all environments and beings, including all Buddhas, into the clear light, and identified this clear light as the Truth Body, which is one with the minds of all Buddhas. From this clear light we arose in the form of the Emanation Body of Vajrayogini. Therefore the self-generation is the synthesis of all Buddhas and so when we make offerings to the self-generation we are making offerings to all Buddhas.

Making offerings to ourself generated as the Deity is an especially powerful method for accumulating merit. If we maintain the awareness that we are Vajrayogini throughout the day, then whatever we enjoy, such as food and drink, becomes an offering to the Deity. It is only in Secret Mantra that we have the opportunity to create merit in this way.

If we fail to make offerings to the self-generation the power of our Tantric practice will diminish. Great Tantric scholars and meditators of the past, including Buddha Shakyamuni, have stated that Tantric practice is characterized by the four complete purities: complete purity of place, complete purity of body, complete purity of deeds, and complete purity of enjoyments. In the practice of Vajrayogini, complete purity of place is the transformation of our environment into Vajrayogini's mandala, complete purity of body is the transformation of our body into Vajrayogini's body, complete purity of deeds is the practice of the yoga of purifying migrators, and complete purity of enjoyments is the viewing of every enjoyment as an offering to the self-generation. If we omit these offerings to the self-generation our practice will not have the fourth complete purity and so it will not be a fully qualified Tantric practice. It will lack the full power, quality and benefits of a Secret Mantra practice. Therefore, it is important to make offerings to ourself generated as Vajrayogini.

The way to bless the eight outer offerings has already been explained. To make the outer offerings to the self-generation we imagine that offering goddesses emanate from our heart, take replica offerings from those blessed previously, and offer them to ourself generated as Vajrayogini. While visualizing this we recite the offering mantras and perform the accompanying hand gestures. After making the eight offerings we make the offerings of the six knowledge goddesses, Rupavajra and so forth, together with their offering mantras and hand gestures. The Heruka sadhana contains the more elaborate offerings of the sixteen knowledge goddesses.

To make the inner offering to the self-generation we imagine that many offering goddesses emanate from our heart and fill their skullcups with inner offering from the large skullcup of blessed nectar. As we recite the three-OM mantra for the inner offering these goddesses offer the nectar to us generated as Vajrayogini, and to the thirty-seven Deities of the body mandala. We then recite OM AH HUM and taste the inner offering.

To make the secret and thatness offerings to the self-generation we visualize that the khatanga we support on our left shoulder transforms into Father Heruka. He enters into embrace with us generated as Vajrayogini. Through this embrace the inner fire at Heruka's navel blazes, causing the white bodhichitta at his crown to melt and flow down his central channel. This white bodhichitta reaches our sex organ and enters the lower tip of our central channel. It then begins to ascend through our central channel. When it reaches our navel we experience joy, when it reaches our heart we experience supreme joy, when it reaches our throat we experience extraordinary joy, and when it reaches our crown we experience spontaneous great joy. As we experience the fourth joy we imagine that the thirty-seven Deities at our heart also experience spontaneous great joy, and we meditate for a short time on this experience of spontaneous great joy. This experience is the secret offering. We then recall emptiness and mix our mind of spontaneous great bliss with emptiness. This is the thatness offering.

Another method for making the secret and thatness offerings is to change our aspect from that of Vajrayogini into that of Heruka and, through embrace with Vajrayogini, called the 'secret Mother' in the sadhana, imagine that we experience the four joys. After making these offerings we then resume the form of Vajrayogini. Both methods are equally valid and we can choose either. Je Phabongkhapa says that the first method may be more suitable for female practitioners and the second for male practitioners.

There is another special method for experiencing the four joys that can be practised at this point. If our motivation is completely pure we should try to receive oral instructions on this method from a qualified Tantric Spiritual Guide.

EIGHT LINES OF PRAISE TO THE MOTHER

When engaging in this practice, first we should know that in ultimate truth there are no impure things, no samsara, no suffering and no mistaken appearance; everything is completely pure in the nature of definitive Heruka, emptiness inseparable from the clear light of bliss. Impure things are only the creation of the ignorance of self-grasping and therefore actually do not exist. With this profound knowledge we engage in the practice of the eight lines of praise to the Mother.

When we have completed the four types of offering we emanate praising goddesses who respectfully press their palms together and recite the eight lines of praise to us generated as Vajrayogini. This praise was taught by Vajradhara and it is an especially blessed practice. For practitioners of Heruka and Vajrayogini these words are the most supreme of all praises. Merely reciting these praises causes Vajrayogini and all the Deities of Heruka's mandala to draw closer to us and remain with us constantly. We can also use these praises to pay homage to other Deities, regarding them and their environment as one in nature with Vajrayogini and her Pure Land. By doing this we glorify all holy beings.

Practitioners of Heruka and Vajrayogini can regard anyone they meet as an emanation of Heruka or Vajrayogini and recite the eight lines of praise of Heruka or Vajrayogini to them. By sincerely reciting these praises we swiftly purify our ordinary appearances and reach outer Dakini Land. Even if we are confronted with an aggressive and vicious criminal we should not dwell upon ordinary appearances but regard him as an emanation of Heruka or Vajrayogini and silently make praises to him with these eight lines. If we gain familiarity with this practice we will come to view all beings as pure. We can even extend this pure view to inanimate objects such as mountains, lakes, buildings, and the earth itself. We should not be misled by the external aspect of any object but should think that its real nature is the same as that of Heruka and Vajrayogini and then praise it with the eight lines. This helps us to overcome ordinary appearances and causes us to attain the outer Pure Land of Vajrayogini.

Many teachings on Heruka Tantra, including *Illuminating All Hidden Meanings* by Je Tsongkhapa, describe Heruka in two ways. The conventional view of Heruka, called interpretative Heruka, is that Heruka is an Emanation Body of Vajradhara with a blue-coloured body, four faces and twelve hands. The ultimate view of Heruka, called definitive Heruka, is that Heruka is a mind of great bliss inseparably mixed with emptiness. Since the ultimate nature of all phenomena is emptiness, definitive Heruka pervades all phenomena. In Tibetan definitive Heruka is called 'kyabdag' Heruka. 'Kyab' means 'pervasive' and 'dag' means 'nature', so 'kyabdag' means 'the same nature as all phenomena'. From this profound viewpoint all the Deities, such as Guhyasamaja, Yamantaka, Heruka and Vajrayogini, are in essence the same. Every Deity, including Vajrayogini, has a definitive and an interpretative nature. By understanding definitive Vajrayogini or Heruka there is great hope that we will be able to perceive whatever appears to our mind as Vajrayogini or Heruka.

Through their devotion and sincere practice of these instructions practitioners draw close to Heruka and Vajrayogini and become as if one with them. If we make offerings and praises to such practitioners we will create great merit and our mind will be blessed.

At this point in the sadhana we recite the eight lines of praise in Sanskrit. An explanation of the English translation is given as follows:

OM I prostrate to Vajravarahi, the Blessed Mother HUM
    HUM PHAT

In each line of this praise, OM symbolizes the body, speech and mind of Vajrayogini to whom we are offering praise. All Buddhas have totally destroyed their ignorance through the perfection of wisdom, and Vajravarahi, or Vajrayogini, is the embodiment of the perfection of wisdom of all Buddhas. The name 'Vajrayogini' emphasizes her nature as the union of great bliss and emptiness, and the name 'Vajravarahi' emphasizes her function of destroying ignorance. The Tibetan translation of the Sanskrit name Vajravarahi is Dorje Pagmo. Here, 'pag' means pig. The pig is a symbol of ignorance, which is why it is depicted at the very centre of the Wheel of Life. By calling Vajrayogini 'Vajravarahi' we are praising her as the essence of the perfection of wisdom that destroys ignorance. She is the

'Blessed Mother' because she has destroyed the four maras and possesses all the good qualities of a Buddha. At the end of each line we recite HUM HUM PHAT. With the first HUM we make the request, 'Please grant me the mundane attainments such as increased wealth, life span and merit.' With the second HUM we make the request, 'Please grant me the supramundane attainments such as the realization of spontaneous great bliss, the union that needs learning, and the Union of No More Learning.' With PHAT we request the destruction of the outer, inner and secret obstacles that prevent us from gaining these attainments.

OM To the Superior and powerful Knowledge Lady
unconquered by the three realms HUM HUM PHAT

Here, 'Superior' refers to Vajrayogini's mind, which sees directly the ultimate nature of all phenomena; and 'powerful Knowledge Lady' means that she has the power to bestow great bliss upon Heruka and upon practitioners. 'Unconquered by the three realms' means that because Vajrayogini has abandoned all delusions of the desire, form and formless realms, the maras of the delusions of the three realms are unable to harm her.

OM To you who destroy all fears of evil spirits with your
great vajra HUM HUM PHAT

Here, 'great vajra' means spontaneous great bliss. Her wisdom of spontaneously born great bliss inseparable from emptiness destroys all harm from evil spirits.

OM To you with controlling eyes who remain as the
vajra seat unconquered by others HUM HUM PHAT

Vajrayogini is the vajra seat of Heruka, who is always in union with her. While remaining unconquered by others she can control them just by looking at them.

153

OM To you whose wrathful fierce form desiccates
Brahma HUM HUM PHAT

Vajrayogini appears in the form of a wrathful, fierce Deity to
subdue the pride of worldly gods such as Brahma and Indra.

OM To you who terrify and dry up demons, conquering
those in other directions HUM HUM PHAT

Vajrayogini dries up the inner demons of ordinary appearances and ordinary conceptions through the blazing of her
inner fire, and through this she conquers all external demons
of the ten directions. If someone has no ordinary appearances
and no ordinary conceptions they cannot be harmed by external demons; therefore they are said to have conquered them.

OM To you who conquer all those who make us dull,
rigid and confused HUM HUM PHAT

Vajrayogini enables us to overcome all harms inflicted by evil
spirits who can interfere with our practice by causing us to
become physically dull or heavy, verbally rigid – for example,
unable to pronounce mantras clearly – or mentally confused
about our practice.

OM I bow to Vajravarahi, the Great Mother, the Dakini
consort who fulfils all desires HUM HUM PHAT

Because Vajrayogini is a manifestation of the perfection of
wisdom, known as the 'Great Mother of all the Buddhas', she
destroys the ignorance of all living beings and has the power
to fulfil their wishes.

The Actual Generation
Stage Meditation

Although it is part of the sixth yoga, the yoga of self-generation, the actual generation stage meditation is explained here because it is at this point in the sadhana that we train in improving our concentration on divine pride and clear appearance.

The actual generation stage meditation is presented in three parts:

1 What is generation stage?
2 Training in gross generation stage meditation
3 Training in subtle generation stage meditation

WHAT IS GENERATION STAGE?

Generation stage is a realization of a creative yoga that is attained as a result of pure concentration on bringing the three bodies into the path, in which we mentally generate ourself as a Tantric Deity and our surroundings as the Deity's mandala. Meditation on generation stage is called a 'creative yoga' because its object is created, or generated, by correct imagination.

The preceding eight yogas are necessary preparations for successful practice of actual generation stage meditation. The eleven yogas are like the limbs of a body and the actual generation stage meditation is like the body itself. This special method of combining actual generation stage meditation with recitation of the sadhana was taught and emphasized by Je Tsongkhapa.

Nagarjuna advised that we should progress step by step from generation stage to completion stage in the same way that we climb a staircase. The main purpose of doing generation stage meditation is to prepare the ground for the later development of completion stage realizations. Without first engaging in generation stage meditation we cannot succeed in completion stage meditation.

TRAINING IN GROSS GENERATION STAGE MEDITATION

This has two parts:

1 Training in divine pride
2 Training in clear appearance

TRAINING IN DIVINE PRIDE

Divine pride is a special way of regarding ourself in which we imagine that we are a Tantric Deity and that our environment is his or her Pure Land. Although it is called 'pride', divine pride is not a delusion. It is utterly different from deluded pride. Deluded pride causes only rebirth in samsara whereas generating the divine pride of being Vajrayogini leads only to liberation from samsara. We begin actual generation stage meditation by cultivating divine pride and then, based on this, develop clear appearance. The principal objects to be abandoned during generation stage meditation are ordinary conceptions and ordinary appearances. Divine pride overcomes ordinary conceptions, and clear appearance overcomes ordinary appearances.

The terms 'ordinary conception' and 'ordinary appearance' are best explained by the following example. Suppose there is a Vajrayogini practitioner called John. Normally he sees himself as John, and his environment, enjoyments, body and mind as John's. These appearances are ordinary appearances. The mind that assents to these ordinary appearances by holding them to be true is ordinary conception. Ordinary conceptions are obstructions to liberation, and ordinary appearances are obstructions to omniscience. All sentient beings, except Bodhisattvas of the tenth ground who have attained the vajra-like concentration of the path of meditation, have ordinary appearances.

Now, if John were to meditate on the generation stage of Vajrayogini, strongly regarding himself as Vajrayogini and believing his surroundings, experiences, body and mind to be those of Vajrayogini, at that time he would have divine pride, which prevents ordinary conceptions. If he were also to attain clear appearance of himself as Vajrayogini, with the environment, enjoyments, body and mind of Vajrayogini, he would then have clear appearance, which prevents him from perceiving ordinary appearances.

At the beginning ordinary conceptions are more harmful than ordinary appearances. How this is so is illustrated by the following analogy. Suppose a magician conjures up an illusion of a tiger in front of an audience. The tiger appears to both the audience and the magician, but whereas the audience believe there actually to be a tiger in front of them and consequently become afraid, the magician does not believe that the tiger actually exists and so remains calm. The problem for the audience is not so much that a tiger appears to them, as their conception that the tiger actually exists. It is this conception rather than the mere appearance of the tiger that causes them to experience fear. If like the magician they had no conception that the tiger existed, then even though they still had an appearance of a tiger they would not be afraid. In the same way, even though things appear to us as ordinary, if we do not conceptually grasp them as ordinary this will not be so harmful. Similarly, it is less damaging to our spiritual development to see our Spiritual Guide as ordinary and yet hold him or her to be in essence a Buddha than it is to see our Spiritual Guide as ordinary and to believe that he or she is ordinary. The conviction that our Spiritual Guide is a Buddha, even though he or she may appear to us as an ordinary person, helps our spiritual practices to progress rapidly.

As already explained, we reduce ordinary conceptions by developing divine pride. For this reason we need to emphasize the development of divine pride at the outset of our training in generation stage. If we continue to perceive our ordinary body and mind this will obstruct our development of divine pride. Therefore, when we meditate on divine pride we must ensure that we lose all awareness of our ordinary body and mind by imagining that we have accomplished Vajrayogini's pure body and mind instead. To subdue our ordinary conceptions and improve our divine pride we can contemplate the following three reasons:

(1) I am no longer an ordinary being because my ordinary body, mind and environment have been purified through the practice of bringing the three bodies into the path. During this practice I actually died and took rebirth as Vajrayogini in her Pure Land.

(2) Later, when I absorbed the wisdom beings, I dissolved all Buddhas in the form of Vajrayogini into myself. Therefore I am one with Vajrayogini, and my nature is the same as that of all Buddhas.

(3) The ordinary deluded pride that I have had until now results only in suffering and continued rebirth in samsara, but divine pride will lead me to liberation and Vajrayogini's Pure Land. Therefore I will never give up this pure pride of being Vajrayogini.

Contemplating these three reasons, or any other helpful reasons, is analytical meditation. When, as a result of this reasoning, divine pride arises in our mind, we try to hold it with single-pointed concentration in placement meditation. We then need continually to strengthen our divine pride through repeated meditation.

It is very important not to mistake the basis upon which we generate divine pride. For example, if a practitioner called John tries to develop divine pride of being Vajrayogini on the basis of his ordinary body and mind, he is completely mistaken. John's body and mind are contaminated aggregates and may be a valid basis for imputing John, but they cannot be a basis for imputing Vajrayogini. The appearances of John's body and mind are ordinary appearances, and assenting to these appearances as true is ordinary conception, which is contrary to divine pride.

When we generate the divine pride of being Vajrayogini in her Pure Land we must first prevent our normal conception and appearance of ourself, as well as of our environment, body and mind. We need to dispel these from our mind completely. Having eliminated ordinary appearances we should then use our imagination to try to perceive Vajrayogini's environment and body, and look upon these as our own environment and body. These are the bases upon which we generate divine pride by firmly deciding 'I am Vajrayogini surrounded by my pure environment and pure enjoyments.'

TRAINING IN CLEAR APPEARANCE

There are two ways to train in clear appearance:

1 Training in clear appearance on the general aspect
2 Training in clear appearance on specific aspects

TRAINING IN CLEAR APPEARANCE ON
THE GENERAL ASPECT

If we have already gained some skill in meditation we can immediately begin training in clear appearance on the general aspect, that is on ourself and the complete mandala of Vajrayogini viewed as a whole; but if we find this too difficult we can begin by training in clear appearance on specific aspects until we gain more familiarity, and then proceed to train in clear appearance on the general aspect.

To meditate on clear appearance on the general aspect we begin by doing analytical meditation to attain a generic image of the entire mandala. We check from the fire circle, vajra fence, charnel grounds and phenomena source up to the lotus, sun, and ourself, Vajrayogini, and then back again. We continue in this way until we have a rough image of ourself, Vajrayogini, together with the entire mandala and all the beings within it.

We then try to hold this image with single-pointed concentration in placement meditation. Gradually, through repeated meditation, we improve our clear appearance of ourself as Vajrayogini in her mandala.

When we have a rough image of ourself as Vajrayogini in her mandala we have found the object of actual generation stage meditation; and we have also reached the first of the nine mental abidings, placing the mind. Through daily practice, and sometimes in short or longer retreat, we should improve this concentration until we reach the fourth mental abiding, close placement. If at this point we enter a strict retreat it is possible for us to accomplish tranquil abiding on generation stage within six months. Then it will not be long before we attain outer Dakini Land. More detailed explanations on the method for attaining tranquil abiding are given in *Joyful Path of Good Fortune* and *Meaningful to Behold*.

TRAINING IN CLEAR APPEARANCE ON SPECIFIC ASPECTS

The specific aspects are specific objects within the mandala. For example, we can focus first on the central eye of Vajrayogini until we perceive it clearly. Without forgetting this we then focus on the other two eyes and then on the face, neck, torso, arms, legs and so forth, until we have a mental image of the entire body. Gradually we can include the phenomena source, eight charnel grounds and protection circle. Contemplating each aspect in this way will help us finally to gain clear appearance of the entire supporting and supported mandala. Once we have accomplished this we train in concentration as before. In this way, through training in analytical and placement meditation, we should improve our clear appearance until we complete the realizations of both gross and subtle generation stages.

TRAINING IN SUBTLE GENERATION STAGE MEDITATION

The protection circle, charnel grounds, phenomena source and self-generation all have gross and subtle features. The vajra ground, fence, tent, canopy, surrounding fires, charnel grounds, phenomena source, lotus, sun, Kalarati, Bhairawa, and our body in the aspect of Vajrayogini are the gross features. They are the objects of gross generation stage meditation. Their constituent parts, such as the tiny vajras within the vajra fence, are the subtle features. A meditation using these subtle features as the object is called 'subtle generation stage meditation'.

Through constant training in meditation to improve clear appearance of the gross objects, eventually we will perceive directly with our mental consciousness the entire mandala, from the fire circle to the self-generation, as clearly as we now see things with our eyes. When we gain this experience in meditation we have attained the complete realization of gross generation stage meditation, and should then switch to training in subtle generation stage meditation.

The supreme object of subtle generation stage meditation is Vajrayogini's body mandala. We should meditate repeatedly on this inner mandala until we can see the thirty-seven Dakinis of the body mandala directly with our mental consciousness as clearly as we now see things with our eyes. When we gain this realization we have completed subtle generation stage. If at the same time our winds gather and dissolve within the central channel at the heart channel wheel we will have attained completion stage realizations. From this we can see that skilful meditation on the body mandala of Vajrayogini is a real wish-fulfilling jewel that satisfies the wishes of pure practitioners.

If we find it difficult to believe that an ordinary being can directly perceive himself or herself as a Deity and his or her environment as a Buddha's Pure Land we should consider the following. Even though our present body and mind are not our I, nevertheless due to strong familiarity with self-grasping we directly and vividly see our I as one with this body and mind. Because of this, whenever our body is unwell we say, 'I am unwell', and whenever our mind is unhappy we say, 'I am unhappy.' If through familiarity with self-grasping ignorance we can come to identify ourself with a contaminated body and

mind, then certainly through familiarity with correct imagination, or correct belief, and pure concentration we can come to
identify ourself with the pure body and mind of Vajrayogini.
Then through familiarizing ourself with generation stage
meditation, eventually we will definitely directly perceive
ourself as Vajrayogini. This has been the experience of many
Tantric meditators.

There is an account of a Yamantaka practitioner who
through his clear appearance of being Yamantaka saw himself
as the real Deity in every detail, including the horns on his
head. He felt as if he could even touch the horns, and whenever he wanted to go through a door he would bend down to
allow room for his horns to pass through! Although he was
not actually Yamantaka, his clear appearance of himself as the
Deity Yamantaka was not a mistaken appearance. If something
is a mistaken appearance it necessarily arises from ignorance,
but if a Tantric practitioner sees himself or herself as a real
Yamantaka or Vajrayogini, this clear appearance arises from
his or her pure concentration and not from ignorance. Such
experiences are evident only to the practitioner himself; other
people will continue to see him as an ordinary person.

People with no experience of Tantric meditation may find
it difficult to believe that it is possible to change our identity
from an ordinary person into a Deity, but by developing a correct understanding of how persons lack true existence and are
mere imputations we will realize that it is definitely possible.
This will help us to experience deep realizations of Tantra and
enable us to gain an understanding of the two truths according to Highest Yoga Tantra – meaning clear light and illusory
body – which is essential for the practice of completion stage.
More information on generation stage can be found in *Tantric
Grounds and Paths*.

The Yoga of Verbal and
Mental Recitation

This has four parts:

1 The mantra to be recited
2 The benefits of reciting this mantra
3 Actual mantra recitation
4 Explanation of close retreat

THE MANTRA TO BE RECITED

Vajrayogini, or Vajravarahi, has many different aspects such as Sangye Khandroma or Buddha Dakini, Dorje Rabngama or Vajra Speech Dakini, and Dorje Nampar Ngangtsema or Vajra Form Dakini. For this reason Buddha Vajradhara taught many different mantras of Vajrayogini, such as the root mantra, the essence mantra, and the close essence mantra. According to the Narokhachö lineage we recite the mantra of Vajrayogini called the 'three-OM mantra'. This mantra is the synthesis of all the mantras of Vajrayogini and Vajravarahi. When we recite this mantra we are directly reciting the mantras of all the thirty-two Dakinis of the body mandala, and we are indirectly reciting the mantras of all Dakas and Dakinis, and therefore of all Buddhas. The three-OM mantra is:

OM OM OM SARWA BUDDHA DAKINIYE VAJRA
WARNANIYE VAJRA BEROTZANIYE HUM HUM HUM
PHAT PHAT PHAT SÖHA

This mantra originally comes from the forty-eighth and fiftieth chapters of the *Root Tantra of Heruka*. The three OMs that begin

Palden Lama Tenpa Sonam Gyaltsen

the mantra and that give it its name signify that Vajrayogini is the embodiment of the three bodies of all Buddhas. The first OM symbolizes the Truth Body of all Buddhas, the second OM the Enjoyment Body of all Buddhas, and the third OM the Emanation Body of all Buddhas.

SARWA BUDDHA DAKINIYE literally means 'All the Buddhas' Dakinis'. In this context, 'Dakini' is the inner Dakini, the clear light mind of a Buddha, and so SARWA BUDDHA DAKINIYE indicates that Vajrayogini is the nature of the clear light mind of all Buddhas.

VAJRA WARNANIYE means 'Vajra Speech Dakini', and indicates that Vajrayogini is the nature of the vajra speech of all Buddhas.

VAJRA BEROTZANIYE means 'Vajra Form Dakini', and indicates that Vajrayogini is the nature of the vajra body of all Buddhas. Here, 'vajra' refers to great bliss inseparable from emptiness.

HUM HUM HUM is a request to Vajrayogini: 'Please grant me the blessings of your body, speech and mind so that I may attain the vajra body, speech and mind of a Buddha.'

PHAT PHAT PHAT is the request: 'Please pacify my outer, inner and secret obstacles.'

SÖHA is the request: 'Please help me to build the foundation of all attainments.'

Some commentaries interpret the letters OM OM OM, HUM HUM HUM and PHAT PHAT PHAT slightly differently, but there are no contradictions between these different interpretations.

By reciting the mantra we are calling Vajrayogini and her thirty-two retinue Dakinis and entreating them. It is important not to regard the letters of the three-OM mantra as ordinary. We should regard them as having the same nature as the thirty-two retinue Dakinis. In the *Root Tantra of Heruka* Vajradhara says:

If you wish to accomplish the supreme attainment
Do not view the mantra as being different from the
    Deities.

The three-OM mantra explicitly contains thirty-two letters, which are like the retinue of the principal letter, the BAM. The letter BAM consists of five letters – YA, RA, LA, WA and short-AH – and so altogether there are thirty-seven letters. These are of one nature with the thirty-seven Dakinis. The short-AH is Vajrayogini, and the letters YA, RA, LA and WA are Lama, Khandarohi, Rupini and Dakini respectively. The letters OM OM OM SAR WA BU DHA DA KI NI YE VAJ RA WAR NA NI YE VAJ RA BE RO TZA NI YE HUM HUM HUM PHAT PHAT PHAT SÖ HA are the retinue of Dakinis: Partzandi, Tzändriakiya, Parbhawatiya, Mahanasa, Biramatiya, Karwariya, Lamkeshöriya, Drumatzaya, Airawatiya, Mahabhairawi, Bayubega, Surabhakiya, Shamadewi, Suwatre, Hayakarne, Khaganane, Tzatrabega, Khandarohi, Shaundini, Tzatrawarmini, Subira, Mahabala, Tzatrawartini, Mahabire, Kakase, Ulukase, Shonase, Shukarase, Yamadhathi, Yamaduti, Yamadangtrini and Yamamatani.

THE BENEFITS OF RECITING THIS MANTRA

By reciting the three-OM mantra we come closer to Vajrayogini, both in the sense of making a connection with a special friend and in the sense of actually becoming the Deity Vajrayogini. When we do a close retreat we emphasize mantra recitation and meditation to bring us closer to the Deity in both these senses, which is why it is called 'close' retreat.

Reciting the three-OM mantra purifies our non-virtuous actions and their imprints, and pacifies the obstacles that prevent success in our practice. It also increases the power of our speech. The speech of most ordinary beings is mundane and possesses little power, but ordinary speech can be transformed through reciting this mantra. With mantra recitation we can pacify all inner obstacles such as sickness and strong delusions, as well as outer obstacles such as being harmed by evil spirits; and we can increase our life span, merit, wealth and, most important, our spiritual realizations. We gain control over the evil actions of others and the ability to lead them into correct paths. We also gain the ability to tame the minds of others and help them by using wrathful actions where necessary. Reciting the three-OM mantra continuously with faith causes us to experience increasing happiness and fulfil our wishes. It causes realizations of completion stage practice of vajra recitation to ripen, and finally it enables us to attain the vajra speech of a Buddha.

The *Root Tantra of Heruka* praises Vajrayogini's mantra as the 'king of all mantras' and states that there is no mantra in all the three realms of existence that is more powerful. This Tantra also explains that Vajrayogini's mantra is in essence the mantra of all Dakinis and that just by remembering or reciting it with faith we remember or recite the mantras of all Dakinis.

Je Phabongkhapa said that only with Vajrayogini's mantra is it possible to receive actual attainments merely by recitation. In the *Root Tantra of Heruka* Vajradhara says:

> Merely by reciting the mantra you can accomplish
>   attainments
> And complete all actions perfectly.

> This, the king of all mantras,
> Causes the completion of every action.
> There is no mantra more supreme than this
> In all the three realms.

> This is the essence of all Dakinis.
> By merely remembering this mantra
> You will accomplish all the attainments.

Here, 'attainments' refers to the temporary happiness of humans and gods, and the ultimate happiness of liberation and enlightenment. It also refers to those attainments that are common to Sutra and Tantra such as renunciation, bodhichitta and correct view, and to the uncommon attainments of Secret Mantra such as the realizations of generation stage and completion stage. Besides accomplishing these attainments, by reciting this mantra we will be cared for by all the Dakas and Dakinis of the twenty-four places, as well as their emanations.

By reciting the three-OM mantra we are reciting the essence mantra of all Dakinis. For example, when we recite this mantra we are also indirectly reciting the mantras of Tara, Sarasvati, Marichi and all other Dakinis. Reciting this mantra also leads to the attainment of outer and inner Dakini Land.

By reciting this mantra we can help others to fulfil their wishes and gain peace, good health, long life and prosperity. We gain the ability to avert others' diseases, such as cancer, strokes and paralysis, as well as all physical pain and dangers from fire, water, earth and wind.

Some practitioners who have a strong karmic link with Vajrayogini, through their daily practice or by merely reciting this mantra attain outer Dakini Land before their death, some-times even without engaging in close retreats or intense medi-tation. Some attain Dakini Land in the bardo, or intermediate state, by remembering as if in a dream their daily recitation of the mantra, thereby enabling Vajrayogini to lead them to her Pure Land. In Dakini Land these practitioners are cared for by Heruka and Vajrayogini and, without ever having to undergo uncontrolled death again, they attain enlightenment during that life. It is for these reasons that the three-OM mantra of Vajrayogini is called the 'king of all mantras'.

ACTUAL MANTRA RECITATION

This has two parts:

1 Verbal recitation
2 Mental recitation with two completion stage meditations

VERBAL RECITATION

At the time of receiving a Vajrayogini empowerment we make a promise to recite a certain number of three-OM mantras as a daily commitment. It is important to keep a suitable rosary, or mala, on which to count mantra recitations. The mala has great meaning and is one of our commitment ritual objects.

Once we have found a suitable mala we should try to bless it every day by performing the following short blessing. We regard our right hand as being the nature of great bliss and our left hand as being the nature of the wisdom of emptiness. We place the mala in the palm of our right hand and cup our left hand over it. Joining our two hands in this way symbolizes the union of great bliss and emptiness. We then recall that the mala is by nature emptiness and recite the three-OM mantra three or seven times. We then blow on the mala while rubbing it between our hands, and with strong concentration imagine that it transforms into Vajrayogini's wisdom, the union of great bliss and emptiness.

Once we have blessed the mala in this way we should always regard it as a holy object. If we bless our mala and continuously use it while reciting the mantra it will gradually become a very powerful object with which we can bestow blessings and avert others' obstacles. Many Tibetans have experienced the spiritual power of the malas of pure practitioners. When they or their children are afflicted by evil spirits they go to pure practitioners, who cure the sick person with the healing action of touching their crown with a blessed mala and praying for their welfare. Through the power of such actions many people have received real benefit.

During mantra recitation there is a special way of using the mala to gather all the Dakinis into our body and to receive their blessings. We begin by suspending the mala over the ring finger of our left hand. We can hold the mala either at the level of our heart or at the level of our navel. We recite the mantra once and then move the first bead towards us with our thumb. We imagine that from the emptiness of each bead arises a Deity in the aspect of Vajrayogini who dissolves into our heart or navel. After reciting a few mantras in this way we can continue by suspending the mala over our middle or index finger, if this is more comfortable, and move the mala beads with our thumb as before. However it is an auspicious sign for our practice to use the ring finger and thumb at least a few times at the beginning of the session of mantra recitation because it symbolizes controlling delusions.

Tantric practitioners have a commitment to benefit sentient beings and to make offerings to the Buddhas. To fulfil these two commitments we can recite the three-OM mantra with the visualization described in the sadhana:

At my heart inside a red phenomena source, a double tetrahedron, in the centre of a moon mandala, is a letter BAM encircled by a red-coloured mantra rosary standing counter-clockwise. From these, immeasurable rays of red light radiate. They purify the negativities and obstructions of all sentient beings and make offerings to all the Buddhas. All the power and force of their blessings is invoked in the form of rays of red light, which dissolve into the letter BAM and mantra rosary, blessing my mental continuum.

This is the recitation of commitment.

To improve our body mandala meditation we can recite the mantra with the following visualization. At the heart of the principal Deity of the body mandala there is a phenomena source. Inside this, on a moon cushion, is a red letter BAM surrounded by the red three-OM mantra. We recite the three-OM mantra with an alert mind and, while observing the letters of the mantra, identify each of the thirty-seven Deities of the body mandala. For example, as we recite the first OM we simultaneously try to identify Partzandi, as we recite the second OM we identify Tzändriakiya, and so forth, until we reach the last syllable HA when we identify Yamamatani.

MENTAL RECITATION WITH TWO COMPLETION STAGE MEDITATIONS

This is presented in three parts:

1 First completion stage meditation
2 Mental recitation
3 Second completion stage meditation

We can practise mental recitation with either generation stage or completion stage meditations. Through this practice we receive benefits both from mantra recitation and from completion stage meditation.

FIRST COMPLETION STAGE MEDITATION

To do this meditation we visualize that at our heart there is a phenomena source about the size of the tip of a little finger. Inside this is a moon cushion, mantra rosary and letter BAM. The phenomena source descends through the central channel to the centre of our navel channel wheel, where we concentrate on it for a few moments. We then gently inhale and imagine that all the winds of the upper part of our body gather and flow down through the central channel, reaching the point just above the phenomena source at our navel. We then slightly tighten the muscles of the lower part of our body and draw up all the lower winds. These rise up through the central channel and reach the point just below the phenomena source at our navel. Both the upper and lower winds of our body are now held together at our navel. This is called the 'vase breath' because the shape of the united upper and lower winds is like the shape of a bulbous vase.

We feel that our mind is inside the phenomena source at the centre of our navel channel wheel. We then focus on the four side corners of the phenomena source where tiny joy swirls spin counter-clockwise. We hold the vase breath and concentrate single-pointedly on the four joy swirls for as long as possible. Just before we begin to feel discomfort we exhale slowly and gently through the nostrils.

Initially we are unable to hold our breath for very long and so we can repeat this process many times in one session. After we have gained some experience in this meditation we can practise actual mental recitation.

MENTAL RECITATION

We begin mental recitation by repeating the previous meditation up to the vase breath. Our mind then dissolves into the letter BAM and becomes one with it. Then, while we hold the vase breath inside the central channel at our navel, our mind, the letter BAM, reads the letters of the three-OM mantra counter-clockwise. We mentally recite the mantra three or seven times and then exhale gently. Then again we draw in the winds to our navel, hold them there while mentally reciting the mantra, and then exhale again. We can repeat this cycle many times in one session.

SECOND COMPLETION STAGE MEDITATION

Regular practice of the following meditation will develop and increase our experience of great bliss, improve our understanding of emptiness, and cause us to realize the clear light of bliss.

We visualize the central channel located exactly midway between the left and right halves of the body, but closer to the back than the front. Inside it is red in colour, smooth and clear. It is in the nature of light and about the thickness of an arrow. From the lower tip, which is at the sex organ, it goes straight up to the crown. Then it arches downwards and ends at the point between the eyebrows. Just inside the lower tip of the central channel is a tiny white joy swirl, which spins very quickly counter-clockwise, and inside the upper tip of the central channel, between the eyebrows, is a tiny red joy swirl also spinning very quickly counter-clockwise.

We focus first on the white joy swirl inside the lower tip of our central channel. We concentrate on it spinning rapidly and imagine that it induces a strong feeling of great bliss. As it spins, the joy swirl slowly rises within the central channel, causing our experience of great bliss to intensify. When the joy swirl reaches the centre of our heart channel wheel we concentrate on it while experiencing bliss. We then focus on the red joy swirl inside the upper tip of our central channel. Spinning continuously, it rises from between our eyebrows to the centre of the crown channel wheel and then slowly descends through the central channel. When it reaches the point just above the white joy swirl at our heart we focus on both joy swirls spinning very rapidly and continuously, one above the other, and we recollect that everything is in the nature of emptiness. As the joy swirls spin, they gradually come closer to each other until finally they merge and transform into one pink joy swirl. The pink joy swirl continues to spin and gradually becomes smaller and smaller until finally it dissolves into the clear light of emptiness. Our mind of great bliss then meditates on emptiness and we concentrate on this experience single-pointedly for as long as possible.

The 'clear light of emptiness' referred to here is the experience of the clear light of bliss mixed inseparably with emptiness, which is the secret Dakini. The letter BAM visualized at our navel during the empowerment and in the first completion stage meditation is the inner Dakini, and the Dakinis of the twenty-four holy places are the outer Dakinis. These three types of Dakini are mentioned in the extensive dedication prayers in the Vajrayogini sadhana, *Quick Path to Great Bliss*, found in Appendix II:

> The beautiful Mother of the Conquerors is the outer
>   Yogini,
> The letter BAM is the supreme inner Vajra Queen,
> The clarity and emptiness of the mind itself is the secret
>   Dakini Mother;
> May I enjoy the sport of seeing the self-nature of each.

EXPLANATION OF CLOSE RETREAT

This has four parts:

1 What is a retreat?
2 Explanation of close retreats of signs, time and
   numbers
3 Preliminary practices for close retreat
4 The actual close retreat

WHAT IS A RETREAT?

On retreat we stop all forms of business and extraneous activities so as to emphasize a particular spiritual practice. There are three kinds of retreat: physical, verbal and mental. We engage in physical retreat when with a spiritual motivation we isolate ourself from other people, activities and noise, and disengage from extraneous and meaningless actions. We engage in verbal retreat when with a spiritual motivation we refrain from meaningless talk and periodically keep silence. We engage in mental retreat by preventing distractions and strong delusions such as attachment, anger, jealousy and strong self-grasping from arising, and by maintaining mindfulness and conscientiousness.

If we remain in physical and verbal retreat but fail to observe mental retreat, our retreat will have little power. Such a retreat may be relaxing, but if we do not prevent strong delusions from arising, our mind will not be at peace, even on retreat. However, keeping physical and verbal retreat will help us to keep mental retreat, and for this reason Shantideva, in *Guide to the Bodhisattva's Way of Life*, praises the first two kinds of retreat.

EXPLANATION OF CLOSE RETREATS OF SIGNS, TIME AND NUMBERS

A close retreat is a retreat in which we practise special methods that cause us to draw closer to the attainments of a Tantric Deity. We engage in a close retreat of signs when we remain in retreat until a correct sign of attainment manifests. We engage in a close retreat of time when we do a retreat for a definite period of time, such as six months; or alternatively when we do either a long or short close retreat every year at the same time.

There are two kinds of close retreat of numbers: a close retreat of actions and a great close retreat. There are also longer and shorter close retreats of actions. On a long close retreat of actions of Vajrayogini we recite the three-OM mantra four hundred thousand times, and on a short close retreat of actions of Vajrayogini we recite the three-OM mantra one hundred thousand times. To conclude both long and short close retreats of actions we should recite ten thousand wisdom-descending mantras and then perform a fire puja.

There are also two kinds of great close retreat: an extensive great close retreat and a short great close retreat. On an extensive great close retreat of Vajrayogini we recite the three-OM mantra ten million times, and on a short great close retreat of Vajrayogini we recite the mantra three million, two hundred thousand times.

PRELIMINARY PRACTICES FOR CLOSE RETREAT

We can do two kinds of practice as preliminaries to engaging in a successful close retreat: distant preliminaries and close preliminaries. Whether or not we attain mundane or supramundane results from doing a close retreat depends upon the preparations that we make. Good preparations bring good results.

DISTANT PRELIMINARIES

There are nine distant preliminary practices:

1 Going for refuge
2 Vajrasattva mantra recitation
3 Prostrations
4 Mandala offerings
5 Guru yoga
6 Samayavajra mantra recitation
7 Vajradaka burning offering
8 Making images of the body or mind of a Buddha
9 Water offerings

We should perform each of these a hundred thousand times. If we are unable to do all nine preliminaries but wish strongly to gain realizations of generation stage and completion stage, we should try to do at least the first five preliminaries, performing each one purely a hundred thousand times. We can do the practices of going for refuge, Vajrasattva mantra recitation, mandala offerings and Guru yoga in conjunction with Je Phabongkhapa's extensive Vajrayogini sadhana, as already explained.

At first we may feel that these preliminaries are too great a task for us, but I, the author, would like to give encouragement by relating my own experience. I have completed four Vajrayogini close retreats. I did my first in a group very soon after receiving the empowerment of Vajrayogini. At that time I had not completed the first five preliminary practices. Later, after completing the first five preliminaries, I did my second and third close retreats. Later still I completed the remaining four preliminaries and I did my fourth close retreat. Since then I have accomplished meditational retreats on Vajrayogini and other Yidams many times. We should not think that by completing just one or two close retreats we will become a Buddha!

It is very important to gain a clear understanding of how to perform each of the nine preliminary practices. The practices of going for refuge, Vajrasattva mantra recitation, mandala offerings and Guru yoga were explained earlier. The way to collect a hundred thousand Guru yogas is to recite the main practice of Guru yoga in the sadhana once at the beginning of each session and then to count the number of recitations of the brief request, the name mantra of our Guru, or the mantra of Guru Sumati Buddha Heruka: OM GURU SUMATI BUDDHA HERUKA SARWA SIDDHI HUM HUM. The way to collect prostrations in conjunction with *The Bodhisattva's Confession of Moral Downfalls* is explained in the book *The Bodhisattva Vow*.

We should do the mantra recitation of Samayavajra and the burning offering of Vajradaka in conjunction with their respective sadhanas, which can be found in Appendix II. Samayavajra mantra recitation mainly purifies degenerated commitments and vows, and the burning offering of Vajradaka purifies our negative karma in general. These two practices and Vajrasattva mantra recitation are principally purification practices. Making prostrations is both a purification practice and a method for accumulating merit.

To perform the burning offering of Vajradaka we need black sesame seeds and a small container for the fire. The container represents the mandala of Vajradaka and serves as the visual object of the practice. The fire that is made inside the container should be smokeless and should last for at least as long as the session. We set up the fire container in front of our meditation seat. We put as many sesame seeds as are to be burned in that session on a plate and arrange the seeds in the shape of a scorpion. When everything has been prepared we sit on the meditation seat and begin the session.

We imagine that all the negative karma created by ourself and other living beings gathers together into a mass of black light, which dissolves into the scorpion-shaped arrangement of sesame seeds. While reciting the offering mantra we take a few sesame seeds with the thumb and ring finger of the right hand and throw them into the fire. We continue in this way until all the sesame seeds on the plate have been burned. While doing this we count the number of mantra recitations and offerings on a mala with our left hand. We should patiently follow this procedure, collecting the mantra recitations and offerings each day in several sessions until we have completed a hundred thousand recitations and offerings.

Je Tsongkhapa compiled instructions specifically for this practice. It is a very powerful method for purifying our own negative actions and it can also be used to purify the negative actions of others, whether they are alive or dead. For example, if our mother has died we can purify her negative actions by performing this burning offering on her behalf. To do this we follow the sadhana as usual, except that we focus mainly on our mother, visualizing her in front of us as if she were alive. We imagine that all the negative karma she has accumulated since beginningless time gathers together in a mass of black smoke, which dissolves into the sesame seeds. While reciting the offering mantra we offer the seeds to the mouth of Vajradaka at the centre of the mandala. We then request that our mother's mental continuum be purified of all faults. We repeat this offering and request many times.

To make a hundred thousand images of a Buddha, or a hundred thousand stupas, we need an authentic mould from which to cast them. We should try to do the casting ourself rather than paying others to do it. As each statue or stupa is produced we imagine that a new living Buddha manifests from the Dharmakaya. While making these images we recite the mantra of the essence of dependent relationship: OM YE DHARMA HETU TRABHAWA HETUN TEKÄN TATHAGATO HÄWADÄ TEKÄNTSAYO NIRODHA EHWAMBHADHI MAHA SHRAMANIYE SÖHA. With one mould we can produce many statues or stupas at the same time, so it will not take very long to make a hundred thousand. The statues or stupas can be either large or small. Even making one statue or stupa with faith creates the cause for us to become a living Buddha in the future.

To make a hundred thousand water offerings, ideally we should obtain a hundred offering bowls and fill these with pure water every day. If we wish to do retreat we can do five sessions each day, offering a hundred water bowls in each session. Gradually we will collect the hundred thousand water offerings. The benefits of offering water and the way to make water offerings are explained in *Joyful Path of Good Fortune*.

At first we may think that we should just do the retreat and not bother with the preliminary practices because they are too difficult. Although it is true that the nine preliminaries take a long time, it is nevertheless important to try to do them. The preliminary practices are like preparing a meal and the actual retreat is like eating the meal. Preparing a meal is more difficult than eating it, but a meal that is prepared with great care is a joy to eat.

Some practitioners may think that once they have finished one retreat there is no need to do the nine or the five preliminaries, but this attitude is incorrect. We cannot say that we have finished meditation retreats until we attain Buddhahood. After completing one close retreat and concluding with a fire puja, in subsequent close retreats we can emphasize meditation and try to gain experience of generation stage and completion stage.

CLOSE PRELIMINARIES

We perform the close preliminary practices just before starting a close retreat. We need to find a quiet and peaceful place with a good, well-built retreat room in a safe and healthy environment. We should make certain that all necessary facilities such as food, water and heating are readily available. We also need a suitable assistant to help us during our retreat. We should have the freedom to practise within our own spiritual tradition.

In addition to these external conditions we need certain inner conditions. In particular we must have studied the instructions and commentaries thoroughly so that we understand how to practise the preliminaries, the eleven yogas of generation stage, and the completion stage meditations.

We should then prepare the retreat room. First we clean the room and set up a shrine with statues or pictures of Buddha Shakyamuni, Je Tsongkhapa, Vajrayogini and our root Guru. If we have other images of Buddhas and Bodhisattvas we can also place them on the shrine. We set up our meditation seat facing the shrine. The seat should, if possible, face west. It should be stable and comfortable, with a slightly raised back. Since the cushion should not be moved throughout the retreat it is important, especially on a long retreat, that it is ventilated underneath. We can do this by raising it on a wooden platform with holes in. We should carry out these preparations a few days before our retreat is due to begin.

On the morning of the day our retreat begins we set up the tormas and other offerings in front of the shrine, placing the tormas on a slightly higher level than the other offerings. In front of these we set out four rows of offering bowls. The first row, nearest the shrine, is for the supramundane Deities, the second row is for the mundane Dakas and Dakinis, and the third row is for the Dharma Protectors. These three rows of outer offerings are set out starting from the statue's left (our right). The fourth row of outer offerings is to the self-generation and is set out starting from our left. Each row of offering bowls is set out in the following order: AHRGHAM, PADÄM, PUPE, DHUPE, DIWE, GÄNDHE and NEWIDE. There is no need to set out a SHAPTA offering because music is not a visual object.

On a small table in front of us we place our ritual objects: our bell and vajra, damaru, inner offering container, ritual vase and mala. The vase should be two-thirds filled with fresh water mixed with saffron, and its spout should point towards us. Until our retreat is finished we should not move or change our meditation seat, nor should we remove the commitment ritual objects from the retreat room.

Outside the retreat house we should mentally make a boundary around the retreat area by choosing various landmarks such as trees, roads or mountains. These can be as near or as far away as we wish. When we have marked the boundary we make a strong determination not to go beyond it until we finish our retreat.

At the beginning of our retreat we make a strong determination not to meet with people for the duration of the retreat. However, we can make exceptions for special people such as our Spiritual Guide, our assistant, our close Dharma friends or our doctor. We should also decide to refrain from all worldly activities, mental busyness and meaningless conversations. In short, we should make a determination to engage in a retreat of body, speech and mind.

We should also prepare two tormas for the preliminary rituals – one, consisting of three small tormas with candles in front of them, which is for dispelling obstacles, and the other for the local guardians. The first torma is taken outside during the preliminary rituals. The torma for the local guardians can be taken outside after these rituals are concluded.

Having completed all the preparations, in the mid-afternoon of the first day of our retreat we should sit on the meditation cushion and perform the preliminary rituals. We recite the preliminary prayers for entering retreat – going for refuge, generating bodhichitta, instantaneous self-generation, blessing the inner offering, accomplishing the cleansing water of the vase, blessing the outer offerings, offering the torma to the mundane Dakas and Dakinis, giving the torma to the local guardians, and giving and sending out the obstacle-dispelling torma. We then mentally generate Khandarohi at each of the boundary landmarks to avert obstacles to our retreat.

At this point we meditate on the protection circle – the vajra ground, fence, tent and canopy, surrounded by the five-coloured wisdom fires. We strongly imagine that we are inside this protection circle. We then bless the meditation seat and again meditate on the protection circle. We then bless our meditation environment and everything within it, and we bless our three bodily places. Then once again we meditate on the protection circle. We should perform all these preliminary rituals in conjunction with the retreat preliminaries sadhana composed by Je Phabongkhapa, or with *Preliminary Jewel*, the condensed Vajrayogini retreat preliminaries, both of which can be found in Appendix II. We should try to finish these preparations in good time so that we can take a break to relax and have supper before sunset. We should start the first session of the actual retreat at dusk.

THE ACTUAL CLOSE RETREAT

We begin the first session of the retreat by generating an especially pure motivation. We think:

> *Through the kindness of Buddha Shakyamuni, and especially through the kindness of my precious root Guru, I now have the great fortune and opportunity to practise the supreme path of Vajrayogini. I must use this opportunity to benefit all living beings.*

With a feeling of great happiness we then recite the sadhana, concentrating on the meaning of the words without being distracted. After *Prayer to Behold the Beautiful Face of Vajrayogini* we make the tsog offerings and then continue with the remaining prayers of the sadhana, concluding with the long dedication prayers and the auspicious prayers. When we go to bed we should remember to practise the yoga of sleeping.

On the next day we should finish the first session before breakfast, the second session before lunch, the third session before supper and the last session before going to bed. We should maintain this, or a similar timetable, for the duration of

THE NEW GUIDE TO DAKINI LAND

the retreat. During the meditation breaks we should improve our renunciation, compassion, bodhichitta and correct view of emptiness by studying and contemplating Lamrim instructions, and also improve our understanding of the generation and completion stages by reading Tantric commentaries.

In each session, after blessing the inner offering, we take one drop of nectar with the tip of our left ring finger and with it draw a triangle on the palm of our right hand. We imagine that this nectar is made of the white and red bodhichittas of Father Heruka and Mother Vajrayogini that came from the Mother's sex organ. We taste the nectar and imagine that our channels, drops and inner winds are blessed and purified of all faults, and we experience the clear light of bliss.

By going for refuge we increase our renunciation and compassion; through meditation and recitation of Vajrasattva we purify our negative karma; by practising Guru yoga we accumulate a vast collection of merit; by meditating on bringing the three bodies into the spiritual path we purify and gain control over death, the intermediate state and rebirth; and through the actual meditation on generation stage and completion stage we purify ordinary appearance and ordinary conception. Through these practices, and through reciting the three-OM mantra, moment by moment we draw closer and closer to Vajrayogini and all the Dakinis. By offering tormas we quickly receive attainments from Vajrayogini, and by making tsog offerings we fulfil our commitments so that we will be cared for by the Heroes and Heroines. During the retreat we should often think about these benefits.

It is very important to keep the commitments of retreat, namely, not to meet with many people, not to engage in meaningless conversations, to maintain mindfulness and conscientiousness, not to engage in worldly activities, not to read books that are unrelated to our main practice, to make torma offerings each day at the same time, not to argue with others, not to show our commitment ritual objects to those with no faith, to be careful not to damage tormas, and not to allow those without faith to touch our mala. We should also try to abandon the ten faults of verbal recitation – breaking the recitation by talking or by coughing, or reciting the mantra too loudly, without any sound, too quickly, too slowly, with sighs, while hiccupping, with a sleepy mind, or with a distracted mind.

When we do a close retreat of actions we should recite the full number of mantras on the same seat. After completing one hundred thousand or four hundred thousand recitations of the three-OM mantra we recite the wisdom-descending mantra ten thousand times: OM OM OM SARWA BUDDHA DAKINIYE VAJRA WARNANIYE VAJRA BEROTZANIYE HUM HUM HUM PHAT PHAT PHAT HUM HA ADZE SÖHA. While reciting this mantra we visualize countless rays of red light radiating from our heart to the ten directions and inviting all the Buddhas in the form of Vajrayogini. These dissolve into our body like a heavy shower of rain falling into an ocean. With strong conviction we think that we have received the blessings of all the Buddhas and we imagine that our mind and body transform into the nature of omniscient wisdom. After completing ten thousand wisdom-descending mantras we do the last session of our retreat in the morning of the last day. In this session we should recite the whole sadhana, including the tsog offering, exactly as we did in the first session of the retreat.

After we have finished the retreat we can take out the tormas and other offerings and put them in a high place, into the sea or a river, or in any clean and pure place. Until we complete the fire puja we should continue to recite once a day the whole sadhana that we used in the retreat, without missing even one day. When we have done the fire puja we have completed our close retreat of actions. In subsequent close retreats on Vajrayogini it is not necessary to do the fire puja at the end of the retreat, unless we specifically wish to.

More information on the preparations for the fire puja and on the design of the hearth can be found by consulting the sadhana and the diagram in Appendix III. When we come to perform the actual fire puja we will require the help of several assistants, or we should perform it with other practitioners.

Je Phabongkhapa

The Yoga of Inconceivability and the Yoga of Daily Actions

THE YOGA OF INCONCEIVABILITY

'Inconceivability' refers to meaning clear light, the mind of spontaneous great bliss that realizes emptiness directly. When we attain this realization we will attain full enlightenment within six months. Training in meditation on the yoga of inconceivability leads us to the attainment of meaning clear light.

All the appearances of this life – our environment, enjoyments, body and mind – arose from the clear light of death of our previous life. Immediately after that clear light of death ceased we perceived the appearance of black near-attainment of reverse order, which was the first moment of the mind of this life. From this mind, all the gross minds that perceive the things of this life gradually developed and we came to experience various pleasant, unpleasant and neutral feelings. Later, when we die, all our gross minds that perceive the things of this world will dissolve back into the clear light of death and at the same time everything that appears to us now will vanish.

Similarly, when we meditate on bringing death into the path of the Truth Body we imagine that all ordinary appearances dissolve into the clear light of death, and that from this mind the gross minds that perceive the pure environment, enjoyments, body and mind of Vajrayogini gradually develop. Then, in the yoga of inconceivability, these minds dissolve back into the clear light of emptiness. Everything we perceive during generation stage meditation disappears and we once again experience only the clear light of emptiness. This process of manifestation and dissolution of the mind and its objects shows very clearly that nothing in samsara or nirvana exists from its own side, from the side of the object. Everything is a mere appearance to the mind, not other than emptiness. When two spaces mix they become one, and likewise when we realize that everything is a mere appearance not other than emptiness we realize non-dual appearance and emptiness, or the union of the two truths. In this context, union means that these two things are one.

The actual practice of this yoga is done by following the sadhana. We visualize as follows:

From the letter BAM and the mantra rosary at my heart, light rays radiate and pervade all three realms. The formless realm dissolves into the upper part of my body in the aspect of rays of blue light. The form realm dissolves into the middle part of my body in the aspect of rays of red light. The desire realm dissolves into the lower part of my body in the aspect of rays of white light. I, in turn, gradually melt into light from below and above and dissolve into the phenomena source. That dissolves into the moon. That dissolves into the thirty-two Yoginis. They dissolve into the four Yoginis, and they dissolve into the Principal Lady of the body mandala. The Principal Lady, in turn, gradually melts into light from below and above and dissolves into the phenomena source. That dissolves into the moon. That dissolves into the mantra rosary. That dissolves into the letter BAM. That dissolves into the head of the BAM. That dissolves into the crescent moon. That dissolves into the drop. That dissolves into the nada, and that, becoming smaller and smaller, dissolves into clear light emptiness.

Having dissolved everything into clear light emptiness we imagine that we experience the clear light of bliss mixed inseparably with emptiness, and we meditate on this belief for as long as possible.

The real inconceivability is the union of great bliss and emptiness. Only qualified Tantric practitioners can experience this. The yoga of inconceivability is principally a method for training in this union, and for attaining meaning clear light and the pure illusory body.

The meditation explained here is the common practice of the yoga of inconceivability, which can be practised by all Vajrayogini practitioners. There is also an uncommon practice of the yoga of inconceivability, which can be practised only by Vajrayogini practitioners who have received special instructions and transmission blessings. The sadhana of this yoga, *The Uncommon Yoga of Inconceivability*, can be found in Appendix II.

THE YOGA OF DAILY ACTIONS

The yoga of daily actions is a method for transforming everyday actions such as eating, sleeping, walking and talking into profound spiritual paths, thereby extracting great meaning from every moment of our life. The yoga of daily actions has two parts:

1 The main practice
2 The branch practices

THE MAIN PRACTICE

With the feeling of great bliss experienced at the time of meditating on the yoga of inconceivability, instantaneously we arise from the state of emptiness as Vajrayogini. We are surrounded by the outer protection circle and wear the inner protection circle of armour marked on our body. We now generate the directional protection circle of the wrathful Dakinis of the ten directions by reciting the wrathful mantra called the 'mantra emanating from the four mouths' while snapping the thumb and index finger of our left hand in each of the ten directions.

We imagine that ten wrathful Dakinis emanate from the letter BAM at our heart. In the east, that is, in front of us, is Kakase, in the north Ulukase, in the west Shonase, in the south Shukarase, in the south-east Yamadhathi, in the south-west Yamaduti, in the north-west Yamadangtrini, and in the north-east Yamamatani. In the space above is Kakase and in the space below is Khandarohi. We visualize all these Deities in the aspect of Vajrayogini, but with wrathful expressions. Powerful flames of wisdom fire emanate from their bodies and pervade the direction they guard, protecting practitioners from harmful spirits.

First we recite OM SUMBHANI SUMBHA HUM HUM PHAT, exhorting the Deity in the east and the Deity in the space above, both of whom are called Kakase, to drive away all the evil spirits from these directions. As we recite this mantra we snap our left thumb and index finger twice, first in front of us and then a little above us. Snapping our fingers reminds us that everything is in the nature of emptiness. Then with the recitation of OM GRIHANA GRIHANA HUM HUM PHAT we exhort Ulukase to drive away all the evil spirits from the north, and we snap our fingers once to the north and recall emptiness. With OM GRIHANA PAYA GRIHANA PAYA HUM HUM PHAT we exhort Shonase in the west and Khandarohi in the space below to drive away all the evil spirits from these directions, and we snap our fingers twice, first behind our head and then behind our neck. With OM ANAYA HO BHAGAWÄN VAJRA HUM HUM PHAT we exhort Shukarase to drive away all the evil spirits from the south, and we snap our fingers once to the south and recall emptiness.

We then recite the four mantras once again. With the recitation of the first mantra we exhort Yamadhathi to drive away all the evil spirits from the south-east, and we snap our fingers once to the south-east and recall emptiness. With the second mantra we exhort Yamaduti to drive away all the evil spirits from the south-west, and we snap our fingers once to the south-west and recall emptiness. With the third mantra we exhort Yamadangtrini to drive away all the evil spirits from the north-west, and we snap our fingers once to the north-west and recall emptiness. With the fourth mantra we exhort Yamamatani to drive away all the evil spirits from the north-east, and we snap our fingers once to the north-east and recall emptiness.

These mantras are called the 'mantra emanating from the four mouths' because the sound of these mantras comes from the mouths of four-faced Heruka. These mantras possess special power that can avert all obstacles.

Having set up this directional protection circle we should maintain the following recognitions throughout our daily activities: (1) whatever appears to our mind is the nature of emptiness, (2) all emptinesses are the nature of our mind of great bliss, and (3) our mind of great bliss is Truth Body Vajrayogini, which means that through experiencing great bliss we develop the thought, 'I am Vajrayogini.' We should try to combine all our daily actions with these three recognitions. Those who can do this practice successfully can transform their everyday actions into acts of great virtue, even though others may think that their actions are neutral, or even evil. Through gaining experience in the correct view of emptiness we will be able to practise the first recognition. Through gaining experience in bringing the three bodies into the path, and through gaining experience of the tenth and eleventh yogas, we will be able to practise the last two recognitions.

THE BRANCH PRACTICES

There are six branch practices:

1 The yoga of eating
2 The tsog offering
3 Burning offerings
4 Offerings of the tenth days
5 Torma offerings
6 Actions of the left

THE YOGA OF EATING

Buddha gave many instructions on how Dharma practitioners should eat. According to Hinayana teachings we should regard food and drink as medicine for curing the pain of hunger and thirst, and eat and drink without attachment. Sutra Mahayana teachings advise us first to cultivate a bodhichitta motivation and then to think: 'My main wish is to help all living beings but to do this I first need to attain Buddhahood. The human body I now have is essential for fulfilling this wish. Therefore I must take care of it by eating and drinking.' With this motivation we then enjoy our food and drink. According to the Vajrayana teachings, in addition to the motivation of bodhichitta we should enjoy every action involving the senses, such as eating and drinking, wearing clothes, washing, singing and dancing, watching television or listening to music, as an offering to our-self generated as a Deity, the synthesis of all Buddhas. With strong conviction in the truth of Vajradhara's words we should recall the two lines from the *Root Tantra of Heruka*:

Making offerings to yourself
Becomes an offering to all Buddhas.

As Vajrayogini practitioners, when we are about to eat or drink we should first bless the food or drink by reciting three times the mantra OM AH HUM HA HO HRIH. OM clears away obstacles; AH purifies the defects of smell, taste and colour; HUM generates the substances, the five meats and the five nectars; and HA HO HRIH transform the substances into nectar. Recalling the thirty-seven Dakinis of the body mandala at our heart we then recite the mantra PHAIM to invite all Buddhas in the aspect of Vajrayogini. We then recite DZA HUM BAM HO, and as we do so we imagine that the wisdom beings arrive, dissolve into the Dakinis of the body mandala, and mix inseparably with them. We then enjoy the food or drink, regarding it as an offering to the thirty-seven Dakinis and thereby delighting all the Buddhas. We should try to memorize the following prayer so that we can recite it before we eat or drink:

OM With a nature inseparable from the three vajras
I generate as the Guru-Deity.
AH This nectar of uncontaminated exalted wisdom and
bliss,

HUM Without stirring from bodhichitta
I partake to delight the Deities dwelling in my body.
AH HO MAHA SUKHA HO

Here, 'the three vajras' are the vajra body, vajra speech and vajra mind of all Buddhas.

THE TSOG OFFERING

For practitioners of Highest Yoga Tantra in general, and of Heruka and Vajrayogini in particular, the tsog offering is very important for renewing commitments and averting obstacles. It is a special method through which we come under the care and guidance of the Dakas and Dakinis who bestow completion stage realizations. Our wealth, merit and great bliss will increase through this practice.

A 'tsog' is an assembly of Heroes and Heroines. The terms 'Hero and Heroine' and 'Daka and Dakini' are interchangeable. Shantideva said that a real Hero or Heroine is someone who has destroyed their enemy, the self-grasping and self-cherishing minds, has conquered their delusions, and has developed the courage to help countless living beings. When we make a tsog offering we should regard both those to whom the offering is made and those who are making the offering as Heroes and Heroines. We offer the tsog offering to the Field for Accumulating Merit, which includes the entire assembly of Heroes and Heroines. When we gather together in a group to do a tsog offering puja it is very important that we regard everyone as an assembly of Heroes and Heroines. If we do this puja alone we should visualize ourself surrounded by all beings in the aspect of Heroes and Heroines.

The substances of a tsog offering can be any pure food and drink such as cakes, chocolate, fruit, honey, biscuits, fruit juice or yoghurt. A true tsog offering must also include meat and alcohol, usually referred to by the Sanskrit terms 'bala' and 'madana' respectively; but if these are not available we can use something else to represent them. If we wish we can make a tsog offering torma in the shape of a Heroine's breast.

Traditionally this torma is coloured red and decorated with a wheel, half moon, drop and nada. All these substances are the basis of the tsog offering.

When we make a tsog offering to Vajrayogini we visualize in the space in front of us the protection circle, charnel grounds and phenomena source. At the centre of the phenomena source stands Vajrayogini surrounded by the four Dakinis, the thirty-two Dakinis, all the Yidams of the four classes of Tantra, all Buddhas and Bodhisattvas, and all Emanation Solitary Realizers and Hearers. In the space above them and a little behind Vajrayogini we visualize the assembly of Gurus. In the front corner of the phenomena source we visualize supramundane Heroes and Heroines, and in the back corner we visualize the Dharma Protectors. Between the charnel grounds and the vajra fence we visualize countless living beings in the aspect of Vajrayogini. We should maintain strong divine pride that we are really Vajrayogini, that our environment is the real Pure Land of Vajrayogini, and that all the beings we see in front of us are emanations of Vajrayogini.

First we bless the tsog offering according to the sadhana. We then recite the tsog offering prayers from the sadhana, making the offerings in the following order: to the assembly of Gurus to receive their blessings; to the assembly of Vajrayogini and her retinue for the attainment of outer and inner Dakini Lands; to the assembly of other Yidams for general Tantric attainments; to the assembly of Buddhas, Bodhisattvas, Solitary Realizers and Hearers for the attainment of general Dharma realizations; to the assembly of Dharma Protectors, Heroes and Heroines to avert obstacles and to gain their assistance in developing great bliss; and to all living beings so that they may attain liberation from ignorance and suffering. As we recite the verses we emanate countless Rasavajra Goddesses from the letter BAM at our heart and imagine that they serve all the guests of the tsog offering. We then offer outer offerings, the inner offering, and the eight lines of praise.

If the Vajrayana Spiritual Guide is present on the throne it is traditional to offer him or her the first portion of the nectar-food of the tsog offering by making up a separate plate of the blessed food. One, two or three representative disciples, depending on how elaborate the offering is, make three prostrations to the Vajrayana Spiritual Guide. If there are two disciples, one should hold the plate containing the first portion and the other should hold the bala and madana. Both should stand respectfully facing the Vajrayana Spiritual Guide. These two disciples begin to chant the first line of the first verse of *Making the tsog offering to the Vajrayana Spiritual Guide*, and the assembled disciples join in. The Vajrayana Spiritual Guide begins the chanting of the second verse, and the disciples join in. The representative disciples begin the third verse, and the Vajrayana Spiritual Guide begins the fourth verse.

With the recitation of the mantra AH HO MAHA SUKHA HO, which means 'O Great bliss!', the Vajrayana Spiritual Guide accepts the first portion of the nectar-food of the tsog offering, the bala and the madana; and the remaining blessed food is then distributed to those present to enjoy with the yoga of eating. Then the whole assembly, together with the Vajrayana Spiritual Guide, chant *Song of the Spring Queen* to generate and increase great bliss. This prayer, which was composed by Je Tsongkhapa, is a very blessed vajra song that expresses the profound essence of Highest Yoga Tantra. It was offered to Je Tsongkhapa by a host of Dakinis when he was living in Ganden Yangpa Chen. There are several commentaries to this song, such as those by Gungtang Tenpai Dronme and Kachen Yeshe Gyaltsen.

After sharing out the tsog offering substances one disciple should collect a piece of blessed food from each disciple and last of all from the Vajrayana Spiritual Guide. The disciple then adds to this plate some of the offering substances that were not distributed, and some bala and madana. If we make the offering at night we can also put a stick of burning incense on the plate. We then bless this offering with the prayer from the sadhana, and give it to the spirits, who live on left-over food that has been dedicated to them by humans.

It is very important for practitioners of Vajrayogini and Heruka to make tsog offerings because it is a principal method for attaining both outer and inner Dakini Land. Khedrubje received a vision of Heruka in which Heruka said to him, 'Practitioners who sincerely practise the tsog offering without missing the two "tenth" days of each month will definitely be reborn in Dakini Land.' We should therefore make sure that we do not miss tsog offerings on these two days.

BURNING OFFERINGS

The real burning offerings that delight the Gurus and Buddhas are the mental practices that consume the fuel of ordinary appearance and ordinary conception. In generation stage meditation we develop the 'fire' of concentration on clear appearance and divine pride, which partially consumes the fuel of ordinary appearance and ordinary conception. Then during completion stage meditation we develop the 'fire' of the wisdom of the union of great bliss and emptiness, which totally consumes the fuel of ordinary appearance and ordinary conception.

The scriptures mention three kinds of burning offering: outer, inner and unsurpassed. Burning offering practices that involve the use of an external fire and material substances are called outer burning offerings. There are many different kinds of outer burning offering, such as the burning offering of black sesame seeds, the burning offering of fulfilling the commitment of close retreat, the burning offering of ten per cent of close retreat, and the burning offerings to attain pacifying, increasing, controlling and wrathful actions.

The Vajradaka burning offering and the burning offering of the candle-flame are both examples of offerings in which only black sesame seeds are burned. The latter was compiled by Je Phabongkhapa to be practised in conjunction with Vajrayogini practice.

To complete a close retreat of action we need to do the burning offering of fulfilling the commitment of close retreat to purify any mistakes we may have made during our retreat. We may have recited the mantra incorrectly, developed doubt or lack of faith, succumbed to distractions or fallen asleep. We may have mispronounced words or omitted or added extra words while reciting the sadhana. It is possible that we practised with a bad motivation, deluded doubt, wrong views, lack of conviction, or without separating our mind from worldly activities. We may have allowed our mindfulness to slacken, engaged in conversation without good reason, developed anger, jealousy or other strong delusions, or ignored or forgotten our Guru's instructions. We can purify all such mistakes by performing the burning offering.

To perform the burning offering of fulfilling the commitment we should first obtain and prepare the traditional substances and make a suitably-sized fire place. We then clean and purify the area where the fire puja is to take place and make the necessary arrangements, such as drawing the mandala on the fire place, arranging the firewood, laying out the substances in the correct order, setting up the seating arrangements, and so forth.

Once we are seated at the fire puja site we pick up our vajra and bell, which we should hold throughout the puja, and we stop speaking. We then imagine that a wisdom fire arises from emptiness. In the centre of the fire we visualize Vajrayogini and mundane Fire Deity, and while reciting the appropriate prayers from the fire puja sadhana we offer to them twelve main substances, a special mixture of substances, outer offerings, the inner offering and torma offerings. We should regard all these substances as having the nature of wisdom nectar.

Each of the twelve substances has a particular significance: (1) offering milk-wood, wood that still contains sap, increases our vitality; (2) offering butter increases our wealth; (3) offering sesame seeds purifies our negative karma; (4) offering couch grass increases our life span; (5) offering rice increases our merit; (6) offering wholemeal flour mixed with yoghurt increases supreme bliss; (7) offering kusha grass purifies our mind; (8) offering mustard seeds averts outer obstacles; (9) offering barley with husks increases harvests; (10) offering barley without husks causes the development of a powerful and quick mind; (11) offering green peas increases the power of our body; and (12) offering wheat alleviates and controls diseases. The thirteenth offering is a special mixture of twelve substances. It is comprised of kusha grass, milk, barley, sesame

seeds, couch grass, rice, flour and yoghurt, sandalwood powder, ti yang ku (a type of grass), thang chu (a special gum),
flowers, and dried, puffed rice.

We perform the burning offering of ten per cent of close
retreat after completing a great close retreat in which we have
recited ten million three-OM mantras. During this puja, which
we perform over a number of days, we recite an additional one
million mantras, a tenth of the total mantra count, and we make
the same number of burning offerings. We can also do this after
retreats of a hundred thousand mantras, four hundred thousand
mantras, or three million, two hundred thousand mantras. In
each case, if we wish, we may perform over a number of days
a fire puja in which we recite additional mantras equal to one
tenth of the total mantra commitment of the retreat.

Once we have accomplished a close retreat of actions and the
concluding fire puja we are authorized to perform four types of
burning offering: burning offerings of pacifying actions to pacify
obstacles for ourself and others; burning offerings of increasing
actions to increase wealth, life span, merit, good fortune and
realizations; burning offerings of controlling actions to gather
and draw in the power of the Buddhas, Bodhisattvas, sentient
beings and the four elements; and burning offerings of wrathful
actions through which we can destroy the power of evil spirits.

When we perform a fire puja we offer the twelve substances
and other material offerings to the Deities, and at the same
time we think that our own and others' ordinary appearances
and conceptions are being consumed in the fire of wisdom.
By thinking like this, our fire puja will be a genuine burning
offering practice.

Any generation stage burning offering that does not involve
the use of an external fire is an inner burning offering, and
any completion stage burning offering is an unsurpassed
burning offering. We can practise both these burning offerings
when we practise the yogas of eating and drinking. Whenever
we eat or drink we focus on the letter BAM at our heart and
imagine making offerings to all the Dakas and Dakinis. To
make such offerings we first generate the divine pride of being
Vajrayogini and imagine that the thirty-seven Dakinis of the

body mandala dissolve and transform into the red letter BAM at our heart. The nada of the BAM then flares up and becomes a blazing wisdom fire, which completely burns up our food and drink as we consume it. While we visualize this we believe that our ordinary appearances and conceptions are completely consumed by the wisdom fire and this causes us to experience the unified wisdom of great bliss and emptiness. This practice causes a healthy body with fewer physical disorders. It also increases our collections of both merit and wisdom.

OFFERINGS OF THE TENTH DAYS

According to the Tibetan calendar, the first tenth day is ten days after the new moon, and the second tenth day is ten days after the full moon. Although in the Tibetan lunar-based calendar the second tenth day is generally regarded as the twenty-fifth day of the month, from this explanation we can understand why each month is said to have two tenth days. When we make special offerings on either of these days it is called an 'offering of the tenth day'. We can also make these offerings on the tenth and twenty-fifth days of the Western calendar. These two days are sacred to the Dakinis, and so if we make offerings or prayers on these days it is especially powerful, and it is easier to receive the blessings of the Dakas and Dakinis. For these reasons sincere practitioners of Heruka and Vajrayogini should not forget to make offerings on the two tenth days. According to the practice of Vajrayogini there are three kinds of offering of the tenth day:

1 Extensive offerings of the tenth days
2 Middling offerings of the tenth days
3 Brief offerings of the tenth days

EXTENSIVE OFFERINGS OF THE TENTH DAYS

This has two parts:

1 The preparations
2 The actual offering

THE PREPARATIONS

We first place a large, high table in front of the shrine, or in any position that is practical. Upon this, on a clean cloth, we place a picture of Vajrayogini's mandala lying flat. In the centre of the mandala we put a small container of sindhura powder. This is called the 'heap mandala of body', and is the visual object in dependence upon which we generate the body of the in-front-generated Vajrayogini. Over this we arrange a tripod upon which we place a real or artificial skullcup, or similar vessel. We pour some alcohol or black tea into the skullcup, sweeten it with honey, and add some inner offering substance. We then cover the vessel with a small, clean red cloth placed on top of a horizontal lattice in the shape of a six-pointed star. This is called the 'nectar mandala of speech', and is the visual object in dependence upon which we generate the speech of Vajrayogini. On top of the cloth we place the sindhura mandala of mind, which is the visual object in dependence upon which we generate the mind of the in-front-generated Vajrayogini. If we do not have a traditional wood block sindhura mandala we can use a clean, circular piece of wood or a round mirror. On the flat surface we paint a red phenomena source, shaped like a six-pointed star formed by two interlocking triangles, with joy swirls in the four side corners. In the centre of the phenomena source we write in gold, preferably with real gold paint, the letter BAM with the three-OM mantra encircling it counter-clockwise. We then sprinkle a little sindhura powder through a small sieve onto the surface of the disc, covering it lightly so that we can still see the letter BAM and mantra. A small amount of sindhura powder should also be placed on each of the four joy swirls. We can use this as the sindhura mandala of mind, and place it on top of the nectar mandala of speech. This method of making the sindhura mandala of mind was explained by Ngulchu Dharmabhadra in accordance with authentic tradition.

Around the mandalas of body, speech and mind we arrange counter-clockwise a set of small offering bowls. Starting in the east, in front of the mandala, we place AHRGHAM, in the north-east, to our right, PADÄM, in the north PUPE, in the north-west DHUPE, in the west DIWE, in the south-west GÄNDHE, in the south NEWIDE, and finally in the south-east a flower to mark the border. In front of these we arrange at least five rows of outer offerings. The first row, closest to the mandala, consists of nine bowls containing in order: AHRGHAM, PADÄM, ÄNTZAMANAM (water for rinsing the mouth), PROKYANAM (water for sprinkling), PUPE, DHUPE, DIWE, GÄNDHE and NEWIDE. These are the offerings to the Deities of the in-front-generated mandala. The second row, laid out in front of the first row, are the general outer offerings: AHRGHAM, PADÄM, PUPE, DHUPE, DIWE, GÄNDHE and NEWIDE. These can be used at any stage in the sadhana, such as for torma offerings, tsog offerings or thanking offerings. In front of these are the outer offerings to the Deity of the vase, from AHRGHAM to NEWIDE, and in front of these are the preliminary offerings, from AHRGHAM to NEWIDE. All these rows of offerings begin from the mandala's left (our right). The front row of offerings, closest to the practitioner, from AHRGHAM to NEWIDE, is for the self-generated Deity. These offerings are laid out in the opposite direction, from our left to our right. We place the torma offerings to the right of the mandala (our left), slightly to the front of the mandala. In front of the main tormas we place a torma for the general Dharma Protectors and a preliminary torma. We place the tsog offerings to the left of the mandala, or wherever there is room.

In front of our seat, on a small table we place a vase or vessel two-thirds filled with saffron water, and add a pinch of the special substance of the vase, if it is available. If we prefer we can set out the offerings to the Deity of the vase in front of the vase rather than in front of the shrine. We place on the table a small conch shell and a miniature vajra that has a long thread of five colours wound around it, together with our bell and vajra, damaru, inner offering container, and some rice or a flower head. In a group practice, only one vase, conch shell and small vajra are necessary for the whole group, and these should be set out on a table in front of the person presiding over the puja.

THE ACTUAL OFFERING

We make the extensive offerings of the tenth days in conjunction with the Vajrayogini self-initiation sadhana, *Feast of Great Bliss*, composed by Je Phabongkhapa, which can be found in Appendix II. The sequence of the sadhana is as follows: performing the preliminaries such as blessing the offerings and offering the preliminary torma, meditation on self-generation, accomplishing the vase, accomplishing the mandala in front, making offerings, receiving the empowerments, offering the tormas, making the tsog offering, making the thanking offering, reciting the dedication prayers, and reciting the auspicious prayers. If Vajrayogini practitioners who have not yet completed a close retreat of action of Vajrayogini wish to do the extensive offering of the tenth day they should make the same preparations, but when they recite the sadhana they should omit the sections on the preliminary torma offering and accomplishing the vase, and then continue from accomplishing the in-front mandala and making extensive offerings up to receiving the empowerments. They should then omit the section on receiving the empowerments, and continue from the torma offerings and tsog offerings to the end of the sadhana.

MIDDLING OFFERINGS OF THE TENTH DAYS

We make the middling offerings of the tenth days by reciting the extensive self-generation sadhana of Vajrayogini together with the tsog offering prayers.

BRIEF OFFERINGS OF THE TENTH DAYS

We make the brief offerings of the tenth days by reciting the condensed sadhana of Vajrayogini, *The Blissful Path*, which can be found in Appendix II, together with the tsog offering prayers.

Since the offering of the tenth days is an important commitment for practitioners of Heruka and Vajrayogini we should

try not to miss them. When we make tsog offerings in conjunction with the *Offering to the Spiritual Guide* puja as a tenth-day
offering we should regard the principal Field for Accumulating
Merit, Lama Losang Tubwang Dorjechang, as having the same
nature as Heruka and Vajrayogini. Whenever we perform a
tsog offering related to any other Deity we should regard the
principal object of the Field for Accumulating Merit as being
one in nature with Heruka and Vajrayogini.

If circumstances prevent us from making a tenth-day offering
we recite twice the number of our usual daily commitment
of the three-OM mantra. If we ignore or completely forget to
make a tenth-day offering we break our commitment.

There is one month of the year that is a very important
time for practitioners of Heruka and Vajrayogini. According
to the Tibetan calendar, this month lasts from the sixteenth
day of the eleventh month of the lunar-based calendar to
the fifteenth day of the twelfth month. Since this usually
falls on or close to the Western month of January, we can
regard this as the special month. This is a powerful time for
practitioners of Heruka and Vajrayogini to make offerings
and to do retreat. The two tenth days within this month are
particularly special. The first is a special day of Vajrayogini,
and the second is a special day of Heruka. It is particularly
important to make special offerings on these two days.

TORMA OFFERINGS

A torma offering is a special offering of food made in order
to gain spiritual attainments. Whereas tsog offerings can be
made only by practitioners of Highest Yoga Tantra, torma
offerings can be made by any practitioner of Sutra or Tantra.
The *Vinaya Sutras* teach that Sangha should offer tormas
to the Three Jewels and to the Dharma Protectors to avert
obstacles and gather all necessary conditions, and that they
should give tormas to the local guardians as a way of making
friends with them. A similar practice is explained in the training the mind teachings. The torma offering in the practice of
Vajrayogini is explained in two parts:

1 The preparations
2 The actual torma offering

THE PREPARATIONS

Generally for the practice of Vajrayogini there are four tormas: the three principal tormas and the torma to the general Dharma Protectors, often called the 'Ogminma torma'. However, according to this tradition, if we wish to offer tormas continually, as part of our daily practice or during close retreat, we can set up five tormas. These tormas are usually coloured red and are decorated. If we wish we can make them in the traditional manner as illustrated in Appendix III. If we cannot make tormas in the traditional manner we can use honey, fresh cakes, alcohol, or any other pure food to represent them.

We set up the tormas in front of a statue or picture of Vajrayogini on the shrine. The central torma is for Vajrayogini and her retinue, who are the main guests of the torma offering. The torma immediately to its right (our left) is for the mundane Dakas and Dakinis, and the torma to the right of this one is the Ogminma torma. Ogmin, or 'Akanishta' in Sanskrit, is a Buddha's Pure Land. The torma immediately to the left of the central torma (our right) is for the Kinkara Dharma Protector. This Protector is a special Protector for practitioners of Heruka and Vajrayogini and is also known as 'Father Mother Lord of the Charnel Grounds'. To the left of this torma is a torma for the Dharma Protector, who is called the 'great Protector of the Guru's words'. In the sadhana the prayer for offering the torma to the general Dharma Protectors contains these two lines:

**I request you, I make offerings to you, O Host of
Protectors of the Conqueror's doctrine,
I propitiate you and rely upon you, O Great Protectors
of the Guru's words.**

The first line refers to Dharma Protectors in general, and the second line refers specifically to our own Spiritual Guide's Dharma Protector. We should find out the name of this special

Dharma Protector by asking our main Spiritual Guide who guides us along Vajrayogini's path. I, the author, have Dorje Shugden as my special Dharma Protector. For me, Dorje Shugden is the great Protector of the Guru's words, and I use the fifth torma as an offering to him. The following special verse for offering the torma to Dorje Shugden can be added to the prayers immediately after the verse to the Kinkara Protector:

From the supreme places such as Tushita, Keajra, and so forth,
Great Protector of the doctrine of the second Conqueror,
Dorje Shugden, five lineages, together with your retinues,
Come here please and partake of this offering and torma.

THE ACTUAL TORMA OFFERING

The visualization of the guests to whom the tormas are offered is exactly the same as the visualization for making the tsog offering and for making the offerings of the tenth days. We bless the tormas according to the sadhana and we then emanate countless Rasavajra Goddesses from the letter BAM at our heart to offer tormas to the guests.

While visualizing the tormas being offered we recite the mantra OM VAJRA AH RA LI HO: DZA HUM BAM HO: VAJRA DAKINI SAMAYA TÖN TRISHAYA HO three times and perform the accompanying mudra. To perform this mudra we hold up both our hands in front of us with the flattened palms facing upwards and the thumbs tucked in. When we recite DZA HUM BAM HO we snap the middle finger and thumb of our right hand. With the first recitation we make torma offerings to Guru Vajrayogini and her retinue of thirty-six Dakinis as well as to the lineage Gurus; with the second we make torma offerings to all the other Yidams, Buddhas, Bodhisattvas, Emanation Solitary Realizers and Emanation Hearers; and with the third we make torma offerings to all Dharma Protectors and supramundane Dakas and Dakinis. The meaning of the offering mantra is as follows:

OM: 'O Vajrayogini'
VAJRA refers to the torma itself
AH RA LI HO: 'please enjoy.'
DZA: we imagine the nectar reaches Vajrayogini's tongue.
HUM: the nectar reaches her throat.
BAM: it reaches her heart.
HO: she experiences spontaneous great bliss.
VAJRA DAKINI: 'O Vajrayogini'
SAMAYA TÖN: 'through your compassionate equanimity'
TRISHAYA HO: 'please care for me.'

We then recite twice the mantra that begins OM KHA KHA, KHAHI KHAHI, SARWA YAKYA RAKYASA . . . . With the first recitation we offer tormas to the mundane Dakas and Dakinis of the four cardinal directions, and with the second we offer tormas to the mundane Dakas and Dakinis of the four intermediate directions. When we recite this mantra we call upon the mundane Dakas and Dakinis – the eleven assemblies such as the assembly of gods and the assembly of nagas, who reside in the eight charnel grounds – to accept the torma and enjoy it, and to assist us in fulfilling our wishes.

After offering these tormas we make outer and inner offerings and recite the long and short prayers to Vajrayogini, requesting her to lead us and all living beings to her Pure Land.

We then offer the torma to the general Dharma Protectors such as four-faced Mahakala, Kalindevi (Palden Lhamo) and the Kinkara Protector, as well as the special torma to the great Protector of the Guru's words. For these offerings we use the prayer from the sadhana called 'Ogminma' in Tibetan.

At the conclusion of the sadhana we recite the Vajrasattva mantra while ringing the bell to recall emptiness. This purifies any mistakes we may have made during our practice.

We ask the holy beings to be patient and to forgive any mistakes. We then recite the dedication prayers and auspicious prayers.

ACTIONS OF THE LEFT

In the *Root Tantra of Heruka* Vajradhara says:

Everything moving and unmoving within the three
   realms
Arises from the left.

Here, 'the left' is the clear light of emptiness. This passage means that everything within the three realms, including all living beings, arises from emptiness. Mother Tantra in general, and Vajrayogini and Heruka Tantras in particular, principally reveal the practice of the clear light of emptiness, that is, a mind of clear light conjoined with a realization of emptiness. Practitioners of Heruka and Vajrayogini should treasure the clear light of emptiness as their heart practice. To remind ourself constantly of this we should try to begin all bodily actions from the left. For example, whenever we are about to touch something or pick something up we should use our left hand, whenever we look at something we should try to think that we are looking at it first with our left eye, whenever we listen to something we should try to think that we are hearing it first with our left ear, and whenever we are about to walk we should take the first step with our left foot. We should apply this to all our bodily actions. Once we gain familiarity with this practice all our activities will be transformed into actions that are similar to those of the Dakinis, who in all their activities remember emptiness. This practice of actions of the left is a commitment of Mother Tantra.

Dorjechang Trijang Rinpoche

How to Attain Outer Dakini Land through the Practice of Generation Stage

There are three types of Vajrayogini practitioner: those who possess great fortune, those who possess middling fortune, and those who possess least fortune.

HOW VAJRAYOGINI PRACTITIONERS WHO POSSESS GREAT FORTUNE ATTAIN OUTER DAKINI LAND, KNOWN AS KEAJRA PURE LAND

A practitioner of great fortune can attain outer Dakini Land before death by engaging in daily practice of generation stage, reciting the three-OM mantra, and making offerings on the tenth days. If we engage in these practices purely, sincerely and continuously for a long time, but do not experience any special signs of attainment, this indicates that we are a being of middling or of least fortune. Some practitioners of middling fortune can attain outer Dakini Land in that life through pure daily practice, maintaining their commitments and vows sincerely, and doing a close retreat of actions. Other practitioners of middling fortune need to do a great close retreat followed by the practice of accomplishing the sindhura mandala using the stem of a langali tree.

Generally it is important for all Vajrayogini practitioners to do close retreats. Once we have completed a close retreat of actions and a fire puja we are qualified to perform self-initiation. With this practice we can renew and strengthen our Tantric vows and commitments and purify our negativities, including our Tantric downfalls. It is important to practise self-initiation regularly because maintaining our vows and commitments is the foundation of all Tantric attainments, and if we break our vows and commitments and do not restore them through an appropriate method, this will be a great obstacle to our gaining Tantric realizations.

HOW VAJRAYOGINI PRACTITIONERS WHO POSSESS MIDDLING FORTUNE ATTAIN OUTER DAKINI LAND

There are three stages:

1 Completing a great close retreat emphasizing self-generation
2 Accomplishing the mandala emphasizing the in-front-generation
3 Actualizing the effect

If a practitioner of middling fortune practises all these three stages with strong faith and conviction, he or she can attain outer Dakini Land.

COMPLETING A GREAT CLOSE RETREAT EMPHASIZING SELF-GENERATION

After completing the nine preliminary practices we can engage in a great close retreat. The preparation and the way to engage in a great close retreat are basically the same as for doing close retreats in general, except that in this case we should collect ten million three-OM mantras and one million wisdom-descending mantras, all on the same seat. Then, mainly using black sesame seeds, we should perform burning offerings of one million mantras, one tenth of the number recited during the great close retreat.

ACCOMPLISHING THE MANDALA EMPHASIZING THE IN-FRONT-GENERATION

After completing a great close retreat we need to accomplish the second stage. The preparations for this – setting up the heap mandala of body, the nectar mandala of speech, the sindhura mandala of mind, the tormas, and the other offerings – are the same as for the extensive offerings of the tenth day, and the retreat itself is basically the same as a close retreat.

During the sessions we should sit facing the west. In each session we recite the self-generation sadhana, from going for refuge up to and including the yoga of inconceivability, and then we continue in accordance with the self-initiation sadhana with accomplishing the sindhura mandala and making extensive offerings and praises, up to just before receiving the empowerments. At this point we recite the mantra to the Vajrayogini generated in front of us.

At the heart of the principal Deity of the sindhura mandala is a phenomena source. Inside this, on a moon cushion, is a red letter BAM surrounded by the three-OM mantra. The BAM and mantra radiate countless red light rays which purify the negative karma of all living beings and make offerings to all the Buddhas. All their power and blessings gather back in the aspect of red light. This dissolves into the red letter BAM and mantra at the heart of the in-front-generated Deity. Then, from the BAM and mantra, wisdom-light radiates to our own heart and we receive the blessings of all the Dakinis. With this visualization we recite the three-OM mantra. We should do this in four sessions a day until we have completed four hundred thousand mantras. This practice is basically the same as that in the self-initiation sadhana except that we do not send out the preliminary torma, accomplish the vase, or receive the four actual empowerments. We should know how the practice can be abbreviated or modified without omitting the essentials.

Each day we need to arrange a new set of the three mandalas and make tsog offerings and other offerings. We should change the sindhura powder every day and keep the old sindhura powder in a special container to be used later in the practice of actualizing the effect.

In the last session of each day we make torma offerings, tsog offerings and thanking offerings, and we recite the long dedication prayers and the auspicious prayers. In this way we finish reciting the four hundred thousand three-OM mantras of the in-front-generated Deity.

When we have completed these mantras we make a container from the stem of a langali tree, a tropical tree that is similar to bamboo but thicker. We cut a section of the stem a few inches long. One end should be closed by a natural blockage in the wood and the other end should be open. Onto a piece of wood, which will be used to plug the open end of the hollow stem like a cork, we carve a joy swirl seal. We divide the sindhura powder that we collected each day into eight small bowls, set them out in front of the mandala, and then recite eight thousand three-OM mantras together with the same practice as in accomplishing the mandala. After we have recited one thousand mantras we empty one bowl of sindhura powder into the langali stem. We continue in this way until we have recited eight thousand mantras and all eight bowls of sindhura have been poured into the langali stem. We then seal the top of the stem with the joy swirl plug. We then wrap the stem in a piece of red cloth which should envelop both ends. We should mark the cloth with a letter BAM, if possible with real gold, to indicate which way up it should stand.

After completing these preparations, on the first tenth day of the month we perform the practice called 'accomplishing the sindhura with the langali stem'. We prepare the three mandalas, the offerings, the tormas and the tsog offerings in exactly the same way as for making extensive offerings of the tenth days. We place the langali stem upright at the centre of the sindhura mandala of mind, with the letter BAM on the cloth facing us.

During the day we do the self-initiation practices according to the sadhana and make extensive offerings. In the evening, just before dark, with a Heruka practitioner to assist us, we take the langali stem to an isolated place that we have found to be suitable and which we should regard as the charnel grounds of Vajrayogini's mandala. When we arrive there we dig a triangular hole about eighteen inches deep, with one point directed towards the west. We place the stem upright inside the hole and then cover it with earth. We should smooth the surface so that it is not noticeable to others, but we should mark or make a mental note of its whereabouts so that we can find it again.

We then sit on that spot, facing west, and perform the self-generation practice from going for refuge up to the mantra recitation while remembering that we and the sindhura in the langali stem are one with emptiness. We then meditate principally on the uncommon yoga of inconceivability, the sadhana for which, *The Uncommon Yoga of Inconceivability*, can be found in Appendix II.

While we are meditating our assistant stays nearby, reciting the mantra emanating from the four mouths and the close essence mantra of Heruka, OM HRIH HA HA HUM HUM PHAT, to prevent interruptions to our meditation. After finishing the session we return to the retreat house and practise the yoga of sleeping. The next day we perform self-initiation with extensive offerings as on the previous day, and at dusk we again go with our assistant to the isolated place, find the place where we buried the langali stem, and do a session in the same way as the previous day but this time slightly longer. After the session we return to the retreat house and practise the yoga of sleeping. We should repeat this every day until the second tenth day of that month, each time lengthening the duration of the night session.

On the second tenth day we again do self-initiation, making even more elaborate offerings. Then at dusk we go to the isolated place with our assistant and begin the session as before, but this time we continue the session throughout the night until dawn. In this session, after reciting the mantra, we practise mainly the uncommon yoga of inconceivability with strong concentration and faith. Then at dawn we conclude the session, remove the langali stem from the ground, and return with it to the retreat house. We place the langali stem in the centre of the sindhura mandala and finally, with extensive offerings, perform the self-initiation practices.

ACTUALIZING THE EFFECT

The great close retreat, the practice of accomplishing the mandala, and the langali stem practice are preparations that enable us eventually to meet with an emanation of Vajrayogini, who will take us by the hand and lead us directly to her Pure Land. When we have accomplished all these preparations the time has come to leave samsaric places. We should think:

Now is the time for me to leave samsara and go to a perfect world, the Pure Land of the Dakinis. There is no reason to be attached to my home, friends or possessions. I must leave the prison of samsara and, guided by Vajrayogini, go to her Pure Land.

Then, without any attachment, doubt or hesitation we leave our home and travel in search of an emanation of Vajrayogini. We take with us the langali stem filled with sindhura, and a small mirror. Every day we mark our forehead with sindhura, using the joy swirl seal on the langali stem. We should wander round cities, towns, big markets, public houses, large parties, wherever many women gather. We can travel to other countries and visit any of the twenty-four auspicious places of Heruka. Maintaining strong divine pride of being Vajrayogini at all times, we imagine that our wisdom eye beholds all women. We continue in this way without discouragement until one day we see a woman, old or young, who has the mark of the sindhura joy swirl seal on her forehead, exactly like our own. When this happens we should immediately look into the mirror to see if our joy swirl mark has disappeared. If it has, this clearly indicates that the woman is an emanation of Vajrayogini. We should not be concerned about whether she is beautiful or ugly, religious or seemingly non-religious. Even if outwardly she appears to deny Dharma we should have no doubt. We should mentally prostrate to her and request her to care for us. If possible we should also make verbal and physical prostrations and request her to accept us. She may not immediately agree to our request, but, knowing that we are now very close to attaining our final goal, we should remain undiscouraged. Sooner or later our wish will be fulfilled.

This is the way practitioners of middling fortune complete the preparations and actualize the effect. By practising in this way they will meet Vajrayogini face to face, and when this happens there is no doubt that they will attain Buddhahood within that life.

HOW VAJRAYOGINI PRACTITIONERS WHO POSSESS LEAST FORTUNE ATTAIN OUTER DAKINI LAND

If we complete a great close retreat, do the langali stem practice and try to actualize the effect, but fail to fulfil our wish, this indicates that we are a practitioner who possesses least fortune. However we should not be discouraged, but should remember that after we die we will come under the care of Vajrayogini, either in the bardo or certainly within seven lives.

Venerable Geshe Kelsang Gyatso Rinpoche

Completion Stage

The commentary to the completion stage practice of Vajra-yogini has two parts:

1 What is completion stage?
2 How to attain inner Dakini Land through the practice of completion stage

WHAT IS COMPLETION STAGE?

'Completion stage' refers to Highest Yoga Tantra realizations that are attained by causing the winds to enter, abide and dissolve within the central channel through the force of meditation.

As mentioned before, outer Dakini Land is the Pure Land of Vajrayogini, Keajra Pure Land. When we attain this as a result of generation stage practice we can attain inner Dakini Land and Buddhahood within that same life through the practice of completion stage meditation. Inner Dakini Land is meaning clear light, the mind of spontaneous great bliss that directly realizes emptiness. To gain this realization we must dissolve all our winds into the indestructible drop at our heart through completion stage meditation.

HOW TO ATTAIN INNER DAKINI LAND THROUGH THE PRACTICE OF COMPLETION STAGE

This has three parts:

1 Explanation of the three basic objects of knowledge
2 Meditations on the path
3 How to attain the results

EXPLANATION OF THE THREE BASIC OBJECTS
OF KNOWLEDGE

This explanation will greatly improve our knowledge of Dharma. Although an extensive explanation of objects of knowledge is presented in Sutra teachings, if we do not study Tantric teachings we will gain only a rough understanding of Buddhadharma. We will not gain a deep understanding of Dharma through studying Sutra teachings alone. The teachings of Highest Yoga Tantra contain the most profound explanations of the basis, the path and the result of practice.

There are innumerable basic objects of knowledge, but here we are concerned principally with three:

1 Objects of knowledge related to the body
2 Objects of knowledge related to the mind
3 Objects of knowledge related to the elements

OBJECTS OF KNOWLEDGE RELATED TO THE BODY

To practise completion stage we need a human body which possesses the six elements: bone, marrow, white drops, flesh, skin and blood. The first three come from our father and the second three from our mother. Anyone, even an advanced Bodhisattva, who lacks these elements has no opportunity to practise completion stage. As human beings we are very fortunate because we have these six elements and we have the opportunity to listen to, contemplate and meditate on the teachings of Highest Yoga Tantra.

Our present body is a gross temporary body originating from the bodies of our parents. Although it is now used by us, in actual fact it is a product of the sperm and egg of our parents. It is therefore a transformation of parts of others' bodies. Due to familiarity with self-grasping we believe that this gross form is our true body. In reality, however, our true body is a very subtle body composed of the inner wind that is inseparable from our very subtle mind. We have had this very subtle body since beginningless time, and it will remain with us forever.

The dream body and the bardo body, the intermediate state body, are subtle bodies, and the illusory body is a very subtle body. In the intermediate state and in our dreams a subtle body naturally becomes manifest, but until we attain the illusory body the very subtle body is never manifest. When we become a Buddha the very subtle inner wind that forms our very subtle body transforms into a Buddha's Form Body and our very subtle mind becomes the omniscient mind of a Buddha. From this we can understand that all living beings have within them the seed of a Buddha's body, and that if they meet the Buddhadharma that explains how to ripen this seed they can become enlightened beings.

Once we have attained the pure illusory body our subtle body is always manifest. It becomes our actual body with which we naturally identify. At this stage our subtle body is our true body and our gross body is like our house. When a highly realized practitioner who has attained the illusory body finally leaves his or her gross body, ordinary beings believe that person has died; but their actual body never dies. The defining characteristic of death is the final separation of body and mind. Since the very subtle body never separates from the very subtle mind, once this body is always manifest we are free from death. When asked by one of his disciples to give an example of a deathless person, Khedrub Sangye Yeshe replied that thousands of Je Tsongkhapa's disciples attained the pure illusory body and that all these beings are deathless because they have attained a vajra body, which is completely free from death.

OBJECTS OF KNOWLEDGE RELATED TO THE MIND

There are three kinds of mind: gross, subtle and very subtle. The five sense consciousnesses and the delusions that manifest within our mental continuum are gross minds because they are produced by gross inner winds and are relatively easy to recognize. As we fall asleep, and as we die, our gross winds gradually dissolve within the central channel. Due to this dissolution we experience eight signs. These signs indicate different levels of absorption of the inner winds. A mind that experiences any of the first seven signs is a subtle mind because it depends upon subtle inner winds and because it is more difficult to recognize than the gross minds. A mind that experiences the eighth sign is a very subtle mind because it is conjoined with the very subtle inner wind and is even more difficult to recognize than the subtle minds.

The very subtle mind is also called the 'continuously residing mind' because it has been with us since beginningless time and will remain with us until we attain Buddhahood. Other minds, such as the deluded minds of attachment, anger and jealousy, are called 'temporary minds' because they will cease when we attain liberation. The terms 'very subtle mind', 'continuously residing mind' and 'mind of clear light' all have the same meaning.

There are two ways to realize the continuously residing mind: intellectually through receiving an introductory explanation, or experientially by meditating on completion stage practices such as the yogas of the channels, drops and winds. When Gampopa told Milarepa of his special experience of concentration, Milarepa replied that although Gampopa's experience was good, he should meditate on tummo as Milarepa himself did, and through this come to recognize the nature of mind. By this, Milarepa meant that by meditating on tummo Gampopa would gain a direct realization of the continuously residing mind.

OBJECTS OF KNOWLEDGE RELATED TO THE ELEMENTS

There are three elements that are important in completion stage meditation: the channels, the drops and the inner winds. It is said that the channels are like a house, the drops are like the furniture, and the winds are like the owner.

By engaging in specific meditations on these three with strong concentration, our winds will gather and dissolve within the central channel and we will experience our continuously residing mind, the mind of clear light. When this mind manifests as a result of meditation, our mind becomes very peaceful and calm, free from distractions and disturbing conceptual thoughts. This experience is greatly superior to the tranquil abiding described in Sutra teachings. It is only by gaining this realization that we can attain the deathless vajra body. Meditating on the continuously residing mind is both a collection of merit and a collection of wisdom, and so it is a cause to attain both the Form Body and the Truth Body of a Buddha.

There are three main channels, six channel wheels or chakras, and seventy-two thousand subsidiary channels. These are explained in *Clear Light of Bliss* and *Modern Buddhism*.

The red drops and the white drops that flow through our channels are the essence of blood and sperm respectively. During sexual intercourse the two lower tips of the central channels of a man and woman join and interpenetrate, thereby causing the heat inside the channels to increase. This causes the white drops of the man and the red drops of the woman to melt and descend through the channels, and this induces bliss. Experienced completion stage practitioners can penetrate their own central channel and thereby increase the heat within it. Because of this, the white or red drops melt and flow down and up within the central channel, causing the practitioner to experience spontaneous great bliss for an extended period of time. These practitioners can then use their continuously residing mind to meditate on emptiness and finally mix with emptiness non-dualistically.

The original red drop, from which the red drops and inner heat originate, is located principally at the centre of the navel channel wheel. The original white drop, from which the white drops and bodily strength originate, is located principally at the centre of the crown channel wheel. The white and red drops are sometimes called 'bodhichittas'. Actual bodhichitta, in this context, is spontaneous great bliss, which is the main cause for attaining enlightenment. Here the white and red drops are given the name of the effect because the melting and flowing of these drops within the central channel is a principal cause for the experience of spontaneous great bliss.

The quintessential drop is the indestructible drop located at our heart inside the central channel. It is about the size of a very small pea. Its upper half is white and its lower half is red. This white and red drop is called 'indestructible' because it will not divide until we die. During the process of dying our winds dissolve into this drop and cause it to open, thereby allowing our very subtle mind to leave and go to the next life.

The inner winds are special energy winds related to the mind that flow through our channels. Our mind cannot function without these winds. Our mind can be likened to a lame person and our winds to a vehicle. Just as a lame person can move from place to place only by using a vehicle, so our mind can move to a fresh object only by depending upon our winds. It is extremely important to develop pure winds because if pure winds predominate, the mind becomes calm and peaceful, whereas if impure winds predominate, negative thoughts and delusions arise. The winds that flow through the right and left channels are impure. These impure winds are a root of samsara because they give rise to many conceptual thoughts that obscure the clarity of our mind. The winds that flow through the central channel are pure. These are the winds that cause the wisdom of great bliss to arise.

The main point of Highest Yoga Tantra practice is to control the winds by gathering them from the subsidiary channels and dissolving them within the central channel. All completion stage meditations are methods to control our winds. When we gain control over our winds we also have full control over our mind. Je Tsongkhapa praised the yoga of winds because it is the principal method for controlling our winds. In *Lamp Thoroughly Illuminating the Five Stages* he says that all completion stage meditations are directly or indirectly included within the yoga of winds.

There are five root winds and five branch winds. The various functions, locations and characteristics of these winds are described in *Clear Light of Bliss* and *Modern Buddhism*.

Any wind that is the vehicle of a gross mind is a gross wind, and any wind that is the vehicle of a subtle mind is a subtle wind. The very subtle wind is the wind related to the very subtle mind. The very subtle wind and the very subtle mind have the same nature and both are called 'indestructible'. It is our very subtle wind that transforms into the illusory body and our very subtle mind that transforms into meaning clear light. Eventually our very subtle wind transforms into the Form Body of a Buddha and our very subtle mind transforms into a Buddha's mind.

MEDITATIONS ON THE PATH

This has two parts:

1 How to gather the inner winds into the central channel: an explanation of tummo meditation
2 Having centralized the inner winds, how to progress through the actual paths

HOW TO GATHER THE INNER WINDS INTO THE CENTRAL CHANNEL: AN EXPLANATION OF TUMMO MEDITATION

The actual methods for gathering the inner winds into the central channel are the yogas of the channels, drops and winds. These three yogas are included within the following tummo meditation. The explanation of tummo meditation has five parts:

1 Visualizing the central channel
2 Visualizing the tummo letter
3 Meditating on the blazing of the tummo fire
4 Purifying imperfections
5 Generating the experience of great bliss and emptiness

These five practices of tummo meditation are revealed in the dedication prayer in the extensive sadhana:

When the reddish-black RAM residing in the centre of
  the three channels at my navel
Has been set ablaze by my upper and lower winds,
And its cleansing fire has burned away the seventy-two
  thousand impure elements,
May my central channel be completely filled with pure
  drops.

221

The first line explains how to visualize the central channel and the tummo letter, the second line reveals the meditation that causes the tummo fire to blaze, the third line refers to purifying impurities through tummo meditation, and the fourth line refers to generating the experience of great bliss and emptiness, which depends upon pure drops flowing through the central channel.

In each session of meditation on tummo we begin by visualizing in front of us our root Guru in the aspect of Buddha Vajradharma. We firmly believe that his body is the synthesis of all Sangha Jewels, his speech the synthesis of all Dharma Jewels, and his mind the synthesis of all Buddha Jewels. We then go for refuge, generate a special bodhichitta motivation, and with strong faith in Guru Vajradharma offer a mandala with the request:

I request you my precious Guru, the essence of all
    Buddhas,
Please bless me to be successful in the profound
    practice of tummo meditation;
Please bless me to generate the union of great bliss and
    wisdom realizing emptiness by gathering my inner
    winds within the central channel;
Please bless me to pacify all outer, inner and secret
    obstacles.

We imagine that Guru Vajradharma dissolves into our heart and becomes one with us. We meditate on the emptiness of our body to prevent all ordinary appearances, and we then generate ourself as Vajrayogini. We imagine that our body is made of pure red light, non-obstructive like a rainbow, and we meditate single-pointedly on this.

VISUALIZING THE CENTRAL CHANNEL

The central channel is as thick as an arrow. From its lower tip at the sex organ it ascends straight to the crown, travelling midway between our right and left sides but slightly closer to our back than to our chest. At the crown it curves forward and terminates between the eyebrows.

We visualize the central channel as having four qualities: (1) it is very straight, like the trunk of a plantain tree; (2) inside it has an oily red colour, like pure blood; (3) it is very clear and transparent, like a candle flame; (4) it is very soft and flexible, like a lotus petal.

The right channel, called 'roma' in Tibetan, is red in colour, and the left channel, called 'kyangma', is white. Both are as thick as straws. The side channels and the central channel ascend from the navel to the crown alongside each other. At the crown, the side channels separate from the central channel and curve down to the two nostrils. The lower tips of the side channels join the central channel at the navel, forming a vacuole inside the central channel. We should contemplate the central channel's nature, colour, shape, location and qualities until we gain a rough mental image of it, and then meditate on this image. By repeatedly contemplating and meditating in this way, we will improve the clarity of our image of the central channel.

VISUALIZING THE TUMMO LETTER

'Tummo', or 'inner fire', refers to the original red drop, at the centre of the navel channel wheel, which has the nature of heat and is the source of all our bodily warmth. We visualize this drop as a red letter RAM, the seed-letter of the fire element, which is located inside the vacuole within the central channel at the centre of our navel channel wheel. This letter RAM, which is about the size of a sunflower seed, is dark red, radiates light, and is capped with a crescent moon, drop and nada. We can visualize the letter RAM either as the English letter R capped with a crescent moon, drop and nada, or as the Tibetan letter, shown in Appendix III. We first form a rough mental image of the RAM and we then imagine that our mind dissolves into it. We then concentrate on this single-pointedly for as long as possible. We need to do this meditation repeatedly over a period of time so that our experience of it improves.

MEDITATING ON THE BLAZING OF THE TUMMO FIRE

First we contract the muscles of the lower doors of the body slightly and draw in the stomach a little. We then imagine that all the lower winds enter the central channel and gather just below the letter RAM at the navel. Next we inhale gently and swallow, imagining that all the upper winds enter the central channel and gather at the point just above the letter RAM. The lower and upper winds now unite at the navel.

We imagine that because of the lower winds moving upwards inside the central channel, the letter RAM at the navel begins to glow like a red hot iron in a furnace, and the nada blazes like a very tiny but intense fire. While holding our breath and the winds at the navel we meditate single-pointedly on the tiny fire of the nada. Just before we feel any discomfort we exhale slowly through both nostrils, not through the mouth. We repeat this process seven, fourteen or twenty-one times in each session.

PURIFYING IMPERFECTIONS

While we are meditating on the blazing tummo fire we imagine that the light of the tummo fire gradually permeates all the channels of our body, and that due to this all the defects and imperfections of our channels, drops and winds are purified.

GENERATING THE EXPERIENCE OF GREAT BLISS
AND EMPTINESS

While meditating on the blazing tummo fire we imagine that all the pure red and white drops of the branch channels flow through the right and left channels into the central channel. They enter the central channel at the point where the side channels join it at the navel. Our central channel fills with pure red and white drops and we imagine that a strong feeling of great bliss arises. With this mind of great bliss we meditate on the emptiness of persons and phenomena.

Through skilful and continuous practice of tummo meditation our winds will enter, abide and dissolve within our central channel without difficulty, and we will experience the eight signs mentioned previously.

If, as a result of meditation, while inhaling and exhaling our breath flows through both nostrils at the same time and with equal strength, this is a sign that our winds have entered the central channel. After this, if, as a result of continued meditation, both the breath and the movement of the abdomen cease, these are signs that our winds are abiding, or remaining, within the central channel. At some point after this we will gradually experience the eight signs which indicate that the winds have actually dissolved within the central channel. A more detailed explanation of these signs is presented in *Clear Light of Bliss* and *Modern Buddhism*.

There are various systems for meditating on tummo. In the tummo meditation described in *Clear Light of Bliss* a short-AH is used instead of the letter RAM, and in other systems a letter BAM is used, but there is no essential difference between these three letters. The tummo meditation that is presented here is simpler than that presented in other instructions, mainly because it is not necessary to visualize channel wheels and so forth.

HAVING CENTRALIZED THE INNER WINDS, HOW TO PROGRESS THROUGH THE ACTUAL PATHS

This has two parts:

1 How to develop and improve great bliss
2 How to develop and improve the rainbow body

The main paths to full enlightenment are the wisdom of great bliss that realizes emptiness, and the illusory body. By improving these two we will attain the Truth Body and the Form Body of a Buddha.

HOW TO DEVELOP AND IMPROVE GREAT BLISS

We visualize our central channel as before, but this time without the side channels and the letter RAM. Just inside the entrance to the upper tip of the central channel, which is between our eyebrows, we visualize a small, red, single phenomena source. This fits neatly into the entrance of the central channel. The long thin point has a hole at its tip and is inside the central channel. Of the remaining three points, which are flush with our skin, one points upwards, one to the right, and one to the left. At the lower tip of our central channel we visualize a similar phenomena source, except that the tip inside the channel entrance has no hole.

Inside the phenomena source between the eyebrows we visualize a small spherical drop made of five-coloured light and having the nature of the wisdom of great bliss of all the Buddhas. The centre of the drop is white, the eastern portion is blue, the southern portion is yellow, the western portion is red, and the northern portion is green. Lights of these five colours radiate from the drop. We meditate on this drop single-pointedly while imagining that we experience bliss. We then imagine that the blissful five-coloured drop begins to ascend through our central channel until it reaches the centre of our crown channel wheel.

We meditate single-pointedly on this drop at our crown, and when a feeling of bliss arises we imagine that a tiny white droplet emerges from the central portion and falls slowly down our central channel. When this droplet reaches our throat we hold it there for a short time and imagine with strong concentration that we experience joy. Then the drop descends further until it reaches our heart. When it reaches our heart we hold it for a short time and experience supreme joy. When the drop descends to our navel we concentrate on the experience of extraordinary joy. We then allow the drop to descend until it reaches the lower tip of our central channel. When it reaches this point we experience spontaneous great joy.

We keep the drop at the lower tip of our central channel for a while and then imagine that it begins to ascend, rising slowly through our central channel. When it reaches our navel we experience joy of reverse order, which is greater than the fourth joy; when it reaches our heart we experience supreme joy of reverse order; when it reaches our throat we experience extraordinary joy of reverse order; and when it reaches our crown it dissolves back into the main drop and we experience spontaneous great joy of reverse order. We now meditate on the emptiness of persons and phenomena, trying to prevent any conventional appearances.

We can repeat this meditation three, seven or more times in one session. By doing this meditation regularly we will improve our experience of great bliss and emptiness.

HOW TO DEVELOP AND IMPROVE THE RAINBOW BODY

At our crown inside the central channel we visualize a five-coloured drop which is in essence the five Buddha families. The drop sparkles with five-coloured lights. We meditate on this drop and experience great bliss. While experiencing great bliss we imagine that the radiance of the five-coloured lights gradually extends until it pervades our whole body. Our body becomes a mass of rainbow light with the nature of the five Buddha families. The five lights continue to spread, gradually pervading our house, the immediate surroundings, the country, the whole world, and finally all three realms, including all living beings. Everything transforms into rainbow light, the nature of the five Buddha families. We meditate on this belief with strong concentration for as long as possible.

We then imagine that from its outer reaches, this expanse of light gradually gathers inward until finally all environments, enjoyments and living beings have dissolved into our body. Our body gradually dissolves, beginning with our feet, until finally it completely absorbs into the drop. This then dissolves into emptiness, and with a mind of great bliss we meditate on emptiness.

We then repeat the whole meditation exactly as before, from visualizing the five-coloured drop at our crown to dissolving everything into the drop and meditating on emptiness with a mind of great bliss. We can do this meditation seven, fourteen or twenty-one times in each session.

As a result of sincere and continuous training in this meditation we will experience certain signs that we will soon attain the rainbow body. We will become aware that our body is becoming lighter than usual, or that our normally dark shadow appears to be less distinct, or that our footprints are less deep, or that in conditions of extreme heat or cold, even if exposed to hot sun or immersed in freezing water for a long time, we experience no physical discomfort and our bliss never diminishes. We may even notice that if someone beats us with a stick we do not experience pain. The authentic rainbow body is the same as the actual illusory body.

HOW TO ATTAIN THE RESULTS

The ultimate result of practising generation stage and completion stage is the Union of No More Learning. In this context 'union' refers to the union of the pure body, the illusory body, and the pure mind, meaning clear light. This union is of two kinds, the union that needs learning and the Union of No More Learning. By progressing through the five stages of completion stage, eventually we will attain the Union of No More Learning, or Buddhahood.

The five stages of completion stage are: isolated speech, isolated mind, illusory body, meaning clear light and union. By doing the meditations described above we can improve our experience of these five stages, and then by relying upon an action mudra we can bring it to completion.

Before we are able to dissolve the winds into the indestructible drop at our heart we can experience the union of great bliss and emptiness by dissolving the winds into the central channel through the navel channel wheel, or through any of the points of entry into the central channel other than the heart channel wheel. This realization of great bliss and emptiness is called 'isolated speech' because with this experience the practitioner is isolated from, or free from, ordinary appearance and conception of his own body and speech. The realization of great bliss and emptiness attained through dissolving the winds into the indestructible drop at the heart is called 'isolated mind', because with this experience the practitioner is isolated from ordinary appearance and conception of his or her mind.

There are two stages in which the winds dissolve into the indestructible drop. The first stage, in which some of the ten winds dissolve, can be attained by solitary meditation. However, to attain the second stage, in which all ten winds, including the pervading wind, dissolve completely into the indestructible drop, it is necessary to rely upon an action mudra.

The correct time to rely upon an action mudra is when we are able to dissolve most of the winds into the indestructible drop through solitary meditation. The moment we dissolve all the winds into the indestructible drop by relying upon an action mudra we attain the isolated mind of ultimate example clear light. When we rise from this concentration we attain the illusory body, the third of the five completion stages. This illusory body is called the 'impure' illusory body because at this stage we have not yet abandoned all delusions completely.

Having attained this illusory body we meditate on emptiness with the clear light mind of bliss. The moment our clear light mind of bliss realizes emptiness directly, we attain meaning clear light and become a Superior being, who has completely abandoned all delusions.

When we rise from the concentration of meaning clear light we attain the pure illusory body, the actual vajra body. The next time we manifest meaning clear light we attain the union of the pure illusory body and meaning clear light. This union is called the union that needs learning and is the fifth of the five completion stages. By continuing to meditate on meaning clear light we will finally become completely free from the obstructions to omniscience, subtle mistaken appearances. Our illusory body will then become a Buddha's body and our meaning clear light will become a Buddha's mind. We shall then have attained Buddhahood – great enlightenment and the Union of No More Learning. This is the union of the ultimate illusory body, a Buddha's body, and the ultimate meaning clear light, a Buddha's mind.

Dedication

We should pray:

> Through the virtues I have collected by reading
> this book,
> May I become a Buddha for the benefit of all
> living beings;
> May all mother living beings be freed from the
> suffering of ignorance,
> And may they attain the omniscient wisdom of
> a Buddha.

Appendix I
The Condensed Meaning
of the Commentary

The following outlines are a condensed summary of the meaning of the commentary. They are like the root text, and the words of the commentary are like branches that grow from them. If possible we should try to memorize these outlines. In this way we will find that even if we cannot remember all the words of the commentary we will still be able to recall their essential meaning. This will be of great benefit if we have to explain the practice to others, and we will also find it easy to apply the meaning of the commentary to our actual practice. For example, if when we practise going for refuge according to the sadhana we recall the relevant outlines, we will be able to remember all the essential stages of going for refuge – visualizing the objects of refuge, developing renunciation, developing compassion, developing conviction in the power of the Three Jewels, and reciting the refuge prayer – and we will then be able to practise accordingly.

The outlines are presented in the traditional manner so as to preserve the blessings of the lineage. In general they correspond to headings within the commentary, although some of the divisions are not listed separately within the commentary. Moreover the sequence of the outlines does not always correspond to the sequence of the commentary. For example, strictly speaking the section on the actual generation stage meditation is the third outline of the yoga of self-generation, and is listed as such, but within the commentary it is explained later, just before the yoga of verbal and mental recitation, because this is the place in the sadhana where we actually do the meditation.

The Condensed Meaning
of the Commentary

———

The commentary to the Highest Yoga Tantra practice of Venerable Vajrayogini has three parts:

1 The preliminary explanation
2 The commentary to the generation and completion stages
3 Dedication

The preliminary explanation has seven parts:

1 Generating a correct motivation
2 The origin and lineage of these instructions
3 The benefits of these instructions
4 Biographies of past Buddhist practitioners who gained realizations through practising these instructions
5 The qualifications necessary for practising these instructions
6 The four special causes of swift attainments
7 What are outer and inner Dakini Lands?

The benefits of these instructions has ten parts:

1 By practising these instructions we quickly receive great and powerful blessings
2 These instructions are a synthesis of all essential instructions
3 These instructions are easy to practise
4 By practising these instructions we can swiftly accomplish attainments
5 These instructions include a special body mandala practice
6 These instructions include an uncommon yoga of inconceivability

7 We can practise both generation stage and completion stage together
8 These instructions are especially suitable for those with strong desirous attachment
9 These instructions are particularly appropriate for this degenerate age
10 Vajrayogini's mantra has many special qualities

The four special causes of swift attainments has four parts:

1 Having unwavering faith
2 Having wisdom that overcomes doubts and misgivings concerning the practice
3 Integrating all our spiritual training into the practice of one Yidam, or Enlightened Deity
4 Practising in secret

The commentary to the generation and completion stages has two parts:

1 Generation stage
2 Completion stage

Generation stage has two parts:

1 The eleven yogas of generation stage
2 How to attain outer Dakini Land through the practice of generation stage

The eleven yogas of generation stage has eleven parts:

1 The yoga of sleeping
2 The yoga of rising
3 The yoga of experiencing nectar
4 The yoga of immeasurables
5 The yoga of the Guru
6 The yoga of self-generation
7 The yoga of purifying migrators
8 The yoga of being blessed by Heroes and Heroines
9 The yoga of verbal and mental recitation
10 The yoga of inconceivability
11 The yoga of daily actions

The yoga of sleeping has two parts:

1 The benefits of practising the yoga of sleeping
2 The way to practise the yoga of sleeping

The benefits of practising the yoga of sleeping has seven parts:

1 We accumulate great merit
2 All our hindrances and obstacles are dispelled
3 We will receive direct care and guidance from Vajrayogini in all our future lives
4 We will be blessed by the Heroines of the twenty-four holy places of Heruka
5 Our practice of generation stage meditation will be strengthened and stabilized
6 We will attain both outer and inner Dakini Lands
7 We will attain enlightenment quickly

The way to practise the yoga of sleeping has two parts:

1 The yoga of sleeping according to generation stage
2 The yoga of sleeping according to completion stage

The yoga of rising has two parts:

1 The yoga of rising according to generation stage
2 The yoga of rising according to completion stage

The yoga of immeasurables has seven parts:

1 Going for refuge
2 Generating the supreme good heart, bodhichitta
3 Receiving blessings
4 Instantaneous self-generation as Vajrayogini
5 Blessing the inner offering
6 Blessing the outer offerings
7 Meditation and recitation of Vajrasattva

Going for refuge has two parts:

1 General explanation
2 The practice of refuge

The practice of refuge has five parts:

1 Visualizing the objects of refuge
2 Developing renunciation
3 Developing compassion
4 Developing conviction in the power of the
   Three Jewels
5 Reciting the refuge prayer

Blessing the inner offering has five parts:

1 The benefits
2 The basis of the inner offering
3 The visual object of the inner offering
4 How to bless the inner offering
5 The significance of the inner offering

How to bless the inner offering has four parts:

1 Clearance
2 Purification
3 Generation
4 Transformation

Generation has two parts:

1 Generating the container
2 Generating the contained substances

Transformation has three parts:

1 Purifying faults
2 Transforming into nectar
3 Increasing

Blessing the outer offerings has two parts:

1 General explanation
2 How to bless the outer offerings

How to bless the outer offerings has four parts:

1 Clearance
2 Purification
3 Generation
4 Actual blessing

Meditation and recitation of Vajrasattva has three parts:

1 Developing the intention to purify
2 Visualizing Vajrasattva
3 Reciting the mantra

Reciting the mantra has three parts:

1 The mantra to be recited
2 How to combine recitation with purification
3 Conclusion

How to combine recitation with purification has two parts:

1 General explanation
2 Purification in seven rounds

Purification in seven rounds has seven parts:

1 Dispelling negativity from above
2 Dispelling negativity from below
3 Destroying negativity at the heart
4 Purification through receiving the vase
   empowerment
5 Purification through receiving the secret
   empowerment
6 Purification through receiving the wisdom-mudra
   empowerment
7 Purification through receiving the word
   empowerment

The yoga of the Guru has two parts:

1 General explanation
2 The practice of Guru yoga

The practice of Guru yoga has six parts:

1 Visualization
2 Prostration
3 Offerings
4 Requesting the lineage Gurus
5 Receiving the blessings of the four empowerments
6 Absorbing the Gurus

Offerings has seven parts:

1 Outer offerings
2 Inner offering
3 Secret offering
4 Thatness offering
5 Offering our spiritual practice
6 Kusali tsog offering
7 Offering the mandala

The yoga of self-generation has three parts:

1 Bringing the three bodies into the path
2 Checking meditation on the mandala and the beings within it
3 The actual generation stage meditation

Bringing the three bodies into the path has two parts:

1 General explanation
2 The practice of bringing the three bodies into the path

The practice of bringing the three bodies into the path has three parts:

1 Bringing death into the path to the Truth Body
2 Bringing the intermediate state into the path to the Enjoyment Body
3 Bringing rebirth into the path to the Emanation Body

The actual generation stage meditation has three parts:

1 What is generation stage?
2 Training in gross generation stage meditation
3 Training in subtle generation stage meditation

Training in gross generation stage meditation has two parts:

1 Training in divine pride
2 Training in clear appearance

Training in clear appearance has two parts:

1 Training in clear appearance on the general aspect
2 Training in clear appearance on specific aspects

THE CONDENSED MEANING OF THE COMMENTARY

The yoga of being blessed by Heroes and Heroines has six parts:

    1 Meditation on the body mandala
    2 Absorbing the wisdom beings and mixing the three messengers
    3 Putting on the armour
    4 Granting empowerment and adorning the crown
    5 Making offerings to the self-generation
    6 Eight lines of praise to the Mother

Meditation on the body mandala has two parts:

    1 General explanation
    2 The actual meditation

Absorbing the wisdom beings and mixing the three messengers has two parts:

    1 Absorbing the wisdom beings into the commitment beings
    2 Mixing the three messengers

The yoga of verbal and mental recitation has four parts:

    1 The mantra to be recited
    2 The benefits of reciting this mantra
    3 Actual mantra recitation
    4 Explanation of close retreat

Actual mantra recitation has two parts:

    1 Verbal recitation
    2 Mental recitation with two completion stage meditations

Mental recitation with two completion stage meditations has three parts:

    1 First completion stage meditation
    2 Mental recitation
    3 Second completion stage meditation

Explanation of close retreat has four parts:

1 What is a retreat?
2 Explanation of close retreats of signs, time and numbers
3 Preliminary practices for close retreat
4 The actual close retreat

Preliminary practices for close retreat has two parts:

1 Distant preliminaries
2 Close preliminaries

Distant preliminaries has nine parts:

1 Going for refuge
2 Vajrasattva mantra recitation
3 Prostrations
4 Mandala offerings
5 Guru yoga
6 Samayavajra mantra recitation
7 Vajradaka burning offering
8 Making images of the body or mind of a Buddha
9 Water offerings

The yoga of daily actions has two parts:

1 The main practice
2 The branch practices

The branch practices has six parts:

1 The yoga of eating
2 The tsog offering
3 Burning offerings
4 Offerings of the tenth days
5 Torma offerings
6 Actions of the left

Offerings of the tenth days has three parts:

1 Extensive offerings of the tenth days
2 Middling offerings of the tenth days
3 Brief offerings of the tenth days

Extensive offerings of the tenth days has two parts:

1 The preparations
2 The actual offering

Torma offerings has two parts:

1 The preparations
2 The actual torma offering

How to attain outer Dakini Land through the practice of generation stage has three parts:

1 How Vajrayogini practitioners who possess great fortune attain outer Dakini Land, known as Keajra Pure Land
2 How Vajrayogini practitioners who possess middling fortune attain outer Dakini Land
3 How Vajrayogini practitioners who possess least fortune attain outer Dakini Land

How Vajrayogini practitioners who possess middling fortune attain outer Dakini Land has three parts:

1 Completing a great close retreat emphasizing self-generation
2 Accomplishing the mandala emphasizing the in-front-generation
3 Actualizing the effect

Completion stage has two parts:

1 What is completion stage?
2 How to attain inner Dakini Land through the practice of completion stage

How to attain inner Dakini Land through the practice of completion stage has three parts:

1 Explanation of the three basic objects of knowledge
2 Meditations on the path
3 How to attain the results

Explanation of the three basic objects of knowledge has three parts:

1 Objects of knowledge related to the body
2 Objects of knowledge related to the mind
3 Objects of knowledge related to the elements

Meditations on the path has two parts:

1 How to gather the inner winds into the central channel: an explanation of tummo meditation
2 Having centralized the inner winds, how to progress through the actual paths

How to gather the inner winds into the central channel: an explanation of tummo meditation, has five parts:

1 Visualizing the central channel
2 Visualizing the tummo letter
3 Meditating on the blazing of the tummo fire
4 Purifying imperfections
5 Generating the experience of great bliss and emptiness

Having centralized the inner winds, how to progress through the actual paths, has two parts:

1 How to develop and improve great bliss
2 How to develop and improve the rainbow body

Appendix II
Sadhanas

CONTENTS

Liberating Prayer

PRAISE TO BUDDHA SHAKYAMUNI

O Blessed One, Shakyamuni Buddha,
Precious treasury of compassion,
Bestower of supreme inner peace,

You, who love all beings without exception,
Are the source of happiness and goodness;
And you guide us to the liberating path.

Your body is a wishfulfilling jewel,
Your speech is supreme, purifying nectar,
And your mind is refuge for all living beings.

With folded hands I turn to you,
Supreme unchanging friend,
I request from the depths of my heart:

Please give me the light of your wisdom
To dispel the darkness of my mind
And to heal my mental continuum.

Please nourish me with your goodness,
That I in turn may nourish all beings
With an unceasing banquet of delight.

Through your compassionate intention,
Your blessings and virtuous deeds,
And my strong wish to rely upon you,

May all suffering quickly cease
And all happiness and joy be fulfilled;
And may holy Dharma flourish for evermore.

Colophon: This prayer was composed by Venerable Geshe Kelsang Gyatso and is recited at the beginning of teachings, meditations and prayers in Kadampa Buddhist Centres throughout the world.

The Blissful Path

———

THE CONDENSED SELF-GENERATION
SADHANA OF VAJRAYOGINI

Compiled by
Geshe Kelsang Gyatso

Guru Vajradharma

The Blissful Path

THE CONDENSED SELF-GENERATION SADHANA OF VAJRAYOGINI

Those who wish to train in the self-generation of Vajrayogini as a daily practice, but who have insufficient time or ability to practise either the extensive or the middling sadhana, can fulfil their aim by practising this short sadhana with strong faith.

THE ACTUAL SADHANA

Visualizing the objects of refuge

In the space before me appears my root Guru in the aspect of Buddha Vajradharma, the manifestation of all Buddhas' speech, with Chakrasambara Father and Mother at his heart, surrounded by the assembly of lineage Gurus; Yidams – the enlightened Deities; Three Precious Jewels – Buddha, Dharma and Sangha; and Dharma Protectors.

We meditate on this great assembly of enlightened holy beings with strong faith. By visualizing our root Guru in this way we will receive the special blessings of the speech of all Buddhas. Through this we can quickly attain the realizations of speech – the realizations of the Dharma instructions of Sutra and Tantra. Only through Dharma realizations can we cease our samsaric problems in general and human problems in particular.

Training in going for refuge, the gateway through which we enter Buddhism

While imagining ourself and all sentient beings going for refuge together, we recite the following refuge prayer three times:

I and all sentient beings as extensive as space, from now
    until we attain enlightenment,
Go for refuge to the Gurus, the supreme Spiritual Guides,
Go for refuge to the Buddhas, the fully enlightened beings,
Go for refuge to Dharma, the precious teachings of Buddha,
Go for refuge to Sangha, the pure spiritual friends.

(3x)

If we sincerely go for refuge to the Gurus, Buddhas, Dharma and Sangha this will lead us to the correct path, the liberating path that directly protects us from suffering and fear. In this practice, principally we should improve our experience of renunciation through continually contemplating and meditating on the instructions of renunciation given in Modern Buddhism. *In this way we should lead ourself to the correct path, such as the realization of renunciation. The realization of renunciation is actual Dharma.*

Generating the supreme good heart, bodhichitta, the gateway through which we enter the path to great enlightenment

We should make the following determination:

Once I have attained the state of complete enlightenment, Buddhahood, I shall free all sentient beings from the ocean of samsara's suffering and lead them to the bliss of full enlightenment. For this purpose I shall practise the stages of Vajrayogini's path.   (3x)

In this practice, principally we should improve our experience of learning to cherish others and compassion for all living beings through continually contemplating and meditating on the instructions of these trainings given in Modern Buddhism. *In this way we should lead ourself to the path to great enlightenment.*

Receiving blessings

Now, from the depths of our heart, we recite:

I prostrate and go for refuge to the Gurus and Three Precious Jewels. Please bless my mental continuum.

(3x)

Due to requesting in this way, the great assembly of enlightened holy beings before me melts into the form of white, red and dark blue rays of light. These dissolve into me and I receive the special blessings of all Buddhas upon my very subtle body, speech and mind.

We meditate on this belief for a short time.

Training in the three bringings

We should engage in the following contemplations and meditations completely free from distractions so that we can easily make progress.

Bringing death into the path to the Truth Body, Buddha's very subtle body

The entire world and its inhabitants melt into light and dissolve into my body. My body also melts into light and slowly diminishes in size until finally it dissolves into emptiness. This resembles the way in which all the appearances of this life dissolve at death. I experience the clear light of death, which in nature is bliss, and my mind the clear light of bliss becomes inseparably one with emptiness, the mere absence of all the things that I normally see. I perceive nothing other than emptiness, ultimate truth. I am Truth Body Vajrayogini.

Venerable Vajrayogini

*We meditate single-pointedly on this divine pride for as long
as possible. If we do this meditation at the time of our death
this will prevent us from taking samsaric rebirth and lead
us to take rebirth in the Pure Land of Keajra. Thus we will
attain permanent liberation from all suffering. Vajrayogini
imputed upon a Buddha's Truth Body is Truth Body
Vajrayogini, definitive Vajrayogini.*

Bringing the intermediate state into the path to the Enjoyment Body, Buddha's subtle Form Body

From the emptiness of the Truth Body, the Dharmakaya, I
instantaneously transform into Enjoyment Body Vajrayogini
in the form of an oval of red light about twelve inches high
and six inches wide, standing vertically on an eight-petalled
lotus and a sun cushion. This resembles the way in which
the body of an intermediate state being arises out of the
clear light of death. I am Enjoyment Body Vajrayogini.

*We meditate on this divine pride for a short time. Vajrayogini
imputed upon a Buddha's subtle Form Body is Enjoyment
Body Vajrayogini.*

Bringing rebirth into the path to the Emanation Body, Buddha's gross Form Body

In the vast space of emptiness of all phenomena, the nature
of my purified mistaken appearance of all phenomena,
which is the Pure Land of Keajra, I appear as Vajrayogini
who is the manifestation of the wisdom of the clear light
of all Buddhas. I have a red-coloured body of light, with
one face and two hands, and I assume the form of a
sixteen-year-old in the prime of my youth. Although I
have this appearance it is not other than the emptiness
of all phenomena. I am Emanation Body Vajrayogini.

*We meditate on this self-generation for as long as possible with
the recognition that ourself as Vajrayogini, the appearance,
and emptiness of all phenomena is one entity not two. Our
meditation on self-generation has the power to reduce and
cease our self-grasping. In this practice we should improve*

253

our experience of training in divine pride and training in clear appearance through continually contemplating and meditating on the instructions of these trainings given on pages 156-162.

We can train in a special tummo meditation at this point. A clear and detailed explanation on how to do this can be found on pages 221-225.

Reciting the mantra

At my heart is wisdom being Vajrayogini, definitive Vajrayogini, who is the synthesis of the body, speech and mind of all Buddhas.

O My Guru Deity Vajrayogini,
Please bestow upon me and all sentient beings
The attainments of the enlightened body, speech
    and mind.
Please pacify our outer, inner and secret obstacles.
Please build within us the basic foundation for all these
    attainments.

For this request we recite the three-OM mantra at least as many times as we have promised.

OM OM OM SARWA BUDDHA DAKINIYE VAJRA WARNANIYE VAJRA BEROTZANIYE HUM HUM HUM PHAT PHAT PHAT SÖHA.

Outer obstacles are harm received from humans and non-humans, as well as from inanimate objects such as fire, water and so forth, inner obstacles are our delusions such as anger, attachment and ignorance, and the secret obstacle is our subtle mistaken appearance of all phenomena.

At this point, if we wish, we can make a tsog offering. The ritual prayer for making a tsog offering can be found on pages 325-331.

Dedication

Through the virtues I have accumulated by meditation and
    recitation of Vajrayogini,

May I receive the special care of Venerable Vajrayogini and
  her emanation Dakinis,
And through receiving their powerful blessings upon my
  very subtle body, speech and mind
May I attain enlightenment quickly to liberate all living
  beings.

Prayers for the Virtuous Tradition

So that the tradition of Je Tsongkhapa,
The King of the Dharma, may flourish,
May all obstacles be pacified
And may all favourable conditions abound.

Through the two collections of myself and others
Gathered throughout the three times,
May the doctrine of Conqueror Losang Dragpa
Flourish for evermore.

The nine-line *Migtsema* prayer

Tsongkhapa, crown ornament of the scholars of the
  Land of the Snows,
You are Buddha Shakyamuni and Vajradhara, the
  source of all attainments,
Avalokiteshvara, the treasury of unobservable
  compassion,
Manjushri, the supreme stainless wisdom,
And Vajrapani, the destroyer of the hosts of maras.
O Venerable Guru-Buddha, synthesis of all Three Jewels,
With my body, speech and mind, respectfully I make
  requests:
Please grant your blessings to ripen and liberate myself
  and others,
And bestow the common and supreme attainments.   (3x)

Colophon: This sadhana or ritual prayer for the spiritual attainment
of Vajrayogini was compiled by Venerable Geshe Kelsang Gyatso from
traditional sources, 2012.

Dakini Yoga

THE MIDDLING SELF-GENERATION
SADHANA OF VAJRAYOGINI

Compiled by
Geshe Kelsang Gyatso

Introduction

Everyone who has received a Highest Yoga Tantra empowerment has a commitment to practise six-session yoga. This six-session yoga has been specially arranged for those who have received a Vajrayogini empowerment.

Six-session yoga can be practised in different ways according to our ability and how much time we have. If we are new to the practice, or if we are very busy, we can keep our basic commitments by reciting the *Condensed Six-session Yoga* according to the instructions given on pages 275-278

If we have more time, we can recite the main six-session practice, *Dakini Yoga*, for one session, and the *Condensed Six-session Yoga* for the remaining five sessions. We can then gradually increase this according to our time and ability, until eventually we are able to recite *Dakini Yoga* in all six sessions.

When we have the time, it is very helpful to read through the vows and commitments listed on pages 279-284.

If we can, it is best to do one session every four hours throughout the day and the night, but if this is not possible we can do three sessions together in the morning and three sessions together in the evening. If we do this using the main six-session yoga, *Dakini Yoga*, it is possible to abbreviate the recitations in the manner explained on page 273.

Guru Vajradharma

Dakini Yoga

Going for refuge

I and all sentient beings, until we achieve enlightenment,
Go for refuge to Buddha, Dharma and Sangha.   (3x)

> *This fulfils the first three commitments of the family of
> Buddha Vairochana, to go for refuge to Buddha, to go for
> refuge to Dharma and to go for refuge to Sangha.*

Generating bodhichitta

Through the virtues I collect by giving and other
     perfections,
May I become a Buddha for the benefit of all.   (3x)

Generating the four immeasurables

May everyone be happy,
May everyone be free from misery,
May no one ever be separated from their happiness,
May everyone have equanimity, free from hatred and
     attachment.

> *The first immeasurable fulfils the fourth commitment of
> the family of Buddha Ratnasambhava, to give love; and the
> fourth immeasurable fulfils the third commitment of the
> family of Buddha Ratnasambhava, to give fearlessness.*

Generating aspiring bodhichitta by means of ritual

From this time forth until I become a Buddha,
I shall keep even at the cost of my life
A mind wishing to attain complete enlightenment
To free all living beings from the fears of samsara and
     solitary peace.

Dorjechang Trijang Rinpoche

Taking the Bodhisattva vows

O Gurus, Buddhas and Bodhisattvas
Please listen to what I now say.
Just as all the previous Sugatas, the Buddhas,
Generated the mind of enlightenment, bodhichitta,
And accomplished all the stages
Of the Bodhisattva's training,
So will I too, for the sake of all beings,
Generate the mind of enlightenment
And accomplish all the stages
Of the Bodhisattva's training.   (3x)

Generating joy

Now my life has borne great fruit,
My human life has attained great meaning;
Today I am born into the lineage of Buddha
And have become a Bodhisattva.

Contemplating conscientiousness

All my actions from now on
Shall accord with this noble lineage;
And upon this lineage, pure and faultless,
I shall never bring disgrace.

Visualizing the Guru

In the space before me arising from the appearance of the
exalted wisdom of non-dual purity and clarity is a celestial
mansion which is square with four doorways, ornaments
and archways, and complete with all the essential features.
In the centre on a jewelled throne supported by eight great
lions, on a seat of a lotus of various colours, a sun, and
a moon, sits my kind root Guru in the aspect of Buddha
Vajradharma. He has a red-coloured body, one face, and
two hands, which are crossed at his heart and hold a vajra
and bell. His hair is tied up in a topknot and he sits with
his legs crossed in the vajra posture. He assumes the form
of a sixteen-year-old in the prime of his youth, adorned
with silks and all the bone and jewelled ornaments.

At his heart is Vajrayogini displaying a sensuous posture and a slightly wrathful smile. At her heart is the concentration being, a red letter BAM, from which light radiates and invites the wisdom beings.

DZA HUM BAM HO
They become non-dual.

This fulfils the fourth commitment of the family of Buddha Akshobya, to rely sincerely upon our Spiritual Guide.

Prostration

Vajra Holder, my jewel-like Guru,
Through whose kindness I can accomplish
The state of great bliss in an instant,
At your lotus feet humbly I bow.

O Glorious Vajrayogini,
Chakravatin Dakini Queen,
Who have five wisdoms and three bodies,
To you Saviour of all I prostrate.

Offering goddesses emanate from my heart and perform the offerings.

Outer offerings

OM AHRGHAM PARTITZA SÖHA
OM PADÄM PARTITZA SÖHA
OM VAJRA PUPE AH HUM SÖHA
OM VAJRA DHUPE AH HUM SÖHA
OM VAJRA DIWE AH HUM SÖHA
OM VAJRA GÄNDHE AH HUM SÖHA
OM VAJRA NEWIDE AH HUM SÖHA
OM VAJRA SHAPTA AH HUM SÖHA

OM AH VAJRA ADARSHE HUM
OM AH VAJRA WINI HUM
OM AH VAJRA GÄNDHE HUM
OM AH VAJRA RASE HUM
OM AH VAJRA PARSHE HUM
OM AH VAJRA DHARME HUM

Inner offering

OM GURU VAJRA YOGINI OM AH HUM

Secret offering

Contemplate that innumerable knowledge goddesses such as Pemachen emanate from your heart and assume the form of Vajrayogini. Guru Father and Mother embrace and experience uncontaminated bliss.

And I offer most attractive illusory mudras,
A host of messengers born from places, born from mantra
    and spontaneously born,
With slender bodies, skilled in the sixty-four arts of love,
And possessing the splendour of youthful beauty.

Thatness offering

Remember that the three circles of the offering are indivisible bliss and emptiness.

I offer you the supreme, ultimate bodhichitta,
A great, exalted wisdom of spontaneous bliss free from
    obstructions,
Inseparable from the nature of all phenomena, the sphere
    of freedom from elaboration,
Effortless, and beyond words, thoughts and expressions.

Making outer, inner, secret and thatness offerings fulfils the first commitment of the family of Buddha Amoghasiddhi, to make offerings to our Spiritual Guide.

Eight lines of praise to the Mother

OM I prostrate to Vajravarahi, the Blessed Mother HUM
    HUM PHAT
OM To the Superior and powerful Knowledge Lady
    unconquered by the three realms HUM HUM PHAT
OM To you who destroy all fears of evil spirits with your
    great vajra HUM HUM PHAT
OM To you with controlling eyes who remain as the vajra
    seat unconquered by others HUM HUM PHAT

OM To you whose wrathful fierce form desiccates Brahma
    HUM HUM PHAT
OM To you who terrify and dry up demons, conquering
    those in other directions HUM HUM PHAT
OM To you who conquer all those who make us dull,
    rigid and confused HUM HUM PHAT
OM I bow to Vajravarahi, the Great Mother, the Dakini
    consort who fulfils all desires HUM HUM PHAT

Kusali tsog offering

My own mind, the powerful Lady of Dakini Land, the size
of only a thumb, leaves through the crown of my head
and comes face to face with my root Guru. Once again
I return and, slicing the skull from my old body, place
it upon a grate of three human heads which has arisen
instantaneously. I chop up the rest of my flesh, blood and
bones, and heap it inside. By staring with wide open eyes
I purify, transform and increase it into an ocean of nectar.
OM AH HUM HA HO HRIH   (3x)

Innumerable offering goddesses holding skullcups emanate
from my heart. With the skullcups they scoop up nectar
and offer it to the guests, who partake by drawing it
through their tongues which are straws of vajra-light.

I offer this nectar of commitment substance
To my root Guru, the nature of the four [Buddha] bodies;
May you be pleased.
OM AH HUM   (7x)

I offer this nectar of commitment substance
To the lineage Gurus, the source of attainments;
May you be pleased.
OM AH HUM

I offer this nectar of commitment substance
To the assembly of Gurus, Yidams, Three Jewels and
    Protectors;
May you be pleased.
OM AH HUM

I offer this nectar of commitment substance
To the guardians who reside in the local places and
    in the regions;
May you assist me.
OM AH HUM

I offer this nectar of commitment substance
To all sentient beings in the six realms and the
    intermediate state;
May you be freed.
OM AH HUM

Through this offering all the guests are satiated with an
    uncontaminated bliss
And the sentient beings attain the Truth Body free from
    obstructions.
The three circles of the offering are the nature of non-dual
    bliss and emptiness,
Beyond words, thoughts and expressions.

Completing the seven limbs

*Within the practice of the seven limbs, the first two,
prostrations and offerings, have been accomplished. Now we
briefly practise the five remaining limbs:*

I confess my wrong deeds from all time,
And rejoice in the virtues of all.
Please stay until samsara ceases,
And turn the Wheel of Dharma for us.
I dedicate all virtues to great enlightenment.

Offering the mandala

*Recite either the long mandala offering and the two short
verses that follow, or just the two short verses:*

OM VAJRA BHUMI AH HUM
Great and powerful golden ground,
OM VAJRA REKHE AH HUM
At the edge the iron fence stands around the outer circle.
In the centre Mount Meru the king of mountains,
Around which are four continents:

265

In the east, Purvavideha, in the south, Jambudipa,
In the west, Aparagodaniya, in the north, Uttarakuru.
Each has two sub-continents:
Deha and Videha, Tsamara and Abatsamara,
Satha and Uttaramantrina, Kurava and Kaurava.
The mountain of jewels, the wish-granting tree,
The wish-granting cow, and the harvest unsown.
The precious wheel, the precious jewel,
The precious queen, the precious minister,
The precious elephant, the precious supreme horse,
The precious general, and the great treasure vase.
The goddess of beauty, the goddess of garlands,
The goddess of song, the goddess of dance,
The goddess of flowers, the goddess of incense,
The goddess of light, and the goddess of scent.
The sun and the moon, the precious umbrella,
The banner of victory in every direction.
In the centre all treasures of both gods and men,
An excellent collection with nothing left out.
I offer this to you my kind root Guru and lineage Gurus,
To all of you sacred and glorious Gurus;
Please accept with compassion for migrating beings,
And having accepted please grant us your blessings.

O Treasure of Compassion, my Refuge and Protector,
I offer you the mountain, continents, precious objects,
    treasure vase, sun and moon,
Which have arisen from my aggregates, sources and
    elements
As aspects of the exalted wisdom of spontaneous bliss
    and emptiness.

I offer without any sense of loss
The objects that give rise to my attachment, hatred and
    confusion,
My friends, enemies and strangers, our bodies and
    enjoyments;
Please accept these and bless me to be released directly from
    the three poisons.

IDAM GURU RATNA MANDALAKAM NIRYATAYAMI

266

Receiving the blessings of the four empowerments

I request you O Guru incorporating all objects of refuge,
Please grant me your blessings,
Please grant me the four empowerments completely,
And bestow on me, please, the state of the four bodies.   (3x)

Contemplate that as a result of your requests:

White light rays and nectars radiate from the OM at the
    forehead of my Guru.
They dissolve into my forehead, purifying the negativities
    and obstructions of my body.
I receive the vase empowerment, and the blessings of my
    Guru's body enter my body.

Red light rays and nectars radiate from the AH at the
    throat of my Guru.
They dissolve into my throat, purifying the negativities
    and obstructions of my speech.
I receive the secret empowerment, and the blessings of my
    Guru's speech enter my speech.

Blue light rays and nectars radiate from the HUM at the
    heart of my Guru.
They dissolve into my heart, purifying the negativities
    and obstructions of my mind.
I receive the wisdom-mudra empowerment, and the
    blessings of my Guru's mind enter my mind.

White, red and blue light rays and nectars radiate from
    the letters at my Guru's three places.
They dissolve into my three places, purifying the
    negativities and obstructions of my body, speech and
    mind.
I receive the fourth empowerment, the precious word
    empowerment, and the blessings of my Guru's body,
    speech and mind enter my body, speech and mind.

Brief request

I request you my precious Guru, the essence of all Buddhas
of the three times, please bless my mental continuum.   (3x)

Absorbing the Guru

Requested in this way, my root Guru, out of affection for
me, melts into the form of red light and, entering through
the crown of my head, mixes inseparably with my mind in
the aspect of a red letter BAM at my heart.

Bringing death into the path to the Truth Body

This very letter BAM expands and spreads to the ends of
space whereby all worlds and their beings become the
nature of bliss and emptiness. Once again, contracting
gradually from the edges, it becomes an extremely minute
letter BAM, which dissolves in stages from the bottom up
into the nada. Then even the nada disappears and becomes
the Truth Body of inseparable bliss and emptiness.
OM SHUNYATA GYANA VAJRA SÖBHAWA ÄMAKO HAM

Bringing the intermediate state into the path to the Enjoyment Body

From the state of emptiness, where all appearance has
gathered like this, there appears a red letter BAM standing
upright in space, in essence an aspect of my own mind,
the exalted wisdom of non-dual bliss and emptiness.

Bringing rebirth into the path to the Emanation Body

From the state of emptiness, from EH EH comes a red
phenomena source, a double tetrahedron. Inside from AH
comes a moon mandala, white with a shade of red. Upon
this, standing in a circle counter-clockwise, rests the mantra
OM OM OM SARWA BUDDHA DAKINIYE VAJRA WARNANIYE
VAJRA BEROTZANIYE HUM HUM HUM PHAT PHAT PHAT
SÖHA.

I, the letter BAM in space, see the moon and, motivated to
take rebirth in its centre, enter the centre of the moon.

Light rays radiate from the moon, letter BAM and mantra
rosary, making all worlds and beings of samsara and
nirvana into the nature of Venerable Vajrayogini. These
gather back and dissolve into the letter BAM and mantra

rosary, which change completely into the supported and supporting mandala of Vajrayogini, fully and all at once.

Checking meditation on the mandala and the beings within it

Furthermore, there is the vajra ground, fence, tent and canopy, outside of which a mass of five-coloured fires blaze, swirling counter-clockwise. Inside these is the circle of the eight great charnel grounds, the Ferocious One and so forth. In the centre of these is a red phenomena source, a double tetrahedron, with its broad neck facing upwards and its fine tip pointing downwards. Except for the front and back, each of the other four corners is marked by a pink joy swirl whirling counter-clockwise.

Inside the phenomena source, in the centre of an eight-petalled lotus of various colours, is a sun mandala. Upon this I arise in the form of Venerable Vajrayogini. My outstretched right leg treads on the breast of red Kalarati. My bent left leg treads on the head of black Bhairawa, which is bent backwards. I have a red-coloured body which shines with a brilliance like that of the fire of the aeon. I have one face, two hands, and three eyes looking towards the Pure Land of the Dakinis. My right hand, outstretched and pointing downwards, holds a curved knife marked with a vajra. My left holds up a skullcup filled with blood which I partake of with my upturned mouth. My left shoulder holds a khatanga marked with a vajra from which hang a damaru, bell and triple banner. My black hair hanging straight covers my back down to my waist. In the prime of my youth, my desirous breasts are full and I show the manner of generating bliss. My head is adorned with five human skulls, and I wear a necklace of fifty human skulls. Naked, I am adorned with five mudras and stand in the centre of a blazing fire of exalted wisdom. My crown is adorned by Father and Mother, Vairochana-Heruka.

Practising the three bringings and meditating on the mandala fulfils the first three commitments of the family of

Venerable Vajrayogini

Buddha Akshobya, to keep a vajra to remind us of great bliss, to keep a bell to remind us of emptiness, and to generate ourself as the Deity.

At this point, if you have time, you can instantaneously generate the body mandala. Meditate briefly on the body mandala and then on the actual generation stage meditation in accordance with the commentary.

Reciting the mantra

At my heart inside a red phenomena source, a double tetrahedron, in the centre of a moon mandala, is a letter BAM encircled by a red-coloured mantra rosary standing counter-clockwise. From these, immeasurable rays of red light radiate. They purify the negativities and obstructions of all sentient beings and make offerings to all the Buddhas. All the power and force of their blessings is invoked in the form of rays of red light, which dissolve into the letter BAM and mantra rosary, blessing my mental continuum.

OM OM OM SARWA BUDDHA DAKINIYE VAJRA WARNANIYE VAJRA BEROTZANIYE HUM HUM HUM PHAT PHAT PHAT SÖHA

Recite at least as many mantras as you have promised to.

Practising giving

From this moment on, without any sense of loss,
I shall give away my body and likewise my wealth,
And my virtues amassed throughout the three times
To help all living beings, my mothers.

This fulfils the first two commitments of the family of Buddha Ratnasambhava, to give material help and to give Dharma.

Generating a determination to keep all vows and commitments purely

I shall never transgress even in my dreams
The most minor rule of the pure moral trainings
Of the Pratimoksha, Bodhisattva and Vajrayana vows.
I shall practise in accordance with Buddha's words.

This fulfils the fourth commitment of the family of Buddha
Vairochana, to refrain from non-virtue; as well as the second
commitment of the family of Buddha Amoghasiddhi, to
strive to maintain purely all the vows we have taken.

Pledging to practise all Dharmas

I shall maintain in accordance with Buddha's intention
All the Dharmas of scripture and realization
Within the three vehicles and four classes of Tantra.
I shall liberate all beings by appropriate means.

This fulfils the three commitments of the family of Buddha
Amitabha, to rely upon the teachings of Sutra, to rely upon
the teachings of the two lower classes of Tantra, and to rely
upon the teachings of the two higher classes of Tantra. It
also fulfils the fifth and sixth commitments of the family of
Buddha Vairochana, to practise virtue and to benefit others.

Dedication

Through the force of the white virtue I have gathered here,
Throughout all my lives may I never transgress
The vows and commitments laid down by Vajradhara,
And may I complete the stages of the twofold path.

By this virtue may I quickly
Accomplish the actual Dakini,
And then lead every living being
Without exception to that ground.

At my deathtime may the Protectors, Heroes, Heroines
    and so forth,
Bearing flowers, parasols and victory banners,
And offering the sweet music of cymbals and so forth,
Lead me to the Land of the Dakinis.

In short, may I never be parted from you, Venerable Guru
    Dakini,
But always come under your care,
And swiftly completing the grounds and paths
Attain the great Dakini state.

If you wish to recite **Dakini Yoga** *three times in one session you should proceed as follows. First recite all the sections from going for refuge through to the brief request. Then repeat this two more times, omitting the sections on visualizing the Guru, the eight lines of praise to the Mother, the kusali tsog offering, and the long mandala offering (but not the two short mandala verses). For the second and third recitations it is necessary to recite the sections on going for refuge, generating bodhichitta, and taking the Bodhisattva vows only once.*

Then recite three times all the sections from absorbing the Guru through to pledging to practise all Dharmas, omitting the sections on the checking meditation on the mandala and reciting the mantra in the second and third recitations.

Finally, recite the dedication prayers once.

Prayers for the Virtuous Tradition

So that the tradition of Je Tsongkhapa,
The King of the Dharma, may flourish,
May all obstacles be pacified
And may all favourable conditions abound.

Through the two collections of myself and others
Gathered throughout the three times,
May the doctrine of Conqueror Losang Dragpa
Flourish for evermore.

The nine-line *Migtsema* prayer

Tsongkhapa, crown ornament of the scholars of the
    Land of the Snows,
You are Buddha Shakyamuni and Vajradhara, the
    source of all attainments,
Avalokiteshvara, the treasury of unobservable
    compassion,
Manjushri, the supreme stainless wisdom,
And Vajrapani, the destroyer of the hosts of maras.
O Venerable Guru-Buddha, synthesis of all Three Jewels,
With my body, speech and mind, respectfully I make
    requests:

273

Please grant your blessings to ripen and liberate myself
and others,
And bestow the common and supreme attainments.

(3x)

Colophon: This sadhana was translated from traditional sources by
Venerable Geshe Kelsang Gyatso.

Condensed Six-session Yoga

When we receive a Highest Yoga Tantra empowerment we promise to maintain the nineteen commitments of the five Buddha families, to liberate all living beings from lower rebirth and from samsaric rebirth, and to lead them to the Vajrayana path, which quickly leads all beings to the state of enlightenment. This practice is our Tantric vow. To fulfil our promise we need to engage in the practice of the nineteen commitments.

As Vajradhara said, we should remember the nineteen commitments six times every day, which means every four hours. This is called 'six-session yoga'. If we are very busy we can fulfil our six-session commitment by doing the following practice six times each day. First we recall the nineteen commitments of the five Buddha families that are listed below, and then, with a strong determination to keep these commitments purely, we verbally or mentally recite the *Condensed Six-session Yoga* that follows, while concentrating on its meaning.

THE NINETEEN COMMITMENTS OF THE FIVE BUDDHA FAMILIES

The six commitments of the family of Buddha Vairochana

1 To go for refuge to Buddha
2 To go for refuge to Dharma
3 To go for refuge to Sangha
4 To refrain from non-virtue
5 To practise virtue
6 To benefit others

The four commitments of the family of Buddha Akshobya

1 To keep a vajra to remind us to emphasize the development of great bliss through meditation on emptiness
2 To keep a bell to remind us to emphasize meditation on emptiness
3 To generate ourself as the Deity while realizing all things that we normally see do not exist
4 To rely sincerely upon our Spiritual Guide who leads us to the practice of the pure moral discipline of the Pratimoksha, Bodhisattva and Tantric vows

The four commitments of the family of Buddha Ratnasambhava

1 To give material help
2 To give Dharma
3 To give fearlessness
4 To give love

The three commitments of the family of Buddha Amitabha

1 To rely upon the teachings of Sutra
2 To rely upon the teachings of the two lower classes of Tantra
3 To rely upon the teachings of the two higher classes of Tantra

The two commitments of the family of Buddha Amoghasiddhi

1 To make offerings to our Spiritual Guide
2 To strive to maintain purely all the vows we have taken

CONDENSED SIX-SESSION YOGA

I go for refuge to the Guru and Three Jewels.
Holding vajra and bell I generate as the Deity and make
    offerings.
I rely upon the Dharmas of Sutra and Tantra and refrain
    from all non-virtuous actions.
Gathering all virtuous Dharmas, I help all living beings
    through the practice of the four givings.

All nineteen commitments are referred to in this verse. The words, 'I go for refuge to the . . . Three Jewels', refer to the first three commitments of the family of Buddha Vairochana – to go for refuge to Buddha, to go for refuge to Dharma, and to go for refuge to Sangha. The word, 'Guru', refers to the fourth commitment of the family of Buddha Akshobya – to rely sincerely upon our Spiritual Guide.

The words, 'Holding vajra and bell I generate as the Deity', refer to the first three commitments of the family of Buddha Akshobya – to keep a vajra to remind us of great bliss, to keep a bell to remind us of emptiness, and to generate ourself as the Deity. The words, 'and make offerings', refer to the first commitment of the family of Buddha Amoghasiddhi – to make offerings to our Spiritual Guide.

The words, 'I rely upon the Dharmas of Sutra and Tantra', refer to the three commitments of the family of Buddha Amitabha – to rely upon the teachings of Sutra, to rely upon the teachings of the two lower classes of Tantra, and to rely upon the teachings of the two higher classes of Tantra. The words, 'and refrain from all non-virtuous actions', refer to the fourth commitment of the family of Buddha Vairochana – to refrain from non-virtue.

The words, 'Gathering all virtuous Dharmas', refer to the fifth commitment of the family of Buddha Vairochana – to practise virtue. The words, 'I help all living beings', refer to the sixth commitment of the family of Buddha Vairochana – to benefit others. The words, 'through the practice of the four givings', refer to the four commitments of the family of Buddha

Ratnasambhava – to give material help, to give Dharma, to give fearlessness and to give love.

Finally, the entire verse refers to the second commitment of the family of Buddha Amoghasiddhi – to strive to maintain purely all the vows we have taken.

More detail on the vows and commitments of Secret Mantra can be found in the book Tantric Grounds and Paths.

Colophon: This prayer and its explanation were compiled
and translated from traditional sources by
Venerable Geshe Kelsang Gyatso.

Vows and Commitments

THE ROOT DOWNFALLS OF THE
BODHISATTVA VOWS

1 Praising ourself and scorning others
2 Not giving wealth or Dharma
3 Not accepting others' apologies
4 Abandoning the Mahayana
5 Stealing the property of the Three Jewels
6 Abandoning Dharma
7 Taking away saffron robes
8 Committing the five heinous actions
9 Holding wrong views
10 Destroying places such as towns
11 Explaining emptiness to those who are likely to
   misunderstand
12 Causing others to abandon the Mahayana
13 Causing others to abandon the Pratimoksha
14 Belittling the Hinayana
15 Speaking falsely about profound emptiness
16 Accepting property that has been stolen from the
   Three Jewels
17 Making bad rules
18 Giving up bodhichitta

THE SECONDARY DOWNFALLS OF THE BODHISATTVA VOWS

Downfalls that obstruct the perfection of giving

1 Not making offerings to the Three Jewels every day
2 Indulging in worldly pleasures out of attachment
3 Being disrespectful to those who received the Bodhisattva vows before us
4 Not replying to others
5 Not accepting invitations
6 Not accepting gifts
7 Not giving Dharma to those who desire it

Downfalls that obstruct the perfection of moral discipline

8 Forsaking those who have broken their moral discipline
9 Not acting in ways that cause others to generate faith
10 Doing little to benefit others
11 Not believing that Bodhisattvas' compassion ensures that all their actions are pure
12 Acquiring wealth or fame through wrong livelihood
13 Indulging in frivolity
14 Claiming that Bodhisattvas need not abandon samsara
15 Not avoiding a bad reputation
16 Not helping others to avoid negativity

Downfalls that obstruct the perfection of patience

17 Retaliating to harm or abuse
18 Not apologizing when we have the opportunity
19 Not accepting others' apologies
20 Making no effort to control our anger

Downfalls that obstruct the perfection of effort

21 Gathering a circle of followers out of desire for profit or respect
22 Not trying to overcome laziness
23 Indulging in senseless conversation out of attachment

Downfalls that obstruct the perfection of mental stabilization

24 Neglecting to train in mental stabilization
25 Not overcoming obstacles to mental stabilization
26 Being preoccupied with the taste of mental stabilization

Downfalls that obstruct the perfection of wisdom

27 Abandoning the Hinayana
28 Studying the Hinayana to the detriment of our Mahayana practice
29 Studying non-Dharma subjects without a good reason
30 Becoming engrossed in non-Dharma subjects for their own sake
31 Criticizing other Mahayana traditions
32 Praising ourself and scorning others
33 Making no effort to study Dharma
34 Preferring to rely upon books rather than upon our Spiritual Guide

Downfalls that obstruct the moral discipline of benefiting others

35 Not going to the assistance of those in need
36 Neglecting to take care of the sick
37 Not acting to dispel suffering
38 Not helping others to overcome their bad habits
39 Not returning help to those who benefit us
40 Not relieving the distress of others
41 Not giving to those who seek charity

42 Not taking special care of disciples
43 Not acting in accordance with the inclinations of others
44 Not praising the good qualities of others
45 Not doing wrathful actions when appropriate
46 Not using miracle powers, threatening actions, and so forth

More detail on the Bodhisattva vows can be found in the book The Bodhisattva Vow.

THE PRECEPTS OF ASPIRING BODHICHITTA

1 To remember the benefits of bodhichitta six times a day
2 To generate bodhichitta six times a day
3 Not to abandon any living being
4 To accumulate merit and wisdom
5 Not to cheat or deceive our Preceptors or Spiritual Guides
6 Not to criticize those who have entered the Mahayana
7 Not to cause others to regret their virtuous actions
8 Not to pretend to have good qualities or hide our faults without a special, pure intention

More detail on the precepts of aspiring bodhichitta can be found in the book Eight Steps to Happiness.

THE FOURTEEN ROOT DOWNFALLS OF THE SECRET MANTRA VOWS

1 Abusing or scorning our Spiritual Guide
2 Showing contempt for the precepts
3 Criticizing our vajra brothers and sisters
4 Abandoning love for any being
5 Giving up aspiring or engaging bodhichitta
6 Scorning the Dharma of Sutra or Tantra
7 Revealing secrets to an unsuitable person
8 Abusing our body

9 Abandoning emptiness
10 Relying upon malevolent friends
11 Not recollecting the view of emptiness
12 Destroying others' faith
13 Not maintaining commitment objects
14 Scorning women

THE BRANCH COMMITMENTS OF
SECRET MANTRA

1 To abandon negative actions, especially killing, stealing, sexual misconduct, lying and taking intoxicants
2 To rely sincerely upon our Spiritual Guide, to be respectful towards our vajra brothers and sisters, and to observe the ten virtuous actions
3 To abandon the causes of turning away from the Mahayana, to avoid scorning gods, and to avoid stepping over sacred objects

THE GROSS DOWNFALLS OF THE
SECRET MANTRA VOWS

1 Relying upon an unqualified mudra
2 Engaging in union without the three recognitions
3 Showing secret substances to an unsuitable person
4 Fighting or arguing during a tsog offering ceremony
5 Giving false answers to questions asked out of faith
6 Staying seven days in the home of someone who rejects the Vajrayana
7 Pretending to be a Yogi while remaining imperfect
8 Revealing holy Dharma to those with no faith
9 Engaging in mandala actions without completing a close retreat
10 Needlessly transgressing the Pratimoksha or Bodhisattva precepts
11 Acting in contradiction to the *Fifty Verses on the Spiritual Guide*

THE UNCOMMON COMMITMENTS OF
MOTHER TANTRA

1 To perform all physical actions first with our left, to make offerings to our Spiritual Guide, and never to abuse him
2 To abandon union with those unqualified
3 While in union, not to be separated from the view of emptiness
4 Never to lose appreciation for the path of attachment
5 Never to forsake the two kinds of mudra
6 To strive mainly for the external and internal methods
7 Never to release seminal fluid; to rely upon pure behaviour
8 To abandon repulsion when tasting bodhichitta

More detail on the Tantric vows can be found in the book Tantric Grounds and Paths.

Colophon: These vows and commitments were translated from traditional sources by Venerable Geshe Kelsang Gyatso.

Quick Path to Great Bliss

THE EXTENSIVE SELF-GENERATION
SADHANA OF VAJRAYOGINI

by
Je Phabongkhapa

Guru Vajradharma

Quick Path to Great Bliss

THE YOGA OF IMMEASURABLES

Going for refuge

In the space before me appear Guru Chakrasambara Father and Mother, surrounded by the assembly of root and lineage Gurus, Yidams, Three Jewels, Attendants, and Protectors.

Imagining yourself and all sentient beings going for refuge, recite three times:

I and all sentient beings, the migrators as extensive as space, from this time forth until we reach the essence of enlightenment,
Go for refuge to the glorious, sacred Gurus,
Go for refuge to the complete Buddhas, the Blessed Ones,
Go for refuge to the sacred Dharmas,
Go for refuge to the superior Sanghas.

Generating bodhichitta

Generate bodhichitta and the four immeasurables while reciting three times:

Once I have attained the state of a complete Buddha, I shall free all sentient beings from the ocean of samsara's suffering and lead them to the bliss of full enlightenment. For this purpose I shall practise the stages of Vajrayogini's path.

Receiving blessings

Now with your palms pressed together, recite:

I prostrate and go for refuge to the Gurus and Three Precious Jewels. Please bless my mental continuum.

Due to reciting this:

The objects of refuge before me melt into the form of white, red, and dark blue rays of light. These dissolve into me and I receive their blessings of body, speech, and mind.

Instantaneous self-generation

In an instant I become Venerable Vajrayogini.

Blessing the inner offering

Purify the inner offering either with the mantra emanating from the four mouths or with the following:

OM KHANDAROHI HUM HUM PHAT
OM SÖBHAWA SHUDDHA SARWA DHARMA SÖBHAWA
   SHUDDHO HAM
Everything becomes emptiness.

From the state of emptiness, from YAM comes wind, from RAM comes fire, from AH a grate of three human heads. Upon this from AH appears a broad and expansive skullcup. Inside from OM, KHAM, AM, TRAM, HUM come the five nectars; from LAM, MAM, PAM, TAM, BAM come the five meats, each marked by these letters. The wind blows, the fire blazes, and the substances inside the skullcup melt. Above them from HUM there arises a white, upside-down khatanga which falls into the skullcup and melts whereby the substances take on the colour of mercury. Above them three rows of vowels and consonants, standing one above the other, transform into OM AH HUM. From these, light rays draw the nectar of exalted wisdom from the hearts of all the Tathagatas, Heroes, and Yoginis of the ten directions. When this is added the contents increase and become vast. OM AH HUM (3x)

Blessing the outer offerings

Now bless the two waters, flowers, incense, lights, perfume, food, and music.

OM KHANDAROHI HUM HUM PHAT
OM SÖBHAWA SHUDDHA SARWA DHARMA SÖBHAWA
  SHUDDHO HAM
Everything becomes emptiness.

From the state of emptiness, from KAM come skullcup
vessels inside which from HUM come offering substances.
By nature emptiness, they have the aspect of the individual
offering substances and function as objects of enjoyment
of the six senses to bestow special, uncontaminated bliss.

OM AHRGHAM AH HUM
OM PADÄM AH HUM
OM VAJRA PUPE AH HUM
OM VAJRA DHUPE AH HUM
OM VAJRA DIWE AH HUM
OM VAJRA GÄNDHE AH HUM
OM VAJRA NEWIDE AH HUM
OM VAJRA SHAPTA AH HUM

Meditation and recitation of Vajrasattva

On my crown, on a lotus and moon seat, sit Vajrasattva
Father and Mother embracing each other. They have
white-coloured bodies, one face, and two hands, and hold
vajra and bell and curved knife and skullcup. The Father
is adorned with six mudras, the Mother with five. They sit
in the vajra and lotus postures. On a moon in his heart is
a HUM encircled by the mantra rosary. From this a stream
of white nectar descends, cleansing all sickness, spirits,
negativities, and obstructions.

OM VAJRA HERUKA SAMAYA, MANU PALAYA, HERUKA
TENO PATITA, DRIDHO ME BHAWA, SUTO KAYO ME BHAWA,
SUPO KAYO ME BHAWA, ANURAKTO ME BHAWA, SARWA
SIDDHI ME PRAYATZA, SARWA KARMA SUTZA ME, TZITAM

SHRIYAM KURU HUM, HA HA HA HA HO BHAGAWÄN,
VAJRA HERUKA MA ME MUNTSA, HERUKA BHAWA, MAHA
SAMAYA SATTÖ AH HUM PHAT

Recite the mantra twenty-one times and then contemplate:

Vajrasattva Father and Mother dissolve into me and my
three doors become inseparable from the body, speech,
and mind of Vajrasattva.

THE YOGA OF THE GURU

Visualization

In the space before me arising from the appearance of the
exalted wisdom of non-dual purity and clarity is a celestial
mansion which is square with four doorways, ornaments,
and archways, and complete with all the essential features.
In the centre on a jewelled throne supported by eight great
lions, on a seat of a lotus of various colours, a sun, and
a moon, sits my kind root Guru in the aspect of Buddha
Vajradharma. He has a red-coloured body, one face, and
two hands, which are crossed at his heart and hold a vajra
and bell. His hair is tied up in a topknot and he sits with
his legs crossed in the vajra posture. He assumes the form
of a sixteen-year-old in the prime of his youth, adorned
with silks and all the bone and jewelled ornaments.

Beginning in front of him and circling counter-clockwise
are all the lineage Gurus from Buddha Vajradhara to my
root Guru. They are in the aspect of Hero Vajradharma
with red-coloured bodies, one face, and two hands. Their
right hands play damarus which reverberate with the
sound of bliss and emptiness. Their left hands hold at their
hearts skullcups filled with nectar, and their left elbows
hold khatangas. They sit with their legs crossed in the
vajra posture. In the prime of their youth, they are
adorned with six bone ornaments.

The Principal and all of his retinue have at their foreheads OM, at their throats AH, and at their hearts HUM. From the HUM at their hearts light rays radiate and invite from their natural abodes the Gurus, Yidams, hosts of mandala Deities, and the assembly of Buddhas, Bodhisattvas, Heroes, Dakinis, Dharmapalas, and Protectors.

OM VAJRA SAMADZA DZA HUM BAM HO
Each becomes a nature which is the synthesis of all objects of refuge.

Prostration

With your palms pressed together, recite:

Vajra Holder, my jewel-like Guru,
Through whose kindness I can accomplish
The state of great bliss in an instant,
At your lotus feet humbly I bow.

Offering goddesses emanate from my heart and perform the offerings.

Outer offerings

OM AHRGHAM PARTITZA SÖHA
OM PADÄM PARTITZA SÖHA
OM VAJRA PUPE AH HUM SÖHA
OM VAJRA DHUPE AH HUM SÖHA
OM VAJRA DIWE AH HUM SÖHA
OM VAJRA GÄNDHE AH HUM SÖHA
OM VAJRA NEWIDE AH HUM SÖHA
OM VAJRA SHAPTA AH HUM SÖHA

OM AH VAJRA ADARSHE HUM
OM AH VAJRA WINI HUM
OM AH VAJRA GÄNDHE HUM
OM AH VAJRA RASE HUM
OM AH VAJRA PARSHE HUM
OM AH VAJRA DHARME HUM

Inner offering

OM GURU VAJRA DHARMA SAPARIWARA OM AH HUM

Secret offering

Contemplate that innumerable knowledge goddesses such as Pemachen emanate from your heart and assume the form of Vajrayogini. Guru Father and Mother embrace and experience uncontaminated bliss.

And I offer most attractive illusory mudras,
A host of messengers born from places, born from mantra, and spontaneously born,
With slender bodies, skilled in the sixty-four arts of love,
And possessing the splendour of youthful beauty.

Thatness offering

Remember that the three circles of the offering are indivisible bliss and emptiness.

I offer you the supreme, ultimate bodhichitta,
A great, exalted wisdom of spontaneous bliss free from obstructions,
Inseparable from the nature of all phenomena, the sphere of freedom from elaboration,
Effortless, and beyond words, thoughts, and expressions.

Offering our spiritual practice

I go for refuge to the Three Jewels
And confess individually all negative actions.
I rejoice in the virtues of all beings
And promise to accomplish a Buddha's enlightenment.

I go for refuge until I am enlightened
To Buddha, Dharma, and the Supreme Assembly,
And to accomplish the aims of myself and others
I shall generate the mind of enlightenment.

Having generated the mind of supreme enlightenment,
I shall invite all sentient beings to be my guests
And engage in the pleasing, supreme practices of
    enlightenment.
May I attain Buddhahood to benefit migrators.

Kusali tsog offering

My own mind, the powerful Lady of Dakini Land, the size
of only a thumb, leaves through the crown of my head
and comes face to face with my root Guru. Once again
I return and, slicing the skull from my old body, place
it upon a grate of three human heads which has arisen
instantaneously. I chop up the rest of my flesh, blood, and
bones and heap it inside. By staring with wide open eyes
I purify, transform, and increase it into an ocean of nectar.
OM AH HUM HA HO HRIH   (3x)

Innumerable offering goddesses holding skullcups emanate
from my heart. With the skullcups they scoop up nectar
and offer it to the guests, who partake by drawing it
through their tongues which are straws of vajra-light.

I offer this nectar of commitment substance
To my root Guru, the nature of the four [Buddha] bodies;
May you be pleased.
OM AH HUM   (7x)

I offer this nectar of commitment substance
To the lineage Gurus, the source of attainments;
May you be pleased.
OM AH HUM

I offer this nectar of commitment substance
To the assembly of Gurus, Yidams, Three Jewels, and
    Protectors;
May you be pleased.
OM AH HUM

I offer this nectar of commitment substance
To the guardians who reside in the local places and in the
    regions;
May you assist me.
OM AH HUM

I offer this nectar of commitment substance
To all sentient beings in the six realms and the
    intermediate state;
May you be freed.
OM AH HUM

Through this offering all the guests are satiated with an
    uncontaminated bliss
And the sentient beings attain the Truth Body free from
    obstructions.
The three circles of the offering are the nature of non-dual
    bliss and emptiness,
Beyond words, thoughts, and expressions.

Offering the mandala

OM VAJRA BHUMI AH HUM
Great and powerful golden ground,
OM VAJRA REKHE AH HUM
At the edge the iron fence stands around the outer circle.
In the centre Mount Meru the king of mountains,
Around which are four continents:
In the east, Purvavideha, in the south, Jambudipa,
In the west, Aparagodaniya, in the north, Uttarakuru.
Each has two sub-continents:
Deha and Videha, Tsamara and Abatsamara,
Satha and Uttaramantrina, Kurava and Kaurava.
The mountain of jewels, the wish-granting tree,
The wish-granting cow, and the harvest unsown.
The precious wheel, the precious jewel,
The precious queen, the precious minister,
The precious elephant, the precious supreme horse,
The precious general, and the great treasure vase.

The goddess of beauty, the goddess of garlands,
The goddess of song, the goddess of dance,
The goddess of flowers, the goddess of incense,
The goddess of light, and the goddess of scent.
The sun and the moon, the precious umbrella,
The banner of victory in every direction.
In the centre all treasures of both gods and men,
An excellent collection with nothing left out.
I offer this to you my kind root Guru and lineage Gurus,
To all of you sacred and glorious Gurus;
Please accept with compassion for migrating beings,
And having accepted please grant us your blessings.

O Treasure of Compassion, my Refuge and Protector,
I offer you the mountain, continents, precious objects,
    treasure vase, sun and moon,
Which have arisen from my aggregates, sources and
    elements
As aspects of the exalted wisdom of spontaneous bliss
    and emptiness.

I offer without any sense of loss
The objects that give rise to my attachment, hatred, and
    confusion,
My friends, enemies, and strangers, our bodies and
    enjoyments;
Please accept these and bless me to be released directly
    from the three poisons.

IDAM GURU RATNA MANDALAKAM NIRYATAYAMI

Requesting the lineage Gurus

Vajradharma, Lord of the family of the ocean of
    Conquerors,
Vajrayogini, supreme Mother of the Conquerors,
Naropa, powerful Son of the Conquerors,
I request you, please bestow the spontaneously born
    exalted wisdom.

Hero Vajradharma

Pamtingpa, holder of the explanations of the great secrets
  for disciples,
Sherab Tseg, you are a treasure of all the precious secrets,
Malgyur Lotsawa, lord of the ocean of Secret Mantra,
I request you, please bestow the spontaneously born
  exalted wisdom.

Great Sakya Lama, you are powerful Vajradhara,
Venerable Sonam Tsemo, supreme vajra son,
Dragpa Gyaltsen, crown ornament of the vajra holders,
I request you, please bestow the spontaneously born
  exalted wisdom.

Great Sakya Pandita, master scholar of the Land of the
  Snows,
Drogon Chogyel Pagpa, crown ornament of all beings
  of the three grounds,
Shangton Choje, holder of the Sakya doctrine,
I request you, please bestow the spontaneously born
  exalted wisdom.

Nasa Dragpugpa, powerful accomplished one,
Sonam Gyaltsen, navigator of scholars and supremely
  accomplished ones,
Yarlungpa, lord of the whispered lineage of the family
  of accomplished ones,
I request you, please bestow the spontaneously born
  exalted wisdom.

Gyalwa Chog, refuge and protector of all migrators, both
  myself and others,
Jamyang Namka, you are a great being,
Lodro Gyaltsen, great being and lord of the Dharma,
I request you, please bestow the spontaneously born
  exalted wisdom.

Jetsun Doringpa, you are unequalled in kindness,
Tenzin Losel, you have practised in accordance with the
  [Guru's] words,

Kyentse, the expounder of the great, secret lineage of
    words,
I request you, please bestow the spontaneously born
    exalted wisdom.

Labsum Gyaltsen, holder of the mantra families,
Glorious Wangchug Rabten, all-pervading lord of the
    hundred families,
Jetsun Kangyurpa, principal of the families,
I request you, please bestow the spontaneously born
    exalted wisdom.

Shaluwa, all-pervading lord of the ocean of mandalas,
Kyenrabje, principal of all the mandalas,
Morchenpa, lord of the circle of mandalas,
I request you, please bestow the spontaneously born
    exalted wisdom.

Nesarpa, navigator of the ocean of whispered lineages,
Losel Phuntsog, lord of the whispered lineages,
Tenzin Trinlay, scholar who furthered the whispered lineages,
I request you, please bestow the spontaneously born
    exalted wisdom.

Kangyurpa, all-pervading lord upholding the Ganden
    doctrine,
Ganden Dargyay, friend of migrators in degenerate times,
Dharmabhadra, holder of the Ganden tradition,
I request you, please bestow the spontaneously born
    exalted wisdom.

Losang Chopel, lord of the Sutras and Tantras,
You have completed the essence of the paths of all the
    Sutras and Tantras.
Jigme Wangpo, scholar who furthered the Sutras and
    Tantras,
I request you, please bestow the spontaneously born
    exalted wisdom.

Dechen Nyingpo, you have the blessings of Naropa
To explain perfectly in accordance with Naropa
The essence of the excellent ripening and liberating paths
    of the Naro Dakini,
I request you, please bestow the spontaneously born
    exalted wisdom.

Losang Yeshe, Vajradhara,
You are a treasury of instructions on the ripening and
    liberating [paths] of the Vajra Queen,
The supreme, quick path for attaining the vajra state,
I request you, please bestow the spontaneously born
    exalted wisdom.

My kind root Guru, Vajradharma,
You are the embodiment of all the Conquerors,
Who grant the blessings of all Buddhas' speech,
I request you, please bestow the spontaneously born
    exalted wisdom.

Please bless me so that through the force of meditation
On the Dakini yoga of the profound generation stage,
And the central channel yoga of completion stage,
I may generate the exalted wisdom of spontaneous great
    bliss and attain the enlightened Dakini state.

Receiving the blessings of the four empowerments

I request you O Guru incorporating all objects of refuge,
Please grant me your blessings,
Please grant me the four empowerments completely,
And bestow on me, please, the state of the four bodies.

(3x)

Contemplate that as a result of your requests:

White light rays and nectars radiate from the OM at the
    forehead of my Guru.
They dissolve into my forehead, purifying the negativities
    and obstructions of my body.

I receive the vase empowerment, and the blessings of my
Guru's body enter my body.

Red light rays and nectars radiate from the AH at the
throat of my Guru.
They dissolve into my throat, purifying the negativities
and obstructions of my speech.
I receive the secret empowerment, and the blessings of my
Guru's speech enter my speech.

Blue light rays and nectars radiate from the HUM at the
heart of my Guru.
They dissolve into my heart, purifying the negativities and
obstructions of my mind.
I receive the wisdom-mudra empowerment, and the
blessings of my Guru's mind enter my mind.

White, red, and blue light rays and nectars radiate from
the letters at my Guru's three places.
They dissolve into my three places, purifying the
negativities and obstructions of my body, speech, and
mind.
I receive the fourth empowerment, the precious word
empowerment, and the blessings of my Guru's body,
speech, and mind enter my body, speech, and mind.

Brief request

I request you my precious Guru, the essence of all Buddhas
of the three times, please bless my mental continuum.

(3x)

Absorbing the Gurus

Requested in this way, the encircling lineage Gurus
dissolve into my root Guru in the centre. My root Guru
too, out of affection for me, melts into the form of red
light and, entering through the crown of my head, mixes
inseparably with my mind in the aspect of a red letter
BAM at my heart.

THE YOGA OF SELF-GENERATION

Bringing death into the path of the Truth Body

This very letter BAM expands and spreads to the ends
of space whereby all worlds and their beings become the
nature of bliss and emptiness. Once again, contracting
gradually from the edges, it becomes an extremely minute
letter BAM, which dissolves in stages from the bottom up
into the nada. Then even the nada disappears and becomes
the Truth Body of inseparable bliss and emptiness.
OM SHUNYATA GYANA VAJRA SÖBHAWA ÄMAKO HAM

Bringing the intermediate state into the path of the
Enjoyment Body

From the state of emptiness, where all appearance has
gathered like this, there appears a red letter BAM standing
upright in space, in essence an aspect of my own mind,
the exalted wisdom of non-dual bliss and emptiness.

Bringing rebirth into the path of the Emanation Body

From the state of emptiness, from EH EH comes a red
phenomena source, a double tetrahedron. Inside from AH
comes a moon mandala, white with a shade of red. Upon
this, standing in a circle counter-clockwise, rests the mantra
OM OM OM SARWA BUDDHA DAKINIYE VAJRA WARNANIYE
VAJRA BEROTZANIYE HUM HUM HUM PHAT PHAT PHAT SÖHA.
I, the letter BAM in space, see the moon and, motivated to
take rebirth in its centre, enter the centre of the moon.

Light rays radiate from the moon, letter BAM, and mantra
rosary, making all worlds and beings of samsara and
nirvana into the nature of Venerable Vajrayogini. These
gather back and dissolve into the letter BAM and mantra
rosary, which change completely into the supported and
supporting mandala, fully and all at once.

301

Venerable Vajrayogini

Checking meditation on the mandala and the beings within it

Furthermore, there is the vajra ground, fence, tent, and canopy, outside of which a mass of five-coloured fires blaze, swirling counter-clockwise. Inside these is the circle of the eight great charnel grounds, the Ferocious One and so forth. In the centre of these is a red phenomena source, a double tetrahedron, with its broad neck facing upwards and its fine tip pointing downwards. Except for the front and back, each of the other four corners is marked by a pink joy swirl whirling counter-clockwise.

Inside the phenomena source, in the centre of an eight-petalled lotus of various colours, is a sun mandala. Upon this I arise in the form of Venerable Vajrayogini. My outstretched right leg treads on the breast of red Kalarati. My bent left leg treads on the head of black Bhairawa, which is bent backwards. I have a red-coloured body which shines with a brilliance like that of the fire of the aeon. I have one face, two hands, and three eyes looking towards the Pure Land of the Dakinis. My right hand, outstretched and pointing downwards, holds a curved knife marked with a vajra. My left holds up a skullcup filled with blood which I partake of with my upturned mouth. My left shoulder holds a khatanga marked with a vajra from which hang a damaru, bell, and triple banner. My black hair hanging straight covers my back down to my waist. In the prime of my youth, my desirous breasts are full and I show the manner of generating bliss. My head is adorned with five human skulls and I wear a necklace of fifty human skulls. Naked, I am adorned with five mudras and stand in the centre of a blazing fire of exalted wisdom.

THE YOGA OF PURIFYING MIGRATORS

At my heart inside a red phenomena source, a double tetrahedron, is a moon mandala. In the centre of this is a letter BAM encircled by a mantra rosary. From these light rays radiate, leaving through the pores of my skin. Touching all sentient beings of the six realms, they purify their negativities and obstructions together with their imprints and transform them all into the form of Vajrayogini.

THE YOGA OF BEING BLESSED BY HEROES AND HEROINES

Meditation on the body mandala

At my heart, in the centre of a phenomena source and moon seat, is a letter BAM which is the nature of the four elements. By splitting it changes into the four letters YA, RA, LA, WA which are the seeds of the four elements. They are the nature of the heart channel petals of the four directions such as the Desirous One. These transform starting from the left into Lama, Khandarohi, Rupini, and Dakini. In the centre, the crescent moon, drop, and nada of the letter BAM, whose nature is the union of my very subtle red and white drops, transform into Venerable Vajrayogini.

Outside these in sequence are the channels such as the Unchanging One of the twenty-four places of the body, such as the hairline and crown, and the twenty-four elements from which come the nails, teeth, and so forth. These channels and elements, which are by nature inseparable, become the nature of the twenty-four letters of the mantra, OM OM and so forth, standing in a circle counter-clockwise from the east. These transform into the eight Heroines of the heart family: Partzandi, Tzändriakiya, Parbhawatiya, Mahanasa, Biramatiya, Karwariya, Lamkeshöriya, and Drumatzaya; the eight Heroines of the speech family: Airawatiya, Mahabhairawi, Bayubega, Surabhakiya, Shamadewi, Suwatre, Hayakarne, and Khaganane; and the eight Heroines of the body family:

Tzatrabega, Khandarohi, Shaundini, Tzatrawarmini, Subira,
Mahabala, Tzatrawartini, and Mahabire. These are the actual
Yoginis who are non-dual with the Heroes of the twenty-four
external places such as Puliramalaya. The channels and
elements of the eight doors such as the mouth, by nature
inseparable from the eight letters HUM HUM and so forth,
transform into Kakase, Ulukase, Shonase, Shukarase,
Yamadhathi, Yamaduti, Yamadangtrini, and Yamamatani.
They all have the bodily form of the Venerable Lady,
complete with ornaments and details.

Absorbing the wisdom beings and mixing the three messengers

Perform the blazing mudra and recite:

PHAIM
Light rays radiate from the letter BAM at my heart and,
leaving from between my eyebrows, go to the ten
directions. They invite all the Tathagatas, Heroes, and
Yoginis of the ten directions in the aspect of Vajrayogini.
DZA HUM BAM HO

*The wisdom beings are summoned, dissolve, remain firm,
and are delighted. Now with the lotus-turning mudra
followed by the embracing mudra, recite:*

OM YOGA SHUDDHA SARWA DHARMA YOGA SHUDDHO HAM
I am the nature of the yoga of completely purified all
phenomena.

Contemplate divine pride.

Putting on the armour

At places in my body arise moon mandalas upon which
at my navel is red OM BAM, Vajravarahi; at my heart blue
HAM YOM, Yamani; at my throat white HRIM MOM,
Mohani; at my forehead yellow HRIM HRIM, Sachalani;
at my crown green HUM HUM, Samtrasani; at all my limbs
smoke-coloured PHAT PHAT, essence of Chandika.

Granting empowerment and adorning the crown

PHAIM

Light rays radiate from the letter BAM at my heart and invite the empowering Deities, the supported and supporting mandala of Glorious Chakrasambara.

O, all you Tathagatas, please grant the empowerment.

Requested in this way, the eight Goddesses of the doorways drive away hindrances, the Heroes recite auspicious verses, the Heroines sing vajra songs, and the Rupavajras and so forth make offerings. The Principal mentally resolves to grant the empowerment and the four Mothers together with Varahi, holding jewelled vases filled with the five nectars, confer the empowerment through the crown of my head.

'Just as all the Tathagatas granted ablution
At the moment of [Buddha's] birth,
Likewise do we now grant ablution
With the pure water of the gods.

OM SARWA TATHAGATA ABHIKEKATA SAMAYA SHRIYE HUM'

Saying this, they grant the empowerment. My whole body is filled, all stains are purified, and the excess water remaining on my crown changes into Vairochana-Heruka, together with the Mother, who adorn my crown.

Offerings to the self-generation

If you are doing self-generation in conjunction with self-initiation it is necessary to bless the outer offerings at this point.

Offering goddesses emanate from my heart and perform the offerings.

Outer offerings

OM AHRGHAM PARTITZA SÖHA
OM PADÄM PARTITZA SÖHA
OM VAJRA PUPE AH HUM SÖHA
OM VAJRA DHUPE AH HUM SÖHA

OM VAJRA DIWE AH HUM SÖHA
OM VAJRA GÄNDHE AH HUM SÖHA
OM VAJRA NEWIDE AH HUM SÖHA
OM VAJRA SHAPTA AH HUM SÖHA

OM AH VAJRA ADARSHE HUM
OM AH VAJRA WINI HUM
OM AH VAJRA GÄNDHE HUM
OM AH VAJRA RASE HUM
OM AH VAJRA PARSHE HUM
OM AH VAJRA DHARME HUM

Inner offering

OM OM OM SARWA BUDDHA DAKINIYE VAJRA WARNANIYE
VAJRA BEROTZANIYE HUM HUM HUM PHAT PHAT PHAT
SÖHA OM AH HUM

Secret and thatness offerings

To perform the secret and thatness offerings either imagine:

I, Vajrayogini, stand in union with Chakrasambara, who
has transformed from my khatanga, and generate
spontaneous bliss and emptiness.

*or imagine that as Vajrayogini you transform into Heruka
and with divine pride perform the secret and thatness
offerings thus:*

With the clarity of Vajrayogini I give up my breasts and
develop a penis. In the perfect place in the centre of my
vagina the two walls transform into two bell-like testicles
and the stamen into the penis itself. Thus I take on the
form of Great Joy Heruka together with the Secret Mother
Vajrayogini who is by nature the synthesis of all Dakinis.

From the sphere of the unobservability of the secret place
of the Father, from a white HUM there arises a white, five-
pronged vajra, and from a red BÄ there arises a red jewel
with a yellow BÄ marking its tip.

From the sphere of the unobservability of the secret place of
the Mother, from an AH there arises a red, three-petalled

lotus, and from a white DÄ there arises a white stamen, signifying white bodhichitta, with a yellow DÄ marking its tip.

OM SHRI MAHA SUKHA VAJRA HE HE RU RU KAM AH
     HUM HUM PHAT SÖHA

Through Father and Mother being absorbed in union, the bodhichitta melts. When from my crown it reaches my throat [I experience] joy. When from my throat it reaches my heart [I experience] supreme joy. When from my heart it reaches my navel [I experience] extraordinary joy. When from my navel it reaches the tip of my jewel I generate a spontaneous exalted wisdom whereby I remain absorbed in the concentration of inseparable bliss and emptiness. Thus, through this bliss inseparably joined with emptiness remaining in single-pointed absorption on the thatness that is the lack of inherent existence of the three circles of the offering, I delight in the secret and thatness offerings.

Then contemplate:

Once again I become Venerable Vajrayogini.

Eight lines of praise to the Mother

OM NAMO BHAGAWATI VAJRA VARAHI BAM HUM HUM
     PHAT
OM NAMO ARYA APARADZITE TRE LOKYA MATI BIYE SHÖRI
     HUM HUM PHAT
OM NAMA SARWA BUTA BHAYA WAHI MAHA VAJRE HUM
     HUM PHAT
OM NAMO VAJRA SANI ADZITE APARADZITE WASHAM
     KARANITRA HUM HUM PHAT
OM NAMO BHRAMANI SHOKANI ROKANI KROTE KARALENI
     HUM HUM PHAT
OM NAMA DRASANI MARANI PRABHE DANI PARADZAYE
     HUM HUM PHAT
OM NAMO BIDZAYE DZAMBHANI TAMBHANI MOHANI
     HUM HUM PHAT
OM NAMO VAJRA VARAHI MAHA YOGINI KAME SHÖRI
     KHAGE HUM HUM PHAT

THE YOGA OF VERBAL AND MENTAL RECITATION

Verbal recitation

At my heart inside a red phenomena source, a double tetrahedron, in the centre of a moon mandala, is a letter BAM encircled by a red-coloured mantra rosary standing counter-clockwise. From these, immeasurable rays of red light radiate. They purify the negativities and obstructions of all sentient beings and make offerings to all the Buddhas. All the power and force of their blessings is invoked in the form of rays of red light, which dissolve into the letter BAM and mantra rosary, blessing my mental continuum.

OM OM OM SARWA BUDDHA DAKINIYE VAJRA WARNANIYE VAJRA BEROTZANIYE HUM HUM HUM PHAT PHAT PHAT SÖHA

Recite at least as many mantras as you have promised to.

Mental recitation

(1) Sit in the sevenfold posture and bring the phenomena source, moon, and mantra letters from the heart down to the secret place if you want to generate bliss, or to the navel if you want to generate a non-conceptual mind, and enclose them with the winds. As if mentally reading the mantra rosary, which stands counter-clockwise in a circle, collect just three, five, or seven recitations. Then, while holding your breath, focus your mind on the pink joy swirls spinning counter-clockwise in the four corners of the phenomena source other than the front and the back, and especially on the nada of the BAM in the centre, which is about to blaze.

(2) The red joy swirl at the upper tip of the central channel and the white joy swirl at the lower tip, each the size of only a grain of barley, travel to the heart while spinning furiously counter-clockwise. At the heart they mix and gradually diminish into emptiness. Place your mind in absorption on bliss and emptiness.

THE YOGA OF INCONCEIVABILITY

From the letter BAM and the mantra rosary at my heart, light
rays radiate and pervade all three realms. The formless realm
dissolves into the upper part of my body in the aspect of
rays of blue light. The form realm dissolves into the middle
part of my body in the aspect of rays of red light. The desire
realm dissolves into the lower part of my body in the aspect
of rays of white light. I, in turn, gradually melt into light
from below and above and dissolve into the phenomena
source. That dissolves into the moon. That dissolves into the
thirty-two Yoginis. They dissolve into the four Yoginis, and
they dissolve into the Principal Lady of the body mandala.
The Principal Lady, in turn, gradually melts into light from
below and above and dissolves into the phenomena source.
That dissolves into the moon. That dissolves into the mantra
rosary. That dissolves into the letter BAM. That dissolves into
the head of the BAM. That dissolves into the crescent moon.
That dissolves into the drop. That dissolves into the nada,
and that, becoming smaller and smaller, dissolves into clear
light emptiness.

THE YOGA OF DAILY ACTIONS

From the state of emptiness in an instant I become Venerable
Vajrayogini. At places in my body arise moon mandalas upon
which at my navel is red OM BAM, Vajravarahi; at my heart
blue HAM YOM, Yamani; at my throat white HRIM MOM,
Mohani; at my forehead yellow HRIM HRIM, Sachalani; at my
crown green HUM HUM, Samtrasani; at all my limbs smoke-
coloured PHAT PHAT, essence of Chandika.

*To protect the main directions and intermediate directions
recite twice:*

OM SUMBHANI SUMBHA HUM HUM PHAT
OM GRIHANA GRIHANA HUM HUM PHAT
OM GRIHANA PAYA GRIHANA PAYA HUM HUM PHAT
OM ANAYA HO BHAGAWÄN VAJRA HUM HUM PHAT

The yoga of the tormas

Set up offerings in the traditional manner and then purify them in the following way:

OM KHANDAROHI HUM HUM PHAT
OM SÖBHAWA SHUDDHA SARWA DHARMA SÖBHAWA
  SHUDDHO HAM
Everything becomes emptiness.

From the state of emptiness, from KAM come skullcup vessels inside which from HUM come offering substances. By nature emptiness, they have the aspect of the individual offering substances and function as objects of enjoyment of the six senses to bestow special, uncontaminated bliss.

OM AHRGHAM AH HUM
OM PADÄM AH HUM
OM VAJRA PUPE AH HUM
OM VAJRA DHUPE AH HUM
OM VAJRA DIWE AH HUM
OM VAJRA GÄNDHE AH HUM
OM VAJRA NEWIDE AH HUM
OM VAJRA SHAPTA AH HUM

Blessing the tormas

OM KHANDAROHI HUM HUM PHAT
OM SÖBHAWA SHUDDHA SARWA DHARMA SÖBHAWA
  SHUDDHO HAM
Everything becomes emptiness.

From the state of emptiness, from YAM comes wind, from RAM comes fire, from AH a grate of three human heads. Upon this from AH appears a broad and expansive skullcup. Inside from OM, KHAM, AM, TRAM, HUM come the five nectars; from LAM, MAM, PAM, TAM, BAM come the five meats, each marked by these letters. The wind blows, the fire blazes, and the substances inside the skullcup melt. Above them from HUM there arises a white, upside-down khatanga which falls into the skullcup and melts whereby

311

the substances take on the colour of mercury. Above them three rows of vowels and consonants, standing one above the other, transform into OM AH HUM. From these, light rays draw the nectar of exalted wisdom from the hearts of all the Tathagatas, Heroes, and Yoginis of the ten directions. When this is added the contents increase and become vast. OM AH HUM (3x)

Inviting the guests of the torma

PHAIM
Light rays radiate from the letter BAM at my heart and invite Venerable Vajrayogini surrounded by the assembly of Gurus, Yidams, Buddhas, Bodhisattvas, Heroes, Dakinis, and both Dharma and mundane Protectors to come from Akanishta to the space before me. From a HUM in the tongue of each guest there arises a three-pronged vajra through which they partake of the essence of the torma by drawing it through straws of light the thickness of only a grain of barley.

Offering the principal torma

Offer the torma while reciting three or seven times:

OM VAJRA AH RA LI HO: DZA HUM BAM HO: VAJRA DAKINI
SAMAYA TÖN TRISHAYA HO

Offering the torma to the mundane Dakinis

Offer the torma while reciting twice:

OM KHA KHA, KHAHI KHAHI, SARWA YAKYA RAKYASA, BHUTA, TRETA, PISHATSA, UNATA, APAMARA, VAJRA DAKA, DAKI NÄDAYA, IMAM BALING GRIHANTU, SAMAYA RAKYANTU, MAMA SARWA SIDDHI METRA YATZANTU, YATIPAM, YATETAM, BHUDZATA, PIWATA, DZITRATA, MATI TRAMATA, MAMA SARWA KATAYA, SÄDSUKHAM BISHUDHAYE, SAHAYEKA BHAWÄNTU, HUM HUM PHAT PHAT SÖHA

Outer offerings

OM VAJRA YOGINI SAPARIWARA AHRGHAM, PADÄM, PUPE,
DHUPE, ALOKE, GÄNDHE, NEWIDE, SHAPTA AH HUM

Inner offering

OM VAJRA YOGINI SAPARIWARA OM AH HUM

Praise

O Glorious Vajrayogini,
Chakravatin Dakini Queen,
Who have five wisdoms and three bodies,
To you Saviour of all I prostrate.

To the many Vajra Dakinis,
Who as Ladies of worldly actions,
Cut our bondage to preconceptions,
To all of you Ladies I prostrate.

Prayer to Behold the Beautiful Face of Vajrayogini

Bliss and emptiness of infinite Conquerors who, as if in a
    drama,
Appear as so many different visions in samsara and nirvana;
From among these you are now the beautiful, powerful Lady
    of Dakini Land,
I remember you from my heart, please care for me with your
    playful embrace.

You are the spontaneously born Mother of the Conquerors in
    the land of Akanishta,
You are the field-born Dakinis in the twenty-four places,
You are the action mudras covering the whole earth,
O Venerable Lady, you are the supreme refuge of myself, the
    Yogi.

You who are the manifestation of the emptiness of the
    mind itself,
Are the actual BAM, the sphere of EH, in the city of the vajra.
In the land of illusion you show yourself as a fearsome
    cannibal
And as a smiling, vibrant, fair young maiden.

313

But no matter how much I searched, O Noble Lady,
I could find no certainty of your being truly existent.
Then the youth of my mind, exhausted by its elaborations,
Came to rest in the forest hut which is beyond expression.

How wonderful, please arise from the sphere of the
    Dharmakaya
And care for me by the truth of what it says
In the Glorious Heruka, King of Tantras,
That attainments come from reciting the supreme close
    essence mantra of the Vajra Queen.

In the isolated forest of Odivisha
You cared for Vajra Ghantapa, the powerful Siddha,
With the bliss of your kiss and embrace and he came to
    enjoy the supreme embrace;
O, please care for me in the same way.

Just as the venerable Kusali was led directly
From an island in the Ganges to the sphere of space,
And just as you cared for the glorious Naropa,
Please lead me also to the city of the joyful Dakini.

Through the force of the compassion of my supreme root
    and lineage Gurus,
The especially profound and quick path of the ultimate,
    secret, great Tantra,
And the pure superior intention of myself, the Yogi,
May I soon behold your smiling face, O Joyful Dakini Lady.

Requesting fulfilment of wishes

O Venerable Vajrayogini, please lead me and all sentient
beings to the Pure Land of the Dakinis. Please bestow on
us every single mundane and supramundane attainment.

(3x)

*If you wish to make a tsog offering you should include it at
this point. The tsog offering is on pages 325-331.*

Offering the torma to the general Dharma Protectors

OM AH HUM HA HO HRIH   (3x)

HUM
From your pure palace of great bliss in Akanishta,
Great powerful one emanating from Vairochana's heart,
Dorje Gur, chief of all the Protectors of the doctrine,
O Glorious Mahakala come here please and partake of
    this offering and torma.

From Yongdui Tsäl and Yama's palace
And from the supreme place of Devikoti in Jambudipa,
Namdrü Remati, chief Lady of the desire realm,
O Palden Lhamo come here please and partake of this
    offering and torma.

From the mandala of the bhaga sphere of appearance and
    existence,
Mother Yingchugma, principal Lady of all samsara and
    nirvana,
Chief of Dakinis and demons, fierce female protector of the
    mantras,
O Great Mother Ralchigma come here please and partake
    of this offering and torma.

From Silwa Tsel and Haha Göpa,
From Singaling and the Ti Se snow mountain,
And from Darlungne and Kaui Dragdzong,
O Zhingkyong Wangpo come here please and partake of
    this offering and torma.

From the eight charnel grounds and Risul in the south,
From Bodhgaya and glorious Samyä,
And from Nalatse and glorious Sakya,
O Legon Pomo come here please and partake of this
    offering and torma.

Kinkara

From the charnel grounds of Marutse in the north-east,
From the red, rocky hills of Bangso in India,
And from the supreme places of Darlung Dagram and so
    forth,
O Yakya Chamdräl come here please and partake of this
    offering and torma.

Especially from Odiyana, Land of the Dakinis,
And from your natural abode,
Completely encircled by mundane and supramundane
    Dakinis,
O Father-Mother Lord of the Charnel Grounds come here
    please and partake of this offering and torma.

From the supreme places such as Tushita, Keajra, and so
    forth,
Great Protector of the doctrine of the second Conqueror,
Dorje Shugdän, five lineages, together with your retinues,
Come here please and partake of this offering and torma.

I request you, I make offerings to you, O Host of
    Protectors of the Conqueror's doctrine,
I propitiate you and rely upon you, O Great Protectors
    of the Guru's words,
I cry out to you and beseech you, O Host of Destroyers
    of the obstructors of Yogis,
Please come here quickly and partake of this offering
    and torma.

I offer a torma adorned with red flesh and blood.
I offer drinks of alcohol, medicine nectars, and blood.
I offer the sound of large drums, thigh-bone trumpets,
    and cymbals.
I offer large, black silk pennants that billow like clouds.

I offer breath-taking attractions equal to space.
I offer loud chants that are powerful and melodious.
I offer an ocean of outer, inner, and secret commitment
    substances.
I offer the play of the exalted wisdom of inseparable bliss
    and emptiness.

Dorje Shugden

May you protect the precious doctrine of Buddha.
May you increase the renown of the Three Jewels.
May you further the deeds of the glorious Gurus,
And may you fulfil whatever requests I make of you.

Requesting forbearance

Now recite the hundred-letter mantra of Heruka:

OM VAJRA HERUKA SAMAYA, MANU PALAYA, HERUKA
TENO PATITA, DRIDHO ME BHAWA, SUTO KAYO ME BHAWA,
SUPO KAYO ME BHAWA, ANURAKTO ME BHAWA, SARWA
SIDDHI ME PRAYATZA, SARWA KARMA SUTZA ME, TZITAM
SHRIYAM KURU HUM, HA HA HA HA HO BHAGAWÄN,
VAJRA HERUKA MA ME MUNTSA, HERUKA BHAWA, MAHA
SAMAYA SATTÖ AH HUM PHAT

Request forbearance by reciting:

Whatever mistakes I have made
Through not finding, not understanding,
Or not having the ability,
Please, O Protector, be patient with all of these.

OM VAJRA MU The wisdom beings, guests of the torma,
dissolve into me and the worldly beings return to their
own places.

Dedication prayers

By this virtue may I quickly
Accomplish the actual Dakini,
And then lead every living being
Without exception to that ground.

At my deathtime may the Protectors, Heroes, Heroines
    and so forth,
Bearing flowers, parasols, and victory banners,
And offering the sweet music of cymbals and so forth,
Lead me to the Land of the Dakinis.

By the truth of the valid Goddesses,
Their valid commitments,
And the supremely valid words they have spoken,
May [my virtues] be the cause for me to be cared for by
the Goddesses.

Extensive dedication

*If you have the time and the wish you can finish with these
prayers, which were composed by Tsarpa Dorjechang:*

In the great ship of freedom and endowment,
Flying the white sail of mindfulness of impermanence,
And blown by the favourable wind of accepting and
abandoning actions and effects,
May I be delivered from the fearsome ocean of samsara.

Relying upon the crown-jewel of the non-deceptive objects
of refuge,
Taking to heart the great purpose of migrators, my mothers,
And cleansing my stains and faults with the nectar of
Vajrasattva,
May I be cared for by the compassionate, venerable Gurus.

The beautiful Mother of the Conquerors is the outer Yogini,
The letter BAM is the supreme inner Vajra Queen,
The clarity and emptiness of the mind itself is the secret
Dakini Mother;
May I enjoy the sport of seeing the self-nature of each.

The worldly environment is the celestial mansion of the
letter EH,
And its inhabitants, the sentient beings, are the Yoginis of
the letter BAM;
Through the concentration of the great bliss of their union,
May whatever appearance arises be pure appearance.

Thus, through the yogas [numbering] the directions and the
moon,
May I eventually be led directly to the city of Knowledge
Holders

By the coral-coloured Lady of joy
With freely hanging vermilion hair and orange, darting
  eyes.

Having practised in a place of corpses with sindhura and
  a langali stem,
And having wandered throughout the land,
May the beautiful Lady to whom the swirl at my forehead
  transfers
Lead me to the Land of the Dakinis.

When the inner Varahi has destroyed the creeping vine of
  apprehender and apprehended,
And the dancing Lady residing in my supreme central
  channel
Has emerged through the door of Brahma into the sphere of
  the pathway of clouds,
May she embrace and sport with the Hero, Drinker of
  Blood.

Through the yoga of unifying [the two winds], meditating
  single-pointedly
On the tiny seed of the five winds at the lotus of my navel,
May my mental continuum be satiated by a supreme bliss
From the fragrant drops pervading the channels of my
  body-mind.

When, through the laughing and smiling play of the
  beautiful Lady
Of normal light tummo within my central channel,
The youthful letter HAM has been completely softened,
May I attain the ground of the great bliss of union.

When the reddish-black RAM residing in the centre of the
  three channels at my navel
Has been set ablaze by my upper and lower winds,
And its cleansing fire has burned away the seventy-two
  thousand impure elements,
May my central channel be completely filled with pure
  drops.

When the five-coloured drop between my eyebrows has
    gone to my crown,
And the stream of moon-liquid originating from it
Has reached the stamen of my secret lotus,
May I be satiated by the four joys of descending and
    ascending.

When, through being struck by the rays of five lights
    radiating from that drop,
All stable and moving phenomena, my body and so forth,
Have been transformed into a mass of brilliant, clear
    rainbows,
May I once again enter the natural abode, the sphere of
    bliss and emptiness.

When the Yogini of my own mind, the union beyond
    intellect,
The primordial state of inexpressible emptiness and clarity,
The original nature free from arising, ceasing, and abiding,
Recognizes its own entity, may I be forever nourished.

When my channels, winds, and drops have dissolved into
    the sphere of EVAM,
And the mind itself has attained the glory of the Truth
    Body of great bliss,
May I care for these migrators as extensive as space
With immeasurable manifestations of countless Form Bodies.

Through the blessings of the Conquerors and their
    marvellous Sons,
The truth of non-deceptive dependent relationship,
And the power and force of my pure, superior intention,
May all the points of my sincere prayers be fulfilled.

Auspicious prayers

May there be the auspiciousness of swiftly receiving the
    blessings
Of the hosts of glorious, sacred Gurus,
Vajradhara, Pandit Naropa, and so forth,
The glorious Lords of all virtue and excellence.

May there be the auspiciousness of the Dakini Truth Body,
Perfection of wisdom, the supreme Mother of the
    Conquerors,
The natural clear light, free from elaboration from the
    beginning,
The Lady who emanates and gathers all things stable and
    moving.

May there be the auspiciousness of the Complete
    Enjoyment Body, spontaneously born,
A body, radiant and beautiful, ablaze with the glory of the
    major and minor marks,
A speech proclaiming the supreme vehicle with sixty
    melodies,
And a mind of non-conceptual bliss and clarity possessing
    the five exalted wisdoms.

May there be the auspiciousness of the Emanation Body,
    born in the places,
Ladies who with various Form Bodies, in various places,
Fulfil by various means the aims of various ones to be
    tamed
In accordance with their various wishes.

May there be the auspiciousness of the supreme Dakini,
    mantra-born,
A venerable Lady with a colour similar to that of a ruby,
With a smiling, wrathful manner, one face, two hands
    holding curved knife and skullcup,
And two legs in bent and outstretched positions.

May there be the auspiciousness of your countless
    millions of emanations
And the hosts of the seventy-two thousand [Dakinis]
Eliminating all the obstructions of practitioners
And bestowing the attainments that are longed for.

Prayers for the Virtuous Tradition

So that the tradition of Je Tsongkhapa,
The King of the Dharma, may flourish,
May all obstacles be pacified
And may all favourable conditions abound.

Through the two collections of myself and others
Gathered throughout the three times,
May the doctrine of Conqueror Losang Dragpa
Flourish for evermore.

The nine-line *Migtsema* prayer

Tsongkhapa, crown ornament of the scholars of the
    Land of the Snows,
You are Buddha Shakyamuni and Vajradhara, the
    source of all attainments,
Avalokiteshvara, the treasury of unobservable
    compassion,
Manjushri, the supreme stainless wisdom,
And Vajrapani, the destroyer of the hosts of maras.
O Venerable Guru-Buddha, synthesis of all Three Jewels,
With my body, speech and mind, respectfully I make
    requests:
Please grant your blessings to ripen and liberate myself
    and others,
And bestow the common and supreme attainments.

(3x)

THE TSOG OFFERING

Blessing the tsog offering

OM KHANDAROHI HUM HUM PHAT
OM SÖBHAWA SHUDDHA SARWA DHARMA SÖBHAWA
  SHUDDHO HAM
Everything becomes emptiness.

From the state of emptiness, from AH comes a broad and
expansive skullcup inside which the five meats, the five
nectars, and the five exalted wisdoms melt and there
arises a vast ocean of the nectar of exalted wisdom.
OM AH HUM HA HO HRIH   (3x)

> *Contemplate that it becomes an inexhaustible ocean of exalted
> wisdom nectar.*

Offering medicine nectars

I offer this supreme nectar
That far transcends vulgar objects;
The supreme commitment of all the Conquerors,
And the foundation of all attainments.

May you be pleased with the great bliss
Of the unsurpassed bodhichitta,
Purified of all stains of obstructions,
And completely free from all conceptions.

Making the tsog offering

HO This ocean of tsog offering of uncontaminated nectar,
Blessed by concentration, mantra, and mudra,
I offer to please the assembly of root and lineage Gurus.
OM AH HUM
Delighted by enjoying these magnificent objects of desire,
EH MA HO
Please bestow a great rain of blessings.

HO This ocean of tsog offering of uncontaminated nectar,
Blessed by concentration, mantra and mudra,

325

I offer to please the divine assembly of powerful Dakinis.
OM AH HUM
Delighted by enjoying these magnificent objects of desire,
EH MA HO
Please bestow the Dakini attainment.

HO This ocean of tsog offering of uncontaminated nectar,
Blessed by concentration, mantra and mudra,
I offer to please the divine assembly of Yidams and their
retinues.
OM AH HUM
Delighted by enjoying these magnificent objects of desire,
EH MA HO
Please bestow a great rain of attainments.

HO This ocean of tsog offering of uncontaminated nectar,
Blessed by concentration, mantra and mudra,
I offer to please the assembly of Three Precious Jewels.
OM AH HUM
Delighted by enjoying these magnificent objects of desire,
EH MA HO
Please bestow a great rain of sacred Dharmas.

HO This ocean of tsog offering of uncontaminated nectar,
Blessed by concentration, mantra and mudra,
I offer to please the assembly of Dakinis and Dharma
Protectors.
OM AH HUM
Delighted by enjoying these magnificent objects of desire,
EH MA HO
Please bestow a great rain of virtuous deeds.

HO This ocean of tsog offering of uncontaminated nectar,
Blessed by concentration, mantra and mudra,
I offer to please the assembly of mother sentient beings.
OM AH HUM
Delighted by enjoying these magnificent objects of desire,
EH MA HO
May suffering and mistaken appearance be pacified.

Outer offerings

OM VAJRA YOGINI SAPARIWARA AHRGHAM, PADÄM, PUPE,
DHUPE, ALOKE, GÄNDHE, NEWIDE, SHAPTA AH HUM

Inner offering

OM VAJRA YOGINI SAPARIWARA OM AH HUM

Eight lines of praise to the Mother

OM I prostrate to Vajravarahi, the Blessed Mother HUM
HUM PHAT
OM To the Superior and powerful Knowledge Lady
unconquered by the three realms HUM HUM PHAT
OM To you who destroy all fears of evil spirits with your
great vajra HUM HUM PHAT
OM To you with controlling eyes who remain as the vajra
seat unconquered by others HUM HUM PHAT
OM To you whose wrathful fierce form desiccates Brahma
HUM HUM PHAT
OM To you who terrify and dry up demons, conquering
those in other directions HUM HUM PHAT
OM To you who conquer all those who make us dull,
rigid and confused HUM HUM PHAT
OM I bow to Vajravarahi, the Great Mother, the Dakini
consort who fulfils all desires HUM HUM PHAT

Making the tsog offering to the Vajrayana
Spiritual Guide

Vajra Holder please listen to me,
This special tsog offering of mine,
I offer to you with a mind of faith;
Please partake as is your pleasure.

EH MA, great peace.
This great, blazing tsog offering burns up delusions
And in that way brings great bliss.
AH HO Everything is great bliss.
AH HO MAHA SUKHA HO

Concerning this, all phenomena are seen as pure,
Of this the assembly should have no doubt.
Since brahmins, outcasts, pigs and dogs
Are of one nature, please enjoy.

The Dharma of the Sugatas is priceless,
Free from the stains of attachment and so forth,
The abandonment of apprehender and apprehended;
Respectfully I prostrate to thatness.
AH HO MAHA SUKHA HO

Song of the Spring Queen

HUM All you Tathagatas,
Heroes, Yoginis,
Dakas and Dakinis,
To all of you I make this request:
O Heruka who delight in great bliss,
You engage in the Union of spontaneous bliss,
By attending the Lady intoxicated with bliss
And enjoying in accordance with the rituals.
AH LA LA, LA LA HO, AH I AH, AH RA LI HO
May the assembly of stainless Dakinis
Look with loving affection and accomplish all deeds.

HUM All you Tathagatas,
Heroes, Yoginis,
Dakas and Dakinis,
To all of you I make this request:
With a mind completely aroused by great bliss
And a body in a dance of constant motion,
I offer to the hosts of Dakinis
The great bliss from enjoying the lotus of the mudra.
AH LA LA, LA LA HO, AH I AH, AH RA LI HO
May the assembly of stainless Dakinis
Look with loving affection and accomplish all deeds.

HUM All you Tathagatas,
Heroes, Yoginis,
Dakas and Dakinis,
To all of you I make this request:
You who dance with a beautiful and peaceful manner,
O Blissful Protector and the hosts of Dakinis,
Please come here before me and grant me your blessings,
And bestow upon me spontaneous great bliss.
AH LA LA, LA LA HO, AH I AH, AH RA LI HO
May the assembly of stainless Dakinis
Look with loving affection and accomplish all deeds.

HUM All you Tathagatas,
Heroes, Yoginis,
Dakas and Dakinis,
To all of you I make this request:
You who have the characteristic of the liberation of great
    bliss,
Do not say that deliverance can be gained in one lifetime
Through various ascetic practices having abandoned great
    bliss,
But that great bliss resides in the centre of the supreme
    lotus.
AH LA LA, LA LA HO, AH I AH, AH RA LI HO
May the assembly of stainless Dakinis
Look with loving affection and accomplish all deeds.

HUM All you Tathagatas,
Heroes, Yoginis,
Dakas and Dakinis,
To all of you I make this request:
Like a lotus born from the centre of a swamp,
This method, though born from attachment, is unstained
    by the faults of attachment.
O Supreme Dakini, through the bliss of your lotus,
Please quickly bring liberation from the bonds of samsara.
AH LA LA, LA LA HO, AH I AH, AH RA LI HO
May the assembly of stainless Dakinis
Look with loving affection and accomplish all deeds.

HUM All you Tathagatas,
Heroes, Yoginis,
Dakas and Dakinis,
To all of you I make this request:
Just as the essence of honey in the honey source
Is drunk by swarms of bees from all directions,
So through your broad lotus with six characteristics
Please bring satisfaction with the taste of great bliss.
AH LA LA, LA LA HO, AH I AH, AH RA LI HO
May the assembly of stainless Dakinis
Look with loving affection and accomplish all deeds.

Blessing the offerings to the spirits

OM KHANDAROHI HUM HUM PHAT
OM SÖBHAWA SHUDDHA SARWA DHARMA SÖBHAWA
  SHUDDHO HAM
Everything becomes emptiness.

From the state of emptiness, from AH comes a broad and
expansive skullcup inside which the five meats, the five
nectars, and the five exalted wisdoms melt and there
arises a vast ocean of the nectar of exalted wisdom.
OM AH HUM HA HO HRIH   (3x)

Actual offering to the spirits

PHAIM
UTSIKTRA BALINGTA BHAKYÄSI SÖHA

HO This ocean of remaining tsog offering of
    uncontaminated nectar,
Blessed by concentration, mantra and mudra,
I offer to please the assembly of oath-bound guardians.
OM AH HUM
Delighted by enjoying these magnificent objects of desire,
EH MA HO
Please perform perfect actions to help practitioners.

> *Send out the remainder of the tsog offering to the*
> *accompaniment of music.*

May I and other practitioners
Have good health, long life, power,
Glory, fame, fortune,
And extensive enjoyments.
Please grant me the attainments
Of pacifying, increasing, controlling and wrathful actions.
You who are bound by oaths please protect me
And help me to accomplish all the attainments.
Eradicate all untimely death, sicknesses,
Harm from spirits and hindrances.
Eliminate bad dreams,
Ill omens and bad actions.

May there be happiness in the world, may the years be
   good,
May crops increase, and may Dharma flourish.
May all goodness and happiness come about,
And may all wishes be accomplished.

By the force of this bountiful giving
May I become a Buddha for the sake of living beings;
And through my generosity may I liberate
All those not liberated by previous Buddhas.

Colophon: This sadhana was translated under the compassionate
   guidance of Venerable Geshe Kelsang Gyatso.

The Uncommon Yoga
of Inconceivability

THE SPECIAL INSTRUCTION OF HOW TO REACH THE
PURE LAND OF KEAJRA WITH THIS HUMAN BODY

**Compiled by
Geshe Kelsang Gyatso**

Guru Sumati Buddha Heruka

Introduction

This sadhana or ritual prayer for the attainment of the Pure Land of Keajra is based on the sadhana written by Je Phabongkhapa. I have presented it in a simple manner to make it easy to understand and practise.

The instruction has two stages:

1 The preparatory practices
2 The actual practice of the uncommon yoga of inconceivability

Preparatory practices often seem more difficult than the actual practice. This is very common. For example, cooking is more difficult than eating, and preparing for a party is more difficult than the actual party!

This uncommon yoga practice is superior to powa practice, the practice of transference of consciousness to a Pure Land. For the effectiveness of this profound practice we should receive the empowerments of Heruka body mandala and Vajrayogini and the special instruction on the uncommon yoga of inconceivability from a qualified Spiritual Guide. We then need to apply effort to practising this instruction continually, thinking, 'With effort I can accomplish anything.' In this way we should lead ourself to the state of Heruka Father and Mother.

Geshe Kelsang Gyatso
10th January 2012
Vajrayogini Day

Venerable Vajrayogini

The Uncommon Yoga
of Inconceivability

THE PREPARATORY PRACTICES

Going for refuge

I and all sentient beings, the migrators as extensive
   as space, from this time forth until we reach the
   essence of enlightenment,
Go for refuge to the glorious, sacred Gurus,
Go for refuge to the complete Buddhas, the Blessed Ones,
Go for refuge to the sacred Dharmas,
Go for refuge to the superior Sanghas.   (3x)

Generating bodhichitta

Once I have attained the state of a complete Buddha,
I shall free all sentient beings from the ocean of
samsara's suffering and lead them to the bliss of full
enlightenment. For this purpose I shall practise the
stages of Vajrayogini's path.   (3x)

Generating special motivation

There is no guarantee that I shall not die today. Death
destroys my precious opportunity to attain the ultimate
goal of enlightenment and to benefit all sentient beings.
Therefore I must transform my body into the deathless
body by attaining Dakini Land, the Pure Land of Keajra.

We meditate on this determination for a short while.

Purifying ordinary appearance of ourself

When I search for my self with wisdom, instead of finding my self, I disappear. This is a clear indication that my self that I normally see does not exist at all.

We meditate on the mere absence of our self that we normally see.

Generating ourself as outer Vajrayogini

In the vast space of emptiness I appear as Venerable Vajrayogini with the usual features but without the phenomena source and cushion. I have a red-coloured body of light, and I assume the form of a sixteen-year-old in the prime of my youth.

We meditate on this belief.

Visualizing the channels

In the very centre of my body, which is the nature of light, is my central channel. As thin as a thread it is very straight, oily-red, and clear and transparent. The lower tip of the central channel is at the level of my navel, from where it ascends in a straight line with its upper tip touching the crown of my head. At either side of the central channel, with no intervening space, are the right and left channels. The right channel is red in colour and the left is white. The right channel begins at the tip of my right nostril and the left channel at the tip of my left nostril. From there, they both ascend in an arch to the crown of my head and from the crown they both descend to one inch below my navel with their tips turned upwards.

Generating our mind Vajrayogini

At my navel between the lower tip of the central channel and the lower tips of the right and left channels, which are turned upwards, there is a small empty space. In this place is my mind in the form of Vajrayogini, as small as the size of a thumb, with the usual features but without the phenomena source and cushion. Her two legs are standing on the lower tips of the right and left channels, which are turned upwards, and her crown is touching the lower tip of the central channel. This inner Vajrayogini is my mind. I am my mind Vajrayogini.

We meditate on this belief.

Purifying and transforming the world and its beings

From the heart of my mind Vajrayogini at the navel immeasurable five-coloured rays of light radiate, the nature of the five omniscient wisdoms. These purify the entire world and all the beings inhabiting it. The world transforms into the Pure Land of Keajra and all beings transform into Vajrayogini. They all melt into light and become one single ball of light. This dissolves into the heart of my mind Vajrayogini at the navel.

At this point we should practise the following meditation. We gently inhale and imagine that all the winds of the upper part of our body gather, flow down and reach the point just above our mind Vajrayogini at our navel. We then slightly tighten the muscles of the lower part of our body and draw up all the lower winds. These rise and reach the point just below our mind Vajrayogini at our navel. Both the upper and lower winds of our body are now held together at our navel. This is called 'vase breath' because the shape of the united upper and lower winds is like the shape of a vase. While holding the vase breath at our navel we concentrate on our mind Vajrayogini and strongly think, 'I am my mind Vajrayogini'. We meditate on this belief. Just before we begin to feel discomfort we exhale slowly and gently through the nostrils. Holding the vase breath helps us to prevent distractions and makes our concentration clear. Initially we will be unable to hold our breath for very long so we need to repeat this practice again and again.

339

THE ACTUAL PRACTICE OF THE UNCOMMON
YOGA OF INCONCEIVABILITY

Having gained deep familiarity with thinking 'I am my mind Vajrayogini', through which we have changed the basis of imputation of ourself, we then engage in the following contemplation and meditation:

When I reach the Pure Land of Keajra I shall be permanently free from sickness, ageing, death and samsara's rebirth, and I shall be able to benefit countless living beings through my emanations. I must go there now.

The two legs and two arms of outer Vajrayogini dissolve into her main body. The lower part of her main body dissolves into my mind Vajrayogini at the navel. My mind Vajrayogini ascends to the heart of outer Vajrayogini. The main body of outer Vajrayogini below the heart dissolves into my mind Vajrayogini at the heart. My mind Vajrayogini ascends to the crown of outer Vajrayogini. The main body of outer Vajrayogini below the crown dissolves into my mind Vajrayogini at the crown. Then the crown of outer Vajrayogini dissolves into my mind Vajrayogini, my mind Vajrayogini instantaneously flies through the higher sky of the Dharmakaya and reaches the Pure Land of Keajra.

We meditate on this belief single-pointedly without distraction.

The body of my mind Vajrayogini becomes smaller and smaller and dissolves into emptiness, which is inseparable from great bliss.

We meditate on the union of great bliss and emptiness, which is the actual inconceivability. We should repeat this actual practice of the uncommon yoga of inconceivability three or seven times in each session.

By gaining deep familiarity with the preparatory practices and the actual practice of this uncommon yoga through continually applying effort and receiving the powerful blessings of Heruka and Vajrayogini, practitioners will reach the Pure Land of Keajra with this human body. This will not be according to common appearance but the uncommon appearance and experience of fortunate practitioners. If a practitioner who is about eighty years old reaches the Pure Land of Keajra his or her body will transform into the body of a sixteen-year-old in the prime of his or her youth and become an uncontaminated body. Thus he or she will be permanently free from sickness, ageing, death and samsara's rebirth, and by continually practising Highest Yoga Tantra he or she will attain full enlightenment in that life.

Dedication

Through the practice of this Yoga of Inconceivability
May the door of Keajra Heaven be open to everyone,
So that all living beings may attain
The state of Heruka Father and Mother.

Through the virtues I have accumulated here,
May the doctrine of Conqueror Losang Dragpa –
The very essence of Buddhadharma –
Flourish for evermore.

Prayers for the Virtuous Tradition

So that the tradition of Je Tsongkhapa,
The King of the Dharma, may flourish,
May all obstacles be pacified
And may all favourable conditions abound.

Through the two collections of myself and others
Gathered throughout the three times,
May the doctrine of Conqueror Losang Dragpa
Flourish for evermore.

The nine-line *Migtsema* prayer

Tsongkhapa, crown ornament of the scholars of the
 Land of the Snows,
You are Buddha Shakyamuni and Vajradhara, the
 source of all attainments,
Avalokiteshvara, the treasury of unobservable
 compassion,
Manjushri, the supreme stainless wisdom,
And Vajrapani, the destroyer of the hosts of maras.
O Venerable Guru-Buddha, synthesis of all Three Jewels,
With my body, speech and mind, respectfully I make
 requests:
Please grant your blessings to ripen and liberate myself
 and others,
And bestow the common and supreme attainments.

(3x)

Colophon: This sadhana or ritual prayer for the attainment of the Pure
Land of Keajra was compiled by Venerable Geshe Kelsang Gyatso
Rinpoche based on traditional sources, 2012.

Feast of Great Bliss

VAJRAYOGINI SELF-INITIATION SADHANA

by
Je Phabongkhapa

Guru Vajradharma

Feast of Great Bliss

*By way of preparation first clean a suitable meditation room
and then, in front of statues or pictures of your Guru, Vajrayogini, and so forth, set up a clean table. On this arrange
the heap mandala of body, the nectar mandala of speech, and
the sindhura mandala of mind, as well as the tormas, outer
offerings, and so forth.*

*On a table in front of you, arrange in the traditional
manner the vase, inner offering, vajra and bell, damaru and
a small container of rice or flowers for scattering.*

As for the practice, there are three parts:

1 *The preliminaries*
2 *The actual practice*
3 *Conclusion*

THE PRELIMINARIES

*The preliminaries begin with the section in the self-generation
sadhana, from going for refuge up to and including blessing
the outer offerings (pp 287-289). This is followed by the
preliminary torma:*

Blessing the preliminary torma

OM KHANDAROHI HUM HUM PHAT
OM SÖBHAWA SHUDDHA SARWA DHARMA SÖBHAWA
  SHUDDHO HAM
Everything becomes emptiness.

From the state of emptiness, from YAM comes wind, from
RAM comes fire, from AH a grate of three human heads.
Upon this from AH appears a broad and expansive skullcup.

Inside from OM, KHAM, AM, TRAM, HUM come the five
nectars; from LAM, MAM, PAM, TAM, BAM come the five
meats, each marked by these letters. The wind blows, the
fire blazes, and the substances inside the skullcup melt.
Above them from HUM there arises a white, upside-down
khatanga which falls into the skullcup and melts whereby
the substances take on the colour of mercury. Above them
three rows of vowels and consonants, standing one above
the other, transform into OM AH HUM. From these, light
rays draw the nectar of exalted wisdom from the hearts of
all the Tathagatas, Heroes and Yoginis of the ten directions.
When this is added the contents increase and become vast.
OM AH HUM   (3x)

Inviting the guests of the torma

Perform the blazing mudra and recite:

PHAIM
Light rays from the letter BAM on the moon seat at my
heart invite the directional guardians, regional guardians,
nagas and so forth who reside in the eight great charnel
grounds. They come to the boundaries in the eight directions,
instantly enter into the clear light, and arise in the form of
Venerable Vajrayogini. From a white HUM in the tongue of
each guest, there arises a white, three-pronged vajra, through
which they partake of the essence of the torma by drawing it
through straws of light the thickness of only a grain of barley.

Offering the torma

OM KHA KHA, KHAHI KHAHI, SARWA YAKYA RAKYASA,
BHUTA, TRETA, PISHATSA, UNATA, APAMARA, VAJRA
DAKA, DAKI NÄDAYA, IMAM BALING GRIHANTU, SAMAYA
RAKYANTU, MAMA SARWA SIDDHI METRA YATZANTU,
YATIPAM, YATETAM, BHUDZATA, PIWATA, DZITRATA,
MATI TRAMATA, MAMA SARWA KATAYA, SÄDSUKHAM
BISHUDHAYE, SAHAYEKA BHAWÄNTU, HUM HUM PHAT
PHAT SÖHA   (2x)

Outer offerings

OM AHRGHAM PARTITZA SÖHA
OM PADÄM PARTITZA SÖHA
OM VAJRA PUPE AH HUM SÖHA
OM VAJRA DHUPE AH HUM SÖHA
OM VAJRA DIWE AH HUM SÖHA
OM VAJRA GÄNDHE AH HUM SÖHA
OM VAJRA NEWIDE AH HUM SÖHA
OM VAJRA SHAPTA AH HUM SÖHA

Inner offering

To the mouths of the directional guardians, regional guardians, nagas, and so forth, OM AH HUM

Requests

Play the damaru and bell while reciting:

You the entire gathering of gods,
The entire gathering of nagas,
The entire gathering of givers of harm,
The entire gathering of cannibals,
The entire gathering of evil spirits,
The entire gathering of hungry ghosts,
The entire gathering of flesh-eaters,
The entire gathering of crazy-makers,
The entire gathering of forgetful-makers,
The entire gathering of dakas,
The entire gathering of female spirits,
All of you without exception
Please come here and listen to me.
O Glorious attendants, swift as thought,
Who have taken oaths and heart commitments
To guard the doctrine and benefit living beings,
Who subdue the malevolent and destroy the dark forces
With terrifying forms and inexhaustible wrath,
Who grant results to yogic actions,
And who have inconceivable powers and blessings,
To you eight types of guest I prostrate.

I request all of you together with your consorts, children and
  servants
To grant me the fortune of all the attainments.
May I and other practitioners
Have good health, long life, power,
Glory, fame, fortune
And extensive enjoyments.
Please grant me the attainments
Of pacifying, increasing, controlling and wrathful actions.
O Guardians, always assist me.
Eradicate all untimely death, sicknesses,
Harm from spirits, and hindrances.
Eliminate bad dreams,
Ill omens and bad actions.

May there be happiness in the world, may the years be
  good,
May crops increase, and may Dharma flourish.
May all goodness and happiness come about,
And may all wishes be accomplished.

To fulfil the intentions of the glorious, sacred Gurus and
accomplish the welfare of all living beings as extensive as
space I must attain the state of Venerable Vajrayogini, the
supreme attainment of the Mahamudra. Therefore, I shall
accomplish the sindhura mandala of Venerable Vajrayogini,
perform the offerings, enter the mandala and receive the
empowerments. All you special guardians who delight in
white actions please accept this vast torma that I offer to
you and guard me from all hindrances that may prevent
me from completing the actions of the great mandala.
Please help me to attain enlightenment. And all you
dark forces, the evil spirits and hindrances who are not
empowered to see the secret practices, do not remain
here but go elsewhere.

Then play the damaru and bell forcefully while reciting:

OM SUMBHANI SUMBHA HUM HUM PHAT
OM GRIHANA GRIHANA HUM HUM PHAT

OM GRIHANA PAYA GRIHANA PAYA HUM HUM PHAT
OM ANAYA HO BHAGAWÄN VAJRA HUM HUM PHAT

Take the torma out.

Blessing the room and the offering substances

OM KHANDAROHI HUM HUM PHAT
OM SÖBHAWA SHUDDHA SARWA DHARMA SÖBHAWA
  SHUDDHO HAM
Everything becomes emptiness.

From the state of emptiness, from DHRUM there arises
a celestial mansion made of jewels of various colours. It
is square with four doorways and adorned with four
archways. It is decorated with all the ornaments and is
complete with all the essential features. Inside from AH
come broad and expansive wisdom skullcups. Inside each
of these there is a HUM. The HUMs melt and there arise
heavenly offering substances: drinking offerings, bathing
offerings, flowers, incense, lights, scented waters, food
and music, all of which are pure and abundant. They
shine and are pervasive, covering all the ground and
filling the whole of space like the billowing clouds of
offerings emanated by the Superior Samantabhadra.
Beyond conception, they arise and abound within the
sight of my Gurus, the divine assembly of Venerable
Vajrayogini, and all the Buddhas and Bodhisattvas.

Now bless the offerings with mudras:

OM AHRGHAM AH HUM
OM PADÄM AH HUM
OM VAJRA PUPE AH HUM
OM VAJRA DHUPE AH HUM
OM VAJRA DIWE AH HUM
OM VAJRA GÄNDHE AH HUM
OM VAJRA NEWIDE AH HUM
OM VAJRA SHAPTA AH HUM

Now perform the space-treasure mudra at the level of your brow and recite:

OM VAJRA PARANA KAM

Whereby the offerings increase many times. Now recite three times:

OM VAJRA GHÄNDE RANITA, PARANITA, SAMPARANITA, SARWA BUDDHA KHYETRA PATZALINI PENJA PARAMITA NADA SÖBHA WI, VAJRA DHARMA HRIDAYA, SANTO KHANI HUM HUM HUM HO HO HO AH KAM SÖHA

The first recitation invites the guests for the offerings to the space in front. With the second the meditation room is blessed by them, and with the third the offerings are blessed by them. Play the great cymbals [or bell and damaru].

THE ACTUAL PRACTICE

The actual practice has four parts:

1 *Meditation on self-generation*
2 *Accomplishing the vase*
3 *Accomplishing the mandala in front and making offerings*
4 *Receiving the empowerments*

MEDITATION ON SELF-GENERATION

This is performed in accordance with the section in the self-generation sadhana, from the meditation and recitation of Vajrasattva up to and including the yoga of daily actions (pp 289-310).

ACCOMPLISHING THE VASE

Generating the vase and the Deity within

OM KHANDAROHI HUM HUM PHAT
OM SÖBHAWA SHUDDHA SARWA DHARMA SÖBHAWA
SHUDDHO HAM
Everything becomes emptiness.

From the state of emptiness, from PAM comes a lotus and
from AH comes a moon. Upon this from DHRUM appears
a jewelled vase possessing all the essential features. Inside
from EH EH comes a red phenomena source, a double
tetrahedron, inside which from AH comes a moon
mandala, white with a shade of red. Upon this stands
a red letter BAM encircled by OM OM OM SARWA BUDDHA
DAKINIYE VAJRA WARNANIYE VAJRA BEROTZANIYE HUM
HUM HUM PHAT PHAT PHAT SÖHA, a red-coloured mantra
rosary standing counter-clockwise. From these, light rays
radiate making offerings to the Superior beings and
fulfilling the welfare of sentient beings. Gathering back,
they transform into an eight-petalled lotus of various
colours with a sun mandala at its centre. Upon this arises
Venerable Vajrayogini. Her outstretched right leg treads on
the breast of red Kalarati. Her bent left leg treads on the
head of black Bhairawa, which is bent backwards. She has
a red-coloured body which shines with a brilliance like
that of the fire of the aeon. She has one face, two hands,
and three eyes looking towards the Pure Land of the
Dakinis. Her right hand, outstretched and pointing
downwards, holds a curved knife marked with a vajra.
Her left holds up a skullcup filled with blood which she
partakes of with her upturned mouth. Her left shoulder
holds a khatanga marked with a vajra from which hang
a damaru, bell and triple banner. Her black hair hanging
straight covers her back down to her waist. In the prime
of her youth, her desirous breasts are full and she shows
the manner of generating bliss. Her head is adorned with
five human skulls and she wears a necklace of fifty human

skulls. Naked, she is adorned with five mudras and stands in the centre of a blazing fire of exalted wisdom.

Absorbing the wisdom beings

Now perform the blazing mudra and recite:

PHAIM
Light rays radiate from the letter BAM at my heart and, leaving from between my eyebrows, go to the ten directions. They invite all the Tathagatas, Heroes and Yoginis of the ten directions in the aspect of Vajrayogini.
DZA HUM BAM HO

The wisdom beings are summoned, dissolve, remain firm, and are delighted. Now with the lotus-turning mudra followed by the embracing mudra, recite:

OM YOGA SHUDDHA SARWA DHARMA YOGA SHUDDHO HAM

Putting on the armour

At places in her body arise moon mandalas upon which at her navel is red OM BAM, Vajravarahi; at her heart blue HAM YOM, Yamani; at her throat white HRIM MOM, Mohani; at her forehead yellow HRIM HRIM, Sachalani; at her crown green HUM HUM, Samtrasani; at all her limbs smoke-coloured PHAT PHAT, essence of Chandika.

Granting empowerment and adorning the crown

PHAIM
Light rays radiate from the letter BAM at my heart and invite the empowering Deities, the supported and supporting mandala of Glorious Chakrasambara, to the space before me.

O, all you Tathagatas, please grant the empowerment.

Requested in this way, the eight Goddesses of the doorways drive away hindrances, the Heroes recite auspicious verses, the Heroines sing vajra songs, and the Rupavajras and so forth make offerings. The Principal mentally resolves to

grant the empowerment and the four Mothers together
with Varahi, holding jewelled vases filled with the five
nectars, confer the empowerment through the crown of
her head.

'Just as all the Tathagatas granted ablution
At the moment of [Buddha's] birth,
Likewise do we now grant ablution
With the pure water of the gods.

OM SARWA TATHAGATA ABHIKEKATA SAMAYA SHRIYE HUM'

Saying this, they grant the empowerment. Her whole body
is filled, all stains are purified, and the excess water
remaining on her crown changes into Vairochana-Heruka,
together with the Mother, who adorn her crown.

Blessing the outer offerings

OM KHANDAROHI HUM HUM PHAT
OM SÖBHAWA SHUDDHA SARWA DHARMA SÖBHAWA
   SHUDDHO HAM
Everything becomes emptiness.

From the state of emptiness, from KAM come skullcup
vessels inside which from HUM come offering substances.
By nature emptiness, they have the aspect of the individual
offering substances and function as objects of enjoyment of
the six senses to bestow special, uncontaminated bliss.

OM AHRGHAM AH HUM
OM PADÄM AH HUM
OM VAJRA PUPE AH HUM
OM VAJRA DHUPE AH HUM
OM VAJRA DIWE AH HUM
OM VAJRA GÄNDHE AH HUM
OM VAJRA NEWIDE AH HUM
OM VAJRA SHAPTA AH HUM

Offering goddesses emanate from my heart and perform the offerings.

Outer offerings

OM VAJRA YOGINI SAPARIWARA AHRGHAM, PADÄM, PUPE, DHUPE, ALOKE, GÄNDHE, NEWIDE, SHAPTA PARTITZA HUM PHAT SÖHA

Inner offering

OM OM OM SARWA BUDDHA DAKINIYE VAJRA WARNANIYE VAJRA BEROTZANIYE HUM HUM HUM PHAT PHAT PHAT SÖHA OM AH HUM

Praise

O Glorious Vajrayogini,
Chakravatin Dakini Queen,
Who have five wisdoms and three bodies,
To you Saviour of all I prostrate.

To the many Vajra Dakinis,
Who as Ladies of worldly actions,
Cut our bondage to preconceptions,
To all of you Ladies I prostrate.

Blessing the water of the vase

First perform the lotus-turning mudra and recite:

HUM

Now hold the mantra thread with your left hand and the mala with your right. Contemplate:

The mantra rosary at my heart leaves by coiling around the mantra thread. It touches the body of the Venerable Lady, causing streams of nectar to flow from her pores and fill the vase.

OM OM OM SARWA BUDDHA DAKINIYE VAJRA WARNANIYE
VAJRA BEROTZANIYE HUM HUM HUM PHAT PHAT PHAT
SÖHA   (108x)

OM SUMBHANI SUMBHA HUM HUM PHAT
OM GRIHANA GRIHANA HUM HUM PHAT
OM GRIHANA PAYA GRIHANA PAYA HUM HUM PHAT
OM ANAYA HO BHAGAWÄN VAJRA HUM HUM PHAT
                                                                               (21x)

OM KHANDAROHI HUM HUM PHAT   (21x)

OM SARWA TATHAGATA ABHIKEKATA SAMAYA SHRIYE HUM
                                                                               (21x)

Outer offerings

OM VAJRA YOGINI SAPARIWARA AHRGHAM, PADÄM, PUPE,
DHUPE, ALOKE, GÄNDHE, NEWIDE, SHAPTA PARTITZA HUM
PHAT SÖHA

Inner offering

OM OM OM SARWA BUDDHA DAKINIYE VAJRA WARNANIYE
VAJRA BEROTZANIYE HUM HUM HUM PHAT PHAT PHAT
SÖHA OM AH HUM

Praise

O Glorious Vajrayogini,
Chakravatin Dakini Queen,
Who have five wisdoms and three bodies,
To you Saviour of all I prostrate.

To the many Vajra Dakinis,
Who as Ladies of worldly actions,
Cut our bondage to preconceptions,
To all of you Ladies I prostrate.

Requesting forbearance

OM VAJRA HERUKA SAMAYA, MANU PALAYA, HERUKA
TENO PATITA, DRIDHO ME BHAWA, SUTO KAYO ME BHAWA,
SUPO KAYO ME BHAWA, ANURAKTO ME BHAWA, SARWA
SIDDHI ME PRAYATZA, SARWA KARMA SUTZA ME, TZITAM
SHRIYAM KURU HUM, HA HA HA HA HO BHAGAWÄN,
VAJRA HERUKA MA ME MUNTSA, HERUKA BHAWA, MAHA
SAMAYA SATTÖ AH HUM PHAT

Whatever was faulty or not obtained,
And actions done with a deluded mind,
Please O Protector
Be patient with all of these.

*Now pour the drinking offering from the conch shell into
the vase.*

OM AH HUM   (3x)

The Venerable Lady inside the vase melts into light and
the water within the vase becomes powerful.

ACCOMPLISHING THE MANDALA IN FRONT AND
MAKING OFFERINGS

Blessing the nectar mandala of speech

Focus on the nectar mandala of speech and contemplate:

OM KHANDAROHI HUM HUM PHAT
OM SÖBHAWA SHUDDHA SARWA DHARMA SÖBHAWA
   SHUDDHO HAM
Everything becomes emptiness.

From the state of emptiness, from AH comes a broad and
expansive skullcup inside which the five meats, the five
nectars, and the five exalted wisdoms melt and there
arises a vast ocean of the nectar of exalted wisdom.

With mudras recite three times:

OM AH HUM HA HO HRIH

The actual practice of accomplishing the mandala

Now focus on all three mandalas:

OM KHANDAROHI HUM HUM PHAT
OM SÖBHAWA SHUDDHA SARWA DHARMA SÖBHAWA
  SHUDDHO HAM
Everything becomes emptiness.

From the state of emptiness, from YAM comes a wind
mandala, from RAM a fire mandala, from WAM a water
mandala, from LAM an earth mandala, and from SUM
Mount Meru. Upon this from AH appears a broad and
expansive wisdom skullcup completely filled with nectar.
Above this from HUM appears a vajra of various colours
with a HUM marking its centre. From this, light rays radiate
to the ten directions and there appear the vajra ground
below, the vajra fence around, and the vajra tent and
canopy above. Outside are the impenetrable hail of arrows
and the fire of exalted wisdom blazing as high as Mount
Meru. Inside is the circle of the eight great charnel grounds.
In the centre of these from EH EH comes a red phenomena
source, a double tetrahedron, inside which from AH comes
a moon mandala, white with a shade of red. In the centre
of this is a red letter BAM encircled by OM OM OM SARWA
BUDDHA DAKINIYE VAJRA WARNANIYE VAJRA BEROTZANIYE
HUM HUM HUM PHAT PHAT PHAT SÖHA, a red-coloured
mantra rosary standing counter-clockwise. From these,
light rays radiate making offerings to the Superior beings
and fulfilling the welfare of sentient beings. Gathering
back, they transform into an eight-petalled lotus of various
colours with a sun mandala at its centre. Upon this arises
Venerable Vajrayogini. Her outstretched right leg treads on
the breast of red Kalarati. Her bent left leg treads on the
head of black Bhairawa, which is bent backwards. She has
a red-coloured body which shines with a brilliance like

that of the fire of the aeon. She has one face, two hands,
and three eyes looking towards the Pure Land of the
Dakinis. Her right hand, outstretched and pointing
downwards, holds a curved knife marked with a vajra.
Her left holds up a skullcup filled with blood which she
partakes of with her upturned mouth. Her left shoulder
holds a khatanga marked with a vajra from which hang
a damaru, bell and triple banner. Her black hair hanging
straight covers her back down to her waist. In the prime
of her youth, her desirous breasts are full and she shows
the manner of generating bliss. Her head is adorned with
five human skulls and she wears a necklace of fifty human
skulls. Naked, she is adorned with five mudras and stands
in the centre of a blazing fire of exalted wisdom.

Absorbing the wisdom beings

PHAIM
Light rays radiate from the letter BAM at my heart and,
leaving from between my eyebrows, go to the ten
directions. They invite all the Tathagatas, Heroes, and
Yoginis of the ten directions in the aspect of Vajrayogini.
DZA HUM BAM HO
OM YOGA SHUDDHA SARWA DHARMA YOGA SHUDDHO HAM

Putting on the armour

At places in her body arise moon mandalas upon which
at her navel is red OM BAM, Vajravarahi; at her heart blue
HAM YOM, Yamani; at her throat white HRIM MOM, Mohani;
at her forehead yellow HRIM HRIM, Sachalani; at her crown
green HUM HUM, Samtrasani; at all her limbs smoke-coloured
PHAT PHAT, essence of Chandika.

Granting empowerment and adorning the crown

PHAIM
Light rays radiate from the letter BAM at my heart and invite
the empowering Deities, the supported and supporting
mandala of Glorious Chakrasambara.

O, all you Tathagatas, please grant the empowerment.

Requested in this way, the eight Goddesses of the doorways drive away hindrances, the Heroes recite auspicious verses, the Heroines sing vajra songs, and the Rupavajras and so forth make offerings. The Principal mentally resolves to grant the empowerment and the four Mothers together with Varahi, holding jewelled vases filled with the five nectars, confer the empowerment through the crown of her head.

'Just as all the Tathagatas granted ablution
At the moment of [Buddha's] birth,
Likewise do we now grant ablution
With the pure water of the gods.

OM SARWA TATHAGATA ABHIKEKATA SAMAYA SHRIYE HUM'

Saying this, they grant the empowerment. Her whole body is filled, all stains are purified, and the excess water remaining on her crown changes into Vairochana-Heruka, together with the Mother, who adorn her crown.

Inviting the guests of the offerings

With mudra, recite:

PHAIM
Light rays radiate from the letter BAM at my heart and invite Venerable Vajrayogini surrounded by the assembly of Gurus, Yidams, Buddhas, Bodhisattvas, Heroes, Dakinis, and both Dharma and mundane Protectors to come from Akanishta to the space before me.

Blessing the offerings

OM KHANDAROHI HUM HUM PHAT
OM SÖBHAWA SHUDDHA SARWA DHARMA SÖBHAWA
   SHUDDHO HAM
Everything becomes emptiness.

From the state of emptiness, from KAM come skullcup
vessels inside which from HUM come offering substances.
By nature emptiness, they have the aspect of the individual
offering substances and function as objects of enjoyment of
the six senses to bestow special, uncontaminated bliss.

OM AHRGHAM AH HUM
OM PADÄM AH HUM
OM ÄNTZAMANAM AH HUM
OM PROKYANAM AH HUM
OM PUPE AH HUM
OM DHUPE AH HUM
OM DIWE AH HUM
OM GÄNDHE AH HUM
OM NEWIDE AH HUM
OM SHAPTA AH HUM

OM RUWA AH HUM
OM SHAPTA AH HUM
OM GÄNDHE AH HUM
OM RASE AH HUM
OM PARSHE AH HUM

Offering goddesses emanate from my heart and perform
the offerings.

Outer offerings

Perform the appropriate mudras and make the offerings:

Offering the four waters

This supreme Tantric offering of water for drinking,
Pleasing, pure and free from stains,
I offer to you with a mind of faith.
Please accept and grant me your kindness.
OM AH HRIH PRAVARA SÄKARAM AHRGHAM PARTITZA
   HUM SÖHA

This supreme Tantric offering of water for the feet,
Pleasing, pure and free from stains,

I offer to you with a mind of faith.
Please accept and grant me your kindness.
OM AH HRIH PRAVARA SÄKARAM PADÄM PARTITZA HUM
  SÖHA

This supreme Tantric offering of water for the mouth,
Pleasing, pure and free from stains,
I offer to you with a mind of faith.
Please accept and grant me your kindness.
OM AH HRIH PRAVARA SÄKARAM ÄNTZAMANAM
  PARTITZA HUM SÖHA

This supreme Tantric offering of water for sprinkling,
Pleasing, pure and free from stains,
I offer to you with a mind of faith.
Please accept and grant me your kindness.
OM AH HRIH PRAVARA SÄKARAM PROKYANAM PARTITZA
  HUM SÖHA

Offering flowers, incense, lights, perfume, and food

With forms that arise from the brush of samadhi,
Their bodies as slender as saplings;
With radiant faces outshining the moon,
Red lips and eyes as blue as upali flowers,
These many young maidens arise from my mind
Holding beautiful garlands of flowers.
They are captured by the bliss of desire
As goddesses who bestow enjoyment.
To generate joy in the mandala beings,
I offer the bliss of these maidens to you.
OM VAJRA PUPE PARTITZA AH HUM

With forms that arise from the brush of samadhi,
Their bodies as slender as saplings;
With radiant faces outshining the moon,
Red lips and eyes as blue as upali flowers,
These many young maidens arise from my mind
Holding vessels of sweet-smelling incense.
They are captured by the bliss of desire

Hero Vajradharma

As goddesses who bestow enjoyment.
To generate joy in the mandala beings,
I offer the bliss of these maidens to you.
OM VAJRA DHUPE PARTITZA AH HUM

With forms that arise from the brush of samadhi,
Their bodies as slender as saplings;
With radiant faces outshining the moon,
Red lips and eyes as blue as upali flowers,
These many young maidens arise from my mind
Holding lights of glittering jewels.
They are captured by the bliss of desire
As goddesses who bestow enjoyment.
To generate joy in the mandala beings,
I offer the bliss of these maidens to you.
OM VAJRA DIWE PARTITZA AH HUM

With forms that arise from the brush of samadhi,
Their bodies as slender as saplings;
With radiant faces outshining the moon,
Red lips and eyes as blue as upali flowers,
These many young maidens arise from my mind
Holding perfumes whose fragrance pervades all worlds.
They are captured by the bliss of desire
As goddesses who bestow enjoyment.
To generate joy in the mandala beings,
I offer the bliss of these maidens to you.
OM VAJRA GÄNDHE PARTITZA AH HUM

With forms that arise from the brush of samadhi,
Their bodies as slender as saplings;
With radiant faces outshining the moon,
Red lips and eyes as blue as upali flowers,
These many young maidens arise from my mind
Holding foods endowed with a hundred flavours.
They are captured by the bliss of desire
As goddesses who bestow enjoyment.
To generate joy in the mandala beings,
I offer the bliss of these maidens to you.
OM VAJRA NEWIDE PARTITZA AH HUM

Offering music

I offer the sound of the beautiful music
Of countless heavenly instruments.
By hearing the sound of these various tunes
All torments of body and mind are removed.
OM VAJRA SHAPTA PARTITZA HUM SÖHA

Offering the sixteen knowledge goddesses

These offering goddesses in the prime of their youth
With beautiful bodies, so finely adorned,
Dancing and singing, give rise to all joys
And bestow perfect bliss on the senses.
With violin, flute, small and large drums
They bring joy to the ear with their music.
These vast clouds of offerings I send forth to you;
Be pleased to accept and bestow the supreme attainments.
OM VAJRA WINI HUM HUM PHAT
OM VAJRA WAMSHE HUM HUM PHAT
OM VAJRA MITAMGI HUM HUM PHAT
OM VAJRA MURANDZE HUM HUM PHAT

These offering goddesses in the prime of their youth
With beautiful bodies, so finely adorned,
Dancing and singing, give rise to all joys
And bestow perfect bliss on the senses.
With delightful smile, sensuous posture,
Melodious song, and beautiful dance,
These vast clouds of offerings I send forth to you;
Be pleased to accept and bestow the supreme attainments.
OM VAJRA HÄSA HUM HUM PHAT
OM VAJRA LASÄ HUM HUM PHAT
OM VAJRA GIRTI HUM HUM PHAT
OM VAJRA NIRTÄ HUM HUM PHAT

These offering goddesses in the prime of their youth
With beautiful bodies, so finely adorned,
Dancing and singing, give rise to all joys
And bestow perfect bliss on the senses.

Holding garlands of flowers, sweet-smelling incense,
Brilliant lights, and conch shells of scent,
These vast clouds of offerings I send forth to you;
Be pleased to accept and bestow the supreme attainments.
OM VAJRA PUPE HUM HUM PHAT
OM VAJRA DHUPE HUM HUM PHAT
OM VAJRA DIWE HUM HUM PHAT
OM VAJRA GÄNDHE HUM HUM PHAT

These offering goddesses in the prime of their youth
With beautiful bodies, so finely adorned,
Dancing and singing, give rise to all joys
And bestow perfect bliss on the senses.
Holding stainless mirrors, vessels of honey,
Various garments, and phenomena sources,
These vast clouds of offerings I send forth to you;
Be pleased to accept and bestow the supreme attainments.
OM RUPA BENZ HUM HUM PHAT
OM RASE BENZ HUM HUM PHAT
OM PARSHE BENZ HUM HUM PHAT
OM DHARMA DHATU HUM HUM PHAT

Offering the five objects of desire

All forms that exist throughout infinite realms
Transform and arise as goddesses
With smiling faces and beautiful bodies;
These Rupavajras I offer to you.
Through the force of all forms that exist
Appearing as Rupavajras,
May I receive unchanging great bliss
And complete the supreme concentration of emptiness
    and bliss.
OM RUPA BENZ HUM HUM PHAT

All sounds that exist throughout infinite realms
Transform and arise as goddesses
Singing sweet songs and playing the lute;
These Shaptavajras I offer to you.

Through the force of all sounds that exist
Appearing as Shaptavajras,
May I receive unchanging great bliss
And complete the supreme concentration of emptiness
   and bliss.
OM SHAPTA BENZ HUM HUM PHAT

All smells that exist throughout infinite realms
Transform and arise as goddesses
Who fill all directions with beautiful smells;
These Gändhavajras I offer to you.
Through the force of all smells that exist
Appearing as Gändhavajras,
May I receive unchanging great bliss
And complete the supreme concentration of emptiness
   and bliss.
OM GÄNDHE BENZ HUM HUM PHAT

All tastes that exist throughout infinite realms
Transform and arise as goddesses
Holding jewelled vessels brimming with nectar;
These Rasavajras I offer to you.
Through the force of all tastes that exist
Appearing as Rasavajras,
May I receive unchanging great bliss
And complete the supreme concentration of emptiness
   and bliss.
OM RASE BENZ HUM HUM PHAT

All touch that exists throughout infinite realms
Transforms and arises as goddesses
Who steal the mind with supremely soft touch;
These Parshavajras I offer to you.
Through the force of all touch that exists
Appearing as Parshavajras,
May I receive unchanging great bliss
And complete the supreme concentration of emptiness
   and bliss.
OM PARSHE BENZ HUM HUM PHAT

Offering parasols

With a thousand spokes of pure, shining gold,
Adorned at the top by a precious blue gem,
Studded with jewels and strings of pearls;
I offer to you these parasols.
OM VAJRA TSATAMGA PARTITZA HUM SÖHA

Offering banners and victory banners

With handles of jewels both straight and pliant,
Adorned at the top with a vajra and moon,
Their three silken tongues are tied with small bells
Which ring softly when stirred by the breeze.
Hanging to form three swirling curves
And adorned with beautiful creatures,
These banners of victory over negative forces,
And others of beauty I offer to you.
OM VAJRA KETU PRATANGI PARTITZA HUM SÖHA

Offering canopies

I offer vast clouds of canopies
Adorning the sky, made of priceless cloth,
With borders of folds of various silks
And emitting a sandalwood fragrance.
OM VAJRA BITANA PARTITZA HUM SÖHA

Offering the seven precious objects

Made from excellent gold from the Dzambu river,
With a thousand spokes spanning five hundred miles,
Aloft in the sky like a second sun,
Travelling thousands of miles in a day,
It carries four armies through the paths of space
To the four continents and the celestial realms.
By my offering to you this precious wheel
May all living beings accomplish Dharma realizations.
OM VAJRA CHAKRA PARTITZA HUM SÖHA

From all the eight corners of this lapiz jewel
Light radiates for a hundred miles
To brighten the night as if it were day
And soothe those stricken with fever.
It destroys disease and untimely death
And fulfils all wishes that come to mind.
By my offering to you this precious jewel
May all living beings fulfil their spiritual hopes.
OM VAJRA MANI RATNA PARTITZA HUM SÖHA

This beautiful lady so pleasing to see
Whose body and breath have the sweetest fragrance,
Who bestows supreme bliss on whoever she touches
And dispels thirst and hunger wherever she reigns,
A lady without the five kinds of faults
And endowed with the eight special features,
By my offering to you this precious queen
May all living beings enjoy a stainless great bliss.
OM VAJRA TRI RATNAPARTITZA HUM SÖHA

Having forsaken non-Dharma and harming others,
With perfect conduct and without dispute,
He knows the wishes of the lords of the earth
And fulfils them without being asked.
Having perfect skill in all the affairs
Of the actions of all kinds of people,
By my offering to you this precious minister
May all living beings fulfil the Conquerors' intentions.
OM VAJRA PARINI YAKA RATNA PARTITZA HUM SÖHA

Like a great snow mountain with seven limbs
And the strength of a thousand elephants,
He travels the world three times in a day,
So wise he is led by a thread.
He walks with care so as not to harm others
And conquers opposing forces.
By my offering to you this precious elephant
May all living beings be conveyed by the supreme vehicle.
OM VAJRA GADZE RATNA PARTITZA HUM SÖHA

Perfectly white, like a water lily,
With a precious jewelled crown and other adornments,
It is perfect in colour, shape, and form
And will travel the world three times in a day.
With a brilliant body free from disease
It can be ridden without ever tiring.
By my offering to you this precious supreme horse
May all living beings have supreme miracle powers.
OM VAJRA ASHÖ RATNA PARTITZA HUM SÖHA

With stores of wealth that last forever,
Precious diamonds, lapis, and sapphire,
Gold and silver and many rare jewels
Abundant in all directions,
He is harmless, honest, and without deceit,
And brings joy to the hearts of all.
By my offering to you this precious householder
May all living beings hold a treasure of teachings.
OM VAJRA GRIHAPATI RATNA PARTITZA HUM SÖHA

Inner offering

Now sprinkle the blessed inner offering as you recite:

OM Glorious and sacred Guru, you are the nature of all
the body, speech, mind, deeds, and qualities of all the
Tathagatas of the three times and the ten directions, you
are source of all the eighty-four thousand classes of
Dharma teaching, you are the principal of all the Superior
Sanghas, to you I make this offering.
OM AH HUM

Vajradharma, Lord of the family of the ocean of
    Conquerors,
Vajrayogini, supreme Mother of the Conquerors,
Naropa, powerful Son of the Conquerors,
I offer you this blissful, pure nectar of commitment
substance.
OM AH HUM

Pamtingpa, holder of the explanations of the great secrets
    for disciples,
Sherab Tseg, you are a treasure of all the precious secrets,
Malgyur Lotsawa, lord of the ocean of Secret Mantra,
I offer you this blissful, pure nectar of commitment
    substance.
OM AH HUM

Great Sakya Lama, you are powerful Vajradhara,
Venerable Sonam Tsemo, supreme vajra son,
Dragpa Gyaltsen, crown ornament of the vajra holders,
I offer you this blissful, pure nectar of commitment
    substance.
OM AH HUM

Great Sakya Pandita, master scholar of the land of the
    snows,
Drogon Chogyel Pagpa, crown ornament of all beings
    of the three grounds,
Shangton Choje, holder of the Sakya doctrine,
I offer you this blissful, pure nectar of commitment
    substance.
OM AH HUM

Nasa Dragpugpa, powerful accomplished one,
Sonam Gyaltsen, navigator of scholars and supremely
    accomplished ones,
Yarlungpa, lord of the whispered lineage of the family
    of accomplished ones,
I offer you this blissful, pure nectar of commitment
    substance.
OM AH HUM

Gyalwa Chog, refuge and protector of all migrators, both
    myself and others,
Jamyang Namka, you are a great being,
Lodro Gyaltsen, great being and lord of the Dharma,
I offer you this blissful, pure nectar of commitment
    substance.
OM AH HUM

Jetsun Doringpa, you are unequalled in kindness,
Tenzin Losel, you have practised in accordance with the
    [Guru's] words,
Kyentse, the expounder of the great, secret lineage of
    words,
I offer you this blissful, pure nectar of commitment
    substance.
OM AH HUM

Labsum Gyaltsen, holder of the mantra families,
Glorious Wangchug Rabten, all-pervading lord of the
    hundred families,
Jetsun Kangyurpa, principal of the families,
I offer you this blissful, pure nectar of commitment
    substance.
OM AH HUM

Shaluwa, all-pervading lord of the ocean of mandalas,
Kyenrabje, principal of all the mandalas,
Morchenpa, lord of the circle of mandalas,
I offer you this blissful, pure nectar of commitment
    substance.
OM AH HUM

Nesarpa, navigator of the ocean of whispered lineages,
Losel Phuntsog, lord of the whispered lineages,
Tenzin Trinlay, scholar who furthered the whispered
    lineages,
I offer you this blissful, pure nectar of commitment
    substance.
OM AH HUM

Kangyurpa, all-pervading lord upholding the Ganden
    doctrine,
Ganden Dargyay, friend of migrators in degenerate times,
Dharmabhadra, holder of the Ganden tradition,
I offer you this blissful, pure nectar of commitment
    substance.
OM AH HUM

Losang Chopel, lord of the Sutras and Tantras,
You have completed the essence of the paths of all the
    Sutras and Tantras,
Jigme Wangpo, scholar who furthered the Sutras and
    Tantras,
I offer you this blissful, pure nectar of commitment
substance.
OM AH HUM

Dechen Nyingpo, you have the blessings of Naropa
To explain perfectly in accordance with Naropa
The essence of the excellent ripening and liberating paths
    of the Naro Dakini,
I offer you this blissful, pure nectar of commitment
    substance.
OM AH HUM

Losang Yeshe, Vajradhara,
You are a treasury of instructions on the ripening and
    liberating [paths] of the Vajra Queen,
The supreme, quick path for attaining the vajra state,
I offer you this blissful, pure nectar of commitment
    substance.
OM AH HUM

My kind root Guru, Vajradharma,
You are the embodiment of all the Conquerors,
Who grant the blessings of all Buddhas' speech,
I offer you this blissful, pure nectar of commitment
    substance.
OM AH HUM

You, the entire assembly of glorious root and lineage
    Gurus,
Who reveal the instructions of the profound path
Of the ripening empowerments and the stainless Tantras,
I offer you this blissful, pure nectar of commitment
    substance.
OM AH HUM

Vajrayogini, you are my Yidam,
Even without moving from the truth of phenomena
    pervading space
You fulfil the welfare of living beings with various
    emanations,
I offer you this blissful, pure nectar of commitment
    substance.
OM AH HUM

And to all you mandala Deities associated with the four
    great classes of Tantra I make this offering.
OM AH HUM

OM GIRANDZA GIRANDZA KUMA KUMA KHUMTI SÖHA
To you Glorious Father and Mother Lord of the Charnel
    Grounds together with your retinue I make this offering.
OM AH HUM

To all the Heroes, Heroines, Dharma Protectors,
    Dharmapalas, directional guardians, regional
    guardians and nagas
I make this offering.
OM AH HUM

To all the guardians of the local places and to all sentient
    beings transformed into the Deity I make this offering.
OM AH HUM

OM AMRITA SÖDANA VAJRA SÖBHAWA ÄMAKO HAM
All the guests are satiated by this nectar of exalted
    wisdom.

Secret and thatness offerings

Venerable Vajrayogini stands in union with Chakrasambara,
who has transformed from her khatanga, and spontaneous
bliss and emptiness is generated in the minds of all the
guests.

Mentally created offerings

NAMO Through the blessings of the truth of phenomena,
the blessings of the completely pure minds of all the

Buddhas and Bodhisattvas, the force of Secret Mantra and mudra, and the power of my aspiration, concentration and prayer, may all the different types of offering in this world, both owned and unowned, together with inconceivable clouds of offerings like those emanated by the Bodhisattva Samantabhadra, appear and multiply before the Gurus, Venerable Vajrayogini and her assembly of Deities, and the Buddhas and Bodhisattvas.

With mudra, recite:

OM SARWA BI, PURA PURA, SURA SURA, AWATAYA AWATAYA
HO, NAMA SAMÄNTA BUDDHA NAM, ABHIMARAYE
PARANA IMAM GA GA NA KAM DHARMADHATU AKASHA
SAMÄNTAMAM, SARWA TATHAGATA APARI SHUDDHALE,
MANDALE MAMA PARANITE, PUNYEGYANA WALEN SARWA
TATHAGATA WALENTA BÄNDHA SÖTANA BALENZAYA SÖHA

Eight lines of praise to the Mother

OM NAMO BHAGAWATI VAJRA VARAHI BAM HUM HUM
PHAT
OM NAMO ARYA APARADZITE TRE LOKYA MATI BIYE SHÖRI
HUM HUM PHAT
OM NAMA SARWA BUTA BHAYA WAHI MAHA VAJRE HUM
HUM PHAT
OM NAMO VAJRA SANI ADZITE APARADZITE WASHAM
KARANITRA HUM HUM PHAT
OM NAMO BHRAMANI SHOKANI ROKANI SHOKANI KROTE
KARALENI HUM HUM PHAT
OM NAMA DRASANI MARANI PRABHE DANI PARADZAYE
HUM HUM PHAT
OM NAMO BIDZAYE DZAMBHANI TAMBHANI MOHANI
HUM HUM PHAT
OM NAMO VAJRA VARAHI MAHA YOGINI KAME SHÖRI
KHAGE HUM HUM PHAT

Extensive praise

If you wish you may recite the following extensive praise:

I respectfully bow to the feet of the Glorious Gurus,
The Lords of the Dharma who hold the treasure of the
    great exalted wisdom,
And with a mind of faith I offer this short praise
To Vajrayogini, the Supreme Mother of the Conquerors.

In the centre of a sun on an eight-petalled lotus,
With one face, two hands, and three blazing, darting eyes,
A venerable Lady, red as a ruby,
I prostrate to the Dakini of Complete Enjoyment.

To subdue those beings with strong attachment
You delight in the spontaneous, non-dual dance
With Glorious Heruka, the Lord of the world;
I prostrate to the Dakini in the great embrace.

Your mind of uncontaminated great bliss
Experiences perfect, unchanging, unsurpassed joy.
O Lady eternally filled with the taste of bliss,
I prostrate to the Dakini of great bliss.

The sphere of space, the completely pure truth of
phenomena free from elaboration,
Beautified by infinite good qualities,
O Lady endowed with all the supreme features,
I prostrate to the Dakini free from inherent existence.

Even though you are naturally free from conception,
Out of great compassion for all living beings
You fulfil all wishes like a wish-granting jewel;
I prostrate to the Dakini filled with compassion.

Having attained the ground of non-abiding nirvana
Free from the extremes of samsara and solitary peace,
You work without interruption to help living beings;
I prostrate to the tireless Dakini.

Through the power of unobservable compassion,
You abide for as long as samsara remains,
Without passing into a state of nirvana;
I prostrate to the unceasing Dakini.

Through meditating in four sessions on the profound path
of generation stage
With the meaning of the four empowerments, and then
making respectful requests,
May I receive a vajra body, the inseparable union of four
bodies;
Please grant me the blessings of the Dakini body.

Through verbal and mental recitation during three times
Of the collection of Secret Mantra letters that begins with
three OMs,
May I receive an inexpressible speech beyond all sounds
in the three worlds;
Please grant me the blessings of the Dakini speech.

Through striving in meditation to purify the two
obstructions
On the central channel path of the completion stages of
the perfect two truths,
May I receive a mind of unchanging bliss spontaneously
accomplishing the two purposes;
Please grant me the blessings of the Dakini mind.

Thus, through the force of making these praises and
requests,
May I be cared for by you, O Great Compassionate One;
And in this life, at death, in the bardo, or before too long,
May I attain the state of the great Dakini.

RECEIVING THE EMPOWERMENTS

As if seeing directly, focus on Venerable Vajrayogini, who is non-dual with your root Guru, surrounded by countless Heroes and Yoginis in front of you:

Ablution

'Just as all the Tathagatas granted ablution
At the moment of [Buddha's] birth,
Likewise do we now grant ablution
With the pure water of the gods.

OM SARWA TATHAGATA ABHIKEKATA SAMAYA SHRIYE HUM'

Taste a little nectar from the vase.

Requesting mandala offering

Contemplate that you are offering your body and enjoyments, together with your roots of virtue, while reciting:

OM VAJRA BHUMI AH HUM
Great and powerful golden ground,
OM VAJRA REKHE AH HUM
At the edge the iron fence stands around the outer circle.
In the centre Mount Meru the king of mountains,
Around which are four continents:
In the east, Purvavideha, in the south, Jambudipa,
In the west, Aparagodaniya, in the north, Uttarakuru.
Each has two sub-continents:
Deha and Videha, Tsamara and Abatsamara,
Satha and Uttaramantrina, Kurava and Kaurava.
The mountain of jewels, the wish-granting tree,
The wish-granting cow, and the harvest unsown.
The precious wheel, the precious jewel,
The precious queen, the precious minister,
The precious elephant, the precious supreme horse,
The precious general, and the great treasure vase.
The goddess of beauty, the goddess of garlands,

The goddess of song, the goddess of dance,
The goddess of flowers, the goddess of incense,
The goddess of light, and the goddess of scent.
The sun and the moon, the precious umbrella,
The banner of victory in every direction.
In the centre all treasures of both gods and men,
An excellent collection with nothing left out.
I offer this to you my kind root Guru inseparable from the
     Venerable Lady,
And request you to grant me your profound blessings.
Please accept with compassion for migrating beings,
And having accepted please grant us your blessings.

O Treasure of Compassion, my Refuge and Protector,
I offer you the mountain, continents, precious objects,
     treasure vase, sun and moon,
Which have arisen from my aggregates, sources and
     elements
As aspects of the exalted wisdom of spontaneous bliss and
     emptiness.

When I become a pure container
Through common paths, bless me to enter
The essence practice of good fortune,
The supreme vehicle, Vajrayana.

IDAM GURU RATNA MANDALAKAM NIRYATAYAMI

Request

Recite the following three times:

Vajra Holder, my jewel-like Guru,
Through whose kindness I can accomplish
The state of great bliss in an instant,
At your lotus feet humbly I bow.
To you, essence of all the Buddhas,
My root Guru, I go for refuge.

O Glorious Vajrayogini,
Chakravatin Dakini Queen,

Who have five wisdoms and three bodies,
To you Saviour of all I prostrate.
O Glorious Vajrayogini,
I request you, please grant your blessings.

Contemplate that from the Vajrayogini of the sindhura mandala there appears another who is similar in aspect, and inseparable from your Guru. Think that she now performs the actions of the Guru.

Putting on the eye ribbon

Put on the eye ribbon.

OM CHAKYU BANDHA WARAMANAYE HUM

Receiving the flower garland

Receive the flower garland.

AH KAM BIRA HUM

Dispelling outer obstacles

Contemplate:

Countless wrathful Khandarohis emanate from the sindhura mandala and banish to a great distance all evil spirits and obstructors who try to prevent me from receiving the profound blessings.
OM KHANDAROHI HUM HUM PHAT

Purifying inner obstacles

Now taste the inner offering.

OM AH HUM
My body and mind are filled with bliss and all inner obstacles are purified.

Venerable Vajrayogini

Answering the questions

'Dear one, who are you and what do you seek?'
I am a Fortunate One seeking great bliss.

'Dear one, why do you seek great bliss?'
To fulfil the commitment of supreme Buddhahood.

Generating the mind of all yogas

At my heart is a moon upon which stands a white vajra.
They are the nature of conventional and ultimate
bodhichitta.

The Venerable Lady touches your heart, stabilizing these minds and blessing them while reciting:

OM SARWA YOGA TSITA UPATAYAMI
OM SURA TE SAMAYA TÖN HO: SIDDHI VAJRA YATA SUKAM

Pledging secrecy

The Venerable Lady touches your crown with her vajra:

'Now you are entering into the lineage of all the Yoginis.
You should not mention these holy secrets of all the Yoginis
to those who have not entered the mandala of all the Yoginis
or to those who have no faith.'

Imagine that you take hold of the vajra in Vajrayogini's hand and are led before the Vajrayogini residing in the centre of the mandala.

DZA HUM BAM HO

Reciting this, you enter the outer [family]. Now to enter the inner [family]:

Taking the Bodhisattva vows

Think that in front of Vajrayogini you generate bodhichitta and take the Bodhisattva vows by reciting the Tantric seven-limb prayer three times:

I go for refuge to the Three Jewels
And confess individually all negative actions.
I rejoice in the virtues of all beings
And promise to accomplish a Buddha's enlightenment.

I go for refuge until I am enlightened
To Buddha, Dharma and the Supreme Assembly,
And to accomplish the aims of myself and others
I shall generate the mind of enlightenment.

Having generated the mind of supreme enlightenment,
I shall invite all sentient beings to be my guests
And engage in the pleasing, supreme practices of
    enlightenment.
May I attain Buddhahood to benefit migrators.

Taking Tantric vows - the nineteen commitments of the five Buddha families

Recite three times:

All Buddhas and your Sons
And all Heroes and Dakinis
Please listen to what I now say.
From this time forth
Until I reach the essence of enlightenment,
I, whose name is . . . ,
Shall generate the sacred, unsurpassed mind of
    enlightenment,
Just as all the Conquerors of the three times
Have assured themselves of enlightenment in this way.

From now on I shall maintain the vows
That come from Buddha [Vairochana],
The unsurpassed Three Jewels
Of Buddha, Dharma and Sangha.
I shall also firmly maintain
The three types of moral discipline:
Training in pure discipline, gathering virtuous Dharmas
And benefiting other living beings.

I shall perfectly maintain
The vajra, bell and mudra,
Of the great, supreme Vajra family,
And shall rely upon my Spiritual Guide.

I shall observe the pleasing commitments
Of the great Ratna family,
Always performing the four types of giving
Six times every day.

Concerning the great, pure Pema family,
Arisen from the great enlightenment,
I shall maintain individually the sacred Dharmas
Of the outer, the secret and the three vehicles.

Concerning the great, supreme Karma family,
I shall perfectly maintain individually
All the vows that I have taken
And make as many offerings as possible.

I shall generate the sacred, unsurpassed mind of
    enlightenment,
And for the sake of all living beings
I shall keep every one of my vows.

I shall deliver those not delivered,
Liberate those not liberated,
Give breath to those unable to breathe,
And lead all beings to a state beyond sorrow.

Taking the uncommon vows of Mother Tantra

Recite three times:

Eternally I shall go for refuge
To Buddha, Dharma and Sangha.
Eternally I shall go for refuge
To all three spiritual vehicles,
The Secret Mantra realizations,
The Dakinis, Heroes, Heroines, Empowering Deities,
And the great beings, the Bodhisattvas,

But most of all, to you my Spiritual Guide.
O Glorious Heruka and all the Heroes,
And all you countless Bodhisattvas,
The Nangdze Yoginis and so forth,
Please listen to what I now say.

From this time forth
Until I abide in non-duality
I shall maintain perfectly
The twenty-two pure practices of non-duality.

Visualizing the inner Yogini

Light rays radiate from the heart of Guru Vajrayogini and
purify my negativities, obstructions, and their imprints
together with my defiled body. They all become emptiness.
From the state of emptiness, from EH EH comes a red
phenomena source, a double tetrahedron, inside which
from AH comes a moon mandala, white with a shade of
red. In the centre of this is a red letter BAM encircled by
OM OM OM SARWA BUDDHA DAKINIYE VAJRA WARNANIYE
VAJRA BEROTZANIYE HUM HUM HUM PHAT PHAT PHAT
SÖHA, a red-coloured mantra rosary standing counter-
clockwise. From these, light rays radiate making offerings
to the Superior beings and fulfilling the welfare of sentient
beings. Gathering back, they transform into an eight-petalled
lotus of various colours with a sun mandala at its centre.
Upon this I arise in the form of Venerable Vajrayogini. My
outstretched right leg treads on the breast of red Kalarati.
My bent left leg treads on the head of black Bhairawa,
which is bent backwards. I have a red-coloured body
which shines with a brilliance like that of the fire of the
aeon. I have one face, two hands, and three eyes looking
towards the Pure Land of the Dakinis. My right hand,
outstretched and pointing downwards, holds a curved
knife marked with a vajra. My left holds up a skullcup
filled with blood which I partake of with my upturned
mouth. My left shoulder holds a khatanga marked with
a vajra from which hang a damaru, bell and triple banner.

My black hair hanging straight covers my back down to
my waist. In the prime of my youth, my desirous breasts
are full and I show the manner of generating bliss. My
head is adorned with five human skulls and I wear a
necklace of fifty human skulls. Naked, I am adorned
with five mudras and stand in the centre of a blazing fire of
exalted wisdom.

At my navel from EH EH comes a red phenomena source, a
double tetrahedron, inside which from AH comes a moon.
mandala, in the centre of which is a red letter BAM. Except
for the front and back, each of the other four corners is
marked by a pink joy swirl whirling counter-clockwise.

Now make requests by reciting three times:

O Precious Guru, please grant me the attainments of all the
body, speech, mind, deeds and qualities of all the Tathagatas
as well as every single mundane and supramundane
attainment. Please stabilize these attainments.

Recite the three-OM mantra and swallow the tinglo.

From the heart of the Venerable Lady before me there
comes a similar Venerable Lady the size of only a thumb.
She enters through my mouth and dances like lightning
from the crown of my head to the soles of my feet.
Finally she dissolves into the letter BAM at my navel. This
completely transforms and there arises an eight-petalled
lotus of various colours with a sun mandala at its centre.
Upon this arises Venerable Vajrayogini. Her outstretched
right leg treads on the breast of red Kalarati. Her bent left
leg treads on the head of black Bhairawa, which is bent
backwards. She has a red-coloured body which shines
with a brilliance like that of the fire of the aeon. She has
one face, two hands, and three eyes looking towards the
Pure Land of the Dakinis. Her right hand, outstretched
and pointing downwards, holds a curved knife marked
with a vajra. Her left holds up a skullcup filled with
blood which she partakes of with her upturned mouth.

Her left shoulder holds a khatanga marked with a vajra from which hang a damaru, bell and triple banner. Her black hair hanging straight covers her back down to her waist. In the prime of her youth, her desirous breasts are full and she shows the manner of generating bliss. Her head is adorned with five human skulls and she wears a necklace of fifty human skulls. Naked, she is adorned with five mudras and stands in the centre of a blazing fire of exalted wisdom.

At places in my body arise moon mandalas upon which at my navel is red OM BAM, Vajravarahi; at my heart blue HAM YOM, Yamani; at my throat white HRIM MOM, Mohani; at my forehead yellow HRIM HRIM, Sachalani; at my crown green HUM HUM, Samtrasani; at all my limbs smoke-coloured PHAT PHAT, essence of Chandika.

Absorbing the outer Yoginis

Contemplate:

The Venerable Lady before me dances with delight and proclaims the sound of the mantra. Light rays radiate from her heart and invite all the Buddhas and Bodhisattvas of the ten directions in the aspect of Venerable Vajrayogini.

Together with countless similar Vajrayoginis who emerge from the heart of the Venerable Lady before me, they dissolve into the crown of my head.

Recite the three-OM mantra and play the damaru and bell.

Recognizing the secret Dakini

Contemplate:

My red central channel, the width of an arrow, goes from between my eyebrows to my secret place. At the lower tip is a white joy swirl the size of only a grain of barley. Spinning furiously counter-clockwise, it ascends to my heart, whereby my whole body and mind are pervaded by bliss.

At the upper tip is a red joy swirl the size of only a grain of barley. Spinning furiously counter-clockwise, it descends to my heart, whereby all appearance dissolves into emptiness. At my heart they mix inseparably and the now pink joy swirl spins furiously counter-clockwise. It becomes smaller and smaller until it dissolves into clear light emptiness.

DHU DHURA GUHYA SAMAYA, OM BAM, HAM YOM, HRIM MOM, HRIM HRIM, HUM HUM, PHAT PHAT

Then, to stabilize, with the vajra touch your crown twice to form a cross and recite:

TIKTRA VAJRA

Now offer the flower:

OM PRATITZA VAJRA HO

Now touch the flower to your crown:

OM PRATI GRIHANA TÖN IMAM SATTÖ MAHABALA

'Today, O Glorious Yogini,
You have sought to open your eyes;
And by opening them you have attained
Vajra eyes that can see everything.'

OM VAJRA NETRA APAHARA PATRA LAM HRIH

Remove the eye ribbon.

HE VAJRA PASHÄ

Thus you are exhorted to look. Think:

I see clearly the entire supported and supporting mandala of Venerable Vajrayogini.

This concludes entering the mandala.

Requesting the four empowerments

Request your Guru for the blessings of the four empowerments by offering a mandala and then reciting three times:

O Glorious Yogini, bestower of empowerments,
Radiant Protector of all living beings,
Since you are the source of all good qualities
I request you now to grant me your blessings.

In an instant I arise as Venerable Vajrayogini in front of
the mandala. I am standing on a lion throne, lotus and
sun, and tread on Kalarati and Bhairawa. Above me are
parasols, to my right are victory banners, to my left are
other banners, and all around me are clouds of offerings.

Receiving the vase empowerment

PHAIM
Light rays radiate from the letter BAM at the heart of
Guru Vajrayogini and invite the empowering Deities,
the supported and supporting mandala of Glorious
Chakrasambara.

O, all you Tathagatas, please grant the empowerment.

Requested in this way, the eight Goddesses of the doorways
drive away hindrances, the Heroes recite auspicious verses,
the Heroines sing vajra songs, and the Rupavajras and so
forth make offerings. The Principal mentally resolves to
grant the empowerment and the four Mothers together with
Varahi, holding jewelled vases filled with the five nectars,
confer the empowerment through the crown of my head.

Now recite the auspicious verses:

O Glorious Heruka with your blazing body,
You shake the three worlds with HA HA, the sound of
    your laughter,
And you confound all the demons with HUM HUM PHAT
    PHAT.
Please grant me now the auspiciousness of Chakrasambara.

Your mantra body is conjoined with EVAM,
Your speech is the play of non-dual AHLIKALI,
Your mind has gone to the essence of ANG,
Please grant me now the auspiciousness of Vajravarahi.

388

'Just as all the Tathagatas granted ablution
At the moment of [Buddha's] birth,
Likewise do we now grant ablution
With the pure water of the gods.

OM SARWA TATHAGATA ABHIKEKATA SAMAYA SHRIYE
HUM TSATRA BIRA TÖN ABHIKINTZA MAM, KAKASE,
ULUKASE, SHONASE, SHUKARASE, YAMADHATI, YAMADUTI,
YAMADANGTRINI, YAMAMATANI BENZI BHAWA
ABHIKINTZA HUM HUM'

Saying this, they grant the empowerment. My whole body
is filled, all stains are purified, and the excess water
remaining on my crown changes into Vairochana-Heruka,
together with the Mother, who adorn my crown.

DZA HUM BAM HO The empowering Deities dissolve
through the crown of my head.

So that they remain firm recite:

OM SUPRA TIKTRA VAJRE YE SÖHA

Transmission of the mantra

A rosary of the three-OM mantra rises from the letter BAM
at the heart of Guru Vajrayogini. Leaving through her
mouth, it enters my mouth and dissolves into the letter
BAM at my heart.

*While contemplating this, recite the three-OM mantra three
times.*

Transmission of the promise

Recite three times:

O Guru Vajrayogini please listen to what I now say. I, whose
name is . . . , from this time forth until I reach the essence
of enlightenment, shall hold you, Venerable Vajrayogini, as
my personal Deity for attaining the Dakini state. I shall
recite the three-OM mantra . . . times each day.

When performing self-initiation it is not necessary to receive the transmission of the promise. It is sufficient to imagine strongly that you will hold the Venerable Lady as your personal Deity and then recite the following:

Transmission of the blessings

Recite three times while scattering flowers or grains:

O Blessed One, may I receive your blessings.
Please grant me your blessings.

Your Guru also says:

O Blessed One, may they receive your blessings. O Blessed One, please grant your blessings. May they receive all the blessings of the body, speech and mind of Venerable Vajrayogini.

Imagine that you place flowers on the crown of your head. Now take a little sindhura with your left ring finger and touch your forehead, throat, and heart while reciting the three-OM mantra. This is the transmission of the blessings.

Now think that the Venerable Lady says:

Thus you have received the vase empowerment in the heap mandala of body. All defilements of your body are purified, you are empowered to meditate on the eleven yogas of generation stage, and you will have the good fortune to attain the resultant Emanation Body.

Receiving the secret empowerment

Visualize as follows:

All the Tathagatas of the ten directions enter into union with the Yogini and the drops of their bodhichitta fall into the skullcup. The Venerable Lady takes these and places them on my tongue.

While reciting the three-OM mantra, take some nectar from the skullcup in front with your left ring finger and place it on your tongue. Contemplate:

I experience these drops flowing through my throat. They mix inseparably and become of one taste with the bodhichitta in the channels of my body, as if dissolving into commitment beings. The eighty conceptual thoughts dissolve into emptiness and I generate within my continuum a concentration held by great bliss and the clarity of emptiness.

Now think that the Venerable Lady says:

Thus you have received the secret empowerment in the nectar mandala of speech. All defilements of your speech are purified, you are empowered to meditate on the central channel path of completion stage, and you will have the good fortune to attain the resultant Complete Enjoyment Body.

Receiving the wisdom-mudra empowerment

Contemplate:

All the Heroes of the ten directions merge into one and transform into Glorious Heruka standing in union with Venerable Vajrayogini. With the clarity of Vajrayogini I receive their drops into my secret place.

Take some sindhura from the sindhura mandala with the tip of your left ring finger and place a drop at your navel, heart, throat, and forehead while reciting the three-OM mantra.

The bodhichitta at my secret place is drawn up to my navel. The entire channel wheel at my navel is filled with bodhichitta and I experience the exalted wisdom of joy.

The bodhichitta is drawn up to my heart. The entire channel wheel at my heart is filled and I experience the exalted wisdom of supreme joy.

The bodhichitta is drawn up to my throat. The entire channel wheel at my throat is filled and I experience the exalted wisdom free from [the appearance of] joy.

The bodhichitta is drawn up to my crown. The entire channel wheel at my crown is filled. At this point my whole body is pervaded by channels, all the channels are pervaded by bodhichitta, the bodhichitta is pervaded by bliss, the bliss is pervaded by emptiness, and I experience the spontaneously born joy that is the union of bliss and emptiness.

Now think that the Venerable Lady says:

Thus you have received the wisdom-mudra empowerment in the sindhura mandala of mind. All defilements of your mind are purified, you are empowered to rely upon the path of a messenger, and you will have the good fortune to attain the resultant Truth Body.

Receiving the word empowerment

The Venerable Lady in front of you says:

The ultimate nature of phenomena has no thing;
Like space, it is without stain.
With the vajra of the exalted wisdom of emptiness,
Meditate perfectly on emptiness.

Contemplate the meaning as follows:

From the beginning the ultimate nature of phenomena has not been polluted by even the slightest truly existent thing. It is like space, completely free from all elaborations of existence and non-existence, permanence and annihilation, samsara and nirvana. Necessarily from the beginning its entity has not been polluted by the elaborations of apprehender and apprehended; therefore it is without stain. Such is the object emptiness. With the object-possessor, the vajra of non-dual exalted wisdom in which all dualistic appearance has subsided, meditate perfectly on emptiness and you will generate great bliss union in your continuum.

Remain in meditative equipoise in this state for a while. Now think that the Venerable Lady says:

Thus you have received the precious word empowerment in the mandala of ultimate bodhichitta. All defilements of your three doors are purified, you are empowered to meditate on the path of inconceivability, and you will have the good fortune to attain the resultant Nature Body.

Receiving the commitment

Now recite three times:

I shall do everything
The Principal has said.

And then recite the following three times:

I offer myself to you
Henceforth to be your servant;
Please keep me as your disciple
And enjoy even my possessions.

Thanking mandala offering

Now offer a thanking mandala to thank your Guru for his kindness in granting the four empowerments:

OM VAJRA BHUMI AH HUM
Great and powerful golden ground,
OM VAJRA REKHE AH HUM
At the edge the iron fence stands around the outer circle.
In the centre Mount Meru the king of mountains,
Around which are four continents:
In the east, Purvavideha, in the south, Jambudipa,
In the west, Aparagodaniya, in the north, Uttarakuru.
Each has two sub-continents:
Deha and Videha, Tsamara and Abatsamara,
Satha and Uttaramantrina, Kurava and Kaurava.
The mountain of jewels, the wish-granting tree,
The wish-granting cow, and the harvest unsown.
The precious wheel, the precious jewel,
The precious queen, the precious minister,
The precious elephant, the precious supreme horse,

The precious general, and the great treasure vase.
The goddess of beauty, the goddess of garlands,
The goddess of song, the goddess of dance,
The goddess of flowers, the goddess of incense,
The goddess of light, and the goddess of scent.
The sun and the moon, the precious umbrella,
The banner of victory in every direction.
In the centre all treasures of both gods and men,
An excellent collection with nothing left out.
I offer this to you my kind root Guru inseparable from the
     Venerable Lady,
And thank you for bestowing upon me the kindness of
your profound blessings.
Please accept with compassion for migrating beings,
And having accepted please grant us your blessings.

The ground sprinkled with perfume and spread with
     flowers,
The Great Mountain, four lands, sun and moon,
Seen as a Buddha Land and offered thus,
May all beings enjoy such Pure Lands.

In short, may I never be parted from you, Venerable Guru
     Dakini,
But always come under your care,
And swiftly completing the grounds and paths
Attain the great Dakini state.

IDAM GURU RATNA MANDALAKAM NIRYATAYAMI

CONCLUSION

Thirdly, there are the concluding stages. First, the tormas.

Blessing the tormas

OM KHANDAROHI HUM HUM PHAT
OM SÖBHAWA SHUDDHA SARWA DHARMA SÖBHAWA
   SHUDDHO HAM
Everything becomes emptiness.

From the state of emptiness, from YAM comes wind, from RAM comes fire, from AH a grate of three human heads. Upon this from AH appears a broad and expansive skullcup. Inside from OM, KHAM, AM, TRAM, HUM come the five nectars; from LAM, MAM, PAM, TAM, BAM come the five meats, each marked by these letters. The wind blows, the fire blazes, and the substances inside the skullcup melt. Above them from HUM there arises a white, upside-down khatanga which falls into the skullcup and melts whereby the substances take on the colour of mercury. Above them three rows of vowels and consonants, standing one above the other, transform into OM AH HUM. From these, light rays draw the nectar of exalted wisdom from the hearts of all the Tathagatas, Heroes and Yoginis of the ten directions. When this is added the contents increase and become vast. OM AH HUM (3x)

Offering the tormas

From a HUM in the tongue of each guest, there arises a three-pronged vajra, through which they partake of the essence of the torma by drawing it through straws of light the thickness of only a grain of barley.

Offering the principal torma

Offer the torma while reciting three or seven times:

OM VAJRA AH RA LI HO: DZA HUM BAM HO: VAJRA DAKINI SAMAYA TÖN TRISHAYA HO

Offering the torma to the mundane Dakinis

Offer the torma while reciting twice:

OM KHA KHA, KHAHI KHAHI, SARWA YAKYA RAKYASI, BHUTA, TRETA, PISHATSA, UNATA, APAMARA, VAJRA DAKA, DAKI, NÄDAYA, IMAM BALING GRIHANTU, SAMAYA RAKYANTU, MAMA SARWA SIDDHI METRA YATZANTU, YATIPAM, YATETAM, BHUDZATA, PIWATA, DZITRATA, MATI TRAMATA, MAMA SARWA KATAYA, SÄDSUKHAM

BISHUDHAYE, SAHAYEKA BHAWÄNTU, HUM HUM PHAT
PHAT SÖHA

Outer offerings

OM VAJRA YOGINI SAPARIWARA AHRGHAM, PADÄM, PUPE,
DHUPE, ALOKE, GÄNDHE, NEWIDE, SHAPTA AH HUM

Inner offering

OM VAJRA YOGINI SAPARIWARA OM AH HUM

Praise

O Glorious Vajrayogini,
Chakravatin Dakini Queen,
Who have five wisdoms and three bodies,
To you Saviour of all I prostrate.

To the many Vajra Dakinis,
Who as Ladies of worldly actions,
Cut our bondage to preconceptions,
To all of you Ladies I prostrate.

Prayer to Behold the Beautiful Face of Vajrayogini

Bliss and emptiness of infinite Conquerors who, as if in
    a drama,
Appear as so many different visions in samsara and
    nirvana;
From among these you are now the beautiful, powerful
    Lady of Dakini Land,
I remember you from my heart, please care for me with
    your playful embrace.

You are the spontaneously born Mother of the Conquerors
    in the land of Akanishta,
You are the field-born Dakinis in the twenty-four places;
You are the action mudras covering the whole earth,
O Venerable Lady, you are the supreme refuge of myself,
    the Yogi.

You who are the manifestation of the emptiness of the
  mind itself,
Are the actual BAM, the sphere of EH, in the city of the
  vajra.
In the land of illusion you show yourself as a fearsome
  cannibal,
And as a smiling, vibrant, fair young maiden.

But no matter how much I searched, O Noble Lady,
I could find no certainty of your being truly existent.
Then the youth of my mind, exhausted by its elaborations,
Came to rest in the forest hut which is beyond expression.

How wonderful, please arise from the sphere of the
  Dharmakaya
And care for me by the truth of what it says
In the Glorious Heruka, King of Tantras,
That attainments come from reciting the supreme close
  essence mantra of the Vajra Queen.

In the isolated forest of Odivisha
You cared for Vajra Ghantapa, the powerful Siddha,
With the bliss of your kiss and embrace and he came to
  enjoy the supreme embrace;
O, please care for me in the same way.

Just as the venerable Kusali was led directly
From an island in the Ganges to the sphere of space,
And just as you cared for the glorious Naropa,
Please lead me also to the city of the joyful Dakini.

Through the force of the compassion of my supreme root
  and lineage Gurus,
The especially profound and quick path of the ultimate,
  secret, great Tantra,
And the pure superior intention of myself, the Yogi,
May I soon behold your smiling face, O Joyful Dakini
  Lady.

Kinkara

Requesting fulfilment of wishes

O Venerable Vajrayogini, please lead me and all sentient beings to the Pure Land of the Dakinis. Please bestow on us every single mundane and supramundane attainment.

Offering the torma to the Lord of the Charnel Grounds

Now it is necessary to offer a torma to Father and Mother Lord of the Charnel Grounds [Kinkara]. First bless the torma by reciting three times:

OM AH HUM HA HO HRIH

Light rays radiate from the letter BAM at my heart and invite from Ogyen, the palace of the Dakinis in the west, the Glorious Father and Mother Lord of the Charnel Grounds, together with their retinues. They partake of all the essence of the torma by drawing it through their tongues, which are straws of vajra light.

OM GIRANDZA GIRANDZA KUMA KUMA KHUMTI SÖHA SHRI SHAMASHANA ADHIPATI MAHA PISHATZI BALIMTA KHA KHA KHAHI KHAHI (3x)

OM SHRI SHAMASHANA ADHIPATI MAHA PISHATZI AHRGHAM, PADÄM, PUPE, DHUPE, ALOKE, GÄNDHE, NEWIDE, SHAPTA AH HUM

OM GIRANDZA GIRANDZA KUMA KUMA KHUMTI SÖHA OM AH HUM

Praise

HUM
I praise the Lord of the Charnel Grounds,
All the deeds of the Conquerors' minds
Assuming a terrifying form
To tame all spirits and fulfil all wishes.

By my praising and making offerings to you
Please fulfil your intended commitments,
And grant me all the attainments
Just as I have requested.

Dorje Shugden

Offering the torma to the general Dharma Protectors

OM AH HUM HA HO HRIH   (3x)

HUM
From your pure palace of great bliss in Akanishta,
Great powerful one emanating from Vairochana's heart,
Dorje Gur, chief of all the Protectors of the doctrine,
O Glorious Mahakala come here please and partake of this
    offering and torma.

From Yongdui Tsel and Yama's palace
And from the supreme place of Devikoti in Jambudipa,
Namdru Remati, chief Lady of the desire realm,
O Palden Lhamo come here please and partake of this
    offering and torma.

From the mandala of the bhaga sphere of appearance and
    existence,
Mother Yingchugma, principal Lady of all samsara and
    nirvana,
Chief of Dakinis and demons, fierce female protector of
    the mantras,
O Great Mother Ralchigma come here please and partake
    of this offering and torma.

From Silwa Tsel and Haha Gopa,
From Singaling and the Ti Se snow mountain,
And from Darlungne and Kaui Dragdzong,
O Zhingkyong Wangpo come here please and partake of
    this offering and torma.

From the eight charnel grounds and Risul in the south,
From Bodhgaya and glorious Samye,
And from Nalatse and glorious Sakya,
O Legon Pomo come here please and partake of this
    offering and torma.

From the charnel grounds of Marutse in the north-east,
From the red, rocky hills of Bangso in India,

And from the supreme places of Darlung Dagram and so
    forth,
O Yakya Chamdrel come here please and partake of this
    offering and torma.

Especially from Odiyana, Land of the Dakinis,
And from your natural abode,
Completely encircled by mundane and supramundane
    Dakinis,
O Father-Mother Lord of the Charnel Grounds come here
    please and partake of this offering and torma.

From the supreme places such as Tushita, Keajra, and so
    forth,
Great Protector of the doctrine of the second Conqueror,
Dorje Shugden, five lineages, together with your retinues,
Come here please and partake of this offering and torma.

I request you, I make offerings to you, O Host of
    Protectors of the Conqueror's doctrine,
I propitiate you and rely upon you, O Great Protectors
    of the Guru's words,
I cry out to you and beseech you, O Host of Destroyers
    of the obstructors of Yogis,
Please come here quickly and partake of this offering and
    torma.

I offer a torma adorned with red flesh and blood.
I offer drinks of alcohol, medicine nectars, and blood.
I offer the sound of large drums, thigh-bone trumpets
    and cymbals.
I offer large, black silk pennants that billow like clouds.

I offer breath-taking attractions equal to space.
I offer loud chants that are powerful and melodious.
I offer an ocean of outer, inner and secret commitment
    substances.
I offer the play of the exalted wisdom of inseparable bliss
    and emptiness.

May you protect the precious doctrine of Buddha.
May you increase the renown of the Three Jewels.
May you further the deeds of the glorious Gurus,
And may you fulfil whatever requests I make of you.

At this point the tsog offering is made in accordance with the rituals in the self-generation sadhana (pp 325-331).

Thanking offering

OM KHANDAROHI HUM HUM PHAT
OM SÖBHAWA SHUDDHA SARWA DHARMA SÖBHAWA
  SHUDDHO HAM
Everything becomes emptiness.

From the state of emptiness, from KAM come skullcup vessels inside which from HUM come offering substances. By nature emptiness, they have the aspect of the individual offering substances and function as objects of enjoyment of the six senses to bestow special, uncontaminated bliss.

OM AHRGHAM AH HUM
OM PADÄM AH HUM
OM VAJRA PUPE AH HUM
OM VAJRA DHUPE AH HUM
OM VAJRA DIWE AH HUM
OM VAJRA GÄNDHE AH HUM
OM VAJRA NEWIDE AH HUM
OM VAJRA SHAPTA AH HUM

Outer offerings

OM VAJRA YOGINI SAPARIWARA AHRGHAM, PADÄM, PUPE,
  DHUPE, ALOKE, GÄNDHE, NEWIDE, SHAPTA AH HUM

Inner offering

OM VAJRA YOGINI SAPARIWARA OM AH HUM

Eight lines of praise to the Mother

OM I prostrate to Vajravarahi, the Blessed Mother HUM
HUM PHAT
OM To the Superior and powerful Knowledge Lady
unconquered by the three realms HUM HUM PHAT
OM To you who destroy all fears of evil spirits with your
great vajra HUM HUM PHAT
OM To you with controlling eyes who remain as the vajra
seat unconquered by others HUM HUM PHAT
OM To you whose wrathful fierce form desiccates Brahma
HUM HUM PHAT
OM To you who terrify and dry up demons, conquering
those in other directions HUM HUM PHAT
OM To you who conquer all those who make us dull,
rigid and confused HUM HUM PHAT
OM I bow to Vajravarahi, the Great Mother, the Dakini
consort who fulfils all desires HUM HUM PHAT

Praise

O Glorious Vajrayogini,
Chakravatin Dakini Queen,
Who have five wisdoms and three bodies,
To you Saviour of all I prostrate

To the many Vajra Dakinis,
Who as Ladies of worldly actions,
Cut our bondage to preconceptions,
To all of you Ladies I prostrate.

Brief dedication

By this virtue may I quickly
Accomplish the actual Dakini,
And then lead every living being
Without exception to that ground.

Requesting fulfilment of wishes

Now with your palms pressed together, recite:

O Venerable Vajrayogini, please lead me and all sentient beings to the Pure Land of the Dakinis. Please bestow on us every single mundane and supramundane attainment.

(3x)

Requesting forbearance

Now recite the hundred-letter mantra of Heruka:

OM VAJRA HERUKA SAMAYA, MANU PALAYA, HERUKA TENO PATITA, DRIDHO ME BHAWA, SUTO KAYO ME BHAWA, SUPO KAYO ME BHAWA, ANURAKTO ME BHAWA, SARWA SIDDHI ME PRAYATZA, SARWA KARMA SUTZA ME, TZITAM SHRIYAM KURU HUM, HA HA HA HA HO BHAGAWÄN, VAJRA HERUKA MA ME MUNTSA, HERUKA BHAWA, MAHA SAMAYA SATTÖ AH HUM PHAT

Request forbearance by reciting:

Whatever mistakes I have made
Through not finding, not understanding,
Or not having the ability,
Please, O Protector, be patient with all of these.

Extensive dedication

Now, with a single-pointed mind, make the following traditional prayers to Guru Vajrayogini in the space before you:

Thus, through the force of meditating correctly on the
    excellent ripening and liberating paths
Of the powerful Lady of Dakini Land, the Mother of the
    Conquerors,
May I always come under the loving care
Of the perfect Guru, the source of attainments.

In the great ship of freedom and endowment,
Flying the white sail of mindfulness of impermanence,
And blown by the favourable wind of accepting and
    abandoning actions and effects,
May I be delivered from the fearsome ocean of samsara.

Through putting on the armour of the great mind of
    enlightenment,
Out of compassion for living beings, my mothers,
May I enter into the ocean of the Bodhisattva's deeds
And thus become a suitable vessel for the ripening
    empowerments.

Through the kindness of the qualified Vajra Holder
I enjoy the nectar of the Highest Yoga Tantra
    empowerments
And the blessings of the Venerable Lady;
Thus may I become a suitable vessel for meditation on the
    liberating paths.

By protecting as I would my eyeballs
The vows and commitments taken at that time,
And through practising the yogas of sleeping, rising and
    experiencing nectar,
May my three doors engage in the three joys.

Relying upon the crown-jewel of the non-deceptive objects
    of refuge,
Taking to heart the great purpose of migrators, my
    mothers,
And cleansing my stains and faults with the nectar of
    Vajrasattva,
May I be cared for by the compassionate, venerable Gurus.

The beautiful Mother of the Conquerors is the outer Yogini,
The letter BAM is the supreme inner Vajra Queen,
The clarity and emptiness of the mind itself is the secret
    Dakini Mother;
May I enjoy the sport of seeing the self-nature of each.

406

May I complete the yoga of generating myself as the Deity,
The marvellous method for bringing into the path of the
    three bodies
The three bases of purification – death, bardo and rebirth –
And the supreme method for ripening the realizations of
    the path and the result.

The worldly environment is the celestial mansion of the
    letter EH,
And its inhabitants, the sentient beings, are the Yoginis of
    the letter BAM;
Through the concentration of the great bliss of their union,
May whatever appearance arises be pure appearance.

Visualizing the inner channels and elements as the
    thirty-seven Deities,
Absorbing all phenomena of samsara and nirvana in the
    nature of the three messengers
And wearing the armour of the mantras,
May I never be disturbed by outer or inner obstacles.

Through verbal and mental recitation focused
    single-pointedly
On the mantra rosary at the emanation wheel and the
    Dharma wheel,
And through the two completion stage messengers arising
    at that time,
May I generate the exalted wisdom of spontaneous bliss
    and emptiness.

When through the hooking lights radiating from the letter
    BAM and mantra rosary
All three realms and their beings melt into light and
    dissolve into me,
And I too dissolve by stages into emptiness,
May my mind remain in the sphere of bliss and emptiness.

When I arise from that state as the Deity marked by the
armour,
Protected from all obstacles by the wrathful sound of the
boundaries,
May all appearance arise as the three secrets of the Deity,
And may I complete the yoga of daily actions and its
branches.

Thus, through the yogas [numbering] the directions and
the moon,
May I eventually be led directly to the city of Knowledge
Holders
By the coral-coloured Lady of joy
With freely hanging vermilion hair and orange, darting
eyes.

Having practised in a place of corpses with sindhura and
a langali stem,
And having wandered throughout the land,
May the beautiful Lady to whom the swirl at my forehead
transfers
Lead me to the Land of the Dakinis.

And if I am not delivered in this life,
Then through the force of my single-pointed effort in
meditation, recitation, and so on,
May the joyful Lady of Dakini Land take me into her care
Either in the bardo or within a few lives.

When, moved by powerful winds, my mind in the form of
the letter BAM
Leaves my central channel through the door of Brahma,
May I attain instant deliverance through the transcending
path
Of mixing with the mind of bliss and emptiness of the
Mother of the Conquerors.

When the inner Varahi has destroyed the creeping vine of
apprehender and apprehended,
And the dancing Lady residing in my supreme central
channel

Has emerged through the door of Brahma into the sphere
   of the pathway of clouds,
May she embrace and sport with the Hero, Drinker of
   Blood.

Through the yoga of unifying [the two winds], meditating
   single-pointedly
On the tiny seed of the five winds at the lotus of my navel,
May my mental continuum be satiated by a supreme bliss
From the fragrant drops pervading the channels of my
   body-mind.

When, through the laughing and smiling play of the
   beautiful Lady
Of blazing light tummo within my central channel,
The youthful letter HAM has been completely softened,
May I attain the ground of the great bliss of union.

When the reddish-black RAM residing in the centre of the
   three channels at my navel
Has been set ablaze by my upper and lower winds,
And its cleansing fire has burned away the seventy-two
   thousand impure elements,
May my central channel be completely filled with pure
   drops.

When the five-coloured drop between my eyebrows has
   gone to my crown,
And the stream of moon-liquid originating from it
Has reached the stamen of my secret lotus,
May I be satiated by the four joys of descending and
   ascending.

When, through being struck by the rays of five lights
   radiating from that drop,
All stable and moving phenomena, my body and so forth,
Have been transformed into a mass of brilliant, clear
   rainbows,
May I once again enter the natural abode, the sphere of
   bliss and emptiness.

When the Yogini of my own mind, the union beyond
    intellect,
The primordial state of inexpressible emptiness and clarity,
The original nature free from arising, ceasing, and abiding,
Recognizes its own entity, may I be forever nourished.

When my channels, winds, and drops have dissolved into
    the sphere of EVAM,
And the mind itself has attained the glory of the Truth
    Body of great bliss,
May I care for these migrators as extensive as space
With immeasurable manifestations of countless Form
    Bodies.

In short, may I never be parted from you, Venerable Guru
    Dakini,
But always come under your care,
And swiftly completing the grounds and paths
Attain the great Dakini state.

Through the blessings of the Conquerors and their
    marvellous Sons,
The truth of non-deceptive dependent relationship,
And the power and force of my pure, superior intention,
May all the points of my sincere prayers be fulfilled.

Requesting the Deity to remain

*If you have an image such as a statue or a painting you
should recite:*

Please remain here inseparable from this image
For the sake of all living beings;
Please grant us long, healthy, and prosperous lives,
And bestow the supreme attainments.
OM SUPRA TIKTRA VAJRE SÖHA

Requesting the Deity to return in the future

If you have no image then recite:

You who fulfil the welfare of all living beings
And bestow attainments as they are needed,
Please return to the Land of the Buddhas,
And return here again in the future.

VAJRA MU The wisdom beings return to their natural
abodes, the commitment beings dissolve into me, and the
other guests return to their own places.

Auspicious prayers

May there be the auspiciousness of swiftly receiving the
    blessings
Of the hosts of glorious, sacred Gurus,
Vajradhara, Pandit Naropa, and so forth,
The glorious Lords of all virtue and excellence.

May there be the auspiciousness of the Dakini Truth Body,
Perfection of wisdom, the supreme Mother of the
    Conquerors,
The natural clear light, free from elaboration from the
    beginning,
The Lady who emanates and gathers all things stable and
    moving.

May there be the auspiciousness of the Complete
    Enjoyment Body, spontaneously born,
A body, radiant and beautiful, ablaze with the glory of the
    major and minor marks,
A speech proclaiming the supreme vehicle with sixty
    melodies,
And a mind of non-conceptual bliss and clarity possessing
    the five exalted wisdoms.

May there be the auspiciousness of the Emanation Body,
    born in the places,
Ladies who with various Form Bodies, in various places,

411

Fulfil by various means the aims of various ones to be
  tamed
In accordance with their various wishes.

May there be the auspiciousness of the supreme Dakini,
  mantra-born,
A venerable Lady with a colour similar to that of a ruby,
With a smiling, wrathful manner, one face, two hands
  holding curved knife and skullcup,
And two legs in bent and outstretched positions.

May there be the auspiciousness of your countless
  millions of emanations
And the hosts of the seventy-two thousand [Dakinis]
Eliminating all the obstructions of practitioners
And bestowing the attainments that are longed for.

Prayers for the Virtuous Tradition

So that the tradition of Je Tsongkhapa,
The King of the Dharma, may flourish,
May all obstacles be pacified
And may all favourable conditions abound.

Through the two collections of myself and others
Gathered throughout the three times,
May the doctrine of Conqueror Losang Dragpa
Flourish for evermore.

The nine-line *Migtsema* prayer

Tsongkhapa, crown ornament of the scholars of the
  Land of the Snows,
You are Buddha Shakyamuni and Vajradhara, the
  source of all attainments,
Avalokiteshvara, the treasury of unobservable
  compassion,
Manjushri, the supreme stainless wisdom,
And Vajrapani, the destroyer of the hosts of maras.
O Venerable Guru-Buddha, synthesis of all Three Jewels,

With my body, speech and mind, respectfully I make
    requests:
Please grant your blessings to ripen and liberate myself
    and others,
And bestow the common and supreme attainments.

(3x)

Colophon: This sadhana was translated under the compassionate
guidance of Venerable Geshe Kelsang Gyatso.

Vajrayogini Retreat Preliminaries

by
Je Phabongkhapa

Venerable Vajrayogini

Vajrayogini Retreat
Preliminaries

Going for refuge and generating bodhichitta

Begin by going for refuge and generating bodhichitta briefly.

Instantaneous self-generation

In an instant I become Venerable Vajrayogini.

Blessing the inner offering

OM KHANDAROHI HUM HUM PHAT
OM SÖBHAWA SHUDDHA SARWA DHARMA SÖBHAWA
    SHUDDHO HAM
Everything becomes emptiness.

From the state of emptiness, from YAM comes wind, from
RAM comes fire, from AH a grate of three human heads.
Upon this from AH appears a broad and expansive skullcup.
Inside from OM, KHAM, AM, TRAM, HUM come the five
nectars; from LAM, MAM, PAM, TAM, BAM come the five
meats, each marked by these letters. The wind blows, the
fire blazes, and the substances inside the skullcup melt.
Above them from HUM there arises a white, upside-down
khatanga which falls into the skullcup and melts whereby
the substances take on the colour of mercury. Above them
three rows of vowels and consonants, standing one above
the other, transform into OM AH HUM. From these, light
rays draw the nectar of exalted wisdom from the hearts of
all the Tathagatas, Heroes, and Yoginis of the ten directions.
When this is added the contents increase and become vast.
OM AH HUM   (3x)

Accomplishing the cleansing water

OM KHANDAROHI HUM HUM PHAT
OM SÖBHAWA SHUDDHA SARWA DHARMA SÖBHAWA
SHUDDHO HAM
Everything becomes emptiness.

From the state of emptiness, from PAM there arises a white jewelled vase complete with all the essential features such as a large belly, a long neck, a down-turned lip and so forth.

OM DAB DE DAB DE MAHA DAB DE SÖHA

The water of the vase and the divine Ganga water become inseparable. Upon this, from PAM, comes a lotus, sun and corpse seat, and upon this, from PAM, comes a curved knife marked by a PAM. From this comes Khandarohi who is red with one face and two hands. Her right hand holds a curved knife and her left hand holds a skullcup. She grips a khatanga in the crook of her left arm. She is naked with bone ornaments and freely hanging hair. Her head is adorned with five human skulls and she wears a necklace of fifty human skulls. She has three eyes and stands with her right side outstretched.

At her crown is an OM, at her throat is an AH, and at her heart is a HUM. Light rays radiate from the HUM at her heart and invite from their natural abodes wisdom beings who are similar in appearance, together with the empowering Deities.

PHAIM
DZA HUM BAM HO They become non-dual.

The empowering Deities grant empowerment and her crown is adorned by Ratnasambhava.

Blessing the outer offerings

OM KHANDAROHI HUM HUM PHAT
OM SÖBHAWA SHUDDHA SARWA DHARMA SÖBHAWA
SHUDDHO HAM
Everything becomes emptiness.

From the state of emptiness, from KAM come skullcup vessels inside which from HUM come offering substances. By nature emptiness, they have the aspect of the individual offering substances and function as objects of enjoyment of the six senses to bestow special, uncontaminated bliss.

OM AHRGHAM AH HUM
OM PADÄM AH HUM
OM VAJRA PUPE AH HUM
OM VAJRA DHUPE AH HUM
OM VAJRA DIWE AH HUM
OM VAJRA GÄNDHE AH HUM
OM VAJRA NEWIDE AH HUM
OM VAJRA SHAPTA AH HUM

This blesses the two waters, flowers, incense, lights, perfume, food and music.

Outer offerings

OM AHRGHAM PARTITZA SÖHA
OM PADÄM PARTITZA SÖHA
OM VAJRA PUPE AH HUM SÖHA
OM VAJRA DHUPE AH HUM SÖHA
OM VAJRA DIWE AH HUM SÖHA
OM VAJRA GÄNDHE AH HUM SÖHA
OM VAJRA NEWIDE AH HUM SÖHA
OM VAJRA SHAPTA AH HUM SÖHA

Inner offering

OM KHANDAROHI HUM HUM PHAT OM AH HUM

Praise

Benzarahi, element of fire,
By nature mindfulness of phenomena,
Principal Dakini of the Lotus Family,
To you, Khandarohi, I prostrate.

Now take hold of the mantra thread and contemplate:

The mantra rosary at my heart leaves by coiling around the mantra thread. It moves the mind of the Deity within the vase whereby light rays radiate from her heart. These invoke all the blessings of the body, speech and mind of the Buddhas and Bodhisattvas of the ten directions in the aspect of light rays and nectars. These dissolve into the Deity in the vase and a stream of nectar flows from her body and fills the vase.

Contemplating this, recite one hundred times:

OM KHANDAROHI HUM HUM PHAT

Recite the hundred-letter mantra to purify anything added or omitted.

Outer offerings

OM AHRGHAM PARTITZA SÖHA
OM PADÄM PARTITZA SÖHA
OM VAJRA PUPE AH HUM SÖHA
OM VAJRA DHUPE AH HUM SÖHA
OM VAJRA DIWE AH HUM SÖHA
OM VAJRA GÄNDHE AH HUM SÖHA
OM VAJRA NEWIDE AH HUM SÖHA
OM VAJRA SHAPTA AH HUM SÖHA

Inner offering

OM KHANDAROHI HUM HUM PHAT OM AH HUM

Praise

Benzarahi, element of fire,
By nature mindfulness of phenomena,
Principal Dakini of the Lotus Family,
To you, Khandarohi, I prostrate.

Through the fire of great bliss the Deity within the vase melts into light and becomes of one taste with the water of the vase, which is the nature of bodhichitta.

In this way the cleansing water is accomplished.

Offering the torma to the general Dakinis

Blessing the torma

OM KHANDAROHI HUM HUM PHAT
OM SÖBHAWA SHUDDHA SARWA DHARMA SÖBHAWA
   SHUDDHO HAM
Everything becomes emptiness.

From the state of emptiness, from YAM comes wind, from RAM comes fire, from AH a grate of three human heads. Upon this from AH appears a broad and expansive skullcup. Inside, from OM, KHAM, AM, TRAM, HUM come the five nectars; from LAM, MAM, PAM, TAM, BAM come the five meats, each marked by these letters. The wind blows, the fire blazes, and the substances inside the skullcup melt. Above them from HUM there arises a white, upside-down khatanga which falls into the skullcup and melts whereby the substances take on the colour of mercury. Above them three rows of vowels and consonants, standing one above the other, transform into OM AH HUM. From these, light rays draw the nectar of exalted wisdom from the hearts of all the Tathagatas, Heroes, and Yoginis of the ten directions. When this is added the contents increase and become vast.
OM AH HUM   (3x)

Inviting the guests of the torma

Perform the blazing mudra and recite:

PHAIM
Light rays from the letter BAM on the moon seat at my heart invite the directional guardians, regional guardians, nagas, and so forth who reside in the eight great charnel grounds. They come to the boundaries in the eight directions,

instantly enter into the clear light, and arise in the form of Venerable Vajrayogini. From a white HUM in the tongue of each guest there arises a white, three-pronged vajra through which they partake of the essence of the torma by drawing it through straws of light the thickness of only a grain of barley.

Offering the torma

Recite two times:

OM KHA KHA, KHAHI KHAHI, SARWA YAKYA RAKYASA, BHUTA, TRETA, PISHATSA, UNATA, APAMARA, VAJRA DAKA, DAKI NÄDAYA, IMAM BALING GRIHANTU, SAMAYA RAKYANTU, MAMA SARWA SIDDHI METRA YATZANTU, YATIPAM, YATETAM, BHUDZATA, PIWATA, DZITRATA, MATI TRAMATA, MAMA SARWA KATAYA, SÄDSUKHAM BISHUDHAYE, SAHAYEKA BHAWÄNTU, HUM HUM PHAT PHAT SÖHA

Outer offerings

OM AHRGHAM PARTITZA SÖHA
OM PADÄM PARTITZA SÖHA
OM VAJRA PUPE AH HUM SÖHA
OM VAJRA DHUPE AH HUM SÖHA
OM VAJRA DIWE AH HUM SÖHA
OM VAJRA GÄNDHE AH HUM SÖHA
OM VAJRA NEWIDE AH HUM SÖHA
OM VAJRA SHAPTA AH HUM SÖHA

Inner offering

To the mouths of the directional guardians, regional guardians, nagas, and so forth, OM AH HUM

Requests

You the entire gathering of gods,
The entire gathering of nagas,
The entire gathering of givers of harm,
The entire gathering of cannibals,

The entire gathering of evil spirits,
The entire gathering of hungry ghosts,
The entire gathering of flesh-eaters,
The entire gathering of crazy-makers,
The entire gathering of forgetful-makers,
The entire gathering of dakas,
The entire gathering of female spirits,
All of you without exception
Please come here and listen to me.
O Glorious attendants, swift as thought,
Who have taken oaths and heart commitments
To guard the doctrine and benefit living beings,
Who subdue the malevolent and destroy the dark forces
With terrifying forms and inexhaustible wrath,
Who grant results to yogic actions,
And who have inconceivable powers and blessings,
To you eight types of guest I prostrate.

I request all of you together with your consorts,
    children and servants
To grant me the fortune of all the attainments.
May I and other practitioners
Have good health, long life, power,
Glory, fame, fortune,
And extensive enjoyments.
Please grant me the attainments
Of pacifying, increasing, controlling and wrathful
    actions.
O Guardians, always assist me.
Eradicate all untimely death, sicknesses,
Harm from spirits, and hindrances.
Eliminate bad dreams,
Ill omens and bad actions.

May there be happiness in the world, may the years be
    good,
May crops increase, and may Dharma flourish.
May all goodness and happiness come about,
And may all wishes be accomplished.

Giving the torma to the local guardians

Blessing the torma

OM KHANDAROHI HUM HUM PHAT
OM SÖBHAWA SHUDDHA SARWA DHARMA SÖBHAWA
    SHUDDHO HAM
Everything becomes emptiness.

From the state of emptiness, from a DHRUM before me comes a broad and expansive jewelled vessel. Inside from OM comes a torma, a vast ocean of uncontaminated nectar of exalted wisdom, which is brilliant and pervasive.
OM AH HUM   (3x)

Offering the torma

Recite three times:

NAMA SARWA TATHAGATA AWALOKITE OM SAMBHARA
    SAMBHARA HUM

Praise

To the Tathagata Rinchen Mang I prostrate.
To the Tathagata Sug Dze Dampa I prostrate.
To the Tathagata Ku Jam Le I prostrate.
To the Tathagata Jigpa Tamche Dang Drelwa I prostrate.

Request

I offer this torma, an ocean of nectar, possessing an excellent collection of the five objects of desire, to Denma, goddess of the earth, to all the regional guardians in the three thousand worlds, to the five long-life goddesses, to the guardians of the doctrine, to the local guardians, the lords of the sites throughout the land, and especially those who reside in this place. Please accept it, and without being jealous or annoyed with any of the actions performed by myself or any of my benefactors, create good conditions that suit our minds.

Through the force of my intention,
Through the force of the blessings of the Tathagatas,
And through the force of the truth of phenomena,
May any suitable purpose
That I wish to come about
Be accomplished without obstruction.

With this recitation request the local guardians to engage in activities that destroy obstacles and accomplish favourable conditions for completing a close retreat.

Giving and sending out the obstacle-dispelling torma

Invocation of the wrathful Deities

Light rays radiate from the letter BAM at my heart and invite the entire assembly of wrathful Deities to the space before me.
OM MAHA KRODHA RADZA SAPARIWARA VAJRA SAMADZA

HUM
O Light of exalted awareness blazing like the fire of the aeon,
Who burn away every trace of ignorance and the darkness
    of desire,
Who destroy all fears of the hateful Yama,
O Great Hero who wear a tiger skin to display your
    courage,
You who suppress all misleading demons and subdue all
    foes,
O Wrathful Knowledge King I beseech you to come to this
    place.
I invite you to subdue all those who mislead us;
Please come through the force of my offerings to help all
    living beings.

OM VAJRA MAHA KRODHA RADZA SAPARIWARA EH HÄ HI
PRAVARA SÄKARAM AHRGHAM PARTITZA SÖHA

Requesting the Deities to remain

PÄMA KA MA LA YE TÖN

Outer offerings

OM VAJRA MAHA KRODHA RADZA SAPARIWARA PRAVARA
SÄKARAM AHRGHAM PARTITZA SÖHA
OM VAJRA MAHA KRODHA RADZA SAPARIWARA PRAVARA
SÄKARAM PADÄM PARTITZA SÖHA
OM VAJRA MAHA KRODHA RADZA SAPARIWARA PUPE
PARTITZA SÖHA
OM VAJRA MAHA KRODHA RADZA SAPARIWARA DHUPE
PARTITZA SÖHA
OM VAJRA MAHA KRODHA RADZA SAPARIWARA ALOKE
PARTITZA SÖHA
OM VAJRA MAHA KRODHA RADZA SAPARIWARA GÄNDHE
PARTITZA SÖHA
OM VAJRA MAHA KRODHA RADZA SAPARIWARA NEWIDE
PARTITZA SÖHA
OM VAJRA MAHA KRODHA RADZA SAPARIWARA SHAPTA
PARTITZA SÖHA

Inner offering

OM VAJRA MAHA KRODHA RADZA SAPARIWARA OM AH
HUM

Praise and prostration

HUM
I prostrate to this assembly ablaze with great wrath,
Who from the non-dual state of emptiness, the nature of
    phenomena,
Display the form of Bhairawa skilled in means,
Never forsaking even worldly deeds.

Even though your exalted wisdom never moves from the
    state of peace,
Your bodily features display a wrathful, devouring manner,
And your voice resounds with the sound of a thousand
    thunderclaps;
I prostrate to you who subdue all [demons].

You display the sport of superior exalted awareness,
And in your hands hold various sharp weapons
To root out and destroy the great poison of the delusions;
I prostrate to you adorned by a canopy of snakes.

I prostrate to you who stand with your legs drawn and
    outstretched in the manner of a Hero
In the midst of a vast blazing fire like the end of the aeon,
Who burn up obstructors and spirits with your fearful eyes,
Which blaze like the sun and the moon.

You are ablaze with a brilliance like the ferocious great fire at
    the end of time,
Your terrifying fangs flash like a thousand bolts of
    lightning,
Your wrathful voice resounds with the roar of a thousand
    thunderclaps;
O King of wrathful Deities who subdue the mass of
    obstructors, to you I prostrate.

HUM
You who proclaim the fearful sound of HUM
And destroy every single obstacle,
O Deity who bestow all the attainments,
Enemy of obstructors, to you I prostrate.

Blessing the torma

*Sprinkle the obstacle-dispelling torma with cleansing water
from the action vase.*

OM KHANDAROHI HUM HUM PHAT
OM SÖBHAWA SHUDDHA SARWA DHARMA SÖBHAWA
    SHUDDHO HAM
Everything becomes emptiness.

From the state of emptiness, from DHRUM comes a vast
and expansive precious vessel. Inside, from OM, comes an
obstacle-dispelling torma, a vast ocean of uncontaminated
nectar.
OM AH HUM   (3x)

Summoning the obstructing spirits

Light rays radiate from the letter BAM at my heart and summon the hosts of obstructors who interfere with the performance of profound close retreat as guests to receive this offering torma.
AH KARA KAYA DZA

Offering the torma

Rotate the torma clockwise while reciting three times:

OM SARWA BIGNÄN NAMA: SARWA TATHAGATO BAYO BISHO MUKE BHÄ: SARWA DÄ KANG UGATE PARANA IMAM GA GA NA KHANG GRIHANA DAM BALIMTAYE SÖHA

Rotate the candles and finger-tormas counter-clockwise while reciting three times:

OM SUMBHANI SUMBHA HUM HUM PHAT
OM GRIHANA GRIHANA HUM HUM PHAT
OM GRIHANA PAYA GRIHANA PAYA HUM HUM PHAT
OM ANAYA HO BHAGAWÄN BYÄ RADZA HUM HUM PHAT

Ordering away the obstructing spirits

Perform the mudra for driving out spirits and recite:

HUM
All you obstructors, worldly gods, and so forth
Who inhabit the site of the great mandala, listen to what
    I now say.
I am going to perform a profound close retreat in this
    place
So you must go elsewhere.

If you act against what I say,
The blazing vajra of exalted wisdom
Will use wrathful methods to control you,
And without doubt all you obstructors will be subdued.

NAMO By the truth of the glorious, sacred Gurus, the venerable root and lineage Gurus, by the truth of Buddha, by the truth of Dharma, by the truth of Sangha, all those who are members of the Tathagata, Vajra, Ratna, Pema and Karma families, the different types of Deity of Essence, Mudra, Secret Mantra and Knowledge Mantra, and especially by the truth of Venerable Vajrayogini and her retinue of Deities, and in dependence upon the power and potential of the blessings of the great truth, all you obstructors, whoever you may be, who are trying to prevent me from performing a profound close retreat in this place should be satisfied by this torma as extensive as space that I am offering to you. You should abandon all harmful thoughts of inflicting harm and injury, and with a peaceful and beneficial mind, with a mind of enlightenment, each of you should now go back to your own places. If you do not go you will be overcome by the blazing vajra fires of wrathful exalted wisdom and you will definitely be completely subdued.

OM SUMBHANI SUMBHA HUM HUM PHAT
OM GRIHANA GRIHANA HUM HUM PHAT
OM GRIHANA PAYA GRIHANA PAYA HUM HUM PHAT
OM ANAYA HO BHAGAWÄN BYÄ RADZA HUM HUM PHAT

OM KHANDAROHI HUM HUM PHAT

While reciting these mantras forcefully, throw white mustard seeds and play the bell and damaru. Take the torma and place it a great distance away. Then think very strongly that until the end of your close retreat all interfering spirits have been banished to a great distance.

Setting up the boundaries

Near to your outer door place a boundary marker in a high place where no one will step over it. This is the boundary beyond which you must not go and inside which those not included within the retreat boundaries may not enter. Arrange offerings and tormas in front of the boundary marker and then sit facing it.

Blessing the outer offerings

OM KHANDAROHI HUM HUM PHAT
OM SÖBHAWA SHUDDHA SARWA DHARMA SÖBHAWA
 SHUDDHO HAM
Everything becomes emptiness.

From the state of emptiness, from KAM come skullcup
vessels inside which from HUM come offering substances.
By nature emptiness, they have the aspect of the individual
offering substances and function as objects of enjoyment
of the six senses to bestow special, uncontaminated bliss.

OM AHRGHAM AH HUM
OM PADÄM AH HUM
OM VAJRA PUPE AH HUM
OM VAJRA DHUPE AH HUM
OM VAJRA ALOKE AH HUM
OM VAJRA GÄNDHE AH HUM
OM VAJRA NEWIDE AH HUM
OM VAJRA SHAPTA AH HUM

Blessing the torma

OM KHANDAROHI HUM HUM PHAT
OM SÖBHAWA SHUDDHA SARWA DHARMA SÖBHAWA
 SHUDDHO HAM
Everything becomes emptiness.

From the state of emptiness, from YAM comes wind, from
RAM comes fire, from AH a grate of three human heads.
Upon this from AH appears a broad and expansive skullcup.
Inside from OM, KHAM, AM, TRAM, HUM come the five
nectars; from LAM, MAM, PAM, TAM, BAM come the five
meats, each marked by these letters. The wind blows, the
fire blazes, and the substances inside the skullcup melt.
Above them from HUM there arises a white, upside-down
khatanga which falls into the skullcup and melts whereby
the substances take on the colour of mercury. Above them
three rows of vowels and consonants, standing one above
the other, transform into OM AH HUM. From these, light

rays draw the nectar of exalted wisdom from the hearts of all the Tathagatas Heroes, and Yoginis of the ten directions. When this is added the contents increase and become vast.
OM AH HUM (3x)

Generating the boundary marker as Khandarohi

Sprinkle the boundary marker with water from the action vase and recite:

OM KHANDAROHI HUM HUM PHAT
OM SÖBHAWA SHUDDHA SARWA DHARMA SÖBHAWA
  SHUDDHO HAM
Everything becomes emptiness.

From the state of emptiness, from PAM comes a lotus, sun and corpse seat upon which, from PAM, comes a curved knife marked by a PAM. From this comes Khandarohi who is red with one face and two hands. Her right hand holds a curved knife and her left hand holds a skullcup. She grips a khatanga in the crook of her left arm. She is naked with bone ornaments and freely hanging hair. Her head is adorned with a crown of five human skulls and she wears a necklace of fifty human skulls. She has three eyes and stands with her right side outstretched.

At her crown is an OM, at her throat is an AH, and at her heart is a HUM. Light rays radiate from the HUM at her heart and invite from their natural abodes wisdom beings who are similar in appearance, together with the empowering Deities.

PHAIM
DZA HUM BAM HO They become non-dual.

The empowering Deities grant empowerment and her crown is adorned by Ratnasambhava.

Khandarohi

Outer offerings

OM AHRGHAM PARTITZA SÖHA
OM PADÄM PARTITZA SÖHA
OM VAJRA PUPE AH HUM SÖHA
OM VAJRA DHUPE AH HUM SÖHA
OM VAJRA ALOKE AH HUM SÖHA
OM VAJRA GÄNDHE AH HUM SÖHA
OM VAJRA NEWIDE AH HUM SÖHA
OM VAJRA SHAPTA AH HUM SÖHA

Inner offering

OM KHANDAROHI HUM HUM PHAT OM AH HUM

Praise

Benzarahi, element of fire,
By nature mindfulness of phenomena,
Principal Dakini of the Lotus Family,
To you, Khandarohi, I prostrate.

Offering the torma

From a HUM in the tongue of Khandarohi there arises a
three-pronged vajra through which she partakes of the
essence of the torma by drawing it through a straw of
light the thickness of only a grain of barley.

Offer the torma by reciting three times:

OM VAJRA AH RA LI HO: DZA HUM BAM HO: VAJRA DAKINI
SAMAYA TÖN TRISHAYA HO

Outer offerings

OM AHRGHAM PARTITZA SÖHA
OM PADÄM PARTITZA SÖHA
OM VAJRA PUPE AH HUM SÖHA
OM VAJRA DHUPE AH HUM SÖHA
OM VAJRA ALOKE AH HUM SÖHA
OM VAJRA GÄNDHE AH HUM SÖHA

OM VAJRA NEWIDE AH HUM SÖHA
OM VAJRA SHAPTA AH HUM SÖHA

Inner offering

OM KHANDAROHI HUM HUM PHAT OM AH HUM

Praise

Benzarahi, element of fire,
By nature mindfulness of phenomena,
Principal Dakini of the Lotus Family,
To you, Khandarohi, I prostrate.

Request

Scatter flowers while reciting:

O Khandarohi, please remain firm in this place until I, the practitioner, have completed my close retreat. Do not allow any outer obstacles to enter, and for the sake of the inner attainments please perform your deeds without wavering.

Imagine that Khandarohi accepts, and until you have finished your practice do not dissolve her into light but think that she remains in that place performing her deeds. Now recite the hundred-letter mantra, the mantra of the essence of dependent relationship for her to remain firm, and auspicious prayers.

The hundred-letter mantra of Heruka

OM VAJRA HERUKA SAMAYA, MANU PALAYA, HERUKA TENO PATITA, DRIDHO ME BHAWA, SUTO KAYO ME BHAWA, SUPO KAYO ME BHAWA, ANURAKTO ME BHAWA, SARWA SIDDHI ME PRAYATZA, SARWA KARMA SUTZA ME, TZITAM SHRIYAM KURU HUM, HA HA HA HA HO BHAGAWÄN, VAJRA HERUKA MA ME MUNTSA, HERUKA BHAWA, MAHA SAMAYA SATTÖ AH HUM PHAT

The mantra of the essence of dependent relationship

OM YE DHARMA HETU TRABHAWA HETUN TEKÄN
TATHAGATO HÄWADÄ TEKÄNTSAYO NIRODHA
EHWAMBHADHI MAHA SHRAMANIYE SÖHA

Meditation on the protection circle

Now return indoors and sprinkle the room with cleansing water and inner offering.

OM KHANDAROHI HUM HUM PHAT
OM SÖBHAWA SHUDDHA SARWA DHARMA SÖBHAWA
    SHUDDHO HAM
Everything becomes emptiness.

While snapping the thumb and forefinger of the left hand recite:

From the state of emptiness, in the east is the black mantra: OM SUMBHANI SUMBHA HUM HUM PHAT; in the north is the green mantra: OM GRIHANA GRIHANA HUM HUM PHAT; in the west is the red mantra: OM GRIHANA PAYA GRIHANA PAYA HUM HUM PHAT; and in the south is the yellow mantra: OM ANAYA HO BHAGAWÄN BYÄ RADZA HUM HUM PHAT. These mantras radiate light rays in their respective colours, forming a mass of blazing light that reaches from the Brahma realm above to the golden base below. The mantras and lights transform into a square vajra fence of various colours: black in the east, green in the north, red in the west, and yellow in the south. It reaches from the Brahma realm above to the golden base below. Simultaneous with the vajra fence, from a HUM there arises a vajra of various colours with a HUM marking its centre. Light radiates from the HUM and, descending to the golden base, transforms into the ground, which is the nature of vajras of various colours. Light rays ascending from the HUM in the variegated vajra transform, outside the fence, into a hail of arrows in the aspect of five-pronged vajras covering all directions above and around. Below these is the vajra tent. Below the tent and upon the fence is the vajra canopy. Together they form one complete unit without even the slightest gap. On the outside they are encircled by the vajra fire, which is like the fire at the end of the world.

Blessing the vajra ground

OM MEDINI VAJRA BHAWA VAJRA BÄNDHA HUM

Blessing the vajra fence

OM VAJRA PARKARA HUM BAM HUM

Blessing the vajra tent

OM VAJRA PANTSA RAM HUM BAM HUM

Blessing the vajra canopy

OM VAJRA BITANA HUM KAM HUM

Blessing the vajra arrows

OM VAJRA SARA DZÖLA TRAM SAM TRAM

Blessing the vajra fire

OM VAJRA DZÖLA ANALARKA HUM HUM HUM

Snapping the fingers as before, recite:

OM SUMBHANI SUMBHA HUM HUM PHAT
OM GRIHANA GRIHANA HUM HUM PHAT
OM GRIHANA PAYA GRIHANA PAYA HUM HUM PHAT
OM ANAYA HO BHAGAWÄN BYÄ RADZA HUM HUM PHAT

Migrators are forever free from hindrances.

This is the meditation on the protection circle. Now you should imagine that those who are included within the boundaries are actually here, within the protection circle. So that you will not forget them, make a note of their names and keep a tally, or at least recall them mentally.

Blessing the meditation seat

Place your left hand in the mudra of meditative equipoise while holding the bell, and place your right hand in the earth-pressing mudra touching the meditation seat while holding the vajra.

This meditation seat and everything beneath to the golden base is firm and solid, the nature of vajra.
OM AH: VAJRA AHSANA HUM SÖHA

Reciting this just seven times, while contemplating the seat to have a vajra nature, blesses the seat.

Protecting the directions

I have the clarity of the Deity. Innumerable light rays and hosts of wrathful Deities emanate from my body and banish all the obstructors who hinder the practices of listening, contemplating, and meditating.

While contemplating the meaning of this, recite each of the four mantras OM SUMBHANI etc. three times, and then recite OM KHANDAROHI etc. many times while sprinkling inner offering over yourself, the room, and your implements, beginning in the east and circling counter-clockwise through all four directions, once again driving out obstructors and providing protection.

Protecting oneself

At my crown, from an OM there arises a white wheel marked by an OM at its centre. At my throat, from an AH there arises a red lotus marked by an AH at its centre. At my heart, from a HUM there arises a blue vajra marked by a HUM at its centre.

Take some inner offering with the ring finger of your left hand and place a drop on your crown, throat, and heart. Recite three times:

OM AH HUM

Contemplate:

Thus light rays radiate from the three letters and bring back all the blessings of the body, speech, and mind of the Buddhas and Bodhisattvas of the ten directions in the aspect of the Deities of the three vajras and rays of light. These all dissolve into my three places and my three doors are blessed in the nature of the three vajras.

Contemplating the meaning of this protects you. At this point you should once again meditate on the protection circle. Together with the previous two, there are altogether three occasions when you should meditate on the protection circle. On the latter two it is not necessary to perform cleansing and purifying (with OM KHANDAROHI . . . and OM SÖBHAWA . . .), rather it is sufficient to visualize it clearly as before with strong meditation.

Having performed all the sections of the preliminaries well you should take a short rest, have something to eat and drink, and refresh yourself. Then, when dusk falls, you should begin the actual session.

Dissolving the boundary marker

When the close retreat and the counting have been properly completed, do a brief dawn session and then set up offerings and tormas in front of the boundary marker as before and bless them in the same way. Then offer the tormas, outer offerings, inner offerings, and praise as before. After that recite:

O Dakini Yingchug Khandarohi,
Just as you have perfectly performed your deeds
To help me in my virtuous actions,
So please return and help me again in the future.

Then recite the hundred-letter mantra three times and request forbearance.

Dissolution

OM
You who fulfil the welfare of all living beings
And bestow attainments as they are needed,
Please return to the Land of the Buddhas
And return here again in the future.

OM VAJRA MU The wisdom being of the boundary marker
returns to her natural abode and the commitment being is
delighted and dissolves into me.

> *Now you should make thanking offerings, make a tsog offering,
> perform the burning offering to fulfil the commitment,
> accomplish the mandala and make offerings, perform self-
> initiation, and finally dedicate your roots of virtue.*

Prayers for the Virtuous Tradition

So that the tradition of Je Tsongkhapa,
The King of the Dharma, may flourish,
May all obstacles be pacified
And may all favourable conditions abound.

Through the two collections of myself and others
Gathered throughout the three times,
May the doctrine of Conqueror Losang Dragpa
Flourish for evermore.

The nine-line *Migtsema* prayer

Tsongkhapa, crown ornament of the scholars of the
    Land of the Snows,
You are Buddha Shakyamuni and Vajradhara, the
    source of all attainments,
Avalokiteshvara, the treasury of unobservable
    compassion,
Manjushri, the supreme stainless wisdom,
And Vajrapani, the destroyer of the hosts of maras.
O Venerable Guru-Buddha, synthesis of all Three
    Jewels,

With my body, speech and mind, respectfully I make
  requests:
Please grant your blessings to ripen and liberate myself
  and others,
And bestow the common and supreme attainments.

(3x)

Colophon: This sadhana was translated under the compassionate
guidance of Venerable Geshe Kelsang Gyatso.

Preliminary Jewel

CONDENSED VAJRAYOGINI
RETREAT PRELIMINARIES

**Compiled by
Geshe Kelsang Gyatso**

Venerable Vajrayogini

Introduction

If you wish to engage in a short retreat on Vajrayogini, or if you do not have the resources or the necessary assistance to perform the more extensive preliminary practices, you may use the following condensed rituals as your retreat preliminaries.

A day or so before your retreat is due to begin you should carry out the following preparations:

(1) First clean the meditation room.
(2) Set up a shrine with a statue or picture of Vajrayogini and representations of your Guru and any other Deities you wish, as well as a stupa and a text.
(3) Set up a meditation seat facing the shrine. Make sure that it is firm and comfortable, with a slightly raised back.
(4) In front of the meditation seat set up a small table covered with a clean cloth. On this, from left to right, arrange your inner offering, vajra, bell, damaru and mala. In front of these place your sadhana texts.
(5) Think about what restrictions you will wish to place on your physical, verbal, and mental activities during your retreat so that you can clearly determine the physical, verbal, and mental boundaries of your retreat.

On the morning of the day that your retreat begins you should set out the following on the shrine:

(1) Five tormas on a slightly raised platform. If you cannot make tormas in the traditional manner you can offer packets of biscuits, jars of honey or jam, or any other pure food as tormas. Remember that the tormas must remain until the end of your retreat, so do not use substances that will deteriorate quickly.

(2) At least two rows of outer offerings. If you set up two rows, the row immediately in front of the tormas is for the in-front-generation and the row in front of that is for the self-generation. If possible, set up four rows. If you do this, the row immediately in front of the tormas is for the supramundane Deities, the next row is for the mundane Dakas and Dakinis, the next row is for the Dharma Protectors, and the row at the front is for the self-generation. All the rows should be set out from the left hand of the Deity. Thus the offerings to the self-generation should start from our left and the others should start from the in-front Deities' left, our right.

On the first day of a retreat it is customary to perform the preliminaries in the mid-afternoon, and then to take a short break and do the first full session of the retreat in the evening.

Preliminary Jewel

Having set up all the offerings, sit on the meditation seat and recite:

Going for refuge

I and all sentient beings, until we achieve enlightenment,
Go for refuge to Buddha, Dharma and Sangha. (3x)

Generating bodhichitta

Through the virtues I collect by giving and other
    perfections,
May I become a Buddha for the benefit of all. (3x)

Instantaneous self-generation

In an instant I become Venerable Vajrayogini.

Meditate briefly on divine pride.

Blessing the inner offering

Remove the lid from the inner offering container and recite:

OM KHANDAROHI HUM HUM PHAT
OM SÖBHAWA SHUDDHA SARWA DHARMA SÖBHAWA
  SHUDDHO HAM
Everything becomes emptiness.

From the state of emptiness, from YAM comes wind, from
RAM comes fire, from AH a grate of three human heads.
Upon this from AH appears a broad and expansive skullcup.
Inside, from OM, KHAM, AM, TRAM, HUM come the five
nectars; from LAM, MAM, PAM, TAM, BAM come the five
meats, each marked by these letters. The wind blows, the
fire blazes, and the substances inside the skullcup melt.

Above them from HUM there arises a white, upside-down khatanga which falls into the skullcup and melts whereby the substances take on the colour of mercury. Above them three rows of vowels and consonants, standing one above the other, transform into OM AH HUM. From these, light rays draw the nectar of exalted wisdom from the hearts of all the Tathagatas, Heroes and Yoginis of the ten directions. When this is added the contents increase and become vast.
OM AH HUM   (3x)

> *With strong concentration contemplate that the nectar in front of you possesses three qualities – it is a medicine nectar that prevents all diseases, it is a life nectar that destroys death, and it is a wisdom nectar that eradicates all delusions. Now taste the nectar and meditate briefly on bliss and emptiness.*

Blessing the meditation room, the implements, and oneself

> *Holding the inner offering container in your right hand, with your left ring finger sprinkle inner offering three times over your room, your seat, your implements, and your body, while reciting:*

OM AH HUM

> *Contemplate that everything is blessed and purified.*

Averting obstacles

> *Imagine that wrathful red Khandarohi Goddesses emanate from your heart and drive away all obstructing spirits and other hindrances from each of the ten directions. While imagining this, play the damaru and bell and recite many times:*

OM KHANDAROHI HUM HUM PHAT

> *Think that until your retreat is finished all obstructing spirits and other hindrances have been banished to a great distance.*

Meditation on the protection circle

Visualize the protection circle. Below is the vajra ground, around is the vajra fence, and above is the vajra tent and canopy. All are blue in colour, and made of indestructible vajras. Outside there is a mass of five-coloured flames: red, white, yellow, green, and blue, which are the nature of the five exalted wisdoms. The flames all swirl counter-clockwise. Imagine this very strongly and then recite:

OM SUMBHANI SUMBHA HUM HUM PHAT
OM GRIHANA GRIHANA HUM HUM PHAT
OM GRIHANA PAYA GRIHANA PAYA HUM HUM PHAT
OM ANAYA HO BHAGAWÄN VAJRA HUM HUM PHAT

Generate a firm conviction that the protection circle actually exists and is completely effective in protecting you from harm and hindrances.

Establishing the retreat boundaries

Now recollect your retreat boundaries of body, speech, and mind, and firmly resolve not to transgress them until your retreat is completed. Meditate on this determination for a while.

Blessing the meditation seat

Hold the bell in your left hand at the level of your navel. Your hand should be palm upwards and the opening of the bell should face your navel. Hold the vajra in your right hand and place the palm of your right hand on your right knee so that the tips of your fingers touch your meditation seat. Contemplate strongly that your meditation seat is the nature of vajra wisdom, indestructible and immovable. Then recite seven times:

OM AH VAJRA AHSANA HUM SÖHA

Blessing the mala

With the divine pride of being Vajrayogini, hold your right hand palm upwards at the level of your heart and contemplate that it is the nature of bliss. Place the mala in your right hand and enclose it with your left hand, which is the nature of emptiness. Then, remembering that the nature of the mala is emptiness, recite three or seven times:

OM OM OM SARWA BUDDHA DAKINIYE VAJRA WARNANIYE VAJRA BEROTZANIYE HUM HUM HUM PHAT PHAT PHAT SÖHA

Now blow on the mala between your hands. With strong concentration contemplate that your mala is now the nature of vajra speech, inseparable from great bliss and emptiness.

Blessing the vajra and bell

Hold the vajra in your right hand at the level of your heart and the bell in your left hand. Contemplate that the vajra is method and the bell is wisdom and then recite:

The vajra is method and the bell is wisdom. Both together are the nature of ultimate bodhichitta.

OM VAJRA AH HUM

Then play the bell while reciting:

OM VAJRA GHANTA HUM

Dedication prayers

By this virtue may I quickly
Accomplish the actual Dakini,
And then lead every living being
Without exception to that ground.

At my deathtime may the Protectors, Heroes, Heroines
    and so forth,
Bearing flowers, parasols and victory banners,
And offering the sweet music of cymbals and so forth,
Lead me to the Land of the Dakinis.

In short, may I never be parted from you, Venerable
    Guru Dakini,
But always come under your care,
And swiftly completing the grounds and paths
Attain the great Dakini state.

> *Now take a short rest, and after dusk begin the first full
> session of your retreat.*

Prayers for the Virtuous Tradition

So that the tradition of Je Tsongkhapa,
The King of the Dharma, may flourish,
May all obstacles be pacified
And may all favourable conditions abound.

Through the two collections of myself and others
Gathered throughout the three times,
May the doctrine of Conqueror Losang Dragpa
Flourish for evermore.

The nine-line *Migtsema* prayer

Tsongkhapa, crown ornament of the scholars of the
    Land of the Snows,
You are Buddha Shakyamuni and Vajradhara, the
    source of all attainments,
Avalokiteshvara, the treasury of unobservable
    compassion,
Manjushri, the supreme stainless wisdom,
And Vajrapani, the destroyer of the hosts of maras.
O Venerable Guru-Buddha, synthesis of all Three Jewels,
With my body, speech and mind, respectfully I make
    requests:
Please grant your blessings to ripen and liberate myself
    and others,
And bestow the common and supreme attainments.   (3x)

Colophon: This sadhana was compiled from traditional sources by
            Venerable Geshe Kelsang Gyatso.

Vajrayogini Burning Offering

by
Je Phabongkhapa

Introduction

In general, with regard to how to perform a burning offering to Venerable Vajrayogini there are many different types such as pacifying, increasing, controlling and wrathful, but these are explained elsewhere. Here we are concerned solely with how to perform a burning offering to fulfil the commitment of a close retreat, for as it says in *Ornament of Vajra Essence Tantra*:

> All faults of excess and omission in Secret Mantra
> Are redressed by a burning offering.

In the place where the burning offering is to be performed, first examine the site, seek permission to use it, and then purify it [by means of the site ritual appended to this sadhana]. Then on ground that is naturally white, or that has been coloured white, begin by determining the very centre, and from that draw lines in each of the cardinal and intermediate directions.

Take a piece of thread half a cubit in length, hold one end at the centre, and describe a circle. Then describe two more circles beyond that, each with a radius four finger-widths longer than the last. These are Muren and Kakyer respectively.

Now hold the thread at the point where the eastern line intersects the inner circle, measure off the distance to the centre, and then swing the thread to the left and right, marking the points where it intersects the inner circle. Then do the same from the western point. By drawing lines to connect these points the outline of a phenomena source will emerge. Draw a second set of lines one finger-width inside these. Now, on the cardinal lines in each of the four directions, mark a point two finger-widths beyond the outer circle. From these, measure the distance to each of the four intermediate lines and join these to form a square. This is the fireplace.

At the heart of the phenomena source in the centre of the hearth either draw a white vajra eight finger-widths in length or arrange a pile of red powder. In each of the four corners [of the phenomena source], apart from the front and the back, draw a joy swirl. The inside of the phenomena source is coloured red but its outline is white. The rest of the hearth and symbols should be only white in colour. Within Kakyer on the hearth draw a rosary of vajras, and within Muren draw either a rosary of curved knives or fire. At each of the four corners of the hearth draw a half-moon marked by a vajra.

When the hearth is drawn, erect a circle of milk-wood and other similar, clean firewood around the inner circle, Muren.

Now you should arrange neatly to hand all the ritual substances, leaving nothing out. These include the burning substances, from milk-wood to the special pacifying substance, that are to be offered to both the mundane and supramundane Deities. These should be prepared according to the general system for pacifying. According to the words of the previous Lamas within this tradition, both alcohol and beef must be included. In addition there should be the tormas, two sets of outer offerings, two sets of garments, tambula tormas, the four waters, cleansing water, inner offering, a wind flag, a small pile of kusha grass, a ladle and a funnel, and materials for lighting the fire.

Vajrayogini Burning Offering

There are three stages to the burning offering:

1 *The preliminaries*
2 *The actual practice*
3 *Subsequent activities*

THE PRELIMINARIES

Begin by practising the stages of self-generation up to and including the yoga of inconceivability (pp 287-310). Then you, Venerable Vajrayogini, radiate rays of white light from your body.

Now, at the fire puja site, accomplish the cleansing water in an action vase by reciting one hundred Khandarohi mantras.

ACCOMPLISHING THE CLEANSING WATER

Accomplishing the cleansing water

OM KHANDAROHI HUM HUM PHAT
OM SOBHAWA SHUDDHA SARWA DHARMA SOBHAWA
  SHUDDHO HAM
Everything becomes emptiness.

From the state of emptiness, from PAM there arises a white jewelled vase complete with all the essential features such as a large belly, a long neck, a down-turned lip and so forth.

OM DAB DE DAB DE MAHA DAB DE SOHA

The water of the vase and the divine Ganga water become inseparable. Upon this, from PAM, comes a lotus, sun and corpse seat, and upon this, from PAM, comes a curved

knife marked by a PAM. From this comes Khandarohi who
is red with one face and two hands. Her right hand holds
a curved knife and her left hand holds a skullcup. She
grips a khatanga in the crook of her left arm. She is naked
with bone ornaments and freely hanging hair. Her head is
adorned with five human skulls and she wears a necklace
of fifty human skulls. She has three eyes and stands with
her right side outstretched.

At her crown is an OM, at her throat is an AH, and at
her heart is a HUM. Light rays radiate from the HUM at
her heart and invite from their natural abodes wisdom
beings who are similar in appearance, together with the
empowering Deities.

PHAIM

DZA HUM BAM HO They become non-dual.

The empowering Deities grant empowerment and her
crown is adorned by Ratnasambhava.

Blessing the outer offerings

OM KHANDAROHI HUM HUM PHAT
OM SOBHAWA SHUDDHA SARWA DHARMA SOBHAWA
  SHUDDHO HAM
Everything becomes emptiness.

From the state of emptiness, from KAM come skullcup
vessels inside which from hum come offering substances.
By nature emptiness, they have the aspect of the individual
offering substances and function as objects of enjoyment of
the six senses to bestow special, uncontaminated bliss.

OM AHRGHAM AH HUM
OM PADÄM AH HUM
OM VAJRA PUPE AH HUM
OM VAJRA DHUPE AH HUM
OM VAJRA DIWE AH HUM
OM VAJRA GÄNDHE AH HUM
OM VAJRA NEWIDE AH HUM
OM VAJRA SHAPTA AH HUM

This blesses the two waters, flowers, incense, lights, perfume, food and music.

Outer offerings

OM AHRGHAM PARTITZA SÖHA
OM PADÄM PARTITZA SÖHA
OM VAJRA PUPE AH HUM SÖHA
OM VAJRA DHUPE AH HUM SÖHA
OM VAJRA DIWE AH HUM SÖHA
OM VAJRA GÄNDHE AH HUM SÖHA
OM VAJRA NEWIDE AH HUM SÖHA
OM VAJRA SHAPTA AH HUM SÖHA

Inner offering

OM KHANDAROHI HUM HUM PHAT OM AH HUM

Praise

Benzarahi, element of fire,
By nature mindfulness of phenomena,
Principal Dakini of the Lotus Family,
To you, Khandarohi, I prostrate.

Now take hold of the mantra thread and contemplate:

The mantra rosary at my heart leaves by coiling around the mantra thread. It moves the mind of the Deity within the vase whereby light rays radiate from her heart. These invoke all the blessings of the body, speech, and mind of the Buddhas and Bodhisattvas of the ten directions in the aspect of light rays and nectars. These dissolve into the Deity in the vase and a stream of nectar flows from her body and fills the vase.

Contemplating this, recite one hundred times:

OM KHANDAROHI HUM HUM PHAT

Recite the hundred-letter mantra to purify anything added or omitted.

Outer offerings

OM AHRGHAM PARTITZA SÖHA
OM PADÄM PARTITZA SÖHA
OM VAJRA PUPE AH HUM SÖHA
OM VAJRA DHUPE AH HUM SÖHA
OM VAJRA DIWE AH HUM SÖHA
OM VAJRA GÄNDHE AH HUM SÖHA
OM VAJRA NEWIDE AH HUM SÖHA
OM VAJRA SHAPTA AH HUM SÖHA

Inner offering

OM KHANDAROHI HUM HUM PHAT OM AH HUM

Praise

Benzarahi, element of fire,
By nature mindfulness of phenomena,
Principal Dakini of the Lotus Family,
To you, Khandarohi, I prostrate.

Through the fire of great bliss the Deity within the vase
melts into light and becomes of one taste with the water
of the vase, which is the nature of bodhichitta.

*In this way the cleansing water is accomplished. After this
you must stop talking.*

GIVING THE TORMA TO THE LOCAL GUARDIANS

Blessing the torma

OM KHANDAROHI HUM HUM PHAT
OM SOBHAWA SHUDDHA SARWA DHARMA SOBHAWA
  SHUDDHO HAM
Everything becomes emptiness.

From the state of emptiness, from a DHRUM before me
comes a broad and expansive jewelled vessel. Inside
from om comes a torma, a vast ocean of uncontaminated
nectar of exalted wisdom.

OM AH HUM   (3x)

Offering the torma

NAMA SARWA TATHAGATA AWALOKITE OM SAMBHARA
  SAMBHARA HUM   (3x)

Praise

To the Tathagata Rinchen Mang I prostrate.
To the Tathagata Sug Dze Dampa I prostrate.
To the Tathagata Ku Jam Lay I prostrate.
To the Tathagata Jigpa Tamche Dang Drelwa I prostrate.

Request

I offer this torma, an ocean of nectar, possessing an
excellant collection of the five objects of desire, to
Denma, Goddess of the earth, to all the regional
guardians in the three thousand worlds, to the five
long-life Goddesses, to the guardians of the doctrine,
to the local guardians, the lords of the sites throughout
the land, and especially those who reside in this place.
Please accept it, and without being jealous or annoyed
with any of the actions performed by myself or any of
my benefactors, create good conditions that suit our minds.

Through the force of my intention,
Through the force of the blessings of the Tathagatas
And through the force of the truth of phenomena
May any suitable purpose
That I wish to come about
Be accomplished without obstruction.

This concludes giving the torma to the local guardians.

Blessing the vajra and bell

The vajra is method and the bell is wisdom. Both together
are the nature of ultimate bodhichitta.

*Hold this thought firmly. Now hold the vajra at your heart
between the thumb and ring finger of your right hand and
recite:*

OM SARWA TATHAGATA SIDDHI VAJRA SAMAYA TIKTA EKA
TÖN DHARAYAMI VAJRA SATTÖ HI HI HI HI HI HUM HUM
HUM PHAT SÖHA

*Now hold the bell between the thumb and ring finger of your
left hand at your left hip while reciting:*

OM VAJRA GHANTA HUM

Now contemplate:

I delight Vajrasattva and the others.

Hold up the vajra while reciting:

HUM
It is excellent to hold the vajra,
The Dharma activity of perfect liberation
That frees all living beings from confusion;
Therefore, with delight I hold the vajra.
HUM HUM HUM HO HO HO

*Hold the vajra at your right hip and play the bell by moving
the clapper from the centre through the eight directions while
reciting:*

OM VAJRA DHARMA RANITA, PARANITA, SAMPARANITA,
SARWA BUDDHA KHYETRA PATZALINI PENJA PARAMITA
NADA SÖBHAWA BENZA SATTÖ HRIDAYA, SANTO KHANI
HUM HUM HUM HO HO HO SÖHA

*From now until the burning offering is completed do not let
either the vajra or the bell leave your hands.*

Cleansing the hearth, the offerings, and oneself

*Now with cleansing water and inner offering sprinkle the
hearth, the substances, and yourself three times counter-
clockwise while reciting:*

OM KHANDAROHI HUM HUM PHAT

Blessing the substances to be offered to mundane Fire Deity

OM KHANDAROHI HUM HUM PHAT
OM SÖBHAWA SHUDDHA SARWA DHARMA SÖBHAWA
  SHUDDHO HAM
Everything becomes emptiness.

From the state of emptiness, from KAM come skullcup
vessels inside which from HUM come offering substances.

By nature emptiness, they have the aspect of the individual
offering substances and function as objects of enjoyment of
the six senses to bestow special, uncontaminated bliss.

OM AHRGHAM AH HUM
OM PADÄM AH HUM
OM ÄNTZAMANAM AH HUM
OM PROKYANAM AH HUM
OM VAJRA PUPE AH HUM
OM VAJRA DHUPE AH HUM
OM VAJRA ALOKE AH HUM
OM VAJRA GÄNDHE AH HUM
OM VAJRA NEWIDE AH HUM
OM VAJRA SHAPTA AH HUM

*This generates and blesses the four waters and the offerings.
Now hold both hands in the mudra for cleansing the
substances by pressing together two vajra fists with the two
middle fingers raised and touching each other at the tips.
Recite:*

OM SÖHA
OM AH SÖHA
OM SHRI SÖHA
OM DZIM SÖHA
OM KURU KURU SÖHA

Contemplate:

The substances are purified of all faults of not possessing
pure qualities, and they become the nature of the five
inner nectars.

Lighting the fire

Set light to the torch while reciting three times:

OM AH HUM

and:

OM KHANDAROHI HUM HUM PHAT

Now purify it by sprinkling it three times with cleansing water and three times with inner offering while reciting:

OM KHANDAROHI HUM HUM PHAT

Place the torch in the centre of the fire and recite:

OM DZÖ LA DZÖ LA HUM

Now fan the fire with the wind flag while reciting:

HUM

Pour seven ladles of butter on the fire while reciting:

OM OM OM SARWA BUDDHA DAKINIYE VAJRA WARNANIYE VAJRA BEROTZANIYE HUM HUM HUM PHAT PHAT PHAT SÖHA

Preparing the kusha grass seat

Holding the kusha grass, recite seven times:

OM VAJRA SATTÖ AH

OM
This kusha grass is clean and virtuous,
The essence of all that grows in the earth.
It pleases the divine Brahmins,
And brings delight to all Three Jewels.
Please pacify all my obstacles,
And make everything auspicious.

Once again recite five times:

OM VAJRA SATTÖ AH

and starting from your left, place four small bundles of kusha grass in the traditional manner around Kakyer on the hearth. Then arrange some kusha grass to resemble a cow's ear and place it in the very centre of the hearth with the tips pointing towards the east. Now with your palms pressed together, recite:

O Blessed One Vajrasattva, please pacify all obstacles and make everything auspicious.

THE ACTUAL PRACTICE

This has three parts:

1 *Initial offering to mundane Fire Deity*
2 *Offering to the supramundane Fire Deity*
3 *Final offering to mundane Fire Deity*

INITIAL OFFERING TO MUNDANE FIRE DEITY

Generating the commitment being

To purify the hearth, sprinkle cleansing water and recite:

OM KHANDAROHI HUM HUM PHAT
OM SÖBHAWA SHUDDHA SARWA DHARMA SÖBHAWA
  SHUDDHO HAM
Everything becomes emptiness.

From the state of emptiness comes a white HUM which melts and there arises an exalted wisdom hearth. It is white in colour, circular in shape, and complete with Muren and Kakyer.

If there are curved knives in Muren, recite 'Within Muren there is a rosary of curved knives' at this point.

Within Kakyer there is a rosary of vajras. Within this from EH EH comes a red phenomena source, a double tetrahedron. In each of the four corners there is a half-moon marked by a vajra. Everything is clear and unobstructed.

Within the hearth, from RAM there arises a blazing fire triangle, in the centre of which is a lotus of various colours

Fire Deity

and a moon seat. Upon this from RAM comes a mala marked by a RAM. This completely transforms into Fire Deity who is red in colour and mounted on a gelded goat. He has one face and four hands. His first right hand is in the mudra of supreme giving and his second holds a mala. His first left hand holds a trident and his second holds a round, long-necked vase brimming with nectar. His hair is tied up in a top-knot and he is adorned with a Brahmin's thread. He wears an upper garment of an antelope's skin and a lower garment of red silk. A radiance of white light emanates from his body. At his heart there is a fire triangle marked by a RAM.

Inviting the wisdom being

Light rays radiate from the seed-letter at the heart of the commitment being and manifest as the wrathful Deity Takkiradza, who invites from the south-east Fire Deity, similar to the visualization, surrounded by a retinue of Rishis.

Hold your right hand in the mudra of fearlessness and move the thumb while reciting:

OM
O Great Being come here, come here please,
Supreme Brahmin, divine Rishi.
Please come to this place
To enjoy the food from the blazing ladle.

Recite either:

OM EH HAYE HI MAHA BHUTA DEWA RIKI DINDZA SATTÖ MAGI HITÖ MAHA ÄMINPANI HITO BHAWA AGNIYE EH HAYE HE: DZA HUM BAM HO

or briefly:

OM AGNIYE EH HAYE HI

Please remain on the seat of kusha grass within Kakyer on the hearth.

Drive away obstacles by sprinkling cleansing water and reciting:

OM KHANDAROHI HUM HUM PHAT

If you wish you can offer the four waters at this point.

DZA HUM BAM HO
The wisdom being becomes non-dual with the commitment being.

Now offer water for sprinkling:

OM AH HRIH PRAVARA SÄKARAM PROKYANAM PARTITZA HUM SÖHA

Likewise, with their individual mudras, offer water for the mouth, water for drinking, and water for the feet:

OM AH HRIH PRAVARA SÄKARAM ÄNTZAMANAM PARTITZA HUM SÖHA
OM AH HRIH PRAVARA SÄKARAM AHRGHAM PARTITZA HUM SÖHA
OM AH HRIH PRAVARA SÄKARAM PADÄM PARTITZA HUM SÖHA

Now offer the close offerings and music thus:

OM AGNIYE AHDIBÄ AHDIBÄ AMBISHA AMBISHA MAHA SHRIYE HAMBÄ KABÄ BAHA NAYE PUPE PARTITZA HUM SÖHA
OM AGNIYE AHDIBÄ AHDIBÄ AMBISHA AMBISHA MAHA SHRIYE HAMBÄ KABÄ BAHA NAYE DHUPE PARTITZA HUM SÖHA
OM AGNIYE AHDIBÄ AHDIBÄ AMBISHA AMBISHA MAHA SHRIYE HAMBÄ KABÄ BAHA NAYE ALOKE PARTITZA HUM SÖHA
OM AGNIYE AHDIBÄ AHDIBÄ AMBISHA AMBISHA MAHA SHRIYE HAMBÄ KABÄ BAHA NAYE GÄNDHE PARTITZA HUM SÖHA
OM AGNIYE AHDIBÄ AHDIBÄ AMBISHA AMBISHA MAHA SHRIYE HAMBÄ KABÄ BAHA NAYE NEWIDE PARTITZA HUM SÖHA
OM AGNIYE AHDIBÄ AHDIBÄ AMBISHA AMBISHA MAHA SHRIYE HAMBÄ KABÄ BAHA NAYE SHAPTA PARTITZA HUM SÖHA

and the inner offering:

OM AGNIYE AHDIBÄ AHDIBÄ AMBISHA AMBISHA MAHA SHRIYE HAMBÄ KABÄ BAHA NAYE OM AH HUM

Praise

Lord of the world, Son of Brahma, powerful Protector,
King of Fire Deities, empowered by Takki,
Who consume all delusions with your supreme wisdom,
To you, O Protector Fire Deity, I bow down.

If you wish to make extensive praises, continue with:

O Son of Brahma, Protector of the world,
King of Fire Deities, supreme Rishi,
You manifest this form out of compassion
To fully protect all living beings.

In the aspect of a Rishi accomplished in knowledge
    mantras,
With the light of wisdom consuming delusions,
And a blazing brilliance like the fire of the aeon,
You are endowed with clairvoyance and miracle powers.

Out of skilful means you ride an emanation vehicle.
Holding a mala you recite knowledge mantras.
You hold a vase of essential nectar
And bring coolness to all with the nectar of Dharma.

You are free from faults and have perfected purity.
Though you abide in the world you have passed beyond
    sorrow;
Though you have attained peace you have great
    compassion;
Therefore I make praises and prostrations to you.

Proclaiming the commitment

*With the mudra of the commitment of Fire Deity proclaim
his commitment by reciting three times:*

OM VAJRA AHNALA MAHA BHUTA DZÖLA DZÖLAYA, SARWA
BHÄMI KURU, SARWA DUTRAM HUM PHAT, TIRSHA DZA
HUM BAM HO: SAMAYA TÖN SAMAYA HO

Making the offerings

Now contemplate:

The tongue of Fire Deity is in the aspect of a white vajra marked by a letter RAM, and the mouth of the funnel is marked by a letter HUM and rays of light.

Initial offering of molten butter

With the mudra of supreme enlightenment take hold of the funnel brimming with butter and make offerings while reciting seven times:

OM AGNIYE AHDIBÄ AHDIBÄ AMBISHA AMBISHA MAHA
  SHRIYE HAMBÄ KABÄ BAHA NAYE SÖHA
For all of us disciples, our benefactors, and others, may all obstacles to attaining liberation and omniscience, all transgressions of the three vows, all natural non-virtues, all inauspiciousness, all unclear concentration, all impure recitation of mantras, and all faults of excess and omission in the rituals [be purified] SHÄNTING KURUYE SÖHA.

At this point you should check to see whether or not there are any obstacles to the fire. If there are, sprinkle cleansing water and attach the words: 'May Khandarohi [pacify] all obstacles SHÄNTING KURUYE SÖHA', while offering seven ladles. Then again sprinkle cleansing water and offer seven, three, or just one ladle with the mantra: OM AGNIYE AHDIBÄ AHDIBÄ AMBISHA AMBISHA MAHA SHRIYE HAMBÄ KABÄ BAHA NAYE SÖHA. If there are no obstacles, this is not necessary.

Offering the milk-wood

Contemplate:

The milk-wood becomes nectar, the nature of the Bodhi Tree.
OM AGNIYE AHDIBÄ AHDIBÄ AMBISHA AMBISHA MAHA
  SHRIYE HAMBÄ KABÄ BAHA NAYE
OM BODHI PIKYAYE
For all of us disciples, our benefactors, and others, may all obstacles to attaining liberation and omniscience, all

transgressions of the three vows, all natural non-virtues,
all inauspiciousness, all unclear concentration, all impure
recitation of mantras, all faults of excess and omission in
the rituals, and especially all obstacles to increased vitality
[be purified] SHÄNTING KURUYE SÖHA.

Offering the molten butter

OM AGNIYE AHDIBÄ AHDIBÄ AMBISHA AMBISHA MAHA
    SHRIYE HAMBÄ KABÄ BAHA NAYE
OM AGNIYE
For all of us disciples, our benefactors, and others, may
all obstacles to attaining liberation and omniscience, all
transgressions of the three vows, all natural non-virtues,
all inauspiciousness, all unclear concentration, all impure
recitation of mantras, all faults of excess and omission in
the rituals, and especially all obstacles to increased wealth
[be purified] SHÄNTING KURUYE SÖHA.

Offering the sesame seeds

OM AGNIYE AHDIBÄ AHDIBÄ AMBISHA AMBISHA MAHA
    SHRIYE HAMBÄ KABÄ BAHA NAYE
OM SARWA PAPAM DAHANA VAJRAYE
For all of us disciples, our benefactors, and others, may
all obstacles to attaining liberation and omniscience, all
transgressions of the three vows, all natural non-virtues,
all inauspiciousness, all unclear concentration, all impure
recitation of mantras, all faults of excess and omission in
the rituals, and especially all our negativities [be purified]
SHÄNTING KURUYE SÖHA.

Offering the couch grass

OM AGNIYE AHDIBÄ AHDIBÄ AMBISHA AMBISHA MAHA
    SHRIYE HAMBÄ KABÄ BAHA NAYE
OM VAJRA AHYUKE
For all of us disciples, our benefactors, and others, may
all obstacles to attaining liberation and omniscience, all
transgressions of the three vows, all natural non-virtues,
all inauspiciousness, all unclear concentration, all impure

recitation of mantras, all faults of excess and omission in the rituals, and especially all obstacles to increased life span [be purified] SHÄNTING KURUYE SÖHA.

Offering the rice

OM AGNIYE AHDIBÄ AHDIBÄ AMBISHA AMBISHA MAHA SHRIYE HAMBÄ KABÄ BAHA NAYE
OM VAJRA PUTRAYE
For all of us disciples, our benefactors, and others, may all obstacles to attaining liberation and omniscience, all transgressions of the three vows, all natural non-virtues, all inauspiciousness, all unclear concentration, all impure recitation of mantras, all faults of excess and omission in the rituals, and especially all obstacles to increased merit [be purified] SHÄNTING KURUYE SÖHA.

Offering the flour and yoghurt

OM AGNIYE AHDIBÄ AHDIBÄ AMBISHA AMBISHA MAHA SHRIYE HAMBÄ KABÄ BAHA NAYE
OM SARWA SAMPA DE
For all of us disciples, our benefactors, and others, may all obstacles to attaining liberation and omniscience, all transgressions of the three vows, all natural non-virtues, all inauspiciousness, all unclear concentration, all impure recitation of mantras, all faults of excess and omission in the rituals, and especially all obstacles to supreme bliss [be purified] SHÄNTING KURUYE SÖHA.

Offering the kusha grass

OM AGNIYE AHDIBÄ AHDIBÄ AMBISHA AMBISHA MAHA SHRIYE HAMBÄ KABÄ BAHA NAYE
OM AHTRATI HATA VAJRAYE
For all of us disciples, our benefactors, and others, may all obstacles to attaining liberation and omniscience, all transgressions of the three vows, all natural non-virtues, all inauspiciousness, all unclear concentration, all impure recitation of mantras, all faults of excess and omission in

the rituals, and especially all obstacles to supreme cleanliness [be purified] SHÄNTING KURUYE SÖHA.

Offering the white mustard seeds

OM AGNIYE AHDIBÄ AHDIBÄ AMBISHA AMBISHA MAHA
  SHRIYE HAMBÄ KABÄ BAHA NAYE
OM SARWA AHRTA SIDDHA YE
For all of us disciples, our benefactors, and others, may all obstacles to attaining liberation and omniscience, all transgressions of the three vows, all natural non-virtues, all inauspiciousness, all unclear concentration, all impure recitation of mantras, all faults of excess and omission in the rituals, and especially all our obstacles [be purified] SHÄNTING KURUYE SÖHA.

Offering the barley with husks

OM AGNIYE AHDIBÄ AHDIBÄ AMBISHA AMBISHA MAHA
  SHRIYE HAMBÄ KABÄ BAHA NAYE
OM VAJRA BINZAYE
For all of us disciples, our benefactors, and others, may all obstacles to attaining liberation and omniscience, all transgressions of the three vows, all natural non-virtues, all inauspiciousness, all unclear concentration, all impure recitation of mantras, all faults of excess and omission in the rituals, and especially all obstacles to wealth and abundant harvests [be purified] SHÄNTING KURUYE SÖHA.

Offering the barley without husks

OM AGNIYE AHDIBÄ AHDIBÄ AMBISHA AMBISHA MAHA
  SHRIYE HAMBÄ KABÄ BAHA NAYE
OM MAHA BEGAYE
For all of us disciples, our benefactors, and others, may all obstacles to attaining liberation and omniscience, all transgressions of the three vows, all natural non-virtues, all inauspiciousness, all unclear concentration, all impure recitation of mantras, all faults of excess and omission in the rituals, and especially all obstacles to excellent quick mental powers [be purified] SHÄNTING KURUYE SÖHA.

Offering the peas

OM AGNIYE AHDIBÄ AHDIBÄ AMBISHA AMBISHA MAHA
SHRIYE HAMBÄ KABÄ BAHA NAYE
OM MAHA BALAYE
For all of us disciples, our benefactors, and others, may
all obstacles to attaining liberation and omniscience, all
transgressions of the three vows, all natural non-virtues,
all inauspiciousness, all unclear concentration, all impure
recitation of mantras, all faults of excess and omission in
the rituals, and especially all obstacles to increased
strength [be purified] SHÄNTING KURUYE SÖHA.

Offering the wheat

OM AGNIYE AHDIBÄ AHDIBÄ AMBISHA AMBISHA MAHA
SHRIYE HAMBÄ KABÄ BAHA NAYE
OM VAJRA GHAMA RI
For all of us disciples, our benefactors, and others, may
all obstacles to attaining liberation and omniscience, all
transgressions of the three vows, all natural non-virtues,
all inauspiciousness, all unclear concentration, all impure
recitation of mantras, all faults of excess and omission in
the rituals, and especially all sickness [be purified]
SHÄNTING KURUYE SÖHA.

Offering the alcohol

OM AGNIYE AHDIBÄ AHDIBÄ AMBISHA AMBISHA MAHA
SHRIYE HAMBÄ KABÄ BAHA NAYE
OM MADANA PÄNJA AMRITA AH HUM
For all of us disciples, our benefactors, and others, may
all obstacles to attaining liberation and omniscience, all
transgressions of the three vows, all natural non-virtues,
all inauspiciousness, all unclear concentration, all impure
recitation of mantras, all faults of excess and omission in
the rituals, and especially all obstacles to accomplishing
supreme attainments [be purified] SHÄNTING KURUYE
SÖHA.

Offering the beef

OM AGNIYE AHDIBÄ AHDIBÄ AMBISHA AMBISHA MAHA
SHRIYE HAMBÄ KABÄ BAHA NAYE
OM BALA PÄNJA AMRITA AH HUM
For all of us disciples, our benefactors, and others, may
all obstacles to attaining liberation and omniscience, all
transgressions of the three vows, all natural non-virtues,
all inauspiciousness, all unclear concentration, all impure
recitation of mantras, all faults of excess and omission in the
rituals, and especially all obstacles to accomplishing supreme
attainments [be purified] SHÄNTING KURUYE SÖHA.

*The previous Lamas of this tradition have said that we should
offer only a small amount of beef.*

Offering the special pacifying substance

OM AGNIYE AHDIBÄ AHDIBÄ AMBISHA AMBISHA MAHA
SHRIYE HAMBÄ KABÄ BAHA NAYE
For all of us disciples, our benefactors, and others, may
all obstacles to attaining liberation and omniscience, all
transgressions of the three vows, all natural non-virtues,
all inauspiciousness, all unclear concentration, all impure
recitation of mantras, all faults of excess and omission in the
rituals, and especially all obstacles to accomplishing supreme
attainments [be purified] SHÄNTING KURUYE SÖHA.

Now offer water for the mouth and water for sprinkling, thus:

OM AH HRIH PRAVARA SÄKARAM ÄNTZAMANAM PARTITZA
HUM SÖHA
OM AH HRIH PRAVARA SÄKARAM PROKYANAM PARTITZA
HUM SÖHA

OFFERINGS TO THE SUPRAMUNDANE FIRE DEITY

Blessing the offering substances

OM KHANDAROHI HUM HUM PHAT
OM SÖBHAWA SHUDDHA SARWA DHARMA SÖBHAWA
SHUDDHO HAM
Everything becomes emptiness.

THE NEW GUIDE TO DAKINI LAND

From the state of emptiness, from KAM come skullcup
vessels inside which from HUM come offering substances.
By nature emptiness, they have the aspect of the individual
offering substances and function as objects of enjoyment
of the six senses to bestow special, uncontaminated bliss.

OM AHRGHAM AH HUM
OM PADÄM AH HUM
OM ÄNTZAMANAM AH HUM
OM PROKYANAM AH HUM
OM VAJRA PUPE AH HUM
OM VAJRA DHUPE AH HUM
OM VAJRA DIWE AH HUM
OM VAJRA GÄNDHE AH HUM
OM VAJRA NEWIDE AH HUM
OM VAJRA SHAPTA AH HUM

OM RUWA AH HUM
OM SHAPTA AH HUM
OM GÄNDHE AH HUM
OM RASE AH HUM
OM PARSHE AH HUM

Now cleanse the substances as before:

OM SÖHA
OM AH SÖHA
OM SHRI SÖHA
OM DZIM SÖHA
OM KURU KURU SÖHA

Contemplate:

The substances are purified of all faults of not possessing
pure qualities, and they become the nature of the five
inner nectars.

Generating the supramundane Fire Deity

At the heart of Fire Deity is a blazing fire triangle. In the
centre of this, from EH EH comes a red phenomena source,
a double tetrahedron, inside which from AH comes a

moon mandala, white with a shade of red. In the centre
of this is a red letter BAM encircled by OM OM OM SARWA
BUDDHA DAKINIYE VAJRA WARNANIYE VAJRA BEROTZANIYE
HUM HUM HUM PHAT PHAT PHAT SÖHA, a red-coloured
mantra rosary standing counter-clockwise. From these,
light rays radiate making offerings to the Superior beings
and fulfilling the welfare of sentient beings. Gathering
back, they transform into an eight-petalled lotus of
various colours with a sun mandala at its centre. Upon
this arises Venerable Vajrayogini. Her outstretched right
leg treads on the breast of red Kalarati. Her bent left leg
treads on the head of black Bhairawa, which is bent
backwards. She has a red-coloured body which shines
with a brilliance like that of the fire of the aeon. She has
one face, two hands, and three eyes looking towards the
Pure Land of the Dakinis. Her right hand, outstretched
and pointing downwards, holds a curved knife marked
with a vajra. Her left holds up a skullcup filled with blood
which she partakes of with her upturned mouth. Her left
shoulder holds a khatanga marked with a vajra from which
hang a damaru, bell, and triple banner. Her black hair
hanging straight covers her back down to her waist. In the
prime of her youth, her desirous breasts are full and she
shows the manner of generating bliss. Her head is adorned
with five human skulls and she wears a necklace of fifty
human skulls. Naked, she is adorned with five mudras
and stands in the centre of a blazing fire of exalted
wisdom. A mass of white light radiates from her body.

Absorbing the wisdom beings

PHAIM
Light rays radiate from the letter BAM at my heart and,
leaving from between my eyebrows, go to the ten
directions. They invite all the Tathagatas, Heroes, and
Yoginis of the ten directions in the aspect of Vajrayogini.
DZA HUM BAM HO
OM YOGA SHUDDHA SARWA DHARMA YOGA SHUDDHO
   HAM

Venerable Vajrayogini

Putting on the armour

At places in her body arise moon mandalas upon which
at her navel is red OM BAM, Vajravarahi; at her heart blue
HAM YOM, Yamani; at her throat white HRIM MOM Mohani;
at her forehead yellow HRIM HRIM, Sachalani; at her crown
green HUM HUM, Samtrasani; at all her limbs smoke-coloured
PHAT PHAT, essence of Chandika.

Granting empowerment and adorning the crown

PHAIM

Light rays radiate from the letter BAM at my heart and
invite the empowering Deities, the supported and
supporting mandala of Glorious Chakrasambara.

O, all you Tathagatas, please grant the empowerment.

Requested in this way, the eight Goddesses of the doorways
drive away hindrances, the Heroes recite auspicious verses,
the Heroines sing vajra songs, and the Rupavajras and so
forth make offerings. The Principal mentally resolves to
grant the empowerment and the four Mothers together with
Varahi, holding jewelled vases filled with the five nectars,
confer the empowerment through the crown of her head.

'Just as all the Tathagatas granted ablution
At the moment of [Buddha's] birth,
Likewise do we now grant ablution
With the pure water of the gods.

OM SARWA TATHAGATA ABHIKEKATA SAMAYA SHRIYE HUM'

Saying this, they grant the empowerment. Her whole body
is filled, all stains are purified, and the excess water
remaining on her crown changes into Vairochana-Heruka,
together with the Mother, who adorn her crown.

Inviting the guests of the offerings

With mudra, recite:

PHAIM

Light rays radiate from the letter BAM at my heart and
invite Venerable Vajrayogini surrounded by the assembly
of Gurus, Yidams, Buddhas, Bodhisattvas, Heroes, Dakinis,
and both Dharma and mundane Protectors to come from
Akanishta to the space before me.

Making offerings

Offering goddesses emanate from my heart and perform the
offerings.

Offering the four waters

OM AH HRIH PRAVARA SÄKARAM AHRGHAM PARTITZA
HUM SÖHA
OM AH HRIH PRAVARA SÄKARAM PADÄM PARTITZA
HUM SÖHA
OM AH HRIH PRAVARA SÄKARAM ÄNTZAMANAM PARTITZA
  HUM SÖHA
OM AH HRIH PRAVARA SÄKARAM PROKYANAM PARTITZA
  HUM SÖHA

Outer offerings

OM SARWA TATHAGATA SARWA BIRA YOGENI SAPARIWARA
  PUPE PUNJA MEGHA SAMUDRA PARANA SAMAYE AH HUM
OM SARWA TATHAGATA SARWA BIRA YOGENI SAPARIWARA
  DHUPE PUNJA MEGHA SAMUDRA PARANA SAMAYE AH HUM
OM SARWA TATHAGATA SARWA BIRA YOGENI SAPARIWARA
  DIWE PUNJA MEGHA SAMUDRA PARANA SAMAYE AH HUM
OM SARWA TATHAGATA SARWA BIRA YOGENI SAPARIWARA
  GÄNDHE PUNJA MEGHA SAMUDRA PARANA SAMAYE AH HUM
OM SARWA TATHAGATA SARWA BIRA YOGENI SAPARIWARA
  NEWIDE PUNJA MEGHA SAMUDRA PARANA SAMAYE AH HUM
OM SARWA TATHAGATA SARWA BIRA YOGENI SAPARIWARA
  SHAPTA PUNJA MEGHA SAMUDRA PARANA SAMAYE AH HUM

Offering the sixteen knowledge goddesses

OM VAJRA WINI HUM HUM PHAT
OM VAJRA WAMSHE HUM HUM PHAT

OM VAJRA MITAMGI HUM HUM PHAT
OM VAJRA MURANDZE HUM HUM PHAT

OM VAJRA HASÄ HUM HUM PHAT
OM VAJRA LASÄ HUM HUM PHAT
OM VAJRA GIRTI HUM HUM PHAT
OM VAJRA NIRTÄ HUM HUM PHAT

OM VAJRA PUPE HUM HUM PHAT
OM VAJRA DHUPE HUM HUM PHAT
OM VAJRA DIWE HUM HUM PHAT
OM VAJRA GÄNDHE HUM HUM PHAT

OM RUPA BENZ HUM HUM PHAT
OM RASA BENZ HUM HUM PHAT
OM PARSHE BENZ HUM HUM PHAT
OM DHARMA DHATU BENZ HUM HUM PHAT

Inner offering

OM OM OM SARWA BUDDHA DAKINIYE VAJRA WARNANIYE
VAJRA BEROTZANIYE HUM HUM HUM PHAT PHAT PHAT
SÖHA OM AH HUM

Eight lines of praise to the Mother

OM I prostrate to Vajravarahi, the Blessed Mother HUM
    HUM PHAT
OM To the Superior and powerful Knowledge Lady
    unconquered by the three realms HUM HUM PHAT
OM To you who destroy all fears of evil spirits with your
    great vajra HUM HUM PHAT
OM To you with controlling eyes who remain as the vajra
    seat unconquered by others HUM HUM PHAT
OM To you whose wrathful fierce form desiccates Brahma
    HUM HUM PHAT
OM To you who terrify and dry up demons, conquering
    those in other directions HUM HUM PHAT
OM To you who conquer all those who make us dull,
    rigid, and confused HUM HUM PHAT
OM I bow to Vajravarahi, the Great Mother, the Dakini
    consort who fulfils all desires HUM HUM PHAT

479

Praise

O Glorious Vajrayogini,
Chakravatin Dakini Queen,
Who have five wisdoms and three bodies,
To you Saviour of all I prostrate.

To the many Vajra Dakinis,
Who as Ladies of worldly actions,
Cut our bondage to preconceptions,
To all of you Ladies I prostrate.

> *If you wish to do these extensively you can perform the garland of offerings, inner offerings, and praises as they occur in the section on the in-front-generation in the self-initiation rituals, from offering the four waters up to and including the extensive praise (pp 360-376).*

Offering the burning substances

> *Now contemplate:*

The tongue of the Deity is in the aspect of a white vajra marked by a letter HUM.

Initial offering of molten butter

> *Offer three or seven ladles [of butter] while reciting the mantra and appended requests seven times:*

OM OM OM SARWA BUDDHA DAKINIYE VAJRA WARNANIYE VAJRA BEROTZANIYE HUM HUM HUM PHAT PHAT PHAT SÖHA

For all of us disciples, our benefactors, and others, may all obstacles to attaining liberation and omniscience, all transgressions of the three vows, all natural non-virtues, all inauspiciousness, all unclear concentration, all impure recitation of mantras, all faults of excess and omission in the rituals [be purified] SHÄNTING KURUYE SÖHA.

Offering the milk-wood

> *Contemplate:*

The milk-wood becomes nectar, the nature of the Bodhi Tree.

OM OM OM SARWA BUDDHA DAKINIYE VAJRA WARNANIYE
VAJRA BEROTZANIYE HUM HUM HUM PHAT PHAT PHAT
SÖHA
OM BODHI PIKYAYE
For all of us disciples, our benefactors, and others, may
all obstacles to attaining liberation and omniscience, all
transgressions of the three vows, all natural non-virtues,
all inauspiciousness, all unclear concentration, all impure
recitation of mantras, all faults of excess and omission in
the rituals, and especially all obstacles to increased vitality
[be purified] SHÄNTING KURUYE SÖHA.

Offer a suitable number.

Offering the molten butter

OM OM OM SARWA BUDDHA DAKINIYE VAJRA WARNANIYE
VAJRA BEROTZANIYE HUM HUM HUM PHAT PHAT PHAT
SÖHA
OM AGNIYE
For all of us disciples, our benefactors, and others, may
all obstacles to attaining liberation and omniscience, all
transgressions of the three vows, all natural non-virtues,
all inauspiciousness, all unclear concentration, all impure
recitation of mantras, all faults of excess and omission in
the rituals, and especially all obstacles to increased wealth
[be purified] SHÄNTING KURUYE SÖHA.

Offering the sesame seeds

OM OM OM SARWA BUDDHA DAKINIYE VAJRA WARNANIYE
VAJRA BEROTZANIYE HUM HUM HUM PHAT PHAT PHAT
SÖHA
OM SARWA PAPAM DAHANA VAJRAYE
For all of us disciples, our benefactors, and others, may
all obstacles to attaining liberation and omniscience, all
transgressions of the three vows, all natural non-virtues,
all inauspiciousness, all unclear concentration, all impure
recitation of mantras, all faults of excess and omission in
the rituals, and especially all our negativities [be purified]
SHÄNTING KURUYE SÖHA.

Offering the couch grass

OM OM OM SARWA BUDDHA DAKINIYE VAJRA WARNANIYE
    VAJRA BEROTZANIYE HUM HUM HUM PHAT PHAT PHAT
    SÖHA
OM VAJRA AHYUKE
For all of us disciples, our benefactors, and others, may
all obstacles to attaining liberation and omniscience, all
transgressions of the three vows, all natural non-virtues,
all inauspiciousness, all unclear concentration, all impure
recitation of mantras, all faults of excess and omission in
the rituals, and especially all obstacles to increased life
span [be purified] SHÄNTING KURUYE SÖHA.

Offering the rice

OM OM OM SARWA BUDDHA DAKINIYE VAJRA WARNANIYE
    VAJRA BEROTZANIYE HUM HUM HUM PHAT PHAT PHAT
    SÖHA
OM VAJRA PUTRAYE
For all of us disciples, our benefactors, and others, may
all obstacles to attaining liberation and omniscience, all
transgressions of the three vows, all natural non-virtues,
all inauspiciousness, all unclear concentration, all impure
recitation of mantras, all faults of excess and omission in
the rituals, and especially all obstacles to increased merit
[be purified] SHÄNTING KURUYE SÖHA.

Offering the flour and yoghurt

OM OM OM SARWA BUDDHA DAKINIYE VAJRA WARNANIYE
    VAJRA BEROTZANIYE HUM HUM HUM PHAT PHAT PHAT
    SÖHA
OM SARWA SAMPA DE
For all of us disciples, our benefactors, and others, may
all obstacles to attaining liberation and omniscience, all
transgressions of the three vows, all natural non-virtues,
all inauspiciousness, all unclear concentration, all impure
recitation of mantras, all faults of excess and omission in
the rituals, and especially all obstacles to supreme bliss
[be purified] SHÄNTING KURUYE SÖHA.

Offering the kusha grass

OM OM OM SARWA BUDDHA DAKINIYE VAJRA WARNANIYE
   VAJRA BEROTZANIYE HUM HUM HUM PHAT PHAT PHAT
   SÖHA
OM AHTRATI HATA VAJRAYE
For all of us disciples, our benefactors, and others, may
all obstacles to attaining liberation and omniscience, all
transgressions of the three vows, all natural non-virtues,
all inauspiciousness, all unclear concentration, all impure
recitation of mantras, all faults of excess and omission in
the rituals, and especially all obstacles to supreme
cleanliness [be purified] SHÄNTING KURUYE SÖHA.

Offering the white mustard seeds

OM OM OM SARWA BUDDHA DAKINIYE VAJRA WARNANIYE
   VAJRA BEROTZANIYE HUM HUM HUM PHAT PHAT PHAT
   SÖHA
OM SARWA AHRTA SIDDHA YE
For all of us disciples, our benefactors, and others, may
all obstacles to attaining liberation and omniscience, all
transgressions of the three vows, all natural non-virtues,
all inauspiciousness, all unclear concentration, all impure
recitation of mantras, all faults of excess and omission in
the rituals, and especially all our obstacles [be purified]
SHÄNTING KURUYE SÖHA.

Offering the barley with husks

OM OM OM SARWA BUDDHA DAKINIYE VAJRA WARNANIYE
   VAJRA BEROTZANIYE HUM HUM HUM PHAT PHAT PHAT
   SÖHA
OM VAJRA BINZAYE
For all of us disciples, our benefactors, and others, may
all obstacles to attaining liberation and omniscience, all
transgressions of the three vows, all natural non-virtues,
all inauspiciousness, all unclear concentration, all impure
recitation of mantras, all faults of excess and omission in
the rituals, and especially all obstacles to wealth and
abundant harvests [be purified] SHÄNTING KURUYE SÖHA.

Offering the barley without husks

OM OM OM SARWA BUDDHA DAKINIYE VAJRA WARNANIYE
VAJRA BEROTZANIYE HUM HUM HUM PHAT PHAT PHAT
SÖHA
OM MAHA BEGAYE
For all of us disciples, our benefactors, and others, may
all obstacles to attaining liberation and omniscience, all
transgressions of the three vows, all natural non-virtues,
all inauspiciousness, all unclear concentration, all impure
recitation of mantras, all faults of excess and omission in
the rituals, and especially all obstacles to excellent quick
mental powers [be purified] SHÄNTING KURUYE SÖHA.

Offering the peas

OM OM OM SARWA BUDDHA DAKINIYE VAJRA WARNANIYE
VAJRA BEROTZANIYE HUM HUM HUM PHAT PHAT PHAT
SÖHA
OM MAHA BALAYE
For all of us disciples, our benefactors, and others, may
all obstacles to attaining liberation and omniscience, all
transgressions of the three vows, all natural non-virtues,
all inauspiciousness, all unclear concentration, all impure
recitation of mantras, all faults of excess and omission in
the rituals, and especially all obstacles to increased
strength [be purified] SHÄNTING KURUYE SÖHA.

Offering the wheat

OM OM OM SARWA BUDDHA DAKINIYE VAJRA WARNANIYE
VAJRA BEROTZANIYE HUM HUM HUM PHAT PHAT PHAT
SÖHA
OM VAJRA GHAMA RI
For all of us disciples, our benefactors, and others, may
all obstacles to attaining liberation and omniscience, all
transgressions of the three vows, all natural non-virtues,
all inauspiciousness, all unclear concentration, all impure
recitation of mantras, all faults of excess and omission in
the rituals, and especially all sickness [be purified]
SHÄNTING KURUYE SÖHA.

Offering the alcohol

OM OM OM SARWA BUDDHA DAKINIYE VAJRA WARNANIYE
VAJRA BEROTZANIYE HUM HUM HUM PHAT PHAT PHAT
SÖHA
OM MADANA PÄNJA AMRITA AH HUM
For all of us disciples, our benefactors, and others, may
all obstacles to attaining liberation and omniscience, all
transgressions of the three vows, all natural non-virtues,
all inauspiciousness, all unclear concentration, all impure
recitation of mantras, all faults of excess and omission in the
rituals, and especially all obstacles to accomplishing supreme
attainments [be purified] SHÄNTING KURUYE SÖHA.

Offering the beef

OM OM OM SARWA BUDDHA DAKINIYE VAJRA WARNANIYE
VAJRA BEROTZANIYE HUM HUM HUM PHAT PHAT PHAT
SÖHA
OM BALA PÄNJA AMRITA AH HUM
For all of us disciples, our benefactors, and others, may
all obstacles to attaining liberation and omniscience, all
transgressions of the three vows, all natural non-virtues,
all inauspiciousness, all unclear concentration, all impure
recitation of mantras, all faults of excess and omission in
the rituals, and especially all obstacles to accomplishing
supreme attainments [be purified] SHÄNTING KURUYE SÖHA.

Offer only a small amount of beef.

Offering the special pacifying substance

OM OM OM SARWA BUDDHA DAKINIYE VAJRA WARNANIYE
VAJRA BEROTZANIYE HUM HUM HUM PHAT PHAT PHAT
SÖHA
For all of us disciples, our benefactors, and others, may
all obstacles to attaining liberation and omniscience, all
transgressions of the three vows, all natural non-virtues,
all inauspiciousness, all unclear concentration, all impure
recitation of mantras, all faults of excess and omission in
the rituals, and especially all obstacles to accomplishing
supreme attainments [be purified] SHÄNTING KURUYE SÖHA.

*When it comes to making many offerings of each substance,
if possible you should recite all three – the Deity's mantra,
the substance mantra, and the appended requests – with each
offering of each burning substance. If this is not possible, then
with each substance you should recite all three with the first
offering, and with subsequent offerings recite just the Deity's
mantra and the requests. If this is not possible, then recite
these with every seventh offering. If none of these is possible,
then for the first and last offering [of each substance] you
should recite all three – the Deity's mantra, the substance
mantra, and the requests – and for the remainder you should
recite the Deity's mantra with each offering. Since there is no
separate mantra for the special pacifying substance it should
be offered with the Deity's mantra.*

*Since the milk-wood and the molten butter are the
principal offerings, each time one of these is offered it is
counted as one burning offering. Here, on the occasion of
fulfilling the commitment, it is good to offer many sesame
seeds. The previous Lamas of this tradition have explained
that we should offer one tenth of the number [of mantras]
we have recited. For example, for a close retreat of a hundred
thousand [mantras] we should make ten thousand offerings
of sesame seeds. This is known as a burning offering of ten
per cent. It is very good if we can do this but it is not strictly
necessary to count exactly ten per cent for the sesame seeds.
More detailed reasons are explained elsewhere.*

Ablution

Now contemplate:

From the Deities' hearts emanate Buddhas holding aloft
white vases brimming with white nectar. I, or those for
whom [the offering] is performed, are sitting on moon
mandalas. We receive ablution, whereby all our sickness,
spirits, negativities, obstructions, and so forth are purified;
and our bodies become as clear as crystal.

*Offer three or seven ladles of butter with the three-OM
mantra. Then offer drinking water by reciting:*

OM OM OM SARWA BUDDHA DAKINIYE VAJRA WARNANIYE
VAJRA BEROTZANIYE HUM HUM HUM PHAT PHAT PHAT SÖHA

Now offer water for sprinkling and water for the mouth:

OM AH HRIH PRAVARA SÄKARAM PROKYANAM PARTITZA
HUM SÖHA

OM AH HRIH PRAVARA SÄKARAM ÄNTZAMANAM PARTITZA
HUM SÖHA

Offering the garments

OM VAJRA WASA SÄ SÖHA

Offering the tambula torma

OM VAJRA TAMBULAYE SÖHA

Outer offerings

OM SARWA TATHAGATA SARWA BIRA YOGINI SAPARIWARA
PUPE PUNJA MEGHA SAMUDRA PARANA SAMAYA SHRIYE
HUM

OM SARWA TATHAGATA SARWA BIRA YOGINI SAPARIWARA
DHUPE PUNJA MEGHA SAMUDRA PARANA SAMAYA
SHRIYE HUM

OM SARWA TATHAGATA SARWA BIRA YOGINI SAPARIWARA
DIWE PUNJA MEGHA SAMUDRA PARANA SAMAYA SHRIYE
HUM

OM SARWA TATHAGATA SARWA BIRA YOGINI SAPARIWARA
GÄNDHE PUNJA MEGHA SAMUDRA PARANA SAMAYA
SHRIYE HUM

OM SARWA TATHAGATA SARWA BIRA YOGINI SAPARIWARA
NEWIDE PUNJA MEGHA SAMUDRA PARANA SAMAYA
SHRIYE HUM

OM SARWA TATHAGATA SARWA BIRA YOGINI SAPARIWARA
SHAPTA PUNJA MEGHA SAMUDRA PARANA SAMAYA
SHRIYE HUM

Offering the sixteen knowledge goddesses

OM VAJRA WINI HUM HUM PHAT
OM VAJRA WAMSHE HUM HUM PHAT

OM VAJRA MITAMGI HUM HUM PHAT
OM VAJRA MURANDZE HUM HUM PHAT

OM VAJRA HASÄ HUM HUM PHAT
OM VAJRA LASÄ HUM HUM PHAT
OM VAJRA GIRTI HUM HUM PHAT
OM VAJRA NIRTÄ HUM HUM PHAT

OM VAJRA PUPE HUM HUM PHAT
OM VAJRA DHUPE HUM HUM PHAT
OM VAJRA DIWE HUM HUM PHAT
OM VAJRA GÄNDHE HUM HUM PHAT
OM RUPA BENZ HUM HUM PHAT
OM RASA BENZ HUM HUM PHAT
OM PARSHE BENZ HUM HUM PHAT
OM DHARMA DHATU BENZ HUM HUM PHAT

Inner offering

OM OM OM SARWA BUDDHA DAKINIYE VAJRA WARNANIYE
VAJRA BEROTZANIYE HUM HUM HUM PHAT PHAT PHAT
SÖHA OM AH HUM

Eight lines of praise to the Mother

OM NAMO BHAGAWATI VAJRA VARAHI BAM HUM HUM PHAT
OM NAMO ARYA APARADZITE TRE LOKYA MATI BIYE SHÖRI
  HUM HUM PHAT
OM NAMA SARWA BUTA BHAYA WAHI MAHA VAJRE HUM
  HUM PHAT
OM NAMO VAJRA SANI ADZITE APARADZITE WASHAM
  KARANITRA HUM HUM PHAT
OM NAMO BHRAMANI SHOKANI ROKANI KROTE KARALENI
  HUM HUM PHAT
OM NAMA DRASANI MARANI PRABHE DANI PARADZAYE
  HUM HUM PHAT
OM NAMO BIDZAYE DZAMBHANI TAMBHANI MOHANI
  HUM HUM PHAT
OM NAMO VAJRA VARAHI MAHA YOGINI KAME SHÖRI
  KHAGE HUM HUM PHAT

Blessing the tormas

OM KHANDAROHI HUM HUM PHAT
OM SÖBHAWA SHUDDHA SARWA DHARMA SÖBHAWA
  SHUDDHO HAM
Everything becomes emptiness.

From the state of emptiness, from YAM comes wind, from
RAM comes fire, from AH a grate of three human heads.
Upon this from AH appears a broad and expansive skullcup.
Inside from OM, KHAM, AM, TRAM, HUM come the five
nectars; from LAM, MAM, PAM, TAM, BAM come the five
meats, each marked by these letters. The wind blows, the
fire blazes, and the substances inside the skullcup melt.
Above them from HUM there arises a white, upside-down
khatanga which falls into the skullcup and melts whereby
the substances take on the colour of mercury. Above them
three rows of vowels and consonants, standing one above
the other, transform into OM AH HUM. From these, light
rays draw the nectar of exalted wisdom from the hearts of
all the Tathagatas, Heroes, and Yoginis of the ten directions.
When this is added the contents increase and become vast.
OM AH HUM   (3x)

Offering the principal torma

Offer the torma while reciting three or seven times:

OM VAJRA AH RA LI HO: DZA HUM BAM HO: VAJRA DAKINI
  SAMAYA TÖN TRISHAYA HO

Offering the torma to the mundane dakinis

Offer the torma while reciting twice:

OM KHA KHA, KHAHI KHAHI, SARWA YAKYA RAKYASA,
BHUTA, TRETA, PISHATA, UNATA, APAMARA, VAJRA DAKA,
DAKI NÄDAYA, IMAM BALING GRIHANTU, SAMAYA
RAKYANTU, MAMA SARWA SIDDHI METRA YATZANTU,
YATIPAM, YATETAM, BHUDZATA, PIWATA, DZITRATA,
MATI TRAMATA, MAMA SARWA KATAYA, SÄDSUKHAM

BISHUDHAYE, SAHAYEKA BHAWÄNTU, HUM HUM PHAT
PHAT SÖHA

Outer offerings

OM VAJRA YOGINI SAPARIWARA AHRGHAM, PADÄM, PUPE,
DHUPE, ALOKE, GÄNDHE, NEWIDE, SHAPTA AH HUM

Inner offering

OM VAJRA YOGINI SAPARIWARA OM AH HUM

Praise

O Glorious Vajrayogini,
Chakravatin Dakini Queen,
Who have five wisdoms and three bodies,
To you Saviour of all I prostrate.

To the many Vajra Dakinis,
Who as Ladies of worldly actions,
Cut our bondage to preconceptions,
To all of you Ladies I prostrate.

Prostration

OM PARNA MAMI SARWA TATHAGATÄN

Now offer drinking water:

OM AH HRIH PRAVARA SÄKARAM AHRGHAM PARTITZA
HUM SÖHA

Requesting forbearance

Whatever has been done out of confusion,
Even the slightest faulty action,
O Protector, because you are the refuge of all beings,
It is fitting for you to be patient with these.

Whatever mistakes I have made
Through not finding, not understanding,
Or not having the ability,
Please, O Protector, be patient with all of these.

Prayer to Behold the Beautiful Face of Vajrayogini

Bliss and emptiness of infinite Conquerors who, as if in a
    drama,
Appear as so many different visions in samsara and
    nirvana;
From among these you are now the beautiful, powerful
    Lady of Dakini Land,
I remember you from my heart, please care for me with
    your playful embrace.

You are the spontaneously born Mother of the Conquerors in
    the land of Akanishta,
You are the field-born Dakinis in the twenty-four places,
You are the action mudras covering the whole earth,
O Venerable Lady, you are the supreme refuge of myself, the
    Yogi.

You who are the manifestation of the emptiness of the mind
    itself,
Are the actual BAM, the sphere of EH, in the city of the vajra.
In the land of illusion you show yourself as a fearsome
    cannibal
And as a smiling, vibrant, fair young maiden.

But no matter how much I searched, O Noble Lady,
I could find no certainty of your being truly existent;
Then the youth of my mind, exhausted by its elaborations,
Came to rest in the forest hut which is beyond expression.

How wonderful, please arise from the sphere of the
    Dharmakaya
And care for me by the truth of what it says
In the Glorious Heruka, King of Tantras,
That attainments come from reciting the supreme close
    essence mantra of the Vajra Queen.

In the isolated forest of Odivisha
You cared for Vajra Ghantapa, the powerful Siddha,
With the bliss of your kiss and embrace and he came to enjoy
    the supreme embrace;
O, please care for me in the same way.

491

Just as the Venerable Kusali was led directly
From an island in the Ganges to the sphere of space,
And just as you cared for the glorious Naropa,
Please lead me also to the city of the joyful Dakini.

Through the force of the compassion of my supreme root and
    lineage Gurus,
The especially profound and quick path of the ultimate,
    secret, great Tantra,
And the pure superior intention of myself, the Yogi,
May I soon behold your smiling face, O Joyful Dakini Lady.

Requesting fulfilment of wishes

O Blessed One Venerable Vajrayogini, for all of us disciples,
our benefactors, and others, please completely pacify all
our adverse circumstances and unfavourable conditions,
our negativities, obstructions, sickness, spirits, obstacles,
and so forth accumulated during beginningless lives in
samsara. Please increase further and further our life span,
merit, glory, wealth, good qualities of scripture and
realization, and so forth. Most especially, please bless us
so that every single stage of the common and uncommon
paths is generated within our mental continuum, and we
quickly attain the state of Venerable Vajrayogini.

Now recite seven times:

OM VAJRA SATTÖ AH

and then recite:

OM VAJRA HERUKA SAMAYA, MANU PALAYA, HERUKA
TENO PATITA, DRIDHO ME BHAWA, SUTO KAYO ME BHAWA,
SUPO KAYO ME BHAWA, ANURAKTO ME BHAWA, SARWA
SIDDHI ME PRAYATZA, SARWA KARMA SUTZA ME, TZITAM
SHRIYAM KURU HUM, HA HA HA HA HO BHAGAWÄN,
VAJRA HERUKA MA ME MUNTSA, HERUKA BHAWA, MAHA
SAMAYA SATTÖ AH HUM PHAT

Departure of Vajrayogini

OM
You who fulfil the welfare of all living beings
And bestow attainments as they are needed,
Please return to the Land of the Buddhas
And return here again in the future.

Contemplate:

OM VAJRA MU The wisdom beings return to their natural
abodes and the commitment beings dissolve into me.

FINAL OFFERING TO MUNDANE FIRE DEITY

Now make offerings to mundane Fire Deity on the hearth:

OM AGNIYE AHDIBÄ AHDIBÄ AMBISHA AMBISHA MAHA SHRIYE
HAMBÄ KABÄ BAHA NAYA PUPE PARTITZA HUM SÖHA
OM AGNIYE AHDIBÄ AHDIBÄ AMBISHA AMBISHA MAHA SHRIYE
HAMBÄ KABÄ BAHA NAYA DHUPE PARTITZA HUM SÖHA
OM AGNIYE AHDIBÄ AHDIBÄ AMBISHA AMBISHA MAHA SHRIYE
HAMBÄ KABÄ BAHA NAYA ALOKE PARTITZA HUM SÖHA
OM AGNIYE AHDIBÄ AHDIBÄ AMBISHA AMBISHA MAHA SHRIYE
HAMBÄ KABÄ BAHA NAYA GÄNDHE PARTITZA HUM SÖHA
OM AGNIYE AHDIBÄ AHDIBÄ AMBISHA AMBISHA MAHA SHRIYE
HAMBÄ KABÄ BAHA NAYA NEWIDE PARTITZA HUM SÖHA
OM AGNIYE AHDIBÄ AHDIBÄ AMBISHA AMBISHA MAHA SHRIYE
HAMBÄ KABÄ BAHA NAYA SHAPTA PARTITZA HUM SÖHA

and the inner offering:

OM AGNIYE AHDIBÄ AHDIBÄ AMBISHA AMBISHA MAHA
SHRIYE HAMBÄ KABÄ BAHA NAYA OM AH HUM

Now offer water for sprinkling and water for the mouth thus:

OM AH HRIH PRAVARA SÄKARAM PROKYANAM PARTITZA
HUM
OM AH HRIH PRAVARA SÄKARAM ÄNTZAMANAM PARTITZA
HUM

Offering the tambula torma

OM VAJRA TAMBULAYE SÖHA

Offering the garments

OM VAJRA WASA SÄ SÖHA

Offering the burning substances

Now offer the remaining burning substances to mundane Fire Deity:

Offering the milk-wood

Contemplate:

The milk-wood becomes nectar, the nature of the Bodhi Tree.
OM AGNIYE AHDIBÄ AHDIBÄ AMBISHA AMBISHA MAHA
  SHRIYE HAMBÄ KABÄ BAHA NAYE
OM BODHI PIKYAYE
For all of us disciples, our benefactors, and others, may
all obstacles to attaining liberation and omniscience, all
transgressions of the three vows, all natural non-virtues,
all inauspiciousness, all unclear concentration, all impure
recitation of mantras, all faults of excess and omission in
the rituals, and especially all obstacles to increased vitality
[be purified] SHÄNTING KURUYE SÖHA.

Offering the molten butter

OM AGNIYE AHDIBÄ AHDIBÄ AMBISHA AMBISHA MAHA
  SHRIYE HAMBÄ KABÄ BAHA NAYE
OM AGNIYE
For all of us disciples, our benefactors, and others, may
all obstacles to attaining liberation and omniscience, all
transgressions of the three vows, all natural non-virtues,
all inauspiciousness, all unclear concentration, all impure
recitation of mantras, all faults of excess and omission in
the rituals, and especially all obstacles to increased wealth
[be purified] SHÄNTING KURUYE SÖHA.

Offering the sesame seeds

OM AGNIYE AHDIBÄ AHDIBÄ AMBISHA AMBISHA MAHA
  SHRIYE HAMBÄ KABÄ BAHA NAYE
OM SARWA PAPAM DAHANA VAJRAYE

For all of us disciples, our benefactors, and others, may
all obstacles to attaining liberation and omniscience, all
transgressions of the three vows, all natural non-virtues,
all inauspiciousness, all unclear concentration, all impure
recitation of mantras, all faults of excess and omission in
the rituals, and especially all our negativities [be purified]
SHÄNTING KURUYE SÖHA.

Offering the couch grass

OM AGNIYE AHDIBÄ AHDIBÄ AMBISHA AMBISHA MAHA
SHRIYE HAMBÄ KABÄ BAHA NAYE
OM VAJRA AHYUKE
For all of us disciples, our benefactors, and others, may
all obstacles to attaining liberation and omniscience, all
transgressions of the three vows, all natural non-virtues,
all inauspiciousness, all unclear concentration, all impure
recitation of mantras, all faults of excess and omission in
the rituals, and especially all obstacles to increased life
span [be purified] SHÄNTING KURUYE SÖHA.

Offering the rice

OM AGNIYE AHDIBÄ AHDIBÄ AMBISHA AMBISHA MAHA
SHRIYE HAMBÄ KABÄ BAHA NAYE
OM VAJRA PUTRAYE
For all of us disciples, our benefactors, and others, may
all obstacles to attaining liberation and omniscience, all
transgressions of the three vows, all natural non-virtues,
all inauspiciousness, all unclear concentration, all impure
recitation of mantras, all faults of excess and omission in
the rituals, and especially all obstacles to increased merit
[be purified] SHÄNTING KURUYE SÖHA.

Offering the flour and yoghurt

OM AGNIYE AHDIBÄ AHDIBÄ AMBISHA AMBISHA MAHA
SHRIYE HAMBÄ KABÄ BAHA NAYE
OM SARWA SAMPA DE
For all of us disciples, our benefactors, and others, may
all obstacles to attaining liberation and omniscience, all

transgressions of the three vows, all natural non-virtues, all inauspiciousness, all unclear concentration, all impure recitation of mantras, all faults of excess and omission in the rituals, and especially all obstacles to supreme bliss [be purified] SHÄNTING KURUYE SÖHA.

Offering the kusha grass

OM AGNIYE AHDIBÄ AHDIBÄ AMBISHA AMBISHA MAHA
  SHRIYE HAMBÄ KABÄ BAHA NAYE
OM AHTRATI HATA VAJRAYE
For all of us disciples, our benefactors, and others, may all obstacles to attaining liberation and omniscience, all transgressions of the three vows, all natural non-virtues, all inauspiciousness, all unclear concentration, all impure recitation of mantras, all faults of excess and omission in the rituals, and especially all obstacles to supreme cleanliness [be purified] SHÄNTING KURUYE SÖHA.

Offering the white mustard seeds

OM AGNIYE AHDIBÄ AHDIBÄ AMBISHA AMBISHA MAHA
  SHRIYE HAMBÄ KABÄ BAHA NAYE
OM SARWA AHRTA SIDDHA YE
For all of us disciples, our benefactors, and others, may all obstacles to attaining liberation and omniscience, all transgressions of the three vows, all natural non-virtues, all inauspiciousness, all unclear concentration, all impure recitation of mantras, all faults of excess and omission in the rituals, and especially all our obstacles [be purified] SHÄNTING KURUYE SÖHA.

Offering the barley with husks

OM AGNIYE AHDIBÄ AHDIBÄ AMBISHA AMBISHA MAHA
  SHRIYE HAMBÄ KABÄ BAHA NAYE
OM VAJRA BINZAYE
For all of us disciples, our benefactors, and others, may all obstacles to attaining liberation and omniscience, all transgressions of the three vows, all natural non-virtues, all inauspiciousness, all unclear concentration, all impure recitation of mantras, all faults of excess and omission in

the rituals, and especially all obstacles to wealth and abundant harvests [be purified] SHÄNTING KURUYE SÖHA.

Offering the barley without husks

OM AGNIYE AHDIBÄ AHDIBÄ AMBISHA AMBISHA MAHA
    SHRIYE HAMBÄ KABÄ BAHA NAYE
OM MAHA BEGAYE
For all of us disciples, our benefactors, and others, may all obstacles to attaining liberation and omniscience, all transgressions of the three vows, all natural non-virtues, all inauspiciousness, all unclear concentration, all impure recitation of mantras, all faults of excess and omission in the rituals, and especially all obstacles to excellent quick mental powers [be purified] SHÄNTING KURUYE SÖHA.

Offering the peas

OM AGNIYE AHDIBÄ AHDIBÄ AMBISHA AMBISHA MAHA
    SHRIYE HAMBÄ KABÄ BAHA NAYE
OM MAHA BALAYE
For all of us disciples, our benefactors, and others, may all obstacles to attaining liberation and omniscience, all transgressions of the three vows, all natural non-virtues, all inauspiciousness, all unclear concentration, all impure recitation of mantras, all faults of excess and omission in the rituals, and especially all obstacles to increased strength [be purified] SHÄNTING KURUYE SÖHA.

Offering the wheat

OM AGNIYE AHDIBÄ AHDIBÄ AMBISHA AMBISHA MAHA
    SHRIYE HAMBÄ KABÄ BAHA NAYE
OM VAJRA GHAMA RI
For all of us disciples, our benefactors, and others, may all obstacles to attaining liberation and omniscience, all transgressions of the three vows, all natural non-virtues, all inauspiciousness, all unclear concentration, all impure recitation of mantras, all faults of excess and omission in the rituals, and especially all sickness [be purified] SHÄNTING KURUYE SÖHA.

Offering the alcohol

OM AGNIYE AHDIBÄ AHDIBÄ AMBISHA AMBISHA MAHA
SHRIYE HAMBÄ KABÄ BAHA NAYE
OM MADANA PÄNJA AMRITA AH HUM
For all of us disciples, our benefactors, and others, may
all obstacles to attaining liberation and omniscience, all
transgressions of the three vows, all natural non-virtues,
all inauspiciousness, all unclear concentration, all impure
recitation of mantras, all faults of excess and omission in
the rituals, and especially all obstacles to accomplishing
supreme attainments [be purified] SHÄNTING KURUYE
SÖHA.

Offering the beef

OM AGNIYE AHDIBÄ AHDIBÄ AMBISHA AMBISHA MAHA
SHRIYE HAMBÄ KABÄ BAHA NAYE
OM BALA PÄNJA AMRITA AH HUM
For all of us disciples, our benefactors, and others, may
all obstacles to attaining liberation and omniscience, all
transgressions of the three vows, all natural non-virtues,
all inauspiciousness, all unclear concentration, all impure
recitation of mantras, all faults of excess and omission in
the rituals, and especially all obstacles to accomplishing
supreme attainments [be purified] SHÄNTING KURUYE
SÖHA.

Offering the special pacifying substance

OM AGNIYE AHDIBÄ AHDIBÄ AMBISHA AMBISHA MAHA
SHRIYE HAMBÄ KABÄ BAHA NAYE
For all of us disciples, our benefactors, and others, may
all obstacles to attaining liberation and omniscience, all
transgressions of the three vows, all natural non-virtues,
all inauspiciousness, all unclear concentration, all impure
recitation of mantras, all faults of excess and omission in
the rituals, and especially all obstacles to accomplishing
supreme attainments [be purified] SHÄNTING KURUYE
SÖHA.

Praise

Lord of the world, Son of Brahma the powerful protector,
King of Fire Deities, empowered by Takki,
Who consume all delusions with your supreme wisdom,
To you, O Protector Fire Deity, I bow down.

If you wish to make extensive praises, continue with:

O Son of Brahma, protector of the world,
King of Fire Deities, supreme Rishi,
You manifest this form out of compassion
To fully protect all living beings.

In the aspect of a Rishi accomplished in knowledge
  mantras,
With the light of wisdom consuming delusions,
And a blazing brilliance like the fire of the aeon,
You are endowed with clairvoyance and miracle powers.

Out of skilful means you ride an emanation vehicle.
Holding a mala you recite knowledge mantras.
You hold a vase of essential nectar
And bring coolness to all with the nectar of Dharma.

You are free from faults and have perfected purity.
Though you abide in the world you have passed beyond
  sorrow;
Though you have attained peace you have great
  compassion;
Therefore I make praises and prostrations to you.

Now offer water for the mouth and water for sprinkling thus:

OM AH HRIH PRAVARA SĀKARAM ĀNTZAMANAM PARTITZA
  HUM SÖHA
OM AH HRIH PRAVARA SĀKARAM PROKYANAM PARTITZA
  HUM SÖHA

Outer offerings

OM AGNIYE AHDIBĀ AHDIBĀ AMBISHA AMBISHA MAHA SHRIYE
  HAMBĀ KABĀ BAHA NAYE PUPE PARTITZA HUM SÖHA

OM AGNIYE AHDIBÄ AHDIBÄ AMBISHA AMBISHA MAHA SHRIYE
HAMBÄ KABÄ BAHA NAYE DHUPE PARTITZA HUM SÖHA
OM AGNIYE AHDIBÄ AHDIBÄ AMBISHA AMBISHA MAHA SHRIYE
HAMBÄ KABÄ BAHA NAYE ALOKE PARTITZA HUM SÖHA
OM AGNIYE AHDIBÄ AHDIBÄ AMBISHA AMBISHA MAHA SHRIYE
HAMBÄ KABÄ BAHA NAYE GÄNDHE PARTITZA HUM SÖHA
OM AGNIYE AHDIBÄ AHDIBÄ AMBISHA AMBISHA MAHA SHRIYE
HAMBÄ KABÄ BAHA NAYE NEWIDE PARTITZA HUM SÖHA
OM AGNIYE AHDIBÄ AHDIBÄ AMBISHA AMBISHA MAHA SHRIYE
HAMBÄ KABÄ BAHA NAYE SHAPTA PARTITZA HUM SÖHA

Blessing the torma

OM KHANDAROHI HUM HUM PHAT
OM SÖBHAWA SHUDDHA SARWA DHARMA SÖBHAWA
SHUDDHO HAM
Everything becomes emptiness.

From the state of emptiness, from YAM comes wind, from
RAM comes fire, from AH a grate of three human heads.
Upon this from AH appears a broad and expansive skullcup.
Inside from OM, KHAM, AM, TRAM, HUM come the five
nectars; from LAM, MAM, PAM, TAM, BAM come the five
meats, each marked by these letters. The wind blows, the
fire blazes, and the substances inside the skullcup melt.
Above them from HUM there arises a white, upside-down
khatanga which falls into the skullcup and melts whereby
the substances take on the colour of mercury. Above them
three rows of vowels and consonants, standing one above
the other, transform into OM AH HUM. From these, light
rays draw the nectar of exalted wisdom from the hearts of
all the Tathagatas, Heroes, and Yoginis of the ten directions.
When this is added the contents increase and become vast.
OM AH HUM   (3x)

Offering the torma

Offer the torma by reciting three times:

OM AGNIYE AHDIBÄ AHDIBÄ AMBISHA AMBISHA MAHA
SHRIYE HAMBÄ KABÄ BAHA NAYA AHKAROMUKAM SARWA
DHARMANÄN ADENUWATEN NADÖ DA OM AH HUM PHAT
SÖHA

Outer offerings

OM AGNIYE AHDIBÄ AHDIBÄ AMBISHA AMBISHA MAHA SHRIYE
HAMBÄ KABÄ BAHA NAYE PUPE PARTITZA HUM SÖHA
OM AGNIYE AHDIBÄ AHDIBÄ AMBISHA AMBISHA MAHA SHRIYE
HAMBÄ KABÄ BAHA NAYE DHUPE PARTITZA HUM SÖHA
OM AGNIYE AHDIBÄ AHDIBÄ AMBISHA AMBISHA MAHA SHRIYE
HAMBÄ KABÄ BAHA NAYE ALOKE PARTITZA HUM SÖHA
OM AGNIYE AHDIBÄ AHDIBÄ AMBISHA AMBISHA MAHA SHRIYE
HAMBÄ KABÄ BAHA NAYE GÄNDHE PARTITZA HUM SÖHA
OM AGNIYE AHDIBÄ AHDIBÄ AMBISHA AMBISHA MAHA SHRIYE
HAMBÄ KABÄ BAHA NAYE NEWIDE PARTITZA HUM SÖHA
OM AGNIYE AHDIBÄ AHDIBÄ AMBISHA AMBISHA MAHA SHRIYE
HAMBÄ KABÄ BAHA NAYE SHAPTA PARTITZA HUM SÖHA

Requesting assistance

O Deity, who eat what is burned in the fire,
King of Rishis and Lord of the spirits,
Together with the hosts of Fire Deities from the south-east,
To you I make offerings, praises and prostrations.
Please enjoy this torma that I offer to you.

May I and other practitioners
Have good health, long life, power,
Glory, fame, fortune,
And extensive enjoyments.
Please grant me the attainments
Of pacifying, increasing, controlling and wrathful actions.
You who are bound by oaths please protect me
And help me to accomplish all the attainments.
Eradicate all untimely death, sicknesses,
Harm from spirits and hindrances.
Eliminate bad dreams,
Ill omens and bad actions.

May there be happiness in the world, may the years be
good,
May crops increase, and may Dharma flourish.
May all goodness and happiness come about,
And may all wishes be accomplished.

Now offer water for drinking:

OM AH HRIH PRAVARA SÄKARAM AHRGHAM PARTITZA
  HUM SÖHA

Requesting forbearance

Whatever has been done out of confusion,
Even the slightest faulty action,
O Protector, because you are the refuge of all beings,
It is fitting for you to be patient with these.

OM VAJRA SATTÖ AH

Departure of mundane Fire Deity

O Eater of burning offerings,
Who accomplish one's own and others' purposes,
Please depart and return at the appropriate time
To help me accomplish all the attainments.

Contemplate:

OM MU
The wisdom being, Fire Deity, returns to his natural abode
and the commitment being assumes the aspect of a blazing
fire.

Putting on the armour

At places in my body arise moon mandalas upon which
at my navel is red OM BAM, Vajravarahi; at my heart blue
HAM YOM, Yamani; at my throat white HRIM MOM, Mohani;
at my forehead yellow HRIM HRIM, Sachalani; at my crown
green HUM HUM, Samtrasani; at all my limbs smoke-
coloured PHAT PHAT, essence of Chandika.

To protect the main directions and intermediate directions
recite twice:

OM SUMBHANI SUMBHA HUM HUM PHAT
OM GRIHANA GRIHANA HUM HUM PHAT
OM GRIHANA PAYA GRIHANA PAYA HUM HUM PHAT
OM ANAYA HO BHAGAWÄN VAJRA HUM HUM PHAT

Auspicious prayers

May there be the auspiciousness of swiftly receiving the
    blessings
Of the hosts of glorious, sacred Gurus,
Vajradhara, Pandit Naropa, and so forth,
The glorious Lords of all virtue and excellence.

May there be the auspiciousness of the Dakini Truth Body,
Perfection of wisdom, the supreme Mother of the
    Conquerors,
The natural clear light, free from elaboration from the
    beginning,
The Lady who emanates and gathers all things stable and
    moving.

May there be the auspiciousness of the Complete Enjoyment
    Body, spontaneously born,
A body, radiant and beautiful, ablaze with the glory of the
    major and minor marks,
A speech proclaiming the supreme vehicle with sixty
    melodies,
And a mind of non-conceptual bliss and clarity possessing
    the five exalted wisdoms.

May there be the auspiciousness of the Emanation Body, born
    in the places,
Ladies who with various Form Bodies, in various places,
Fulfil by various means the aims of various ones to be
    tamed
In accordance with their various wishes.

May there be the auspiciousness of the supreme Dakini,
    mantra-born,
A venerable Lady with a colour similar to that of a ruby,
With a smiling, wrathful manner, one face, two hands
holding curved knife and skullcup,
And two legs in bent and outstretched positions.

May there be the auspiciousness of your countless
    millions of emanations
And the hosts of the seventy-two thousand [Dakinis]
Eliminating all the obstructions of practitioners
And bestowing the attainments that are longed for.

Prayers for the Virtuous Tradition

So that the tradition of Je Tsongkhapa,
The King of the Dharma, may flourish,
May all obstacles be pacified
And may all favourable conditions abound.

Through the two collections of myself and others
Gathered throughout the three times,
May the doctrine of Conqueror Losang Dragpa
Flourish for evermore.

The nine-line *Migtsema* prayer

Tsongkhapa, crown ornament of the scholars of the
    Land of the Snows,
You are Buddha Shakyamuni and Vajradhara, the
    source of all attainments,
Avalokiteshvara, the treasury of unobservable
    compassion,
Manjushri, the supreme stainless wisdom,
And Vajrapani, the destroyer of the hosts of maras.
O Venerable Guru-Buddha, synthesis of all Three Jewels,
With my body, speech and mind, respectfully I make
    requests:
Please grant your blessings to ripen and liberate myself
    and others,
And bestow the common and supreme attainments.

(3x)

A RITUAL FOR PURIFYING AND BLESSING THE SITE

If a burning offering has already been performed on the site of the hearth, or if it is above ground level, there is no need to perform a site ritual. However, if neither is the case, and if a ritual has not already been performed in that place, the following site ritual should be performed there.

On the site where the hearth will be made, set out a torma for the local guardians, as well as outer offerings, and inner offering. Those who are to perform [the offering] should assemble and if they have already performed self-generation on that day should proceed with the ritual. If not, they should begin with:

In an instant I become Venerable Vajrayogini.

Now bless the inner offering, outer offerings, and torma. Then:

Light rays radiate from my heart and invite the local guardians and their retinues.

Outer offerings

OM KYETRA PALA SAPARIWARA AHRGHAM PARTITZA HUM SÖHA
OM KYETRA PALA SAPARIWARA PADÄM PARTITZA HUM SÖHA
OM KYETRA PALA SAPARIWARA PUPE PARTITZA HUM SÖHA
OM KYETRA PALA SAPARIWARA DHUPE PARTITZA HUM SÖHA
OM KYETRA PALA SAPARIWARA ALOKE PARTITZA HUM SÖHA
OM KYETRA PALA SAPARIWARA GÄNDHE PARTITZA HUM SÖHA
OM KYETRA PALA SAPARIWARA NEWIDE PARTITZA HUM SÖHA
OM KYETRA PALA SAPARIWARA SHAPTA PARTITZA HUM SÖHA

Inner offering

OM KYETRA PALA SAPARIWARA OM AH HUM

Offering the torma

AHKAROMUKAM SARWA DHARMANÄN ADENUWATEN
NADÖ DA OM AH HUM PHAT SÖHA   (3x)

Request

Recite three times:

All you who abide in this place,
Gods, nagas, givers of harm, cannibals, and others,
I request you to grant me permission
To make use of this site.

Requested in this way:

Having been requested, they gladly depart to their own places.

Now, to purify the ground, with divine pride, sprinkle the site of the hearth with white mustard seeds, water, and ashes from a wood stove while reciting OM KHANDAROHI HUM HUM PHAT. With this mantra spread the ground with the five bovine substances, starting from the east, and then sprinkle scented water and cleansing water. Then sit in the vajra posture and with the earth-pressing mudra recite:

OM BHUKE The ground becomes emptiness.

HUM LAM HUM The ground becomes the nature of atoms.

OM MEDINI BENZI BHAWA VAJRA BHÄNDHA HUM The ground becomes completely firm, the nature of vajra.

OM HANA HANA VAJRA KRODHA HUM PHAT Wrathful Vajra destroys all obstacles.

Reciting this, while touching the ground with your hand, blesses the site. Now for the supreme purification contemplate:

All phenomena, the ground and so forth, are of one taste with emptiness.

Colophon: This sadhana was translated under the compassionate guidance of Venerable Geshe Kelsang Gyatso.

Vajradaka Burning Offering

A PRACTICE FOR PURIFYING
MISTAKES AND NEGATIVITIES

by
Ngulchu Dharmabhadra

Vajradaka

Vajradaka Burning Offering

Going for refuge

I and all sentient beings, until we achieve enlightenment,
Go for refuge to Buddha, Dharma and Sangha.   (3x)

Generating bodhichitta

Through the virtues I collect by giving and other
    perfections,
May I become a Buddha for the benefit of all.   (3x)

Generating special bodhichitta

And especially for the sake of all mother sentient beings,
I must attain the state of complete Buddhahood as quickly
as possible. Therefore I shall engage in a burning offering to
Vajradaka.

Visualizing the commitment being

OM VAJRA AMRITA KUNDALI HANA HANA HUM PHAT
OM SÖBHAWA SHUDDHA SARWA DHARMA SÖBHAWA
    SHUDDHO HAM
The fire becomes emptiness.

From the state of emptiness there arises a fiercely blazing
fire of exalted wisdom. In the centre of this, from a HUM
and a vajra, there arises wrathful Vajradaka, dark blue in
colour. He has one face and two hands, which are joined
in the mudra of a Hungdze and hold a vajra and bell.
With his mouth wide open, he snarls into space, baring
his four sharp fangs. His head is adorned with five dry
skulls and he wears a long necklace of fifty moist skulls. He
wears a tiger's skin for a lower garment and is complete

with all the features of a wrathful manifestation. He sits
with his legs forming a circle, in the manner of a Hero
destroying negativities and obstructions. At his crown is a
white OM, at his throat a red AH, at his heart a blue HUM.

Inviting and absorbing the wisdom beings

Light rays radiate from the HUM at his heart and invite
from their natural abodes wisdom beings in the same
aspect, together with the empowering Deities.

DZA HUM BAM HO
They become non-dual.

Granting empowerment

The empowering Deities grant empowerment and his
crown is adorned by Akshobya.

Offerings

OM VAJRADAKA SAPARIWARA AHRGHAM PARTITZA HUM SÖHA
OM VAJRADAKA SAPARIWARA PADÄM PARTITZA HUM SÖHA
OM VAJRADAKA SAPARIWARA PUPE PARTITZA HUM SÖHA
OM VAJRADAKA SAPARIWARA DHUPE PARTITZA HUM SÖHA
OM VAJRADAKA SAPARIWARA ALOKE PARTITZA HUM SÖHA
OM VAJRADAKA SAPARIWARA GÄNDHE PARTITZA HUM SÖHA
OM VAJRADAKA SAPARIWARA NEWIDE PARTITZA HUM SÖHA
OM VAJRADAKA SAPARIWARA SHAPTA PARTITZA HUM SÖHA

Prostration

O Vajra Akshobya, great exalted wisdom,
Great skilful one from the vajra sphere,
Supreme among the three vajras and three mandalas,
To you Vajradaka I prostrate.

Visualization for making the burning offering

I remain in my ordinary form. At my heart is a black letter
PAM, the seed of negativity. At my navel, from RAM, comes
a red fire mandala. On the soles of both my feet, from YAM,
comes a blue wind mandala.

Light rays radiate from the letter PAM and draw back all
the negativities and obstructions of my three doors in the
aspect of black rays of light. These dissolve into the PAM.

Below, the wind blows and enters through the soles of my
feet. The fire at my navel blazes and light rays from the
fire drive the PAM out through my nostrils. My negativities
take on the aspect of a scorpion which dissolves into the
sesame seeds. I offer these to the mouth of Vajradaka.

OM VAJRA DAKA KHA KHA KHAHI KHAHI SARWA PAPAM
DAHANA BHAKMI KURU SÖHA

May all the negativities, obstructions, and degenerated
commitments I have accumulated during beginningless
lives in samsara [be purified] SHÄNTING KURUYE SÖHA

*Offer the sesame seeds to Vajradaka while reciting the mantra
and the brief request prayer. Continue in this way until all
the sesame seeds have been offered.*

Thanking offering

OM VAJRADAKA SAPARIWARA AHRGHAM, PADÄM, PUPE,
DHUPE, ALOKE, GÄNDHE, NEWIDE, SHAPTA PARTITZA HUM
SÖHA

Prostration

Merely by our remembering your dark-blue form of a
    wrathful cannibal,
Amidst a blazing mass of exalted wisdom fire,
You destroy all maras, negativities, and obstructions;
To you Vajradaka I prostrate.

Requesting forbearance

Whatever mistakes I have made
Through not finding, not understanding,
Or not having the ability,
Please, O Protector, be patient with all of these.

Dissolution

The wisdom beings return to their natural abodes and
the commitment being transforms into the aspect of a
blazing fire.

Dedication

By this virtue, throughout all my lives
May I never be parted from the Mahayana Guru who
    reveals the unmistaken path,
And by always remaining under his care
May I drink continuously from the nectar of his speech.

Due to this, may I and others complete the practices
Of renunciation, bodhichitta, correct view,
The six perfections, and the two stages,
And may we swiftly attain the state endowed with the
    ten powers.

Through the blessings of the non-deceptive Guru and
    Three Jewels,
And the power of the immutable nature of phenomena
    and non-deceptive dependent relationship,
May everything be auspicious for my excellent prayers
    to be accomplished
So that I may swiftly attain omniscient Buddhahood.

Prayers for the Virtuous Tradition

So that the tradition of Je Tsongkhapa,
The King of the Dharma, may flourish,
May all obstacles be pacified
And may all favourable conditions abound.

Through the two collections of myself and others
Gathered throughout the three times,
May the doctrine of Conqueror Losang Dragpa
Flourish for evermore.

The nine-line *Migtsema* prayer

Tsongkhapa, crown ornament of the scholars of the
Land of the Snows,
You are Buddha Shakyamuni and Vajradhara, the
source of all attainments,
Avalokiteshvara, the treasury of unobservable
compassion,
Manjushri, the supreme stainless wisdom,
And Vajrapani, the destroyer of the hosts of maras.
O Venerable Guru-Buddha, synthesis of all Three Jewels,
With my body, speech and mind, respectfully I make
requests:
Please grant your blessings to ripen and liberate myself
and others,
And bestow the common and supreme attainments.

(3x)

Colophon: This sadhana was translated under the compassionate
guidance of Venerable Geshe Kelsang Gyatso.

Samayavajra Sadhana

by
Je Phabongkhapa

Samayavajra

Samayavajra Sadhana

Going for refuge

I and all sentient beings, until we achieve enlightenment,
Go for refuge to Buddha, Dharma and Sangha.　　(3x)

Generating bodhichitta

Through the virtues I collect by giving and other
　　perfections,
May I become a Buddha for the benefit of all.　　(3x)

Visualizing the commitment being

I have the clarity of the Deity. At my heart, on a lotus of
various colours and a moon mandala, there arises, from HA,
a sword with its handle marked by a HA. This completely
transforms into Samayavajra, who has a green-coloured
body and three faces, one green, one black and one white.
He has six hands. The first two embrace his consort who is
similar in appearance. The other two right hands hold a
vajra and a sword, and the other two left hands hold a bell
and a lotus. Both the Father and the Mother are adorned
with various jewelled ornaments. At their crown is an OM,
at their throat is an AH, and at their heart is a HUM.

Inviting and absorbing the wisdom beings

From the HUM at the heart, light rays radiate and invite from
their natural abodes wisdom beings in the same aspect.

DZA HUM BAM HO
They become non-dual.

Granting empowerment

Once again light rays radiate from the HUM at the heart
and invite the five families together with their retinues.

OM PÄNZA KULA SAPARIWARA AHRGHAM, PADÄM, PUPE,
DHUPE, ALOKE, GÄNDHE, NEWIDE, SHAPTA PARTITZA HUM
SÖHA

O, all you Tathagatas, please grant him the empowerment.

Requested in this way, with vases brimming with the
nectar of exalted wisdom, they grant the empowerment
through the crown of my head.

'OM SARWA TATHAGATA ABHIKEKATA SAMAYA SHRIYE HUM'

The entire body of Samayavajra is filled and he experiences
great bliss. All stains are purified. The excess water at the
crown completely transforms and the Father's crown is
adorned by Akshobya and the Mother's by Amoghasiddhi.

Recitation of the mantra

On a moon at the heart of Samayavajra is a vajra of
various colours. At its centre is a green HA from which
flows a fine stream of nectar. This is encircled by OM AH
PANGYA DHIKA HA HUM. A stream of nectar flows out
through the points of the multi-coloured vajra, gradually
filling my whole body. I experience uncontaminated bliss
and all the stains of my degenerated commitments leave
through the pores of my skin in the form of black liquid.

*While contemplating this, recite the mantra as many times
as you wish.*

OM AH PANGYA DHIKA HA HUM

Prayer of confession and resolve

Out of unknowing and confusion
I have transgressed and broken my commitments.
O Guru Protector, please protect me.

Principal Holder of the Vajra,
To you whose nature is great compassion,
Lord of all beings I go for refuge.

Samayavajra replies: Dear One, all your negativities,
obstructions, and degenerated commitments are cleansed
and purified.

Absorption

Having said this, he dissolves into me, and my three doors
become inseparable from the body, speech and mind of
Samayavajra.

Dedication

By this virtue may I purify
All defilements and hindrances
That obstruct my progress on the spiritual paths,
And may I attain Buddhahood for the benefit of all.

Prayers for the Virtuous Tradition

So that the tradition of Je Tsongkhapa,
The King of the Dharma, may flourish,
May all obstacles be pacified
And may all favourable conditions abound.

Through the two collections of myself and others
Gathered throughout the three times,
May the doctrine of Conqueror Losang Dragpa
Flourish for evermore.

The nine-line *Migtsema* prayer

Tsongkhapa, crown ornament of the scholars of the
    Land of the Snows,
You are Buddha Shakyamuni and Vajradhara, the
    source of all attainments,
Avalokiteshvara, the treasury of unobservable
    compassion,

Manjushri, the supreme stainless wisdom,
And Vajrapani, the destroyer of the hosts of maras.
O Venerable Guru-Buddha, synthesis of all Three Jewels,
With my body, speech and mind, respectfully I make
 requests:
Please grant your blessings to ripen and liberate myself
 and others,
And bestow the common and supreme attainments.

(3x)

Colophon: This sadhana was translated under the compassionate
guidance of Venerable Geshe Kelsang Gyatso.

The Root Tantra of Heruka
and Vajrayogini

CHAPTERS ONE AND FIFTY-ONE OF THE
CONDENSED HERUKA ROOT TANTRA

Translated by
Venerable Geshe Kelsang Gyatso

Buddha Shakyamuni

Introduction

The *Heruka Root Tantras* belong to the Highest Yoga Tantra of Vajrayana Buddhism. Buddha taught the extensive, middling and condensed *Heruka Root Tantras*. The *Condensed Heruka Root Tantra*, which has fifty one chapters, was translated from Sanskrit into Tibetan.

Commentaries to the *Condensed Heruka Root Tantra* given by Buddha Shakyamuni, and many other commentaries written by Indian Buddhist Masters such as Mahasiddha Naropa and Lawapa, were also translated. Later, commentaries were written by Tibetan Tantric scholars based on Je Tsongkhapa's commentary to the *Condensed Heruka Root Tantra* entitled *Clear Illumination of All Hidden Meanings*.

I have translated the first and last chapters of the *Condensed Heruka Root Tantra* from Tibetan to English. As Je Tsongkhapa said, each word of the root Tantra has many different meanings; I have translated the hidden meaning, not the words. My purpose in doing this is to benefit the people of this modern world.

Geshe Kelsang Gyatso
2003

Twelve-armed Heruka

The Root Tantra of
Heruka and Vajrayogini

Spoken by the Blessed One, Buddha Shakyamuni, at the request of Vajrapani

Thus I shall explain the great secret –
The instructions on the stages of Heruka's path –
The unsurpassed of all the unsurpassed
That fulfils the wish for all attainments.

Generate the Pure Land of Heruka with the celestial
    mansion,
And yourself as glorious Buddha Heruka embracing
    Vajravarahi
With a retinue of thirty-six Dakinis and twenty-four
    Heroes;
In the supreme secret of great bliss
Always gather the nature of all.
Thus Heruka, who is imputed upon this great bliss,
Which is inseparable from the emptiness of all,
Is the Blessed One, definitive Heruka,
The synthesis of all Dakas and Dakinis.
And Heruka who appears with a blue-coloured body
With four faces and twelve arms,
Is the interpretative Heruka taught for commitment.
The supreme secret of great bliss
Arises through melting the drops inside the central channel;
Thus it is hard to find in the world
A person who experiences such bliss.
When examined there is no body;
You should know all things in the same way.

The commitments, meditations, recitations,
And other rituals will be explained.

Practitioners should always make offerings,
Either extensively or briefly,
To the assembly of Deities of Heruka's mandala,
Especially on the tenth and twenty-fifth days of each
     month.
With the motivation of the compassionate mind of
     bodhichitta
And the wisdom realizing the emptiness of all
     phenomena,
A practitioner can rely upon the three messengers:
An emanation, one who possesses realizations, or
One who is keeping the commitments purely.
The bliss arising through melting your own drops
Should be offered to Heruka who abides at your heart.
Because Heruka is always at the practitioner's heart,
Inseparable from him or her,
Anyone who sees, hears, touches or remembers such a
     practitioner
Will definitely receive Heruka's blessings.
Practitioners have the great power to heal themselves
And to accumulate merit and wisdom;
They can quickly accomplish attainments
Through meditation and recitation of the mantras.
As a basic practice you should always keep the
     commitments;
Breaking these would destroy the blessings
That you received when granted the empowerment,
And thus you would not accomplish any attainments.
Bliss through melting the drops inside the central channel,
Mixed completely with the emptiness of all,
Is the supreme secret of great bliss
That gives rise to all five attainments:
Pacifying, increasing and controlling attainments,
Attainments through wrathful actions,
And the attainment of supreme enlightenment.

By penetrating the point of the lower tip of your central
    channel,
When joined with the lower tip of the central channel of
    the mudra,
Wisdom wind will enter your central channel;
Through gaining deep experience with this meditation
You will attain the supreme secret of great bliss.
You can also rely on and practise the four mudras:
Commitment, action, phenomenon and great;
The four different ways of embracing should be known.
The bliss experienced by such a pure practitioner
Is unequalled by any bliss experienced by gods or
    humans.
The place where you meditate on the great secret
Can be a mountain, forest, cemetery, town or city.
Having found a suitable place with no obstacles
You should continually strive to accomplish
The supporting and supported mandala of Heruka.

This concludes Chapter One: *The Condensation of the Heruka
Root Tantra.*

The other instructions, which are hard to find,
That are hidden in the scriptures –
The way to accomplish the mandalas of Heruka –
Will also be briefly explained.

To begin, you should meditate on the meaning of Shri
    Heruka,
The union of great bliss and emptiness.
Then, meditate on the correct imaginations that believe:
The place is the actual Pure Land of Heruka
Appearing in the aspect of the supporting mandala,
The protection circle and celestial mansion;
Your body is the supreme secret of great bliss
Appearing in the form of Heruka's blue-coloured body,
Adorned with the five ornaments
And embracing the wisdom consort Vajravarahi;
Your speech is the nature of the mantra of AHLIKALI,
The source of all the mantras;
You are receiving the blessings and empowerment;
Your body is adorned with the inner protection,
The protection circle of the armour mantras;
The Deities of the five wheels appear in the celestial
    mansion;
The migrators of the six realms are purified
By emanating rays of wisdom light;
Outer, inner and eight-line mantra offerings are made;
Training in clear appearance and divine pride
Beyond ordinary appearance and conceptions –
Thus I have explained the fourteen essential points.
Those who sincerely engage in this practice
Will quickly purify all negativities,
Always take higher rebirth with good fortune,
And attain the state of the Conqueror Buddha.

Just as fire quickly destroys objects,
The recitations and meditations of Heruka and
    Vajrayogini
Quickly destroy suffering.
When such practitioners experience death,

Various emanations will appear to them
With offerings such as flowers and beautiful music,
And lead them to the Pure Land of Keajra.
For such practitioners, death is just mere name –
They are simply moved from the prison of samsara
To the Pure Land of Buddha Heruka.
The good fortune of Heruka Tantra practice
Will be extremely hard to find in the future –
Thus you should not waste the opportunity you have
    now.
The twelve arms of Heruka indicate that the practitioner
    will be freed
From the twelve dependent-related links of samsara;
Treading on Bhairawa and Kalarati shows victory over
    the maras –
Thus you should strive to practise these instructions.
Generate yourself as the principal of the mandala,
Surrounded by the Heroes and Yoginis of the five
    wheels
Who are all delighted with the supreme secret of great
    bliss.
At the end of the session, the supporting and
    supported
All dissolve into great bliss and emptiness –
Meditate on this union of bliss and emptiness.
From this, arise as the action Deity Heruka
Who engages in subsequent practices.

The Blessed One appears in many different aspects
To benefit all living beings who have different wishes.
Among the various methods that the Blessed One has
    shown
To fulfil the various wishes of living beings,
Supreme are the instructions of Sutra and the four
    classes of Tantra:
Action, Performance, Yoga and Highest Yoga Tantra.
You should never abandon Highest Yoga Tantra,
But realize that it has inconceivable meaning

And is the very essence of Buddhadharma.
It is hard to understand the profound meaning of
   Highest Yoga Tantra
For those who do not understand the real nature of
   things, emptiness.
However, the emanations of Buddha Vajradhara
   pervade everywhere
And the Buddha lineage of all beings is always with
   them;
Thus finally all living beings without exception
Will attain the supreme state of enlightenment,
   Buddhahood.

This concludes Chapter Fifty-One: *The Conclusion of the
Heruka Root Tantra.*

The condensed mantra of Heruka, Vajrayogini, the thirty-six
Dakinis and the twenty-four Heroes:

OM HUM BAM RIM RIM LIM LIM, KAM KHAM GAM GHAM
NGAM, TSAM TSHAM DZAM DZHAM NYAM, TRAM THRAM
DRAM DHRAM NAM, TAM THAM DAM DHAM NAM, PAM
PHAM BAM BHAM, YAM RAM LAM WAM, SHAM KAM SAM
HAM HUM HUM PHAT

For the sake of all living beings,
May I become Heruka;
And then lead every living being
To Heruka's supreme state.

Colophon: This text was translated by Venerable
Geshe Kelsang Gyatso, 2003

Appendix III
Diagrams and Illustrations

———

CONTENTS

Hand Gestures

AHRGHAM

PADÄM

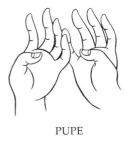

PUPE

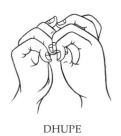

DHUPE

ALOKE/DIWE

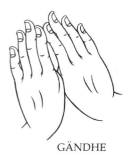

GÄNDHE

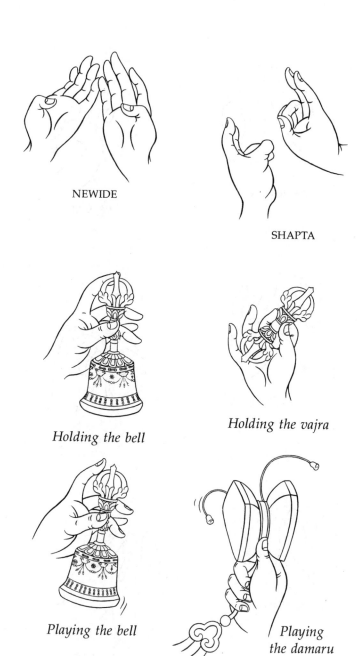

NEWIDE

SHAPTA

Holding the bell

Holding the vajra

Playing the bell

Playing
the damaru

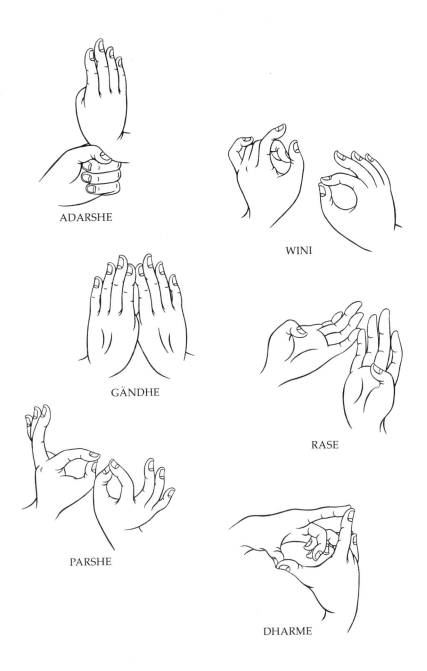

ADARSHE

WINI

GÄNDHE

RASE

PARSHE

DHARME

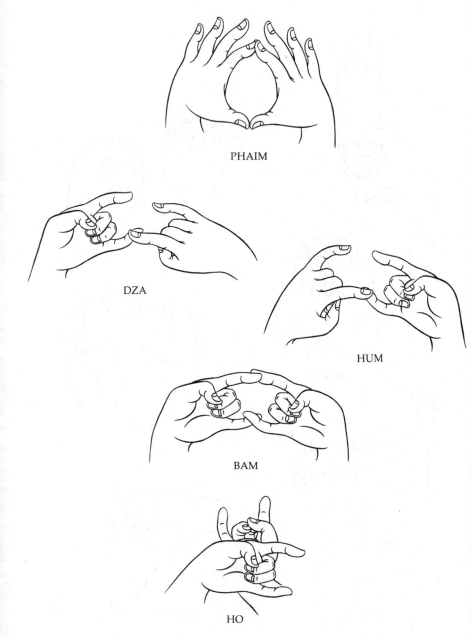

PHAIM

DZA

HUM

BAM

HO

HAND GESTURES

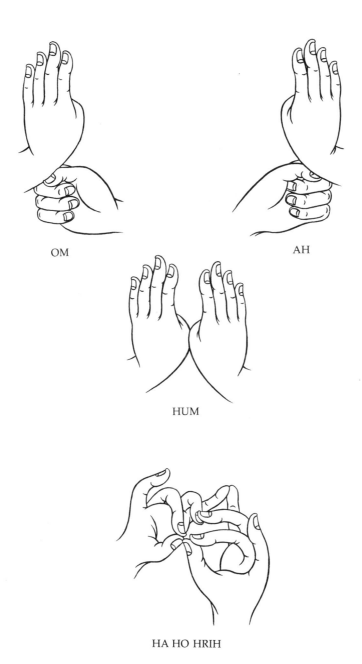

OM

AH

HUM

HA HO HRIH

537

Seed-letters and Ritual Objects

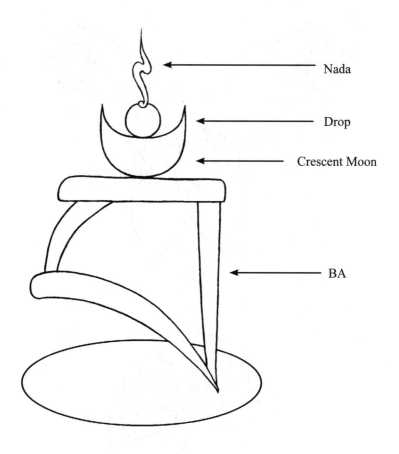

— Nada

— Drop

— Crescent Moon

— BA

Letter BAM

Letter BAM and mantra rosary on a moon disc
inside the phenomena source

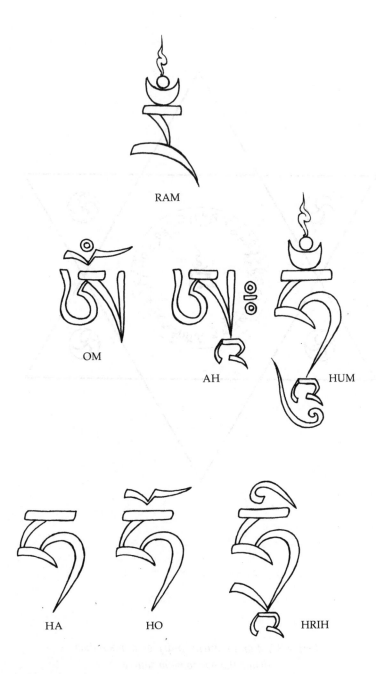

RAM

OM

AH

HUM

HA

HO

HRIH

540

Tormas

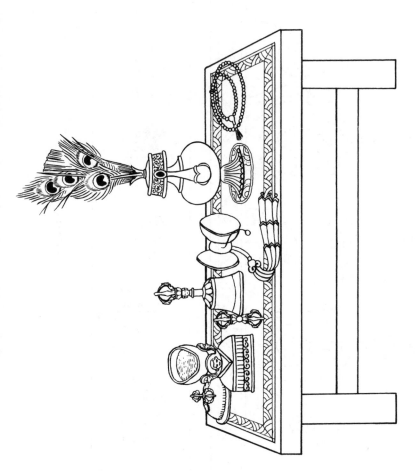

Inner offering in skullcup, vajra, bell, damaru, action vase, mala

Fire puja mandala

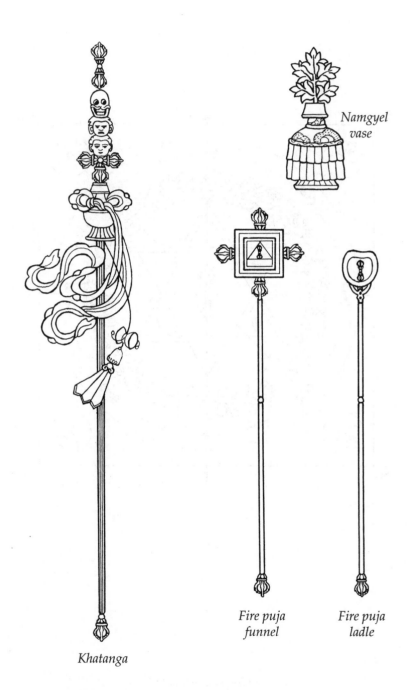

Namgyel vase

Khatanga

Fire puja funnel

Fire puja ladle

Glossary

Aggregate In general, all functioning things are aggregates because they are an aggregation of their parts. In particular, a person of the desire or form realm has five aggregates: the aggregates of form, feeling, discrimination, compositional factors and consciousness. A being of the formless realm lacks the aggregate of form but has the other four. A person's form aggregate is his or her body. The remaining four aggregates are aspects of his mind. See also *Contaminated aggregates*. See *The New Heart of Wisdom*.

Akanishta A Pure Land where Bodhisattvas attain enlightenment. See *Clear Light of Bliss* and *Tantric Grounds and Paths*.

Akshobya The manifestation of the aggregate of consciousness of all Buddhas. He has a blue-coloured body.

Alertness A mental factor that is a type of wisdom which examines our activity of body, speech and mind, and knows whether or not faults are developing. See *Understanding the Mind*.

Amitabha The manifestation of the aggregate of discrimination of all Buddhas. He has a red-coloured body.

Amoghasiddhi The manifestation of the aggregate of compositional factors of all Buddhas. He has a green-coloured body.

Analytical meditation The mental process of investigating a virtuous object – analyzing its nature, function, characteristics and other aspects. See *Joyful Path of Good Fortune* and *The New Meditation Handbook*.

Arya See Superior being.

Aspiring bodhichitta A bodhichitta that is a mere wish to attain enlightenment for the benefit of all living beings. See also *Bodhichitta*.

Atisha (AD 982-1054) A famous Indian Buddhist scholar and meditation master. He was Abbot of the great Buddhist monastery of Vikramashila at a time when Mahayana Buddhism was flourishing in India. He was later invited to Tibet where he reintroduced pure Buddhism. He is the author of the first text on the stages of the path, *Lamp for the Path*. His tradition later became known as the 'Kadampa Tradition'. See *Modern Buddhism* and *Joyful Path of Good Fortune*.

Attachment A deluded mental factor that observes a contaminated object, regards it as a cause of happiness and wishes for it. See *Joyful Path of Good Fortune* and *Understanding the Mind*.

Basis of imputation All phenomena are imputed upon their parts, therefore any of the individual parts, or the entire collection of the parts, of any phenomenon is its basis of imputation. A phenomenon is imputed by mind in dependence upon its basis of imputation appearing to that mind. See *Modern Buddhism*, *The New Heart of Wisdom* and *Ocean of Nectar*.

Beginningless time According to the Buddhist world view there is no beginning to mind, and so no beginning to time. Therefore all living beings have taken countless previous rebirths.

Benzarahi A female Buddha who is the manifestation of the fire element of all Buddhas. She is the consort of Buddha Amitabha.

Blessing The transformation of our mind from a negative state to a positive state, from an unhappy state to a happy state, or from a state of weakness to a state of strength, through the inspiration of holy beings such as our Spiritual Guide, Buddhas and Bodhisattvas.

Bodhichitta Sanskrit word for 'mind of enlightenment'. 'Bodhi' means enlightenment, and 'chitta' means mind. There are two types of bodhichitta: conventional bodhichitta and ultimate bodhichitta. Generally speaking, the term 'bodhichitta' refers to conventional bodhichitta, which is a primary mind motivated by great compassion that spontaneously seeks enlightenment to benefit all living beings. There are two types of conventional bodhichitta: aspiring bodhichitta and engaging bodhichitta. Ultimate bodhichitta is a wisdom motivated by conventional bodhichitta that directly realizes emptiness, the ultimate nature of phenomena. See also *Aspiring bodhichitta* and *Engaging bodhichitta*. See *Joyful Path of Good Fortune, Modern Buddhism* and *Meaningful to Behold*.

Bodhisattva A person who has generated spontaneous bodhichitta but who has not yet become a Buddha. From the moment a practitioner generates a non-artificial, or spontaneous, bodhichitta he or she becomes a Bodhisattva and enters the first Mahayana path, the path of accumulation. An ordinary Bodhisattva is one who has not realized emptiness directly, and a Superior Bodhisattva is one who has attained a direct realization of emptiness. See *Joyful Path of Good Fortune* and *Meaningful to Behold*.

Buddha family There are five main Buddha families: the families of Vairochana, Ratnasambhava, Amitabha, Amoghasiddhi, and Akshobya. They are the five purified aggregates – the aggregates of form, feeling, discrimination, compositional factors, and consciousness, respectively;

and the five exalted wisdoms – the exalted mirror-like wisdom, the exalted wisdom of equality, the exalted wisdom of individual realization, the exalted wisdom of accomplishing activities and the exalted wisdom of the Dharmadhatu, respectively. See *Great Treasury of Merit*.

Buddha lineage The root mind of a sentient being, and its ultimate nature. Buddha lineage, Buddha nature and Buddha seed are synonyms. All sentient beings have Buddha lineage and therefore have the potential to attain Buddhahood. See *Mahamudra Tantra*.

Buddha Shakyamuni The Buddha who is the founder of the Buddhist religion. See *Introduction to Buddhism* and *Modern Buddhism*.

Channels Subtle inner passageways of the body through which flow subtle drops moved by inner winds. See *Modern Buddhism*, *Mahamudra Tantra* and *Clear Light of Bliss*.

Channel wheel 'Chakra' in Sanskrit. A focal centre where secondary channels branch out from the central channel. Meditating on these points can cause the inner winds to enter the central channel. See *Modern Buddhism*, *Mahamudra Tantra* and *Clear Light of Bliss*.

Commitment being A visualized Buddha or ourself visualized as a Buddha. A commitment being is so called because in general it is the commitment of all Buddhists to visualize or remember Buddha, and in particular it is a commitment of those who have received an empowerment into Highest Yoga Tantra to generate themselves as a Deity.

Contaminated aggregates Any of the aggregates of form, feeling, discrimination, compositional factors and consciousness of a samsaric being. See also *Aggregate*. See *The New Heart of Wisdom* and *Joyful Path of Good Fortune*.

Conventional truth Any phenomenon other than emptiness. Conventional truths are true with respect to the minds of ordinary beings, but in reality they are false. See *The New Heart of Wisdom*, *Modern Buddhism*, *Meaningful to Behold* and *Ocean of Nectar*.

Deity body Divine body. When a practitioner attains an illusory body he or she attains an actual divine body, or Deity body, but not a Deity's body. A Deity's body is necessarily a body of a Tantric enlightened being. See *Tantric Grounds and Paths*.

Delusion A mental factor that arises from inappropriate attention and that functions to make the mind unpeaceful and uncontrolled. There are three main delusions: ignorance, desirous attachment and anger. From these all other delusions such as jealousy, pride and deluded doubt arise. See *Joyful Path of Good Fortune* and *Understanding the Mind*.

547

Demon See *Mara*.

Desire realm The environment of humans, animals, hungry spirits, hell beings, and the gods who enjoy the five objects of desire.

Dharma Protector A manifestation of a Buddha or Bodhisattva, whose main function is to eliminate obstacles and gather all necessary conditions for pure Dharma practitioners. Also called 'Dharmapala' in Sanskrit. See *Heart Jewel*.

Dorje Shugden A Dharma Protector who is an emanation of the Wisdom Buddha Manjushri. See *Heart Jewel*.

Dorjechang Trijang Rinpoche (AD 1901-1981) A special Tibetan Lama of the twentieth century who was an emanation of Buddha Shakyamuni, Heruka, Atisha, Amitabha and Je Tsongkhapa. Also known as 'Kyabje Trijang Rinpoche' and 'Lama Losang Yeshe Trijang Rinpoche'.

Drops There are two types of drop in the body. These are the essence of blood and sperm. When the drops melt and flow through the inner channels they give rise to an experience of bliss. See *Modern Buddhism*, *Mahamudra Tantra* and *Clear Light of Bliss*.

Emptiness Lack of inherent existence, the ultimate nature of all phenomena. See *Modern Buddhism*, *The New Heart of Wisdom* and *Ocean of Nectar*.

Engaging bodhichitta After we have taken the Bodhisattva vow, our aspiring bodhichitta transforms into engaging bodhichitta, which is a mind that actually engages in the practices that lead to enlightenment. See also *Bodhichitta*.

Example clear light A mind of clear light that realizes emptiness by means of a generic image. See *Clear Light of Bliss* and *Tantric Grounds and Paths*.

Faith A mental factor that functions principally to eliminate non-faith. See *Modern Buddhism*, *Joyful Path of Good Fortune* and *Understanding the Mind*.

Five elements (Tib. jung.wa) Earth, water, fire, wind and space. All matter can be said to be composed of a combination of these elements. There are five inner elements (those that are conjoined with the continuum of a person), and five outer elements (those that are not conjoined with the continuum of a person).

Five omniscient wisdoms The five exalted wisdoms of a Buddha: the exalted mirror-like wisdom, the exalted wisdom of equality, the exalted wisdom of individual realization, the exalted wisdom of accomplishing activities, and the exalted wisdom of the Dharmadhatu. See also *Buddha family*.

Form realm The environment of the gods who possess form and who are superior to desire realm gods. So-called because the gods who inhabit it have subtle form. See *Ocean of Nectar*.

Formless realm The environment of the gods who do not possess form. See *Ocean of Nectar*.

Four Noble Truths True sufferings, true origins, true cessations and true paths. They are called 'noble' truths because they are supreme objects of meditation. Through meditation on these four objects we can realize ultimate truth directly and thus become a noble, or Superior, being. Sometimes referred to as the 'Four truths of Superiors'. See *How to Solve Our Human Problems*, *Modern Buddhism* and *Joyful Path of Good Fortune*.

Geshe A title given by the Kadampa monasteries to accomplished Buddhist scholars.

God 'Deva' in Sanskrit. A being of the god realm, the highest of the six realms of samsara. There are many different types of god. Some are desire realm gods, while others are form or formless realm gods. See *Joyful Path of Good Fortune*.

Guhyasamaja A Highest Yoga Tantra Deity. See *Great Treasury of Merit*.

Guru Sanskrit word for 'Spiritual Guide'.

Heroes and Heroines A Hero is a male Tantric Deity embodying method. A Heroine is a female Tantric Deity embodying wisdom.

Hinayana Sanskrit word for 'Lesser Vehicle'. The Hinayana goal is to attain merely one's own liberation from suffering by completely abandoning delusions. See *Joyful Path of Good Fortune*.

Illusory body The subtle divine body that is principally developed from the indestructible wind. When a practitioner of Highest Yoga Tantra rises from the meditation of the isolated mind of ultimate example clear light, he or she attains a body that is not the same as his or her ordinary physical body. This new body is the illusory body. It has the same appearance as the body of the personal Deity of generation stage except that it is white in colour. It can be perceived only by those who have already attained an illusory body. See *Tantric Grounds and Paths*, *Mahamudra Tantra* and *Clear Light of Bliss*.

Imprint There are two types of imprint: imprints of actions and imprints of delusions. Every action we perform leaves an imprint on the mental consciousness, and these imprints are karmic potentialities to experience certain effects in the future. The imprints of delusions remain even after the delusions themselves have been abandoned, rather as the smell of garlic lingers in a container after the garlic has been removed. Imprints of delusions are obstructions to omniscience, and are completely abandoned only by Buddhas.

THE NEW GUIDE TO DAKINI LAND

Indestructible drop The most subtle drop, which is located at the heart. It is formed from the essence of the white and red drops received from our parents at conception, and encloses the very subtle mind and its mounted wind. These red and white drops do not separate until the time of death, when they open and allow the very subtle mind and its mounted wind to depart to the next life. See *Modern Buddhism, Mahamudra Tantra, Clear Light of Bliss* and *Tantric Grounds and Paths.*

Ishvara A god who abides in the Land Controlling Emanations, the highest state of existence within the desire realm. Ishvara has limited, contaminated miracle powers which make him more powerful than other beings in the desire realm. If we entrust ourselves to Ishvara we may receive some temporary benefit in this life, such as an increase in wealth or possessions, but wrathful Ishvara is the enemy of those who seek liberation and he interferes with their spiritual progress. He is therefore said to be a type of Devaputra demon. See also *Mara.*

Je Phabongkhapa (AD 1878-1941) A great Tibetan Lama who was an emanation of Heruka. He is also known as 'Dorjechang Phabongkha Trinlay Gyatso' and as 'Dechen Nyingpo Phabongkha Dorjechang'. Je Phabongkhapa or Phabongkha Rinpoche was the holder of many lineages of Sutra and Secret Mantra. He was the root Guru of Dorjechang Trijang Rinpoche.

Je Tsongkhapa (AD 1357-1419) An emanation of the Wisdom Buddha Manjushri, whose appearance in fourteenth-century Tibet as a monk, and the holder of the lineage of pure view and pure deeds, was prophesised by Buddha. He spread a very pure Dharma throughout Tibet, showing how to combine the practices of Sutra and Tantra, and how to practise pure Dharma during degenerate times. His tradition later became known as the 'Gelug' or 'Ganden Tradition'. See *Heart Jewel* and *Great Treasury of Merit.*

Kadampa Tradition The pure tradition of Kadampa Buddhism established by Atisha. Followers of this tradition up to Je Tsongkhapa are known as 'Old Kadampas', and those after the time of Je Tsongkhapa are known as 'New Kadampas'. See *Modern Buddhism* and *Joyful Path of Good Fortune.*

Kangyur The collection of all the Sutras and Tantras that have been translated from Sanskrit into Tibetan. See also *Tengyur.*

Khedrubje One of the principal disciples of Je Tsongkhapa who did much to promote the tradition of Je Tsongkhapa after he passed away. See *Heart Jewel* and *Great Treasury of Merit.*

Lama Losang Tubwang Dorjechang A special manifestation of Je Tsongkhapa revealed directly to the great Yogi Dharmavajra. In this manifestation Je Tsongkhapa appears as a fully ordained monk wearing a long-eared Pandit's hat, with Buddha Shakyamuni at his heart, and Conqueror Vajradhara at his heart. In the practice of Offering to the Spiritual Guide we visualize our Spiritual Guide in this aspect. 'Lama' indicates that he is our Spiritual Guide, 'Losang' that he is Je Tsongkhapa (whose ordained name was Losang Dragpa), 'Tubwang' that he is Buddha Shakyamuni, and 'Dorjechang' that he is Vajradhara. In Tibetan, this aspect of our Spiritual Guide is also known as 'je sempa sum tseg', which means 'Je Tsongkhapa, the Unification of Three Holy Beings'. This indicates that in reality our Spiritual Guide is the same nature as Je Tsongkhapa, Buddha Shakyamuni, and Conqueror Vajradhara. See *Great Treasury of Merit*.

Liberation Complete freedom from samsara and its cause, the delusions. See *Joyful Path of Good Fortune*.

Lineage A line of instruction that has been passed down from Spiritual Guide to disciple, with each Spiritual Guide in the line having gained personal experience of the instruction before passing it on to others.

Lineage Gurus The line of Spiritual Guides through whom a particular instruction has been passed down.

Lochana A female Buddha who is the manifestation of the earth element of all Buddhas. She is the consort of Buddha Vairochana.

Lord of Death Although the mara, or demon, of uncontrolled death is not a sentient being, it is personified as the Lord of Death, or 'Yama'. The Lord of Death is depicted in the diagram of the Wheel of Life clutching the wheel between his claws and teeth. See *Joyful Path of Good Fortune*.

Mahakaruna Sanskrit term for 'great compassion', and also an epithet for Buddha Avalokiteshvara.

Mahasiddha Sanskrit word for 'Greatly Accomplished One', which is used to refer to Yogis or Yoginis with high attainments.

Mahayana Sanskrit word for 'Great Vehicle', the spiritual path to great enlightenment. See *Joyful Path of Good Fortune*, *Universal Compassion* and *Meaningful to Behold*.

Mahayana path A clear realization in the mental continuum of a Bodhisattva or a Buddha. There are five Mahayana paths: the Mahayana path of accumulation, the Mahayana path of preparation, the Mahayana path of seeing, the Mahayana path of meditation and the Mahayana Path of No More Learning. The first four are necessarily in the continuum of a Bodhisattva and the last is necessarily in the continuum of a Buddha. See *Joyful Path of Good Fortune* and *Tantric Grounds and Paths*.

Mamaki A female Buddha who is the manifestation of the water element of all Buddhas. She is the consort of Buddha Ratnasambhava.

Mara Sanskrit for 'demon', and refers to anything that obstructs the attainment of liberation or enlightenment. There are four principal types of mara: the mara of the delusions, the mara of contaminated aggregates, the mara of uncontrolled death, and the Devaputra maras. Of these, only the last are actual sentient beings. The principal Devaputra mara is wrathful Ishvara, the highest of the desire realm gods, who inhabits the Land Controlling Emanations. A Buddha is called a 'Conqueror' because he or she has conquered all four types of mara. See *The New Heart of Wisdom*.

Meditation A mind that concentrates on a virtuous object, and is a mental action that is the main cause of mental peace. See also Analytical meditation and Placement meditation. See *Joyful Path of Good Fortune* and *The New Meditation Handbook*.

Merit The good fortune created by virtuous actions. It is the potential power to increase our good qualities and produce happiness.

Method Any spiritual path that functions to ripen our Buddha lineage. Training in renunciation, compassion and bodhichitta are examples of method practices.

Mindfulness A mental factor that functions not to forget the object realized by its primary mind. See *Clear Light of Bliss*, *Meaningful to Behold* and *Understanding the Mind*.

Mudra Generally, the Sanskrit word for 'seal', as in Mahamudra, the 'great seal'. More specifically, 'mudra' is used to refer to a consort, as in 'action mudra' or 'wisdom mudra', and to hand gestures used in Tantric rituals. See *Clear Light of Bliss*, *Mahamudra Tantra* and *Great Treasury of Merit*.

Naga A non-human being not normally visible to humans. Nagas usually live in the oceans of the world but they sometimes inhabit land in the region of rocks and trees. They are very powerful, some being benevolent and some malevolent.

Nagarjuna A great Indian Buddhist scholar and meditation master who revived the Mahayana in the first century AD by bringing to light the teachings on the *Perfection of Wisdom Sutras*. See *Ocean of Nectar* and *The New Heart of Wisdom*.

Nine mental abidings Nine levels of concentration leading to tranquil abiding: placing the mind, continual placement, replacement, close placement, controlling, pacifying, completely pacifying, single-pointedness and placement in equipoise. See *Meaningful to Behold* and *Joyful Path of Good Fortune*.

Nirvana Sanskrit term meaning 'state beyond sorrow'. Complete freedom from samsara and its cause, the delusions.

Offering to the Spiritual Guide 'Lama Chopa' in Tibetan. A special Guru yoga of Je Tsongkhapa, in which our Spiritual Guide is visualized in the aspect of Lama Losang Tubwang Dorjechang. The instruction for this practice was revealed by Buddha Manjushri in the *Kadam Emanation Scripture* and written down by the first Panchen Lama. It is an essential preliminary practice for Vajrayana Mahamudra. See also *Lama Losang Tubwang Dorjechang*. See *Great Treasury of Merit*.

Ordinary being Anyone who has not realized emptiness directly.

Perfection of wisdom Any wisdom maintained by bodhichitta motivation. See *The New Heart of Wisdom* and *Ocean of Nectar*.

Person An I imputed in dependence upon any of the five aggregates. See *Understanding the Mind*.

Placement meditation Single-pointed concentration on a virtuous object. See *Joyful Path of Good Fortune* and *The New Meditation Handbook*.

Pride A deluded mental factor that, through considering and exaggerating one's own good qualities or possessions, feels arrogant. See *Joyful Path of Good Fortune* and *Understanding the Mind*.

Ratnasambhava The manifestation of the aggregate of feeling of all Buddhas. He has a yellow-coloured body.

Sadhana A ritual prayer that is a special method for attaining realizations, usually associated with a Tantric Deity.

Samsara Sometimes known as 'cyclic existence'. This can be understood in two ways: as uninterrupted rebirth without freedom or control, or as the aggregates of a being who has taken such a rebirth. It is characterized by suffering and dissatisfaction. There are six realms of samsara. Listed in ascending order according to the type of karma that causes rebirth in them, they are the realms of the hell beings, hungry spirits, animals, humans, demi-gods and gods. The first three are lower realms or unhappy migrations, and the second three are higher realms or happy migrations. Although from the point of view of the karma that causes rebirth there, the god realm is the highest realm in samsara, the human realm is said to be the most fortunate realm because it provides the best conditions for attaining liberation and enlightenment. See *The New Heart of Wisdom* and *Joyful Path of Good Fortune*.

Sangha According to the Vinaya tradition, any community of four or more fully ordained monks or nuns. In general, ordained or lay people who take Bodhisattva vows or Tantric vows can also be said to be Sangha.

Self-cherishing A mental attitude that considers oneself to be precious or important. It is regarded as a principal object to be abandoned by Bodhisattvas. See *Modern Buddhism, Eight Steps to Happiness, Universal Compassion* and *Meaningful to Behold*.

Self-grasping A conceptual mind that holds any phenomenon to be inherently existent. The mind of self-grasping gives rise to all other delusions such as anger and attachment. It is the root cause of all suffering and dissatisfaction. See *Modern Buddhism, The New Heart of Wisdom, Transform Your Life* and *Ocean of Nectar*.

Sentient being Any being who possesses a mind that is contaminated by delusions or their imprints. Both 'living being' and 'sentient being' are terms used to distinguish beings whose minds are contaminated by any of the two obstructions from Buddhas, whose minds are completely free from these obstructions.

Shantideva (AD 687-763) A great Indian Buddhist scholar and meditation master. He composed *Guide to the Bodhisattva's Way of Life*. See *Meaningful to Behold* and *Guide to the Bodhisattva's Way of Life*.

Sindhura A red powder from any of the twenty-four auspicious places of Heruka.

Six perfections The perfections of giving, moral discipline, patience, effort, mental stabilization and wisdom. They are called 'perfections' because they are motivated by bodhichitta. See *Joyful Path of Good Fortune, Meaningful to Behold* and *The Bodhisattva Vow*.

Solitary peace A Hinayana nirvana.

Spontaneous great bliss A special bliss that is produced by the drops melting inside the central channel. It is attained by gaining control over the inner winds. See *Clear Light of Bliss* and *Tantric Grounds and Paths*.

Stages of the path 'Lamrim' in Tibetan. A special arrangement of all Buddha's teachings that is easy to understand and put into practice. It reveals all the stages of the path to enlightenment. See *Joyful Path of Good Fortune, Modern Buddhism* and *The New Meditation Handbook*.

Stupa A symbolic representation of Buddha's mind.

Sukhavati The Pure Land of Buddha Amitabha.

Superior being 'Arya' in Sanskrit. A being who has a direct realization of emptiness. There are Hinayana Superiors and Mahayana Superiors.

Sutra The teachings of Buddha that are open to everyone to practise without the need for empowerment. These include Buddha's teachings of the three turnings of the Wheel of Dharma.

Tengyur The collection of commentaries to Buddha's teachings that have been translated from Sanskrit into Tibetan. See also *Kangyur*.

Ten directions The four cardinal directions, the four intermediate directions, and the directions above and below.

Tranquil abiding A concentration that possesses the special bliss of suppleness of body and mind that is attained in dependence upon completing the nine mental abidings. See *Clear Light of Bliss*, *Joyful Path of Good Fortune* and *Meaningful to Behold*.

Tushita 'Ganden' in Tibetan, 'Joyful Land' in English. The Pure Land of Buddha Maitreya. Both Je Tsongkhapa and Atisha went to this Pure Land after they passed away. See *Heart Jewel*.

Twenty-four holy places Twenty-four special places in this world where the mandalas of Heruka and Vajrayogini still remain. They are: Puliramalaya, Dzalandhara, Odiyana, Arbuta, Godawari, Rameshöri, Dewikoti, Malawa, Kamarupa, Ote, Trishakune, Kosala, Kalinga, Lampaka, Kancha, Himalaya, Pretapuri, Grihadewata, Shauraktra, Suwanadvipa, Nagara, Sindhura, Maru and Kuluta.

Ultimate bodhichitta A wisdom motivated by conventional bodhichitta that directly realizes emptiness. See *Modern Buddhism*, *The New Heart of Wisdom*, *Universal Compassion* and *Great Treasury of Merit*.

Ultimate nature All phenomena have two natures: a conventional nature and an ultimate nature. In the case of a table, for example, the table itself, its shape, colour and so forth are all the conventional nature of the table. The ultimate nature of the table is the table's lack of inherent existence. The conventional nature of a phenomenon is a conventional truth, and its ultimate nature is an ultimate truth. See *Modern Buddhism*, *The New Heart of Wisdom* and *Ocean of Nectar*.

Uncontaminated bliss A realization of bliss conjoined with a wisdom directly realizing emptiness. See *Tantric Grounds and Paths* and *Great Treasury of Merit*.

Union of No More Learning A union of the pure illusory body and meaning clear light that has abandoned the obstructions to omniscience. Synonymous with Buddhahood. See *Clear Light of Bliss*, *Tantric Grounds and Paths* and *Great Treasury of Merit*.

Union that needs learning A union of the pure illusory body and meaning clear light that has not yet abandoned the obstructions to omniscience. See *Clear Light of Bliss*, *Tantric Grounds and Paths* and *Great Treasury of Merit*.

Vairochana The manifestation of the aggregate of form of all Buddhas. He has a white-coloured body.

Vajra Generally the Sanskrit word 'vajra' means indestructible like a diamond and powerful like a thunderbolt. In the context of Secret Mantra it can mean the indivisibility of method and wisdom, omniscient wisdom or spontaneous great bliss. See *Tantric Grounds and Paths*.

Vajra body Generally, the channels, drops and inner winds. More specifically, the pure illusory body. The body of a Buddha is known as the 'resultant vajra body'. See *Clear Light of Bliss*, *Tantric Grounds and Paths* and *Great Treasury of Merit*.

Vajra brothers/sisters Practitioners who have received any Highest Yoga Tantra empowerment from the same Vajra Master, either at the same time or at different times.

Vajradhara The founder of Vajrayana, or Tantra. He appears directly only to highly realized Bodhisattvas to whom he gives Tantric teachings. To benefit other living beings with less merit, he manifested in the more visible form of Buddha Shakyamuni. He also said that in degenerate times he would appear in an ordinary form as a Spiritual Guide. See *Great Treasury of Merit*.

Vajrayana Spiritual Guide A fully qualified Tantric Spiritual Guide. See *Great Treasury of Merit*.

Vow A virtuous determination to abandon particular faults that is generated in conjunction with a traditional ritual. The three sets of vows are the Pratimoksha vows of individual liberation, the Bodhisattva vows and the Secret Mantra vows. See *The Bodhisattva Vow* and *Tantric Grounds and Paths*.

Wisdom A virtuous, intelligent mind that makes its primary mind realize its object thoroughly. A wisdom is a spiritual path that functions to release our mind from delusions or their imprints. An example of wisdom is the correct view of emptiness. See *The New Heart of Wisdom*, *Understanding the Mind* and *Ocean of Nectar*.

Yamantaka A Highest Yoga Tantra Deity who is a wrathful manifestation of Manjushri.

Yoga A term used for various spiritual practices that entail maintaining a special view, such as Guru yoga and the yogas of sleeping, rising and experiencing nectar. 'Yoga' also refers to union, such as the union of tranquil abiding and superior seeing.

Yogi/Yogini Sanskrit terms usually refering to a male or female meditator who has attained the union of tranquil abiding and superior seeing.

Bibliography

Geshe Kelsang Gyatso is a highly respected meditation master and scholar of the Mahayana Buddhist tradition founded by Je Tsongkhapa. Since being invited to the West in 1977, Geshe Kelsang has worked tirelessly to establish pure Buddhadharma throughout the world. Over this period he has given extensive teachings on the major scriptures of the Mahayana. These teachings provide a comprehensive presentation of the essential Sutra and Tantra practices of Mahayana Buddhism.

Books

The following books by Geshe Kelsang are all published by Tharpa Publications.

The Bodhisattva Vow A practical guide to helping others. (2nd. edn., 1995)

Clear Light of Bliss A Tantric meditation manual. (2nd. edn., 1992)

Eight Steps to Happiness The Buddhist way of loving kindness. (2nd. edn., 2012)

Essence of Vajrayana The Highest Yoga Tantra practice of Heruka body mandala. (1997)

Great Treasury of Merit How to rely upon a Spiritual Guide. (1992)

Guide to the Bodhisattva's Way of Life How to enjoy a life of great meaning and altruism. (A translation of Shantideva's famous verse masterpiece.) (2002)

Heart Jewel The essential practices of Kadampa Buddhism. (2nd. edn., 1997)

How to Solve Our Human Problems The four noble truths. (2005)

Introduction to Buddhism An explanation of the Buddhist way of life. (2nd. edn., 2001)

Joyful Path of Good Fortune The complete Buddhist path to enlightenment. (2nd. edn., 1995)

Living Meaningfully, Dying Joyfully The profound practice of transference of consciousness. (1999)

Mahamudra Tantra The supreme Heart Jewel nectar. (2005)

Meaningful to Behold Becoming a friend of the world. (5th. edn., 2007)

Modern Buddhism The path of compassion and wisdom. (2011)

The New Guide to Dakini Land The Highest Yoga Tantra practice of Buddha Vajrayogini. (3rd. edn., 2012)

The New Heart of Wisdom Profound teachings from Buddha's heart (An explanation of the Heart Sutra). (5th. edn., 2012)

The New Meditation Handbook Meditations to make our life happy and meaningful. (2003)

Ocean of Nectar The true nature of all things. (1995)

Tantric Grounds and Paths How to enter, progress on, and complete the Vajrayana path. (1994)

Transform Your Life A blissful journey. (2001)

Understanding the Mind The nature and power of the mind. (3rd. edn., 2002)

Universal Compassion Inspiring solutions for difficult times. (4th. edn., 2002)

Sadhanas and Other Booklets

Geshe Kelsang has also supervised the translation of a collection of essential sadhanas, or ritual prayers for spiritual attainments, available in booklet or audio formats.

Avalokiteshvara Sadhana Prayers and requests to the Buddha of Compassion.

The Blissful Path The condensed self-generation sadhana of Vajrayogini.

The Bodhisattva's Confession of Moral Downfalls The purification practice of the *Mahayana Sutra of the Three Superior Heaps*.

Condensed Essence of Vajrayana Condensed Heruka body mandala self-generation sadhana.

Dakini Yoga The middling self-generation sadhana of Vajrayogini.

Drop of Essential Nectar A special fasting and purification practice in conjunction with Eleven-faced Avalokiteshvara.

Essence of Good Fortune Prayers for the six preparatory practices for meditation on the stages of the path to enlightenment.

Essence of Vajrayana Heruka body mandala self-generation sadhana according to the system of Mahasiddha Ghantapa.

Feast of Great Bliss Vajrayogini self-initiation sadhana.

Great Liberation of the Father Preliminary prayers for Mahamudra meditation in conjunction with Heruka practice.

Great Liberation of the Mother Preliminary prayers for Mahamudra meditation in conjunction with Vajrayogini practice.

The Great Mother A method to overcome hindrances and obstacles by reciting the *Essence of Wisdom Sutra* (the *Heart Sutra*)

A Handbook for the Daily Practice of Bodhisattva and Tantric Vows.

Heartfelt Prayers Funeral service for cremations and burials.

Heart Jewel The Guru yoga of Je Tsongkhapa combined with the condensed sadhana of his Dharma Protector.

The Kadampa Way of Life The essential practice of Kadam Lamrim.

Liberation from Sorrow Praises and requests to the Twenty-one Taras.

Mahayana Refuge Ceremony and Bodhisattva Vow Ceremony.

Medicine Buddha Prayer A method for benefiting others.

Medicine Buddha Sadhana A method for accomplishing the attainments of Medicine Buddha.

Meditation and Recitation of Solitary Vajrasattva.

Melodious Drum Victorious in all Directions The extensive fulfilling and restoring ritual of the Dharma Protector, the great king Dorje Shugden, in conjunction with Mahakala, Kalarupa, Kalindewi and other Dharma Protectors.

Offering to the Spiritual Guide (Lama Chopa) A special way of relying upon a Spiritual Guide.

Path of Compassion for the Deceased Powa sadhana for the benefit of the deceased.

Pathway to the Pure Land Training in powa – the transference of consciousness.

Powa Ceremony Transference of consciousness for the deceased.

Prayers for Meditation Brief preparatory prayers for meditation.

Prayers for World Peace.

A Pure Life The practice of taking and keeping the eight Mahayana precepts.

Quick Path to Great Bliss The extensive self-generation sadhana of Vajrayogini.

The Root Tantra of Heruka and Vajrayogini Chapters One & Fifty-one of the *Condensed Heruka Root Tantra.*

The Root Text: Eight Verses of Training the Mind.

Treasury of Wisdom The sadhana of Venerable Manjushri.

The Uncommon Yoga of Inconceivability The special instruction of how to reach the Pure Land of Keajra with this human body

Union of No More Learning Heruka body mandala self-initiation sadhana.

Vajra Hero Yoga The brief practice of Heruka body mandala self-generation.

The Vows and Commitments of Kadampa Buddhism.

Wishfulfilling Jewel The Guru yoga of Je Tsongkhapa combined with the sadhana of his Dharma Protector.

The Yoga of Buddha Amitayus A special method for increasing lifespan, wisdom and merit.

The Yoga of Buddha Heruka The essential self-generation sadhana of Heruka body mandala & Condensed six-session yoga.

The Yoga of Buddha Maitreya Self-generation sadhana.

The Yoga of Buddha Vajrapani Self-generation sadhana.

The Yoga of Enlightened Mother Arya Tara Self-generation sadhana.

The Yoga of Great Mother Prajnaparamita Self-generation sadhana.

The Yoga of Thousand-armed Avalokiteshvara Self-generation sadhana.

The Yoga of White Tara, Buddha of Long Life.

To order any of our publications, or to request a catalogue, please visit www.tharpa.com or contact your nearest Tharpa office listed on pages 565-566.

Study Programmes of
Kadampa Buddhism

Kadampa Buddhism is a Mahayana Buddhist school founded by the great Indian Buddhist Master Atisha (AD 982-1054). His followers are known as 'Kadampas'. 'Ka' means 'word' and refers to Buddha's teachings, and 'dam' refers to Atisha's special Lamrim instructions known as `the stages of the path to enlightenment'. By integrating their knowledge of all Buddha's teachings into their practice of Lamrim, and by integrating this into their everyday lives, Kadampa Buddhists are encouraged to use Buddha's teachings as practical methods for transforming daily activities into the path to enlightenment. The great Kadampa Teachers are famous not only for being great scholars but also for being spiritual practitioners of immense purity and sincerity.

The lineage of these teachings, both their oral transmission and blessings, was then passed from Teacher to disciple, spreading throughout much of Asia, and now to many countries throughout the Western world. Buddha's teachings, which are known as 'Dharma', are likened to a wheel that moves from country to country in accordance with changing conditions and people's karmic inclinations. The external forms of presenting Buddhism may change as it meets with different cultures and societies, but its essential authenticity is ensured through the continuation of an unbroken lineage of realized practitioners.

Kadampa Buddhism was first introduced into the West in 1977 by the renowned Buddhist Master, Venerable Geshe Kelsang Gyatso. Since that time, he has worked tirelessly to spread Kadampa Buddhism throughout the world by giving extensive teachings, writing many profound texts on Kadampa Buddhism, and founding the New Kadampa Tradition – International Kadampa Buddhist Union (NKT-IKBU), which now has over a thousand Kadampa Buddhist Centres worldwide. Each Centre offers study programmes on Buddhist psychology, philosophy, and meditation instruction, as well as retreats for all levels of practitioner. The emphasis is on integrating Buddha's teachings into daily life to solve our human problems and to spread lasting peace and happiness throughout the world.

The Kadampa Buddhism of the NKT-IKBU is an entirely independent Buddhist tradition and has no political affiliations. It is an association of Buddhist Centres and practitioners that derive their inspiration and guidance from the example of the ancient Kadampa Buddhist Masters and their teachings, as presented by Geshe Kelsang.

There are three reasons why we need to study and practise the teachings of Buddha: to develop our wisdom, to cultivate a good heart, and to maintain a peaceful state of mind. If we do not strive to develop our wisdom, we will always remain ignorant of ultimate truth – the true nature of reality. Although we wish for happiness, our ignorance leads us to engage in non-virtuous actions, which are the main cause of all our suffering. If we do not cultivate a good heart, our selfish motivation destroys harmony and good relationships with others. We have no peace, and no chance to gain pure happiness. Without inner peace, outer peace is impossible. If we do not maintain a peaceful state of mind, we are not happy even if we have ideal conditions. On the other hand, when our mind is peaceful, we are happy, even if our external conditions are unpleasant. Therefore, the development of these qualities is of utmost importance for our daily happiness.

Geshe Kelsang Gyatso, or 'Geshe-la' as he is affectionately called by his students, has designed three special spiritual programmes for the systematic study and practice of Kadampa Buddhism that are especially suited to the modern world – the General Programme (GP), the Foundation Programme (FP), and the Teacher Training Programme (TTP).

GENERAL PROGRAMME

The General Programme provides a basic introduction to Buddhist view, meditation, and practice that is suitable for beginners. It also includes advanced teachings and practice from both Sutra and Tantra.

FOUNDATION PROGRAMME

The Foundation Programme provides an opportunity to deepen our understanding and experience of Buddhism through a systematic study of six texts:

1 *Joyful Path of Good Fortune* – a commentary to Atisha's Lamrim instructions, the stages of the path to enlightenment.
2 *Universal Compassion* – a commentary to Bodhisattva Chekhawa's *Training the Mind in Seven Points*.
3 *Eight Steps to Happiness* – a commentary to Bodhisattva Langri Tangpa's *Eight Verses of Training the Mind*.
4 *The New Heart of Wisdom* – a commentary to the *Heart Sutra*.
5 *Meaningful to Behold* – a commentary to Bodhisattva Shantideva's *Guide to the Bodhisattva's Way of Life*.
6 *Understanding the Mind* – a detailed explanation of the mind, based on the works of the Buddhist scholars Dharmakirti and Dignaga.

The benefits of studying and practising these texts are as follows:

(1) *Joyful Path of Good Fortune* – we gain the ability to put all Buddha's teachings of both Sutra and Tantra into practice. We can easily make progress on, and complete, the stages of the path to the supreme happiness of enlightenment. From a practical point of view, Lamrim is the main body of Buddha's teachings, and the other teachings are like its limbs.

(2) and (3) *Universal Compassion* and *Eight Steps to Happiness* – we gain the ability to integrate Buddha's teachings into our daily life and solve all our human problems.

(4) *The New Heart of Wisdom* – we gain a realization of the ultimate nature of reality. By gaining this realization, we can eliminate the ignorance of self-grasping, which is the root of all our suffering.

(5) *Meaningful to Behold* – we transform our daily activities into the Bodhisattva's way of life, thereby making every moment of our human life meaningful.

(6) *Understanding the Mind* – we understand the relationship between our mind and its external objects. If we understand that objects depend upon the subjective mind, we can change the way objects appear to us by changing our own mind. Gradually, we will gain the ability to control our mind and in this way solve all our problems.

TEACHER TRAINING PROGRAMME

The Teacher Training Programme is designed for people who wish to train as authentic Dharma Teachers. In addition to completing the study of fourteen texts of Sutra and Tantra, which include the six texts mentioned above, the student is required to observe certain commitments with regard to behaviour and way of life, and to complete a number of meditation retreats.

All Kadampa Buddhist Centres are open to the public. Every year we celebrate Festivals in many countries throughout the world, including two in England, where people gather from around the world to receive special teachings and empowerments and to enjoy a spiritual holiday. Please feel free to visit us at any time!

For further information about NKT-IKBU study programmes or to find your nearest centre visit www.kadampa.org, or please contact:

NKT-IKBU Central Office
Conishead Priory
Ulverston
Cumbria LA12 9QQ
England
Tel: 01229-588533
Tel: 01229-580080
Email: info@kadampa.org
Website: www.kadampa.org

or

KMC New York
47 Sweeney Road,
Glen Spey, NY 12737,
USA
Tel: +1 845-856-9000
Fax: +1 845-856-2110
Email: info@kadampanewyork.org
Website: www.kadampanewyork.org

Tharpa Offices Worldwide

Tharpa books are currently published in English (UK and US), Chinese, French, German, Italian, Japanese, Portuguese and Spanish. Most languages are available from any Tharpa office listed below.

UK Office

Tharpa Publications UK
Conishead Priory, ULVERSTON
Cumbria, LA12 9QQ, UK
Tel: +44 (0)1229-588599
Fax: +44 (0)1229-483919
Web: www.tharpa.com/uk/
E-mail: info.uk@tharpa.com

US Office

Tharpa Publications US
47 Sweeney Road
GLEN SPEY NY 12737, USA
Tel: +1 845-856-5102
Toll-free: 888-741-3475
Fax: +1 845-856-2110
Web: www.tharpa.com/us/
E-mail: info.us@tharpa.com

Asia Office

Tharpa Asia
Zhong Zheng E Rd., Sec 2,
Lane 143, Alley 10, No 7,
Tamsui District, NEW TAIPEI
CITY, 25159, TAIWAN
Tel: +886-(02)-8809-4313
Web: www.tharpa.com/hk-en/
E-mail: info.asia@tharpa.com

Australian Office

Tharpa Publications Australia
25 McCarthy Road,
MONBULK VIC 3793
AUSTRALIA
Tel: +61 (0)3 9752 0277
Web: www.tharpa.com/au/
E-mail: info.au@tharpa.com

Brazilian Office

Editora Tharpa Brasil
Rua Fradique Coutinho 701
VILA MADALENA, 05416-011
São Paulo - SP, BRAZIL
Tel/Fax: +55 (11) 3812 7509
Web: www.tharpa.com.br
E-mail: info.br@tharpa.com.br

Canadian Office

Tharpa Publications Canada
631 Crawford St.,
TORONTO ON M6G 3K1,
CANADA
Tel: +1 416-762-8710
Toll-free: 866-523-2672
Fax: +1 416-762-2267
Web: www.tharpa.com/ca/
E-mail: info.ca@tharpa.com

French Office
Editions Tharpa
Château de Segrais
72220 SAINT-MARS-D'OUTILLÉ,
FRANCE
Tél : +33 (0)2 43 87 71 02
Fax : +33 (0)2 76 01 34 10
Web: www.tharpa.com/fr/
E-mail: info.fr@tharpa.com

German Office
Tharpa-Verlag Deutschland
Sommerswalde 8
16727 OBERKRÄMER
OT Schwante, GERMANY
Tel: +49 (033055) 222 135
Fax: +49 (033055) 222 139
Web: www.tharpa.com/de/
E-mail: info.de@tharpa.com

Japanese Office
Tharpa Japan
c/o Kazuko Numata,
Amitabha Buddhist Centre,
Shimagahara 11399-35, IGA-SHI,
Mie 519-1711, JAPAN
Tel/Fax: +81 (0)595-59-2008
Web: www.meditationinjapan.com
E-mail: info.jp@tharpa.com

Mexican Office
Tharpa México
Enrique Rébsamen No. 406,
Col. Narvate, entre Xola y
Diagonal de San Antonio,
C.P. 03020, MÉXICO D.F.,
MÉXICO
Tel: +01 (55) 56 39 61 86
Tel/Fax: +01 (55) 56 39 61 80
Web: www.tharpa.com/mx/
E-mail: tharpa@kadampa.org/mx

South African Office
c/o Mahasiddha Kadampa
Buddhist Centre
2 Hollings Road, Malvern
DURBAN 4093
REP. OF SOUTH AFRICA
Tel: +27 (0)31 464 0984
Web: www.tharpa.com/za/
E-mail: info.za@tharpa.com

Spanish Office
Editorial Tharpa España
Camino Fuente del Perro s/n
29120 ALHAURÍN EL GRANDE
(Málaga), SPAIN
Tel: +34 952 596808
Fax: +34 952 490175
Web: www.tharpa.com/es/
E-mail: info.es@tharpa.com

Swiss Office
Tharpa Verlag AG
Mirabellenstrasse 1
CH-8048 ZÜRICH,
SWITZERLAND
Tel: +41-44-401 0220
Fax: +41-44-461 3688
Web: www.tharpa.com/ch/
E-mail: info.ch@tharpa.com

Index

The letter 'g' indicates an entry in the glossary

wind element 59
winds, inner 33, 114, 143, 144,
171-2, 220-1. *See also* yoga of
winds
downward-voiding 64, 65
entering central channel 115,
130, 136, 143, 215, 218, 225
pervading 229
wisdom, g
collection of 113, 115, 219.
See also five omniscient
wisdoms; perfection of
wisdom
overcoming doubts 16-7
wisdom beings
absorbing 137-41, 144
inviting 85

Y

Yama. *See* Lord of Death
Yamani 145
Yamantaka 5, 7, 19, 129, 152,
162, g
Yarlungpa 84
Yeshe Tsondru 81
Yidam. *See* Deity
yoga g
yoga of being blessed by Heroes
and Heroines 129-54. *See also*
body mandala

yoga of daily actions 27,
187-205
yoga of drops 143, 221. *See also*
inner fire
yoga of eating 27, 189-91, 196-7
yoga of experiencing nectar 27,
36-40, 57, 66
yoga of immeasurables 41-79
yoga of inconceivability
common 185-7
uncommon 7, 187, 211
yoga of purifying migrators 128
yoga of rising 27, 34
completion stage 35-6
generation stage 34-5
yoga of self-generation. *See*
self-generation
yoga of sleeping 27-34
benefits 30
completion stage 32-4
generation stage 30-2
yoga of the Guru. *See* Guru yoga
yoga of verbal and mental
recitation 163-83
yoga of winds 143, 220
yogas, eleven. *See also* individual
yogas
yogas of three purifications 27
Yogis and Yoginis g. *See* Heroes
and Heroines; Dakinis and
Dakas